the Unofficial Guide®

DISNEY
Cruise Line

Len Testa with Erin Foster, Laurel Stewart, and Ritchey Halphen

Helmsman Mickey greets guests in the *Magic*'s lobby (Photo: Laurel Stewart)

Cabanas buffet, found on the *Magic, Dream,* and *Fantasy,* is a great spot for breakfast and lunch. (Photo: Laurel Stewart)

The big finale of the *All Aboard* welcome show on the *Magic* (Photo: Scott Smith)

Getting started with the excellent Midship Detective Agency interactive adventure game on the *Dream* (Photo: Laurel Stewart)

Belle drops in to tell stories during *Disney Dreams—An Enchanted Classic.* (Photo: bright_shadows56)

Dumbo and Timothy Q. Mouse busy themselves sprucing up the stern of the *Fantasy*. (Photo: Laurel Stewart)

Disney's plush buses can provide round-trip service between the Orlando airport and Port Canaveral. (Photo: Laurel Stewart)

Donald's Pool on the *Fantasy*. You can see the AquaDuck waterslide and Mickey's Pool in the background. (Photo: Laurel Stewart)

The *Magic*'s new Twist 'n' Spout waterslide (Photo: Len Testa)

The AquaDuck waterslide (*Dream* and *Fantasy*) provides thrills aplenty for kids and grown-ups alike. (Photo: Laurel Stewart)

The *Fantasy*'s AquaLab splash area (Photo: Ricky Brigante)

The *Fantasy*'s adult pool at night (Photo: Laurel Stewart)

The *Magic*'s Quiet Cove Pool at night (Photo: Laurel Stewart)

The *Magic*'s new Oceaneer Club
(Photo: Len Testa)

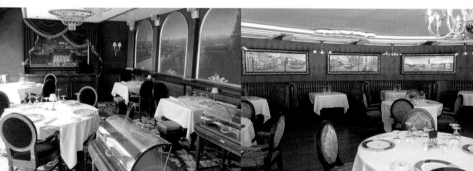

Back dining room at Remy, the best restaurant on the *Dream* (Photo: Len Testa)

Each DCL ship has an Italian restaurant called Palo; the versions on the *Dream* (shown) and the *Fantasy* are the prettiest. (Photo: Len Testa)

The version of Vibe teen club on the *Magic* and *Wonder* (left) is markedly different in theme and decor from the version on the *Dream* and *Fantasy* (right).
(Photos: left, Laurel Stewart; right, Joe Tolley)

Stern-side view of the *Fantasy* in port (Photo: Laurel Stewart)

The *Wonder* in port at Nassau (Photo: Laurel Stewart)

Daytime view of one of the *Magic*'s funnels (Photo: Laurel Stewart)

Castaway Cay's Pelican Plunge: a floating platform of fun (Photo: Scott Smith)

Castaway Cay's Mount Rustmore makes for a fun photo opportunity. (Photo: Laurel Stewart)

Mush! Dogsledding in Alaska (Photo: Erin Foster)

Mayan ruins are part of DCL's Western Caribbean itineraries. (Photo: Chad Klotzle)

A typical Deluxe Inside Stateroom. This one is from the *Wonder*. (Photo: Len Testa)

Deluxe Oceanview Stateroom with Verandah on the *Dream*. (Photo: Scott Sanders/disneycruise lineblog.com)

Big-city vistas unfold behind the bar at Skyline Lounge on the *Dream*. (Photo: Laurel Stewart)

687 is the *Dream*'s upscale sports bar. (Photo: Laurel Stewart)

The *Dream*'s Walt Disney Theatre hosts the ship's live shows. (Photo: Laurel Stewart)

The *Magic*'s Brazilian-themed restaurant, Carioca's (Photo: Len Testa)

Selection of port wines at Palo on the *Wonder* (Photo: Laurel Stewart)

The *Fantasy*'s Enchanted Garden restaurant has a ceiling whose lighting changes from day to night. (Photos: Laurel Stewart)

THE *unofficial* GUIDE®
to Disney
Cruise Line

2015

Other *Unofficial Guides*:

THE *unofficial* GUIDE

TO Disney Cruise Line

2015

LEN TESTA with ERIN FOSTER,
LAUREL STEWART, and
RITCHEY HALPHEN

keen
communications

Please note that prices fluctuate in the course of time and that travel information changes under the impact of many factors that influence the travel industry. We therefore suggest that you write or call ahead for confirmation when making your travel plans. Every effort has been made to ensure the accuracy of information throughout this book, and the contents of this publication are believed to be correct at the time of printing. Nevertheless, the publishers cannot accept responsibility for errors or omissions, for changes in details given in this guide, or for the consequences of any reliance on the information provided by the same. Assessments of attractions and so forth are based upon the author's own experience; therefore, descriptions given in this guide necessarily contain an element of subjective opinion, which may not reflect the publisher's opinion or dictate a reader's own experience on another occasion. Readers are invited to write the publisher with ideas, comments, and suggestions for future editions.

Published by:
Keen Communications, LLC
PO Box 43673
Birmingham, AL 35243

Editor: Ritchey Halphen
Cover and color-insert design: Scott McGrew
Text design: Vertigo Design with Annie Long
Cartography and illustrations: Steve Jones
Proofreaders: Emily C. Beaumont, Julie Hall Bosché
Indexer: Sylvia Coates

For information on our other products and services or to obtain technical support, please contact us from within the United States at 888-604-4537 or by fax at 205-326-1012.

Keen Communications, LLC, also publishes its books in a variety of electronic formats. Some content that appears in print may not be available in electronic formats.

ISBN-13: 978-1-62809-032-1; eISBN: 978-1-62809-033-8

Distributed by Publishers Group West

Manufactured in the United States of America

5 4 3 2 1

CONTENTS

LIST *of* MAPS *and* DIAGRAMS

ABOUT *the* AUTHORS

LEN TESTA is the coauthor of *The Unofficial Guide to Walt Disney World; The Unofficial Guide to Disneyland; The Unofficial Guide to Walt Disney World with Kids; The Unofficial Guide Color Companion to Walt Disney World; Mini-Mickey: The Pocket-Sized Unofficial Guide to Walt Disney World;* and *The Unofficial Guide to Britain's Best Days Out: Theme Parks and Attractions.* A computer scientist, Len created both the *Unofficial Guides* touring plan software and the **touringplans .com** website. The father of a teenage daughter, he lives in Greensboro, North Carolina.

As a charter member of the official Disney Parks Moms Panel, **ERIN FOSTER** has researched and written answers to more than 10,000 guest questions about Disney travel. In a quest to consume absolutely everything Disney Destinations has to offer, Erin has visited Walt Disney World, Disneyland, Disneyland Paris, and Hong Kong Disneyland. (Somebody send her to Tokyo Disneyland—please!) Her travels also include Disney Cruise Line voyages throughout the world and Adventures by Disney journeys on four continents. She is a regular contributor to the **touringplans.com** blog and **disneyfoodblog.com** and has been a guest on many other Disney-related websites and podcasts, including **allears.net**, PassPorter Moms, Be Our Guest, Disney Wedding Blog, WDW Today, and WDW Radio. Erin lives near New York City with her husband and three teenage daughters.

LAUREL STEWART has contributed to *The Unofficial Guide to Walt Disney World* and *The Unofficial Guide Color Companion to Walt Disney World* and works for **touringplans.com**. Despite not enjoying sand, seawater, or direct sunlight, she's always up for a cruise. Laurel was born in the Bahamas and lives in North Carolina.

RITCHEY HALPHEN is an editor at Keen Communications in Birmingham, Alabama. He is also a coauthor (with Bob Sehlinger and Len Testa) of *Mini-Mickey: The Pocket-Sized Unofficial Guide to Walt Disney World.*

ACKNOWLEDGMENTS

IT TOOK A LIFEBOAT FULL OF PEOPLE to produce this book and its companion web content. David Davies created our website for Disney Cruise Line (DCL) information, wrote the Fare Tracker tool, and lent an expert eye to the proofreading of the text. Scott Sanders from **disney cruiselineblog.com** keeps us updated on the latest DCL news. Also, thanks to Emily and Isabelle Sanders for testing the waterslides with us.

DCL kids' club research was done by Alex Duncan, "Captain" Kieran Duncan, Jacklyn Scirica, and Hannah Testa. Kelsey and Kathy Lubetich bravely navigated the waters and lumberjacks of Alaska for that coverage. Thanks also to Tammy Whiting of Storybook Destinations, Beci Mahnken and Stephanie Hudson of Mouse Fan Travel, and Sue Pisaturo and Lynne Amodeo of Small World Vacations for their help in determining cruise-pricing trends.

—*Len Testa and Laurel Stewart*

I WOULD LIKE TO THANK my husband, Jeff, who was the first person to hire me as a writer, and my daughters, Charlie, Josie, and Louisa, who make me go on the scary rides. Additional thanks to the women and men of the Disney Parks Moms Panel, whose passion for all things Disney is a constant inspiration. Special thanks to the Moms Panel's Bernie Edwards for proofreading and suggestions, for this and every *Unofficial Guide*.

—*Erin Foster*

MANY THANKS TO THE CREW at Keen Communications who contributed to this book: Amber Kaye Henderson, my right-hand editor and organizer for the first edition; Annie Long, our indefatigable typesetter; Steve Jones, who produced the maps and diagrams; Scott McGrew, who designed the cover and color insert; proofreaders Emily Beaumont and Julie Bosché; and indexer Sylvia Coates.

—*Ritchey Halphen*

INTRODUCTION

◼ ABOUT *This* GUIDE

WHY "UNOFFICIAL"?

THE MATERIAL HEREIN originated with the authors and has not been reviewed, edited, or approved by the Walt Disney Company, Inc., or Disney Cruise Line (DCL). To the contrary, we represent and serve you, the consumer: If a ship serves mediocre food or has subpar entertainment, we say so. Through our independence, we hope that we can make selecting a cruise efficient and economical and help make your cruise experience on-target and fun.

Toward that end, our *unofficial* guide offers the following:

- Our recommendations for which ship to choose for your first cruise
- How to find the perfect itinerary, including specific cruises and dates
- When to book your cruise to get the cheapest fares
- What to pack, including travel documents for you and your children
- Color photos from throughout the ships, plus deck and stateroom diagrams
- Unbiased reviews of onboard restaurants, live entertainment, and nightlife
- The best family activities, including children's clubs, family games, outdoor sports, and more
- Where and when to meet Disney characters on board
- Full coverage of Disney's private island, Castaway Cay, along with ports and shore excursions

DISNEY CRUISE LINE:
An Overview

IN 1998, THE WALT DISNEY COMPANY LAUNCHED—literally—its own cruise line with the 2,400-passenger *Disney Magic.* An almost identical ship, the *Disney Wonder,* entered service in 1999. Two larger ships, the *Disney Dream* and the *Disney Fantasy,* joined the fleet in 2011 and 2012, respectively.

In starting a cruise line, Disney put together a team of respected industry veterans, dozens of the world's best-known ship designers, and its own unrivaled creative talent. Together, they created the Disney ships, recognizing that every detail would be critical to the line's success.

The result? They've succeeded, starting with the ships' appearance: simultaneously classic and innovative. Exteriors are traditional, reminiscent of the great ocean liners of the past, but even here you'll find a Disney twist or two. Inside, the ships feature up-to-the-minute technology and are full of novel ideas for dining, entertainment, and cabin design. Even Disney's exclusive cruise terminal at Port Canaveral, Florida, is part of the overall strategy, aiming to make even embarking and disembarking enjoyable.

unofficial **TIP**
Because the ships' decor and entertainment are based almost entirely on Disney films and characters, we don't recommend a DCL cruise to anyone who isn't at least mildly fond of Mickey and the gang.

For Port Canaveral and Miami cruises, Disney's private island, **Castaway Cay,** was chosen to avoid the hassle of tendering. As for dining, Disney practically reinvented the concept for cruises when it introduced rotational dining (see Part Seven), where each evening you dine in a different restaurant with a different motif, but your waiters and dining companions move with you.

The foundation of DCL's business is built on Bahamian and Caribbean cruises out of Port Canaveral, about 90 minutes from Walt Disney World, and Miami. Disney also offers Alaskan, Californian, Canadian, and European cruises, as well as repositioning cruises. Other departure ports include Barcelona, Spain; Galveston, Texas; San Diego, California; San Juan, Puerto Rico; Vancouver, Canada; and Venice, Italy.

All Bahamian cruises originating in Port Canaveral and Miami make at least one port call at Castaway Cay. DCL's Alaskan and European itineraries are well conceived and interesting; by comparison, its Bahamian and Caribbean itineraries are unimaginative and prosaic, but they are good for first-time cruisers.

DCL'S TARGET MARKET

DISNEY CRUISES ARE TAILORED to families who are new to cruising. But like the theme parks, the cruise line is a Disney product for kids of all ages.

DISNEY CRUISE LINE SHIPS IN A NUTSHELL				
	Disney Magic	Disney Wonder	Disney Dream	Disney Fantasy
YEAR LAUNCHED	1998	1999	2011	2012
CAPACITY				
PASSENGERS (maximum)	2,713	2,713	4,000	4,000
CREW	950	950	1,458	1,458
TOTAL	3,663	3,663	5,458	5,458
PASSENGER DECKS	11	11	14	14
STATEROOMS				
INSIDE	256	256	150	150
OCEANVIEW	362	362	199	199
OUTSIDE VERANDAH	259	259	901	901
TOTAL	877	877	1,250	1,250
THEME	Art Deco	Art Nouveau	Art Deco	Art Nouveau

To cater to varied constituencies, some facilities, services, activities, and programs are designed specifically for adults without kids, including seniors and honeymooning couples. For example, in addition to the themed restaurants, each ship has at least one alternative restaurant, swimming pool, and nightclub for adults only, as well as entertainment for all the family. Disney continues trying to enhance the adult experience with such facilities as adults-only cafés, adult-oriented sports bars, and areas for teens.

Initially, cruise experts questioned whether Disney could fill its ships when kids are in school, but Disney determined that if 1–2% of the estimated 40 million annual visitors to its resorts and parks bought a Disney cruise vacation, the ships would sell out. Disney was right—now, after more than 15 years of success, no one is questioning them.

Disney offers a "seamless vacation package" to those who want to combine a stay at Walt Disney World with a cruise departing from Florida. DCL passengers are met at the airport by Disney staff and transported to the terminal in easily identifiable buses. When your cruise is packaged with a stay at most Disney hotels, you check into both your land and sea portions of your vacation at once.

COMPETITORS AND PRICES

DCL USES ITS REPUTATION for high quality, service, and entertainment to dispel novices' doubts about cruise vacations. Disney's main competitor seems to be **Royal Caribbean International,** which offers Caribbean, Mediterranean, and Alaskan cruises similar to Disney's, with most of the same departure and destination ports. The two cruise lines often have ships departing within days—sometimes hours—of each other, headed mostly to the same places.

Beyond staterooms, you'll find everything from bars and lounges to small art galleries, expansive spas, dedicated shopping areas, and specialty restaurants on both cruise lines. Here's how those offerings, plus pre- and post-cruise services, compare between DCL and Royal Caribbean's newer ships, such as the *Allure of the Seas, Oasis of the Seas,* and *Quantum of the Seas.*

AREA YOUTH CLUBS
WHO'S BETTER: Disney The children and teens we've interviewed, including our own, prefer Disney's kids clubs by a wide margin. During our observations, DCL staff ensured that every child new to the club was introduced to the existing members, and the staff actively participated in planning and keeping organized a continuous set of games, crafts, and play time.

If your vacation includes letting your children use one of the kids' clubs for any length of time, this is all you need to know.

AREA PRE-TRIP PLANNING AND RESERVATIONS
WHO'S BETTER: Disney Both cruise lines have good phone-based customer service. Disney's website is easier to use, especially for booking activities. On Royal Caribbean's website, we were never able to link reservations between our cabins, and we had to reenter all of our credit card information each time we booked a shore excursion or specialty meal.

AREA BOARDING PROCESS
WHO'S BETTER: Royal Caribbean Its boarding is faster and more efficient, even on ships such as the *Allure,* which holds 50% more passengers than Disney's largest ships.

AREA GETTING AROUND AND GETTING ORIENTED
WHO'S BETTER: Disney DCL's daily *Personal Navigator* and free smartphone app let you see quickly what's going on at any time of day. We do like Royal Caribbean's touchscreen maps, near the elevators.

AREA THEMING AND DETAIL OF PUBLIC SPACES
WHO'S BETTER: Tie DCL's stem-to-stern theming, based on the decor of classic ocean liners, makes its ships far prettier than Royal Caribbean's, which, as one of our dinner companions remarked, feel "like a really nice mall."

That said, Royal Caribbean's largest ships are big enough to have scaled-down versions of New York's Central Park and Atlantic City's boardwalk, which Disney can't match. Royal's collection of onboard art, curated from contemporary artists worldwide and found in walkways and stairwells, is more interesting to many adults than Disney's collection, which comes from its animated films.

AREA DINING
WHO'S BETTER: Disney Both cruise lines provide breakfast, lunch, and

dinner in standard restaurants as part of your fare. Disney's food is tastier and its restaurants more elaborately themed.

On the other hand, Royal Caribbean's larger ships have more than 20 optional dining locations (where you pay extra to eat), while DCL's ships have just 1 or 2. If you think you'll tire of visiting the same restaurant several times, Royal is a better choice.

Service is excellent on both lines.

AREA **LIVE ENTERTAINMENT**

WHO'S BETTER: Royal Caribbean Both lines put on large, elaborate stage shows: Royal Caribbean's lineup includes *Chicago;* Disney generally rehashes its animated stories. Royal's shows are more varied and appeal more to adults; what's more, we think its performers and musicians are better than DCL's.

AREA **NIGHTCLUBS, BARS, AND LOUNGES**

WHO'S BETTER: Disney Surprised? Where Royal Caribbean's bars tend to be large, open to pedestrian traffic, and barely themed, Disney's are more intimate and have appropriately atmospheric music and decor, and many sit in a dedicated adults-only area, far away from crowded public spaces. (Case in point: Disney's Champagne bars play Édith Piaf and Frank Sinatra in the background, as the good Lord intended; Royal's bars play The Eagles and Gordon Lightfoot.) Plus, service is more personal on DCL.

AREA **SHOPPING**

WHO'S BETTER: Royal Caribbean Its larger ships carry a wider variety of men's and women's clothing, art, housewares, and more. Both lines sell men's and women's jewelry, duty-free alcohol, and sundries.

AREA **SPA**

WHO'S BETTER: Disney Another area where DCL wins on theming and detail. While Senses Spa on the *Dream* and the *Fantasy* are smaller than Royal Caribbean's spas, Disney's overlook the ocean and have more heated stone loungers, more themed showers, and better steam rooms.

AREA **POOLS**

WHO'S BETTER: Disney for kids, Royal Caribbean for adults The children's play areas, slides, and water rides on Disney's ships are better than Royal Caribbean's. For adults, Royal's newer ships have larger pools and more of them, spread across an even wider area than on Disney's largest ships.

AREA **DEBARKATION**

WHO'S BETTER: Royal Caribbean Both DCL and Royal Caribbean can get you off the ship in a hurry, although Royal does it a bit faster. Disney's baggage-claim area is better organized, however, making it easier to find your checked luggage.

Cost Considerations

Disney's fares include unlimited fountain soda, plain coffee, tea, and water (bottled versions cost extra), while Royal Caribbean charges around $20 per person per day for fountain soda as part of a beverage package (which also includes bottled water, orange juice, premium coffee, and nonalcoholic cocktails), or about $560 for a family of four for a seven-night cruise. We don't recommend Royal's beverage package—for one thing, their free coffee is better than Disney's, and our family was happy to drink water, tea, and lemonade throughout our cruise. We each had an occasional soda at mealtime, but we didn't spend anything close to $560 on extra drinks on our weeklong cruise.

When it comes to the bottom line, however, the fact is that Disney charges a premium for its cruise product. For example, on seven-night Eastern Caribbean cruises out of Port Canaveral during the second half of 2015, Disney's prices were over $7,200 for one inside cabin, depending on the specific date; Royal Caribbean's prices were $2,200–$3,000, around 60–70% less than Disney for very similar cruises. (All cruise prices assume two adults and two children ages 12 and 6 in one cabin.)

We initially thought Disney was charging more for these cruises because its Orlando theme parks provide a built-in audience for Port Canaveral sailing; the port is, after all, within 90 minutes of Walt Disney World. But Disney is more expensive for ports far away from its theme parks: We spot-checked Disney's seven-night Alaska cruises out of Vancouver for 2013 and 2014 and found that they run around 80% more than Royal Caribbean's—a difference of $2,400–$2,700 per cruise. That kind of money buys a lot of ice.

One area where Disney seems to be price-competitive with Royal Caribbean is on seven-night Mediterranean cruises out of Barcelona, Spain. Fares for random dates in 2015 for Disney cruises were slightly lower or the same, on average, than Royal Caribbean.

HOW *to* CONTACT
the AUTHORS

MANY WHO USE THE *UNOFFICIAL GUIDES* write to us with questions, comments, or their own strategies for planning and enjoying travel. We appreciate all such input, both positive and critical. Readers' comments are frequently incorporated into revised editions and have contributed immeasurably to their improvement. Please write to:

Len, Erin, Laurel, and Ritchey
The Unofficial Guide to Disney Cruise Line
PO Box 43673
Birmingham, AL 35243
unofficialguides@menasharidge.com

When you write, put your address on both your letter and envelope; the two sometimes get separated. It's also a good idea to include your phone number. If you e-mail us, please tell us where you're from. Remember, as travel writers, we're often out of the office for long periods of time, so forgive us if our response is slow. *Unofficial Guide* e-mail isn't forwarded to us when we're traveling, but we'll respond as soon as possible after we return.

READER SURVEY

OUR WEBSITE HOSTS A QUESTIONNAIRE you can use to express opinions about your Disney cruise, at **touringplans.com/disney-cruise-line/survey**. The questionnaire lets every member of your party, regardless of age, tell us what he or she thinks about attractions, restaurants, and more.

If you'd rather print out and send us the survey, mail it to **Reader Survey, *The Unofficial Guides*, P.O. Box 43673, Birmingham, AL 35243.**

PART ONE

DOLLARS *and* SENSE

WHAT'S INCLUDED *in* YOUR DISNEY CRUISE FARE

A DISNEY CRUISE ISN'T CHEAP. Given the cost, you might be wondering how much more you'll have to pay once you're aboard the ship. Here's a quick rundown of what is and isn't included in your cruise fare. We've included some rough estimates of the optional items to help with budgeting.

FOOD

INCLUDED: LOTS OF FOOD All meals, including snacks, are free at all of the ship's restaurants except for Remy and Palo. You can order as much food as you like.

NOT INCLUDED: FANCY RESTAURANTS Meals at Remy and Palo require an additional charge of $75 and $25, respectively, for dinner; Palo also charges $25 for its brunch, while Remy's brunch is $50. Wine is an extra charge beyond those prices, at each meal.

INCLUDED: MOST ROOM-SERVICE ITEMS Your fare includes room-service meals, except as noted below. Room service is a great option for when you don't feel like dressing up for dinner.

NOT INCLUDED: PACKAGED SNACKS AND BOTTLED DRINKS Beverages such as bottled water ($3), soda not served as part of meal service or from the self-service dispensers on the pool deck ($3), beer ($6), and wine ($8 and up) cost extra, as do packaged snacks such as popcorn and peanuts. Tips are another additional charge.

INCLUDED: ALL-YOU-WANT SOFT DRINKS AND ICE CREAM Complimentary soda, coffee, water, cocoa, and hot and iced tea are unlimited at meals, and beverages served from drink dispensers on deck are also free of charge. Self-serve ice cream from the onboard dispensers is free.

NOT INCLUDED: BOTTLED WATER, ALCOHOLIC BEVERAGES, AND FANCY COFFEES Bottled water, beer, wine, and cocktails cost extra. A wine package is available. You'll also pay out-of-pocket for specialty coffees, espresso, cappuccinos, and teas from bars and cafés (such as the Cove Café). A 15% gratuity is automatically added to bar and beverage tabs. Adults 21 and older may also bring their own wine and liquor aboard in their carry-on luggage; a $20 corking fee applies if you bring your own wine or Champagne to a full-service restaurant on board.

The 10 Best Bangs for Your Buck (*and One Freebie*) on a Disney Caribbean Cruise

1. Rainforest at Senses Spa (*Dream* and *Fantasy*) At around $25 per day, this is a must-do. Only a limited number of passes are sold per cruise, so make a point of buying your pass soon after boarding. Because of the limits on how many passes are sold (we've heard 20 per cruise), there are many times when you'll have the entire Rainforest to yourself. This is the ultimate in quiet relaxation for adults, and a total bargain at that. The package is also available at Senses Spa on the *Magic* and Vista Spa on the *Wonder* (about $16 per day), but the smaller Rainforest area means that you're more likely to have company, and the number of showers and saunas is a little disappointing if you've ever experienced the spa on the larger ships. Try the body scrubs (extra charge) at least once.

2. Porters for your bags The $2–$5 per bag you'll tip your porter both boarding and returning home through Customs is money well spent. These guys work hard and make our lives so much easier. When boarding, not having to handle your own bags is one less hassle in a hectic process. When you leave the ship, it helps you end your cruise on a high note.

3. Bicycles on Castaway Cay These wheels cost $10 per hour and make getting around the island a breeze. But more than that, they're fun for the whole family. Between riding out to the observation tower (off the airstrip) for a great view of the island and getting to your destination on the island faster than the tram can get you there, this decision is as easy as riding a . . . well, you know.

4. Snorkeling on Castaway Cay A mask, flippers, and life vest will set you back $29 per adult and $14 per kid. The sea life is copious in the lagoon, and the hidden treasures Disney has added under water are a delight. Go in the morning and again in the afternoon. Hours of entertainment aren't usually this cheap when Disney's name is attached.

5. Palo A quiet, no-rush brunch or dinner for adults with great service and food for $25 plus gratuity? Heck, yeah! Let's face it: Your kids are probably ready to spend some time away from you too. Come for the food; linger for the atmosphere. Dress up and remember that a meal this good would cost several times as much on shore.

The 10 Best Bangs for Your Buck
(*and One Freebie*) on a Disney Caribbean Cruise

6. Adult-beverage tastings For around $15, you're treated to several wines, liquors, or cocktails. (*Remember:* No one is spitting out the spirits, and they can sneak up on you, so try to eat something first.) We've been lucky enough to be the only participants on a few occasions, allowing us to really interact with the guides. Our favorite is the Champagne tasting, but we haven't been let down by any of them. One author discovered a new favorite wine during a tasting at Meridian on the *Fantasy*. Another time, we were asked, "How would you like to try the most expensive whiskey we sell?" Our reply: "Yes, please!"

7. Castaway Ray's Stingray Adventure This is both less expensive and better organized than stingray encounters in other ports. It's a winner with kids ($36) and adults ($45). There's no time wasted getting back and forth to your port adventure because it's on Castaway Cay—just show up at the ray area at your appointed time, and have fun.

8. Flounder's Reef Nursery (*Wonder*)/It's a Small World Nursery Parents of children younger than age 3 can enjoy some downtime and let the excellent staff watch their little ones for $9 per hour for the first child and $8 per hour per additional child in the same family. Feedback from parents is extremely positive.

9. Coffee The "coffee" at the beverage stations can best be described as a tepid, vaguely coffee-flavored substance that will make you question your will to live. Pony up for the real thing at Cove Café, Vista Café, or the coffee bar at the buffets. Sure, it's around $3–$5 plus tip, but that's less than you'd pay at Starbucks, and it doesn't make you regret your caffeine habit. Ask for a Café Fanatic rewards card and get every sixth coffee drink free. (For us, that's sometime early in day two of any cruise.) Didn't fill all the punches on your card? Hang on to it for your next cruise.

10. Castaway Cay 5K This port adventure is free, and you get the moral superiority of knowing you've gotten in your exercise for the day while being among the first to exit the ship at the island. There are race bibs and plastic medals, and the whole family can join in. Try to beat your Castaway Cay personal best every time you come to the island.

11. Gratuities DCL ships are full of energetic young men and women, many of whom are far away from home, who make your trip magical. In addition to tipping our servers and stateroom attendants generously—yes, that means more than the recommended amount—we also start our trip off right by meeting our baristas and bartenders on the first day and night of the cruise and treating them well. We don't do it because we expect anything extra (though being known as good customers never hurts), but because we get fantastic service. And don't forget these folks when you're filling out your comment cards at the end of the cruise. It's always good to help a deserving person's career when you can.

ENTERTAINMENT AND ACTIVITIES

INCLUDED: LOTS OF ENTERTAINMENT There's no extra charge for live performances, movies, and character greetings.

NOT INCLUDED: BINGO, SOME ONBOARD SEMINARS, AND MOVIE SNACKS A few activities, such as bingo, cost money to play. Beverage seminars, which typically offer several kinds of spirits for sampling, cost $15–$25 depending on the alcohol. Likewise, at the movie theater, candy bars and such cost extra.

INCLUDED: GYM FACILITIES Covered in your fare is use of the fitness center, including free weights and other fitness equipment. The center also has changing rooms with showers and sauna.

NOT INCLUDED: SPA AND SALON SERVICES Spa treatments (including massages, facials, steam rooms, and upscale showers) cost from $115 to upwards of $500 per person, per treatment. Salon services range from $50 to $70 for manicures and pedicures, and from $35 to around $75 for hairstyling, depending on hair length.

INCLUDED: POOLS, GAMES, AND MOST SPORTS These include all of the pools and waterslides and activities, such as miniature golf, basketball, Ping-Pong, and shuffleboard. Board games are available at no charge in some lounges.

NOT INCLUDED: VIDEO GAMES The video arcades on the ships charge 25¢–$2 per game.

INCLUDED: CASTAWAY CAY BEACHES AND RESTAURANTS Food, lounge chairs, and beach umbrellas are free, as is Castaway Cay's 5K road run.

NOT INCLUDED: CASTAWAY CAY RECREATION AND ALCOHOL Disney Cruise Line (DCL) charges for bike rentals ($10 per hour), snorkeling ($14–$29 for one day, $18–$36 for two days), and use of boats ($14–$27 per half-hour) and watercraft ($95 per hour for one rider, $160 per hour for two riders). The same goes for private cabanas—a whopping $400 or $529 per day—and alcoholic drinks at Castaway Cay's bars.

KID STUFF

INCLUDED: KIDS' CLUBS (AGES 3 AND UP) These include the Oceaneer Club/Oceaneer Lab for kids ages 3–12, the Edge club for tweens ages 11–14, and the Vibe club for teens ages 14–17.

NOT INCLUDED: CHILD CARE FOR KIDS UNDER 3 The Flounder's Reef and It's a Small World Nurseries charge $9 per hour for the first child and $8 per hour for a second child in the same family.

MISCELLANEOUS

INCLUDED: CALLS TO ANYWHERE ON THE SHIP Use of the ships' Wave Phones is free.

NOT INCLUDED: SHIP-TO-SHORE CALLS AND INTERNET Ship-to-shore calls from onboard phones cost $8 per minute. Each stateroom has a standard phone with voice mail, plus a Wave Phone, a mobile phone you may use free of charge on the ship and Castaway Cay for calls, voice mail, and text messaging (only from Wave Phone to Wave Phone).

Rather than charge cruisers for their Internet usage based on how long they're online, Disney Cruise Line charges based on the amount of bandwidth used. The following is a list of the packages available, with our recommendations:

PLAN	DATA (MB)	COST	NOTES
Pay as You Go	1	25¢	Use if you have a one-off need for the Internet to check or send e-mail
Small	100	$19 (19¢/MB)	For guests who need to check e-mail from time to time but don't need to surf the Internet during their cruise
Medium	300	$39 (13¢/MB)	For guests who wish to use social media to let their friends know how much fun they're having on board
Large	1,000	$89 (9¢/MB)	For guests who are unable to leave their work at home or who wish to stream music. (Many movies will take up more than the 1GB allowance, and an HD movie can take up to four times this much.)

Other items not included:

PHOTOS Disney offers packages of prints or CDs similar to its Memory Maker packages at Walt Disney World. Pricing begins at around $150 for a package of 10 prints and up to $450 for a package of all your onboard photos on a CD as well as printed. Onboard photographers will also shoot pictures for free with your own camera.

SHORE EXCURSIONS Known in DCL-speak as port adventures, these cost anywhere from $10 (for a 1-hour bike rental on Castaway Cay) to $1,900 (for a private catamaran tour of St. Maarten). Be aware that many shore excursions carry additional optional costs beyond the stated price. For example, many excursion operators offer souvenir photo packages for an additional fee. Additionally, meals are not included in the price of many shore excursions.

LAUNDRY It costs $2 to wash and $2 to dry a load of clothes. Soap, fabric softener, and dryer sheets are available for $1 each, per load. Dry cleaning is also available for an additional fee.

GRATUITIES Disney automatically adds gratuities of around $12 per person per day to your onboard account. A 15% gratuity is automatically added to bar and beverage tabs. See pages 57–58 for more information.

TRANSPORTATION TO THE PORT Round-trip service between Walt Disney World and Port Canaveral runs $70 per person; transportation costs between any city's cruise terminal and airport may vary. See the section starting on page 40 for more details.

CRUISING *with* KIDS

WE'LL START BY SAYING that there's a good chance your kids will have a great time.

As parents, we know that one of the most difficult parts of planning a vacation with kids is ensuring that they're entertained throughout the trip. For us, this usually means making sure that every travel day has at least a couple of things specifically designed to appeal to our kids and their friends—things we'd prefer didn't involve shopping or sitting passively in front of a screen.

It can be exhausting to plan this way (and we're *professionals!*). In fact, we think this is one of the main reasons why a trip to Disney World is so appealing to parents: Disney's theme parks provide a nearly constant and wide-ranging set of entertainment options for kids and adults. A family that hasn't planned a thing can show up and find something fun to do. Disney cruises work the same way—family activities, including trivia contests, scavenger hunts, and shuffleboard, are scheduled throughout the day, on virtually every day of every sailing.

If you think your kids would benefit from spending some time with their peers, Disney provides organized activities throughout the day for children ages 3–17. Some activities for younger children get started as early as 7 a.m., while activities for older teens can run until 2 a.m. Off the ships, Castaway Cay offers dedicated beach and recreation spots for families, teens, and tweens, plus a splash area for little ones. There are shore excursions created just for families too. Some sailings also offer teen-only excursions and sightseeing events.

*un*official TIP
See page 142 for our advice on cruising with teens and tweens.

Disney is also keeping up with two recent trends in the cruise industry. The first is setting aside more space per ship for kids' clubs. On the newer *Dream* and *Fantasy,* these clubs take up substantially more space than on older DCL ships. Second, Disney frequently runs concurrent, age-appropriate activities within the same club. For example, the Oceaneer Club accepts children ages 3–12; however, Disney may group together the younger kids for a game with marshmallows in one area of the club while the older kids sing karaoke in another.

Our own children have found Disney's children's activities more fun than hanging around with us on the ship. It may be a cliché, but it's true: We saw the kids only during meals, at bedtime, or when we specifically scheduled things to do as a family. Thanks to the web, our kids are still in contact with the friends they've made on their cruises, even though some are an ocean away.

CRUISING *Without* KIDS

GIVEN DISNEY'S REPUTATION for family-friendly entertainment, it's natural for those who travel without children to wonder if DCL is a good choice for adult cruisers. Happily, just as with the Disney parks, there's something for folks of all ages to enjoy on a Disney cruise. Disney ships have an adults-only pool and coffeehouse, the spa is limited to guests age 18 and up (with the exception of the Chill teen spa on the *Dream* and *Fantasy*), and some of the entertainment districts are limited to cruisers age 18 and up every night after around 9 p.m. For those wanting to dine in an adults-only atmosphere, Remy (*Dream* and *Fantasy* only) and Palo (see Part Seven) are likewise restricted to those age 18 and older. Castaway Cay has an adult beach with its own dining, bar, and cabanas (which must be reserved in advance). We recommend traveling when school is in session if you're looking for a more adult-oriented vacation, and the good news is that these times tend to be far less expensive. Disney cast members have told us that the long ship-repositioning cruises (such as the Panama Canal itinerary) or transatlantic voyages tend to have the lowest percentage of children on board.

unofficial **TIP**
DCL seems to be very popular for girls' trips because of its safe atmosphere.

If your idea of a fun cruise is a party boat, then DCL probably isn't for you. There's no casino, and honestly the nightlife is more mild than wild. But we've traveled several times with only adults in our party and had a fantastic time. Spend some time at the spa, get to know the bartenders and baristas at the various bars and lounges, skip the shows, dine at Palo or Remy (or both!), and enjoy some downtime.

WHERE *to* FIND
MORE INFORMATION

DISNEY CRUISE LINE'S OFFICIAL WEBSITE is **disneycruise.disney .go.com.** Here, you can see which itineraries are served by each ship; search for cruises by destination, month, and length; and see prices for various kinds of staterooms. Once you've made a reservation, you can book shore excursions, restaurants, and children's activities through the site.

PassPorter's Disney Cruise Line and Its Ports of Call guidebook ($21.95 for the basic edition) provides a good overview of DCL. The deluxe edition ($47.95) includes paper worksheets that you can use to plan everything from a cruise budget to a daily schedule. The book's companion website, **passporter.com,** has user-led discussion forums, where folks from all over can ask questions and provide answers to almost any cruise-related scenario.

Muelle , E

8699

Thu Aug 11 2016

The unofficial guide to Disney

3350801502491S

Another good online resource is **disneycruiselineblog.com,** which posts almost-daily updates, including everything from new-itinerary rumors to new shopping merchandise on board. The site also has a neat feature that lets you see the current location of every ship in the Disney fleet.

Despite the somewhat confusing name, the **Disney Parks Moms Panel (disneyworldforum.disney.go.com)** features Disney Cruise Line specialists. These folks are veterans of many DCL voyages and have received training from DCL cast members. They're able to answer any individual Disney cruise–planning question, big or small.

Popular general Disney sites with dedicated DCL forums include **disboards.com, forums.wdwmagic.com, micechat.com,** and, for Brits, **thedibb.co.uk** (*DIBB* stands for "Disney Information Bulletin Board").

PART TWO

PLANNING YOUR CRUISE

CHOOSING *an* ITINERARY

DISNEY CRUISE LINE OFFERS ALMOST 50 SEPARATE ITINER-ARIES, ranging from 2-night weekend getaways to 15-night voyages between two oceans using the Panama Canal. The cruise you select is likely to be determined by how much vacation time you have, the ship on which you want to sail, the cost, and the ports that interest you.

ITINERARY RECOMMENDATIONS FOR FIRST-TIME CRUISERS

WE THINK THE IDEAL ITINERARY for first-time cruisers is four or five nights aboard the *Dream* or *Fantasy*. Why? They're newer ships, with better restaurants, bars, and spas; interactive areas, such as the Midship Detective Agency; more space for kids' activities; and more space on deck for pools and lounging.

unofficial **TIP**
The average Disney cruise lasts five nights, sails somewhere in the Caribbean, and stops at Disney's Castaway Cay island in the Bahamas.

An ideal cruise for first-timers also includes two stops at Castaway Cay, Disney's private island (see Part Ten). You'll need one visit to become familiar with the island and its features; by the second day, you'll be more relaxed, knowing that you're taking advantage of the best the island has to offer.

There are 10 "double dip" sailings on the *Dream* in 2015, all leaving Port Canaveral and all between June 22 and July 29, 2015. The next-best alternative is a 7-Night Eastern Caribbean cruise aboard the *Fantasy*, with three days at sea plus stops at St. Maarten; San Juan, Puerto Rico; and Castaway Cay. Three days at sea allows you plenty of time to relax and explore the ship. Dozens of these cruises are available, so finding one should be easy at any time of year.

GENERAL RECOMMENDATIONS

IF YOU'RE TRYING TO DECIDE among Eastern Caribbean, Western Caribbean, and Bahamian cruises, you only have two questions to answer: First, are you interested in exploring the culture of the ports you're visiting? Second, if so, are you more interested in Caribbean towns or Mayan history?

If the answer to the first question is no—if your perfect vacation involves lying on a beach, taking the kids snorkeling, scuba diving, or swimming with dolphins—you can do that in every port from Barbados to Cozumel. Pick any itinerary that includes Castaway Cay and that also fits your schedule and budget, and you're set.

If you're interested in local color, choose between the Eastern and Western Caribbean itineraries. The Eastern itineraries offer the best ports to explore. **St. John** and **St. Thomas** are great stops, but Disney gives you only 5 or 6 hours there. **St. Maarten** is fun because it's Dutch.

On Western Caribbean cruises, **Costa Maya** and **Cozumel** are notable only for their inland tours of Mayan ruins. If those interest you more than Caribbean towns, pick a Western itinerary.

Now, lest you think we're making an "all those people look the same" argument in advising you how to choose between Bahamian and Caribbean itineraries, rest assured we're not. Rather, our advice is based on the observation that the cruise industry's overbooking of the same Caribbean ports has led to a certain sameness of experience virtually everywhere. As Julia Cosgrove, editor-in-chief of *Afar* magazine, observes, "There's no sense of 'I should go to this island as opposed to that because I'm going to get this deeper cultural experience by connecting with people in one place versus another.' "

Disney's seven- and nine-day Alaska itineraries are virtually identical, and all are served by the *Wonder*. Pick whichever itinerary suits your budget and schedule.

Disney's Mediterranean cruises are distinguished primarily by their length (typically 4, 5, 7, 9, or 12 nights), departure port, and whether they visit Venice. The main distinction among the 12-night cruises is whether they include that visit to Venice: Three of the four itineraries do, with only the "A" itinerary skipping it. If you really want to see Venice, however, the 12-night "B" and "C" itineraries include an overnight stop, which would allow you to stay out to the wee hours.

Guests with special needs (see Part Five, pages 67–69) will want to think about the port-adventure options available with the itineraries they're considering. Because some ports have a preponderance of excursions that prohibit wheelchair access, you may not want to book a trip where your choice of off-ship activities could be limited.

unofficial **TIP**
When you're combing through the DCL website for discounts, look for stateroom categories with the codes **IGT, OGT,** and **VGT.** These indicate heavily discounted inside, outside, and verandah staterooms.

SAVING MONEY

YOU HAVE FOUR PRIMARY STRATEGIES for saving money on a Disney cruise:

1. **Book as early as possible.** Most cruise fares start low and begin to rise as the ship fills up. It's possible to save 10–20% by booking a year in advance.

2. **Book at the last minute.** Conversely, if your travel schedule is very flexible, savings of up to 25% off are possible when you book a cruise within two weeks of its sailing date. These deals are especially good if you live within a day's drive of the departure port because you can avoid the last-minute price hikes on airline tickets. Offers including last-minute deals can be found on DCL's website (**disneycruise.disney.go.com**), as well as on our favorite money-saving site, **MouseSavers (mousesavers.com)**, under "Disney Cruise Line."

3. **Book your next cruise while on board.** DCL offers discounts up to 10% off the lowest prevailing rates, occasionally along with onboard ship credits. Stop by the Future Cruise Sales Desk, usually on Deck 4 Midship, for details. Be aware that discount blackout dates may apply—when we tried to book a cruise coinciding with Easter, we were told that the standard 10% discount was unavailable. We were, however, able to get an onboard credit and a reduced deposit.

4. **Depart from a less popular port.** Disney offers aggressive discounts on cruises from ports that aren't in great demand. Disney cruises out of the poor-selling Galveston, Texas, port, for example, were discounted throughout most of 2013 and early 2014. Your travel agents should know which ports aren't selling as quickly as others. Armed with that information, you'll find it easy to compare transportation costs to the ports you're considering. (See Part Four for more tips on choosing a port.)

5. **Take advantage of onboard credit offers.** While pricing for cruise fares is consistent from Disney to independent travel agents to larger online sites, such as Orbitz and Expedia, some agencies are able to sweeten the pot with generous onboard credits. Shop around for the best packages.

 # SURF *and* TURF, DISNEY-STYLE

COMBINING YOUR CRUISE WITH A WALT DISNEY WORLD VACATION

DISNEY SELLS PACKAGES THAT COMBINE A DISNEY CRUISE and a trip to Walt Disney World, for cruises departing from Port Canaveral. Called **Land and Sea** packages, the itineraries include the Bahamas, Eastern and Western Caribbean, and the *Magic*'s Eastbound Transatlantic cruise to Barcelona. Land and Sea packages include lodging at a Disney World resort; theme park admission, dining plans, and other extras can be added to the Disney World portion of the trip. Because of the lack of flexibility with a Land and Sea package through DCL, and due to better prices when booking à la carte, we recommend making reservations for each part of a theme park and cruise vacation separately. Regardless of whether you book land and sea together or separately, you will be able to arrange bus transportation between Port Canaveral and your Walt Disney World resort for a fee.

The most frequent question we're asked about combining a theme park and cruise vacation is whether to visit Disney World before or after the cruise. The majority of people who've done both say they were more relaxed on the cruise than at Walt Disney World, so they prefer to take the cruise after the park visit. Some families don't have a preference either way. A relatively small number prefer to see Walt Disney World second because they prefer the faster pace of WDW after a cruise. Our recommendation, though, is to see the World first—chances are that your tired legs (and wallet) will appreciate some downtime at sea.

COMBINING YOUR CRUISE WITH AN ADVENTURES BY DISNEY TRIP

MANY EUROPEAN CRUISES out of Barcelona, Venice, Dover, and Copenhagen can be combined with a pre-cruise Adventures by Disney guided vacation. Your trip includes lodging, meals, and tours. For more details, see **adventuresbydisney.com** (click "Destinations," then "Europe").

 The **BOOKING PROCESS**

GETTING STARTED

ONCE YOU'VE SETTLED ON A SHIP, an itinerary, and dates, it's time to book your trip. You have three ways to do this:

1. Use the Disney Cruise Line website (**disneycruise.disney.go.com**).

2. Call DCL at ☎ 800-951-3532.

3. Use a travel agent.

There are advantages to each. The main advantage to booking yourself, either online or by phone, is that you can usually do it immediately. If you have booked a cruise before, have access to each traveler's information, don't have questions about the ship or itinerary, and want instant gratification, this may be your best option.

The advantage of using a travel agent is that he or she can save you time by doing most of the tedious data entry for you, and the agent may also offer onboard credits. Many agents have booked dozens, if not hundreds, of cruises, and have a single-page form for you to fill out, where you provide your preferences for everything from what time you prefer to board the ship to when you prefer to eat. Some travel agencies will also rebook your cruise automatically if a lower fare becomes available. A travel agent might also be able to save you money because he or she might have access to group space for a particular cruise. The traveler doesn't have to participate in any group activities but receives the price advantage of being part of the group booking.

DEPOSIT TERMS AND CANCELLATION POLICY

MOST CRUISE RESERVATIONS REQUIRE A DEPOSIT equal to 20% of the cruise's price (not including taxes) for each passenger age 3 and older on that reservation. Some DCL promotions, such as booking a follow-up cruise while you're already on a current cruise, require only a 10% deposit. Booking a future cruise while you're on the ship almost always includes an onboard credit for the cruise you're booking too.

DCL's full cancellation policy can be found online at the DCL website; click "Terms and Conditions" at the bottom of the home page. You can cancel a reservation in writing or by phone; also, moving the date of your cruise or changing the name of someone on your reservation is considered a cancellation.

If your cruise starts or ends in the United States and your cruise is fewer than 10 days long, your refund amount depends on how much advance notice you give Disney. The following table summarizes the criteria used:

SUITES AND CONCIERGE STATEROOMS	
If You Cancel This Many Days Before Start of Cruise	**DCL Charges This for Cancellation**
90 days or more	Your entire deposit (typically 20%)
89–56 days	50% of vacation price, per person
55–30 days	75% of vacation price, per person
29 days or fewer	100% of vacation price, per person

For staterooms that are not suites or in the concierge section, a "holiday" cancellation policy applies if your sailing starts or ends in the United States, is fewer than 10 days long, and includes these US holiday dates: January 1, July 4, Thanksgiving (the fourth Thursday in November), or December 25:

HOLIDAY CANCELLATION POLICY *(Excludes suites and concierge staterooms)*	
If You Cancel This Many Days Before Start of Cruise	**DCL Charges This for Cancellation**
89–65 days	Your entire deposit (typically 20%)
64–43 days	50% of vacation price, per person
42–15 days	75% of vacation price, per person
14 days or fewer	100% of vacation price, per person

The nonholiday cancellation policy is less restrictive:

STANDARD CANCELLATION POLICY *(Excludes suites and concierge staterooms)*	
If You Cancel This Many Days Before Start of Cruise	**DCL Charges This for Cancellation**
74–45 days	Your entire deposit (typically 20%)
44–30 days	50% of vacation price, per person
29–15 days	75% of vacation price, per person
14 days or fewer	100% of trip price, per person

If your cruise starts and ends outside the United States or lasts 10 days or more, the cancellation terms are as follows:

SAILINGS OUTSIDE THE US OR 10+ DAYS IN LENGTH	
If You Cancel This Many Days Before Start of Cruise	DCL Charges This for Cancellation
56+ days (suites and concierge rooms) or 119–56 days (other than suites and concierge rooms)	Your entire deposit (typically 20%)
55–30 days	50% of vacation price, per person
29–15 days	75% of vacation price, per person
14 days or fewer	100% of trip price, per person

If you booked a cruise before October 1, 2014, the cancellation fees will be based on the schedule listed on your original confirmation, unless the sailing date or vacation package is modified.

Finally, cruises booked with a "restricted rate" discount code are always nonrefundable and nontransferable—you forfeit 100% of the cruise fee if you don't sail.

THE DCL PLANNING CENTER

A KEY PART OF YOUR Disney Cruise Line booking is the Planning Center at the DCL website: **disneycruiseline.com/plan.** You can access the Planning Center only with a reservation number—available after you've paid your deposit and received your confirmation e-mail. In addition to the reservation number, you'll need access to the birth date of at least one member of your party. If you've cruised with Disney previously, you may also access your reservation without your reservation number through the Castaway Club section of the DCL site.

The Planning Center includes the following:

- **Reservation Summary** Basic info such as your stateroom number; dining-time assignment; names of the guests in your party; air transportation, ground transportation, and WDW hotel information, if you've booked any of these through Disney; and trip itinerary, including ashore and onboard times for port days. Remember that if your party has booked multiple staterooms, you'll have multiple reservation numbers. To reserve excursions or onboard activities, you'll need the correct reservation number for each member of your party, and you'll need to be in the Planning Center for the correct stateroom.

- **My Cruise Activities** Descriptions of the port adventures and onboard activities available during your sailing, including excursions, spa treatments, adult dining, child care, and more. After you've paid your cruise fee in full and as your travel date nears, this becomes the booking center for these items.

- **My Online Check-In** You may check in online up to three days before your sailing. This is where you'll give DCL specifics about your travel, authorize credit card payment for onboard purchases, and provide additional information about your party. While Online Check-In is optional, it can reduce your wait time at the port terminal. If you're using My Online Check-In, you'll be able to print a signature and payment-authorization form. Bring this with you to your embarkation port.

- **Fun Aboard the Ship** Information on amenities specific to your sailing vessel.

- **Character Calls** Arrange for a Disney character to place a recorded phone call to your home welcoming members of your party to their cruise (which is particularly fun if the cruise is a surprise for those with whom you're cruising).

- **Packing List** General recommendations for what to pack, along with some specifics based on your cruise itinerary.

- **Air & Ground Transportation** This is where you'll enter your flight/port-transfer information or add port transfers and so on to your package.

- **Passport & Travel Documentation** Notifications about specific travel documents required for your itinerary.

- **Stay Connected** Allows you to register for e-mail or text reminders about your trip.

- **In-Room Gifts & Shopping** Lets you buy presents and floral arrangements for members of your party who may be celebrating birthdays, anniversaries, or other milestones during your voyage. Gifts will be delivered to your stateroom during your sailing.

- **Driving Directions** Detailed directions to your port. Also includes the correct address to make your GPS happy.

- **Custom Pre-Arrival Guide** You can download a PDF of most of the information provided at the Planning Center. The file will include your booking information as well as your general itinerary and any excursions, spa treatments, or adult dining you may have booked.

If you're like most guests, you'll visit the Planning Center more than a few times before your trip. One of our most recent DCL voyages was a four-day quickie, with just two guests. Even with this relatively simple profile, we stopped by the Planning Center nearly a dozen times before our trip—sometimes just to feel good knowing we were headed out on a cruise.

OTHER PREP WORK

PACKING

HAVING TRAVELED WITH LOTS OF PEOPLE over many years, we realize that asking "What do I need to pack?" is like asking "What is art?" Everyone will have their own answer based on their experience and preferences. Some people assume that they're going to do laundry on the ship and pack three days' worth

unofficial **TIP**
Check out *Unofficial Guide* blogger Scott Sanders's excellent DCL packing tips at **blog.touringplans.com.**

of clothes for a seven-night cruise. Others would rather pay for an extra suitcase to carry more clean clothes. The amount you pack is up to you.

Knowing what to pack is equally important, and the range of opinions regarding packing essentials is huge. The DCL Planning Center has a pretty good page with suggestions on appropriate clothing for the ship's restaurants and ports of call, along with a short, reasonable list of incidentals to pack (as well as stuff you can't bring aboard).

unofficial **TIP**
When you're searching for outlets in your stateroom, be thorough: We've often found unoccupied outlets behind the TV. And feel free to unplug your Wave Phone if you know you won't be using it.

Beyond that, type "Disney Cruise Line packing list" into any search engine and you'll see thousands of lists with hundreds of items. Some of them read like an Amazon jungle-trek prep list (mosquito netting appears on more than one). It's useful to read through a couple of lists to see if they mention anything you can't live without. Our most important packing advice is this: Don't drive yourself crazy trying to pack for every scenario. You're going to lug those bags a lot farther than you might think. If you're not absolutely certain you're going to use something, *leave it at home.*

You can buy most everyday personal items on board the ship if needed. We generally don't make a special trip to the drugstore to buy motion-sickness pills, antibiotic/anti-itch creams, or over-the-counter pain relievers if we don't already have them on hand at home. To avoid bringing extra luggage, guests with young children may want to purchase supplies through **Babies Travel Lite** (babiestravellite .com/?AFFIL=DCL), which offers such items as diapers, wipes, and bath supplies. They can also deliver baby-care items to your pre- or post-cruise hotel in Orlando, Los Angeles, or Vancouver.

Besides appropriate clothing, our short packing list includes the following essentials:

- **Prescription medication** Pack these in carry-on luggage, in their original containers.

- **Tablet computer** Load enough books, music, movies, TV shows, games, and apps for the cruise, plus the trip to and from the port.

- **White-noise mobile app** This is useful for drowning out noise from hallways, next-door cabins, and ship machinery. A good one to try is **Sleepmaker Rain** (available in free and paid versions on iTunes and Google Play).

- **Hats, sunglasses, and sunscreen** Sunscreen is reasonably priced on the ships, in case you don't want to pack it.

- **Water shoes or flip-flops** You'll need these for the pool and beach.

ELECTRICAL OUTLETS

ALL OUTLETS ON THE SHIPS conform to the North American 110V/60Hz standard. If you live in the US or Canada, any device you have that operates normally at home should work on board. All staterooms have hair dryers, so if you're tight on space or not attached to your own model, you won't need to pack one.

If you're visiting from outside the US, you may need an adapter or converter for your electric gadgets. What's the difference? An adapter ensures that the plug on your device will fit into the electrical receptacle in the wall, but it doesn't change the electrical voltage. A converter does both (and costs more). Your local version of Amazon almost certainly has an excellent selection. Our advice is to have one converter per person, or two if you're traveling alone.

Be aware that there is a real scarcity of electrical outlets in most staterooms, particularly on the *Wonder*. If you'll have more than two people over age 8 in one stateroom, you will almost certainly need to bring some mechanism to add outlet access. Power strips and extension cords are technically prohibited on board; we've never had one confiscated, though other cruisers reportedly have. To hedge your bets, bring along a plug-in USB hub: Many inexpensive models allow four or five USB devices (phones, tablets, and the like) to charge on one outlet, without any extra wires.

PASSPORTS AND TRAVEL DOCUMENTS

EVERYONE IN YOUR FAMILY, including children, will need to provide proof of citizenship before boarding the ship. If you're a US citizen and you have a valid passport or passport card, it's easiest if you bring that.

If you don't have a passport but (1) you're a US citizen traveling from an American port such as Port Canaveral, Miami, or San Juan; (2) you're traveling only within the Western Hemisphere (the US, Canada, Mexico, or the Caribbean); and (3) you're returning to the same port on the same ship, you may be able to present a valid government-issued photo ID (such as a driver's license) along with proof of citizenship (an original or copy of a birth certificate, a Consular Report of Birth Abroad, or a Certificate of Naturalization). Most Disney cruises to Canada, Alaska, the Caribbean, and the Bahamas qualify. See **getyouhome.gov** for details (click "USA" on the home page, then click the "Special Groups" link).

unofficial **TIP**
If you're a US citizen taking a cruise that begins or ends outside the States, you *must* have a passport.

Other valid forms of identification include a state-issued Enhanced Driver's License (currently available only in Michigan, Minnesota, New York State, Vermont, and Washington State) or a valid Trusted Traveler Card. For the latter, see **getyouhome.gov** for details (click "USA" on the home page, then click "Trusted Traveler Programs"). Children under age 16 can present a birth certificate (original or copy), a Consular Report of Birth Abroad, or a Certificate of Naturalization.

If you're a divorced, separated, or single parent traveling abroad with your child and without your child's other parent, it's recommended that you obtain a signed, notarized letter from the child's other parent stating that you have his or her permission to take your child on the trip. This letter is in addition to the ID requirements listed above and should include the following:

- The child's full name and birth date
- The other parent's full name, address, and phone number
- Your full name, address, and phone number
- A description of the entire trip, including dates, countries, and cruise information, plus transportation information if available
- The purpose of the trip
- The other parent's original signature, in ink, and the date of his or her signature

Depending on where you live, it may take a couple of days to find a notary public, so don't wait until the last minute to get this done. Banks and post offices usually have notaries on staff. Keep in mind that the notary will have to witness the other parent signing the form, so it's best to have the other parent present the form to the notary. The same advice holds for aunts, uncles, and grandparents traveling with someone else's child, and families who have invited their children's friends along for the cruise.

Requirements for Canadian citizens are almost identical: A Canadian passport, a Canadian Enhanced Driver's License, and a Trusted Traveler Card are all valid forms of ID.

Citizens of countries other than the US and Canada should remember that some countries may require that you present a visa or passport to enter, regardless of their rules for US citizens.

You should also read the fine print when choosing excursions. For example, some excursions on Alaska voyages require a valid passport because they dip in and out of Canada during the trip. Even if you didn't need a passport for the cruise, you might need one for a particular excursion.

CREDIT CARDS AND PAYMENT METHODS

DCL SHIPS ACCEPT CASH, traveler's checks, Visa, MasterCard, American Express, Discover, Diners Club, JCB, and the Disney Visa card for payment. They also accept Disney gift cards, Disney Rewards Dollars (available to Disney Chase Visa–card holders), and Disney Dollars.

Cash is rarely used on board—your stateroom key serves as a credit card. (In fact, cash is not accepted as payment for beverages, spa or salon services, photography, laundry, or retail purchases.) It's still useful to have some cash available for luggage attendants and while you're in port, however. You can cash checks and obtain change from the Guest Services desk. You can also use other credit cards while on board.

US dollars are widely accepted throughout most of the Caribbean and in the Bahamas, and most prices are quoted in dollars. US-based credit cards are also accepted at many shops and stores, but don't expect smaller stores, bodegas, markets, and taxis to take them.

If you're traveling to Europe, Mexico, or Canada, you have a few options:

- **Ask your local bank to convert your US dollars before you leave home.** Many US banks will do this at a reasonable exchange rate; some charge a small exchange fee. Give your bank about a week to obtain the foreign currency because many branches don't keep euros, pesos, or Canadian dollars on hand. Your bank will likely convert any unspent foreign currency back to dollars when you return too.

- **Use a local ATM that's part of your bank's network.** If you're traveling in Europe and you're not sure how much cash to bring, you can usually get a fair exchange rate by withdrawing money at a local cash machine. Visa's website has a handy worldwide ATM locator (**visa.com/atmlocator**), and in our experience there are usually many more ATMs available than the ones listed online. Keep in mind that your local bank will probably add a withdrawal fee and a foreign-transaction fee, so it's better to make a few large withdrawals than lots of small ones.

- **Exchange traveler's checks for local currency when you disembark.** Traveler's checks are safer than carrying cash because they can be replaced if lost or stolen. The downside: Converting them to local currency takes more time than using an ATM or obtaining local currency before you leave home.

unofficial **TIP**
To prevent any sudden stops on your accounts, let your bank and credit card companies know that you're traveling abroad before you leave home.

If you want to convert your traveler's checks to cash, try to find a local bank willing to do the exchange, and verify the exchange calculations by hand. We've heard from readers who were promised one exchange rate outside a local currency-exchange stand (not a bank) and got another, lower rate when the conversion was done inside.

Finally, note that the US dollar is unofficially accepted in many markets, bodegas, and taxis throughout Mexico, but you'll rarely get a good deal that way. You'll probably be offered a simple exchange rate of 10 pesos per dollar, whereas the current exchange rate is something like 12 pesos per dollar—almost 17% more than what you're likely to be offered.

HEALTH INSURANCE

US RESIDENTS TRAVELING OUTSIDE OF THE STATES should contact their health-insurance providers to check their coverage for emergencies outside the country. While Disney offers trip insurance for its cruises, it currently limits coverage to $10,000 per person for medical and dental emergencies. Ten grand at most hospitals these days is going to get you some ice, a Band-Aid, and a kiss from the doctor to make your boo-boo better . . . if you're lucky. If you're going to pay for additional insurance, make sure it's enough to be helpful in an emergency.

Residents of most European countries taking a Disney cruise in Europe should also investigate the use of the **European Health Insurance Card,** which covers travel through much of Europe (visit **ehic .org.uk** for details). If you need additional travel insurance, companies such as American Express offer it for around 3% of the total cost of your trip.

Finally, some websites, such as **insuremytrip.com,** offer a handy feature for comparing travel-insurance policies from different companies. **MouseSavers (mousesavers.com)** also contains some good tips.

unofficial **TIP**
As you pack for your trip, plan to carry three copies of your health insurance information: one in a wallet or purse, one in carry-on luggage, and one in checked luggage.

CELL PHONES

MOST US MOBILE CARRIERS, including AT&T, Sprint, T-Mobile, and Verizon, have international calling plans at reasonable rates, while data plans tend to be very expensive. (The notable exception is T-Mobile, which includes free unlimited international data in its Simple Choice Plan.) In addition, many of these plans can be turned on and off from the carrier's website, so you only need to pay for coverage while you're traveling. Check with your carrier website for details on its international plans, including whether there's coverage in the countries you plan to visit.

You'll also need to check whether your phone's communications technology is compatible with the wireless infrastructure of the countries you plan to visit. Almost all cell phones throughout the world use either CDMA or GSM to transmit calls. (GSM phones have SIM cards; CDMA phones don't.) The two technologies don't work together, so a CDMA phone won't work on a GSM network (except as noted in the tip at right), and vice versa.

unofficial **TIP**
Sprint and Verizon's US versions of the iPhone 4s, 5, 5c, 5s, 6, and 6 Plus have both CDMA and GSM support.

Most carriers in the US, including Verizon, Sprint, MetroPCS, and U.S. Cellular, use CDMA, while AT&T and T-Mobile in the US use GSM, which is also the standard for most phones in the rest of the world. If you use AT&T or T-Mobile, your phone will likely work almost anywhere you're headed.

If you're using a CDMA carrier, check with your carrier to see whether your phone supports GSM anyway. Some newer phones, including some iPhones as well as some BlackBerry, HTC, Motorola, and Samsung devices, support both protocols and will automatically detect when they're on a GSM network.

Again, using mobile data outside the US can be obscenely expensive, with typical rates anywhere from 5 to 20 times as much as you're likely paying at home, and it's common to hear stories of unwitting travelers racking up thousands of dollars in charges without ever making a call, because they didn't know to do the following:

1. **Turn off your phone completely when you're not using it.** This prevents your phone from using a foreign carrier's data network to check e-mail and other messages.

2. **Disable data roaming unless you absolutely need it.** Look for an icon or button called "Settings" on your phone, and from there something called "Data," "Data Settings," or "Mobile Data." Make sure that's turned off.

If the prospect of turning off your phone gives you the shakes, you have a third option, recommended by a reader:

Put your phone in airplane mode instead of turning it off. This way you can still use your camera, listen to music, or use Wi-Fi.

Remember that cell service in Alaskan and Hawaiian ports is included at no additional charge on most US wireless calling plans (check with your carrier), so you won't need to modify your plan if you just want to talk in these ports. However, you may experience service levels different from what you might expect on the mainland. For example, our AT&T service in Skagway, Alaska, was acceptable, but our Verizon service was spotty at best.

 CASTAWAY CLUB

DCL USES THIS PROGRAM TO REWARD REPEAT CRUISERS. It works somewhat along the lines of a frequent-flyer program—the more you cruise with Disney, the better your status and the more perks you get.

Castaway Club status is determined solely by the number of DCL voyages you've completed, not by how much money you've spent. A guest who's sailed on five 3-day cruises in the smallest inside cabin belongs to a higher level than a guest who has spent more money on one 12-day voyage in the largest cabin.

The club levels are as follows:

- If you've never taken a Disney cruise before, you're a **First-Time Guest.**
- Guests who have completed 1–5 Disney cruises have **Silver** status.
- Guests who have completed 6–10 Disney cruises have **Gold** status.
- Guests who have completed more than 10 Disney cruises have **Platinum** status.

Most guests will be able to count all of their cruising toward their status level, with a few rare exceptions, such as a Disney cast member cruising on business (tough life, eh?).

A number of perks are available to all Castaway Club members, including "Welcome Back" stateroom gifts and priority check-in at the port terminal. As your membership level increases, so do your benefits. For many guests, one of the chief benefits of Castaway Club membership is that the higher your status level, the earlier you can reserve many aspects of your cruise, including port excursions, on-board dining at the adults-only Palo and Remy, spa visits, and some child-care situations:

- **First-Time Guests** may make reservations 75 days prior to sailing.
- **Silver** Castaway Club members may make reservations 90 days prior to sailing.
- **Gold** members may make reservations 105 days prior to sailing.
- **Platinum** members may make reservations 120 days prior to sailing.

Castaway Club status may not make much of a difference in some situations. For example, nearly everyone will be able to rent a bike at Castaway Cay. In other circumstances, however, belonging to a higher level can be a real boon. For example, Castaway Cay has only 21 private cabanas, split between the family and adult beach areas. With several thousand guests aboard your ship, competition for these private oases can be fierce, and Castaway Club members get first crack at them. It may be impossible for a First-Time Guest traveling during peak season to reserve a cabana. Other popular experiences include dining at Palo and Remy on days at sea, massages at Castaway Cay, and Flounder's Reef babysitting during showtimes.

Sometimes not everyone in a single stateroom has the same Castaway Club status. In that case, the benefits for each guest are determined by the Castaway Club member with the highest status in that room. For example, if I (Erin) have been on a few more cruises than my husband (lucky me!) and my status is higher than his, I can make reservations for both of us at my level. However, if we're also traveling with First-Time Guests staying in another stateroom, they *can't* take advantage of my higher status level, even though they're in our party. Effectively, then, Castaway Club status on any particular cruise is applied by stateroom, not by party. Keep this in mind if you're planning activities for a large group—not everyone will have equal access to reservations if members of your party have different status levels.

PART THREE

STATEROOMS

DISNEY CRUISE LINE'S SHIPS BOAST some of the largest cabins in the cruise industry, which helps explain—a bit—why their fares are correspondingly high. An inside cabin, generally the least expensive on any ship, is 169–184 square feet on Disney's ships, compared with 114–165 square feet on Royal Caribbean and 160–185 on Carnival. Disney's ocean-view and verandah (balcony) cabins are larger than Royal Caribbean's and Carnival's too.

In addition to space, Disney's bathroom layout is an improvement over those of other cruise lines. Disney staterooms in Categories 10–4 feature a split-bath design, in which the shower and toilet are in separate compartments, each with its own door and sink. The advantage of this design is that two people can get ready at the same time. (Category 11 staterooms have the shower and toilet in the same compartment.)

Disney's clever incorporation of storage space is one of the things we were most impressed with on our first few cruises. Most cabins have two sliding-door closets, each big enough for one large or two small suitcases; under-bed storage for carry-on or soft-sided luggage; and several drawers built in to the cabin's desk area. In addition, some cabins on the *Wonder* offer a steamer trunk for storage, while the *Magic* has dressers instead of trunks. (For a list of these cabins, see **tinyurl.com/steamertrunklist**.)

> *un**official** **TIP***
> On the *Dream* and *Fantasy*, some inside cabins have "virtual portholes"—video screens that combine real-time views from outside the ship with animated snippets of various Disney characters. Many children strongly prefer these to actual verandah views, and inside cabins are usually much less expensive.

While Disney's staterooms are well designed and large for the cruise industry, most are smaller than the typical hotel room. A room at a Walt Disney World Value hotel, such as Pop Century Resort, is about 260 square feet—about 40% larger than a DCL inside cabin. Even a well-appointed Family Oceanview State-room with Verandah is 304 square feet, a little smaller than a room at a Disney Moderate hotel, such as Caribbean Beach Resort.

OUR STATEROOM RECOMMENDATIONS

AT 169–184 SQUARE FEET, an **Inside Stateroom** has enough room for two adults, or two adults and one small child. (Just remember: They give you 60 square feet per person in prison.) These are Category 10 and 11 cabins, so a family of this size shouldn't have much contention for bathrooms when getting ready.

If you're a family of three or four and you have two tweens or teens, you'll appreciate the extra space of a **Deluxe Oceanview with Verandah Stateroom** (246 or 268 square feet) or **Deluxe Family Oceanview with Verandah Stateroom** (about 300 square feet). Alternatively, you could book two cabins: two inside connecting rooms or an inside and outside cabin across the hall from each other. The advantage to two rooms, besides the extra space and extra bathroom, is that the kids can sleep late if they want.

CABIN APPOINTMENTS

EVERY DISNEY CRUISE LINE (DCL) stateroom is outfitted with the following:

- Private bath with sink and toilet
- Desk with chair and dedicated lighting—big enough to actually get work done
- Sleeper sofa
- Satellite television with remote
- Closet with two sliding doors (*Magic* and *Wonder*) or two hinged doors (*Dream* and *Fantasy*)
- Hooks (for towels) and hangers (for clothes)
- Electronic safe—just big enough for passports, wallets, and other small valuables
- Coffee table—the top opens for storage (*Dream* and *Fantasy* only).
- Privacy curtain—separating the sleeping area from the sofa
- Beverage cooler—keeps drinks cool, not necessarily cold. No freezer.
- In-room phone with voice mail
- Wave Phone—a mobile phone you can use aboard the ship
- Digital alarm clock—typically an iHome. (Bring a Lightning-to-30-pin converter if you have a newer iPhone.)
- Toiletries—H2O Plus soap, shampoo, conditioner, and body lotion
- Hair dryer

- Life jackets
- Room-service menus
- Bedside lamps
- Ice bucket and glasses
- In-room thermostat (digital on the *Dream* and *Fantasy;* older-style dial on the *Magic* and *Wonder*)
- Custom artwork—usually depicts Disney characters and themes relevant to the cruise line, ships, islands, or travel

Cabins with exterior windows also include blackout curtains, which do an amazing job of blocking the sun. If you need light to wake up in the morning, don't shut them unless you want to sleep until noon.

WHAT YOU *WON'T* FIND Cabins don't have minibars, coffeemakers, microwaves, teakettles, steam irons, or ironing boards. An iron and ironing board are available in most of the ships' laundry rooms.

STATEROOM CATEGORIES

CATEGORIES 11A–11C: Standard Inside Stateroom

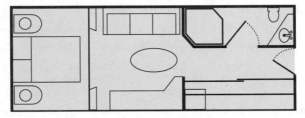

MAXIMUM OCCUPANCY 4 people
SIZE (square feet) *Magic/Wonder,* 184; *Dream/Fantasy,* 169
DESCRIPTION Has one queen-size bed or two twin beds (which can be pushed together), a sleeper sofa, and combined bath with tub and shower. Some rooms have a pull-down upper berth. These cabins are on Decks 2, 5, 6, and 7 on the *Magic* and *Wonder,* and on Decks 2, 5, 6, 7, 8, 9, and 10 on the *Dream* and *Fantasy.* They're generally available in the Forward (toward the bow/front), Midship (center), and Aft (toward the stern/rear) sections of the ships.

CATEGORY 10A (all ships), CATEGORIES 10B and 10C (*Magic* and *Wonder*): Deluxe Inside Stateroom

MAXIMUM OCCUPANCY 4 people
SIZE (square feet) *Magic/Wonder,* 214; *Dream/Fantasy,* 204
DESCRIPTION These cabins on the *Magic, Dream,* and *Fantasy* have one queen-size bed; cabins on the *Wonder* have one queen or two twin beds (which can be pushed together). Cabins on all ships have a one-person sleeper sofa and split bath; some rooms have a pull-down upper berth. Category 10C rooms, on the *Magic* and *Wonder,* are located entirely on

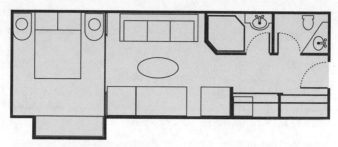

DELUXE INSIDE STATEROOM

Deck 1 Midship and Deck 2 Aft. Category 10B rooms, also found on the *Magic* and *Wonder*, are located entirely on Deck 2 Midship. Category 10A rooms are on Decks 5 and 7 on the *Magic* and *Wonder* and Decks 5, 6, 7, 8, and 9 on the *Dream* and *Fantasy*, anywhere along the ship.

CATEGORIES 9A–9D: Deluxe Oceanview Stateroom

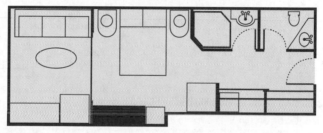

MAXIMUM OCCUPANCY 4 people

SIZE (square feet) *Magic/Wonder*, 214; *Dream/Fantasy*, 204

DESCRIPTION Same size and features as a Category 10 Deluxe Inside, plus a window view of the ocean. These cabins on the *Magic, Dream,* and *Fantasy* have one queen-size bed; cabins on the *Wonder* have one queen or two twin beds (which can be pushed together). All cabins on all ships have a sleeper sofa and split bath; some rooms have a pull-down upper berth. Categories 9B–9D are found only on Decks 1 and 2 on the *Magic* and *Wonder* and only on Deck 2 Midship on the *Dream* and *Fantasy*. Category 9A cabins are found on the Forward section of Decks 5, 6, and 7 on the *Magic* and *Wonder*, and on Decks 5, 6, 7, and 8 of the *Dream* and *Fantasy*. The 9A cabins on Decks 6, 7, and 8 of the *Dream* and *Fantasy* are interesting because they're at the extreme Forward and Aft ends of the ships, affording them unique views at a relatively low cost.

CATEGORIES 8A–8D (exclusive to the *Dream* and *Fantasy*): Deluxe Family Oceanview Stateroom

MAXIMUM OCCUPANCY 5 people

SIZE (square feet) 241

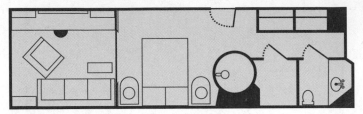

DELUXE FAMILY OCEANVIEW STATEROOM

DESCRIPTION These cabins have one queen-size bed. Most have a one-person pull-down bed in the wall; a few also have one-person pull-down beds in the ceiling. All cabins have a one-person sleeper sofa as well as a split bath; most have round tubs and showers.

CATEGORY 7A: Deluxe Oceanview Stateroom with Navigator's Verandah

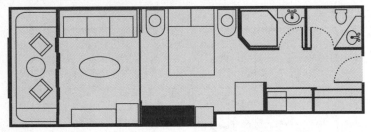

MAXIMUM OCCUPANCY 3 people

SIZE (square feet) *Magic/Wonder,* 268 (including verandah); *Dream/Fantasy,* 246 (including verandah)

DESCRIPTION Found on Decks 5, 6, and 7 on all ships (Fore and Aft on the *Dream* and *Fantasy;* Aft only on the *Magic* and *Wonder*), these cabins have one queen or two twin beds (which can be pushed together). All cabins have a one-person sleeper sofa and split bath. The interesting feature about these cabins is the Navigator's Verandah: a small, semi-enclosed, teak-floored deck attached to the stateroom and featuring either a large exterior window or open railing. The window doesn't open, so in those rooms the extra space and teak deck are the difference between these cabins and the Category 9 staterooms on the *Magic* and *Wonder.* On the *Dream* and *Fantasy,* these cabins have an undersize or obstructed-view verandah.

CATEGORIES 6A (all ships) and 6B (*Dream* and *Fantasy* only): Deluxe Oceanview Stateroom with Verandah

MAXIMUM OCCUPANCY 4 people

SIZE (square feet) *Magic/Wonder,* 268 (including verandah); *Dream/Fantasy,* 246 (including verandah)

DESCRIPTION These cabins have a queen-size bed, a one-person sleeper sofa, and a one-person pull-down bed, typically above the sofa. All have

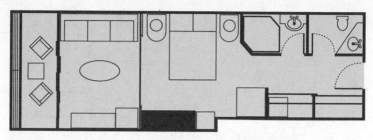

DELUXE OCEANVIEW STATEROOM WITH VERANDAH

a split bath, most with round tubs and showers. Category 6A cabins are found Aft on Decks 5, 6, and 7 of the *Magic* and *Wonder* and Aft on Decks 8, 9, and 10 on the *Dream* and *Fantasy*. Category 6B staterooms are found only on the *Dream* and *Fantasy*, Aft on Decks 5, 6, and 7. These staterooms differ from Category 5 staterooms because they have private verandahs with a short white wall instead of a railing with Plexiglas. In addition, some of the Category 5 cabins are found Midship, whereas all Category 6 cabins seem to be Aft.

CATEGORIES 5A–5C (all ships), 5D and 5E (*Dream* and *Fantasy* only): Deluxe Oceanview Stateroom with Verandah

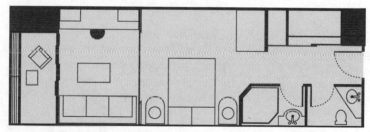

MAXIMUM OCCUPANCY 4 people
SIZE (square feet) *Magic/Wonder,* 268 (including verandah); *Dream/Fantasy,* 246 (including verandah)
DESCRIPTION There seems to be little difference between these and the Category 6 cabins on the *Magic* and *Wonder.* All have the same square footage and amenities, and all are on Decks 5, 6, and 7. Category 5E cabins have oversize verandahs, and some have a white wall instead of a railing with Plexiglas. No other Category 5 cabins have a white wall on the verandah.

CATEGORIES 4A and 4B (all ships), 4C and 4D (*Dream* and *Fantasy* only), 4E (*Magic* and *Wonder* only): Deluxe Family Oceanview Stateroom with Verandah
MAXIMUM OCCUPANCY 5 people
SIZE (square feet) *Magic/Wonder,* 304 (including verandah); *Dream/Fantasy,* 299 (including verandah)

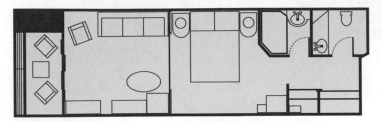

DELUXE FAMILY OCEANVIEW STATEROOM WITH VERANDAH

DESCRIPTION These cabins have a queen-size bed and sleeper sofa (fits one person); most have a pull-down wall bed (sleeps one). Some also have a pull-down upper-berth bed. All have a split bath, most with round tubs and showers. One issue with the pull-down wall bed in these cabins is that you'll have to move the desk chair in order to use the bed. The Category 4E cabins are found only Aft on Decks 7 and 8 of the *Magic* and *Wonder*. There are only two 4E cabins on Deck 7, and what makes them interesting is that they have an angled view directly off the ship's stern. They're also adjacent to Deck 7's "secret" sun deck. On the *Dream* and *Fantasy*, the A–D designations for this category represent the deck on which the stateroom is located: 4A staterooms are on Decks 9 and 10 Midship, 4B staterooms are on Deck 8 Midship, 4C staterooms are on Deck 7 Midship, and 4D staterooms are on Deck 6 Midship.

CATEGORY V (*DREAM* AND *FANTASY* ONLY):
Concierge Family Oceanview Stateroom with Verandah

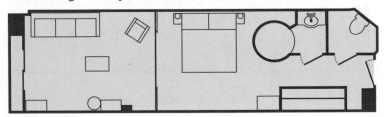

MAXIMUM OCCUPANCY 5 people
SIZE (square feet) 306 (including verandah)
DESCRIPTION These cabins have a queen bed, a sleeper sofa for two, and an upper-berth pull-down bed that sleeps one. These rooms have an extra half-bath, giving the shower side of the split bath a sink and vanity. Category V staterooms are on Decks 11 and 12 Forward.

CATEGORY T: Concierge 1-Bedroom Suite with Verandah
MAXIMUM OCCUPANCY 5 people
SIZE (square feet) *Magic/Wonder,* 614 (including verandah); *Dream/Fantasy,* 622 (including verandah)

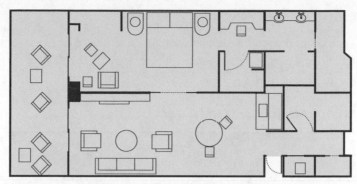

CONCIERGE 1-BEDROOM SUITE WITH VERANDAH

DESCRIPTION These cabins feature a separate bedroom with queen bed and a bathroom with whirlpool tub and separate shower. The living room has upholstered chairs and a sofa, plus a separate table and chairs. The living room also sleeps three: two on the convertible sofa and one in the pull-down bed. These staterooms are found all along Deck 8 on the *Magic* and *Wonder* and the Forward sections of Decks 11 and 12 on the *Dream* and *Fantasy*.

CATEGORY S (*Magic* and *Wonder* only):
Concierge 2-Bedroom Suite with Verandah

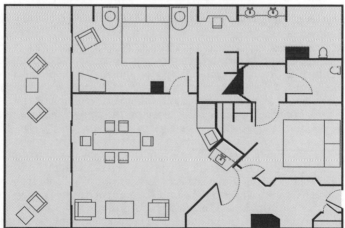

MAXIMUM OCCUPANCY 7 people
SIZE (square feet) 954 (including verandah)
DESCRIPTION The master bedroom has a queen bed, a walk-in closet, a vanity, two sinks, and a walk-in shower. The other bedroom has twin

beds, a bathroom with tub and sink, and a walk-in closet. Two others can sleep on the convertible sofa in the living room, and a pull-down bed sleeps one more. In addition, the 2-Bedroom Suite features a large living room with seating for 10 people, a huge private verandah suitable for entertaining a few guests, and another half-bath. Category S cabins are on Deck 8 Forward.

CATEGORY R: Concierge Royal Suite

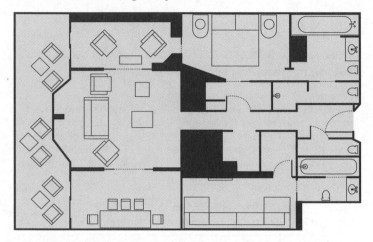

MAXIMUM OCCUPANCY 7 people (*Magic/Wonder*); 5 people (*Dream/Fantasy*)

SIZE (square feet) *Magic/Wonder,* 1,029 (including verandah); *Dream/Fantasy,* 1,781 (including verandah)

DESCRIPTION On the *Magic* and *Wonder,* the master bedroom has a queen bed, a walk-in closet, a vanity, two sinks, and a walk-in shower. The other bedroom has twin beds, a bathroom with tub and sink, and a walk-in closet. Two others can sleep on the convertible sofa in the living room, and a pull-down bed sleeps one more. On the *Magic* and *Wonder,* the Royal Suite includes a separate dining room, living room, and media room, plus a private verandah that you should rent out to other families for birthdays (it'll fit an elephant) and another half-bath. Royal Suites on the *Dream* and *Fantasy* have one long room separated into dining and living areas. The master bedroom features a queen bed and bath with two sinks, a shower, and a tub. An in-wall pull-down double bed and a single pull-down bed in the living room complete the sleeping arrangements. The most impressive feature of these suites on the *Dream* and *Fantasy* may be the verandah, which curves around the suite to follow the contour of the deck. Besides being large enough to land aircraft, it includes a whirlpool tub.

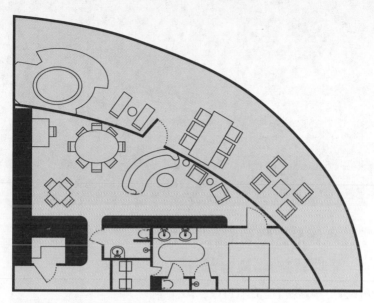

CONCIERGE ROYAL SUITE WITH VERANDAH

PART FOUR

ARRIVING, GETTING YOUR SEA LEGS, *and* DEPARTING

TRANSPORTATION *to* YOUR CRUISE

CHOOSING A DEPARTURE PORT BASED ON TIME AND MONEY

MOST DISNEY ITINERARIES depart from two or three different ports at various times of the year. While the differences in the ports' quality are relatively small, your departure port is more likely to affect your trip's transportation cost.

If you live within a few hours' drive of one of Disney's ports, your least expensive option is almost certainly going to be using that port. Otherwise, consider flying in the day before you depart to account for flight cancellations.

If you're taking a European cruise and flying in from North America, consider arriving two days before your cruise. This will protect you against most flight cancellations and also give you a bit more time to adjust to the time-zone difference.

As for quality, Disney's Port Canaveral terminal is the nicest in the United States, with easy, ample parking; good directional signage; and a comfortable waiting area. We wouldn't choose a cruise, however, based on the hour or so spent in the terminal. Instead, include the transportation cost to and from the port, plus lodging, in the total cost of the cruises you're considering to see how the overall cost shakes out.

GETTING TO AND FROM THE PORT

MOST NORTH AMERICAN DISNEY CRUISE LINE (DCL) GUESTS have three options when arranging transportation to the cruise terminal: book transportation through Disney, book through a third-party service, or drive themselves. This section covers all three options in detail, including driving directions, GPS settings, and terminal parking rates for those taking their own car.

Using Disney Transportation from the Airport or a Disney-Approved Hotel

If you're flying in to Orlando, you can use Disney's shuttle service to get to Port Canaveral. The cost is $70 per person, free for kids under age 3, and should be arranged ahead of time through your travel agent or Disney. DCL recommends that your flight into Orlando arrive by 1:45 p.m. and your flight out depart after 11:30 a.m.

Disney also provides shuttle service from other city airports to its cruise terminals. Round-trip prices in Barcelona, Spain, for instance, are $60–$120 per person, depending on whether you're staying at a hotel the night before and/or the night after your cruise. It's $40–$80 in Miami; $90 in Galveston; $100 in San Diego; $40 in San Juan, Puerto Rico; $50–$66 in Vancouver, British Columbia (depending on the airport); and $60–$340 (not a typo) in Venice. See **tinyurl.com /dclgroundtransfers** for more details.

If you've purchased ground transfers from Disney, you must give them your flight information. You can do this on the DCL website at **disneycruise.com/plan.** Disney provides few details about where to find your ground-transportation driver. Unless you hear otherwise, assume that a uniformed DCL greeter will be stationed near the airport baggage-claim area holding either a DCL sign or a sign with your party's name on it.

Using Disney Transportation from Walt Disney World to Port Canaveral

Disney provides round-trip transfer service among Walt Disney World hotels at a cost of $70 per person, round-trip.

LUGGAGE TRANSFER If you're taking a DCL cruise after staying at a Disney-owned resort at Walt Disney World and you've booked transportation from the resort to the ship through Disney, cruise representatives can transfer your luggage from your hotel room to your ship's stateroom.

Contact DCL at least three days before you leave home to take advantage of this service. They'll ask you for the number of bags and tell you when and where to meet for your drive to the ship. They'll also give you instructions on what to do with your bags; typically, you'll simply leave them in your hotel room, with your DCL luggage tags attached, and Disney will transfer them directly to your stateroom.

Surprisingly, you may not find this service as smooth as one might expect from Disney, as this reader reports:

> *The staff at Pop Century Resort want nothing to do with helping you get ready for your cruise. When I stopped at the concierge desk to ask*

about luggage transfer, they simply gave me a card with the DCL phone number on it and told me to call it myself. When I called the number, I got an automated message telling me what time I would be picked up, but no indication of the meeting spot or what to do with our bags. We finally did get printed instructions about the port transfer at 9:30 p.m. We were told to leave our luggage in the room, by the door, with the DCL tags attached no later than 8:30 a.m. and that we should meet in the Pop Century lobby at 12:30 p.m. to check in with the cruise-line staff.

You really do have to be ready on time—cast members were at our door at 8:31 to collect our luggage. Also, the DCL staff was in the Pop lobby at noon; we left as soon as everyone scheduled to be on the bus was there.

One thing to note: If you use Disney transportation to get to Port Canaveral, you don't have any control over what time you get to the port. They tell you where to be and when to be there. So if you want a few more minutes in the parks, you can't leave WDW a bit later, and if you want more time to explore the ship, you can't leave earlier.

Third-Party Shuttle Services

If you have more than four people, it's often less expensive to hire a third-party shuttle service to transport you to your cruise terminal.

GALVESTON SuperShuttle (☎ 800-258-3826; **supershuttle.com**) offers town-car, SUV, and van-shuttle service between Houston and Galveston. Round-trip costs are $302 for the town car for up to 4 people, $338 for a 10-passenger van, or $338 for a 5-passenger SUV.

PORT CANAVERAL Mears Transportation (☎ 407-423-5566; **mears transportation.com**) offers private-town-car, SUV, and van shuttles from Orlando to Port Canaveral. Round-trip costs are $270 for up to 3 people in a town car ($90 per person), $360 for up to 5 in an SUV ($72 per person), or $360 for up to 10 in a van ($36 per person). The big advantage to using a third-party service is that you can depart as soon as your group is ready. One-way rates are half of the round-trip figures listed; tips aren't included.

SAN DIEGO If you're flying in for a cruise out of San Diego, **SuperShuttle** (☎ 800-258-3826; **supershuttle.com**) offers one-way and round-trip transfers from virtually every airport in the region. Cost is about $12 per person between San Diego's airport and port. Check SuperShuttle's website for details; use "San Diego Cruise Ship Terminal" as your destination when you reserve online.

Driving Yourself

This section provides driving directions for Disney's ports in Florida, California, and Canada, plus information on on-site versus off-site parking rates at the various cruise terminals.

TO PORT CANAVERAL It takes about an hour to drive from Orlando to Port Canaveral under normal conditions. Traffic and road construction on the Beachline Expressway (FL 528), a toll road, can turn that 60-minute trip into a 3-hour ordeal. And because Port Canaveral and Orlando are linked by only three main roads— with limited connections between them—there are a couple of points along the Beachline where you have no way of taking an alternate route if traffic is delayed. Our advice is to allow at least 2 hours for this trip or, better yet, 2½ hours. If you get to the port early, Disney's cruise terminal is air-conditioned and comfortable, with enough room for restless kids to run around in while you wait to board.

unofficial TIP
Text the location and a photo of your parking spot to other members of your group before you leave the parking facility. This will help you remember where you parked when you return from your cruise.

If you're using a GPS, enter this address as your destination: **Port Canaveral Terminal A, 9155 Charles M. Rowland Dr., Port Canaveral, FL 32920.** Use "Cape Canaveral" if your GPS doesn't recognize Port Canaveral as a city.

If you're not using a GPS, DCL's Planning Center (**disneycruiseline .com/plan**) has very clear driving directions for getting to Port Canaveral. If you're driving from Walt Disney World, the most direct route uses eastbound FL 536 to the Central Florida GreeneWay (FL 417) and then to the Beachline Expressway. The GreeneWay and Beachline are toll roads, so have $10 in cash available for the round-trip.

You're on the Beachline almost the entire way to Port Canaveral. Once you arrive, the port's terminals function almost exactly like an airport's. The same kinds of signs for airline terminals are posted for cruise-line terminals at Port Canaveral. DCL ships usually depart from Terminal A, so you'll be looking for road signs to that effect. If you want to see what the drive looks like, the Canaveral Port Authority has an excellent video (complete with catchy reggae soundtrack) that shows what the exits, terminal, and parking options look like from a car passenger's perspective: **portcanaveral.com/drive.**

Once you arrive at Terminal A, you'll park and walk to the security checkpoint. Parking rates at DCL's Port Canaveral terminal are $60 for three days, $75 for four days, $90 for five days, and $120 for seven days. You may also prepay for your parking at the terminal online at **portcanaveral.com/cruising/parking.php.** There is no price cut for booking ahead of time.

TO MIAMI Driving here is a challenge because of the traffic, one-way streets, and constant construction. We recommend using a GPS, preferably one with traffic information, to guide you to the port. Use this address: **Port of Miami, 1015 N. America Way, Miami, FL 33132.** DCL recommends turning off your GPS once you've reached the port's bridge, and then staying in the left lane and following the signs to the parking garage closest to your terminal.

Like Port Canaveral, Miami has both parking garages and open-air lots. Parking is $20 per day. If the lots closest to your ship are full, drop off some of your family and luggage near the cruise terminal, and then swing around and find a spot in one of the other garages—the nearest open garages can be half a mile from the terminal, and there's no reason to have everyone haul their luggage that far.

Miami's ports are supposed to have shuttles running between the parking garages and terminals, but we've never seen them operating. (We *have* seen giant iguanas running around, though, so keep your eyes open!)

Once inside the terminal, you'll be directed to a check-in line. Miami's terminals are older and smaller than Port Canaveral's, but DCL's section is well maintained and efficient. Once you're checked in, you'll go up a set of escalators and then through a long corridor to board the ship.

TO GALVESTON   The port is about 71 miles from Houston's George Bush Intercontinental Airport (IAH), roughly a 90-minute drive with traffic. If you're only dropping off passengers, the address to use for your GPS for Terminal Number 1 is **2502 Harborside Dr., Galveston, TX 77550;** Terminal Number 2 is at **2702 Harborside Dr.** If you're parking, the GPS address for the parking lots is the **intersection of 33rd Street and Harborside Drive.**

TO SAN DIEGO   You will need to park in the Economy Lot on Pacific Highway (**3302 Pacific Hwy., San Diego, CA 92101**) at the San Diego International Airport, and take a shuttle from the lot to the Port of San Diego. Parking is $11 per day.

TO VANCOUVER   The port is about a 30-minute drive from Vancouver's airport: **Cruise Terminal, 999 Canada Place, Vancouver, BC, Canada V6C 3C1.** Traffic in the several blocks surrounding Canada Place can be quite congested on cruise-departure mornings, so budget an extra 20 minutes for the last three blocks of travel if you're planning to arrive at the port during the late morning of your sail date. The cruise terminal has 775 parking spaces, which cost $32 CDN (about $32 US) or $184 CDN ($184 US) per week. Reservations are recommended and can be made online at **vinciparkcanadaplace.ca/reserve -a-space.html.**

If you're a group of able-bodied adults with a reasonable amount of luggage, the easiest and cheapest way to get from the airport to the cruise terminal is Vancouver's clean and efficient **subway–light rail service.** The one-way trip costs about $8 CDN (about $7 US) and takes about half an hour, with no transfers needed. Visit **translink.ca** for more information. (Input **YVR** as your start point and **Canada Place** as your end point.)

Adding Air Travel to Your Package? *Don't!*

While you can purchase airfare through Disney, we don't recommend it—rarely do you save money by doing so, not to mention if you book through Disney, you lose all control of your flight selection—they'll do it for you.

We've been cautioned by both Disney-specialist travel agents and a travel-specialist Disney cast member that DCL air bookers will get you from point A to point B, but they generally won't pay attention to the presence or length of layovers, fine details about departure times, the size of the aircraft, local airport selection, or other particulars that can turn a good trip into a logistical headache.

You may also find that flight refunds are more difficult to obtain if you arrange your air travel through Disney. Book your flight yourself, or use a travel agent who will consider personal factors and logistics as well as pricing.

 # The DAY *Before* YOUR CRUISE

STAYING AT A LOCAL HOTEL THE NIGHT BEFORE

YOUR CRUISE WILL START ON TIME, even if you're not on the ship. One way to minimize the chance of that happening is to arrive at the port the day before your cruise and spend the night at a local hotel. While it adds a night's lodging to your trip's cost and another day to your trip's length, we think the peace of mind you get from knowing you'll make your cruise is worth it.

DCL has relationships with hotels in each of its port cities. You can book your pre- or post-cruise hotel stay through Disney as part of your vacation package, no matter which port you're sailing from. The pros: Disney has vetted the property, so you're unlikely to end up with a real clinker, and transportation to/from the port will be seamless if you've also purchased ground transfers. The cons include the limited range of price-point options and a lack of choices at nonmainstream properties—if, say, you've got your heart set on staying at a hip new boutique hotel in Barcelona, you'll likely have to book it on your own rather than through DCL.

If you have Disney book your hotel stay, be prepared to have the process feel somewhat different than if you booked on your own. For example, during a recent Alaskan DCL voyage, we had Disney book our pre-trip hotel stay, at the convenient Fairmont Vancouver Airport Hotel. Because we booked through Disney, we got no direct information from the Fairmont, not even a confirmation number. This proved slightly problematic when we called about six weeks before our trip to inquire about the type of room we were in: We learned that Disney doesn't even tell the hotel the names of its guests or their room needs until about two weeks in advance. Rest assured that if you've booked a room through Disney, you'll have one. But for hyper-planners used to having every detail mapped out, the process may feel somewhat unsettling.

If you're driving to your cruise, most hotels near cruise ports offer their guests inexpensive parking and taxi and shuttle transportation to the port; some offer these services to the general public too. The hotel's parking rates are often substantially less than what you'd pay at the cruise terminal. For example, parking at many Port Canaveral hotels costs around $6 per day, compared with $17–$20 per day at the terminal.

If You're Cruising out of Port Canaveral

You have the option of spending the night at a hotel in Port Canaveral or Orlando. We've done both, and there are advantages to each. The advantage to staying in Port Canaveral is that you're only a few minutes from the cruise terminal. You can have a relaxed breakfast on the morning of your cruise, take a swim in the pool, and pick up any last-minute items at one of Port Canaveral's grocery stores. The one downside to Port Canaveral is that it doesn't offer as many entertainment options as Orlando, and you may find yourself staying at your hotel for the evening, either watching TV or swimming. While many families find this relaxing, some would prefer to maximize their vacation activities.

Our favorite hotel in Port Canaveral is the **Residence Inn Cape Canaveral Cocoa Beach** (8959 Astronaut Blvd.; ☎ 321-323-1100; **tinyurl.com/residenceinncanaveral**). This hotel offers studio, one-bedroom, and two-bedroom suites that sleep up to six people, plus a free breakfast buffet and Internet access at reasonable prices. There's no restaurant on-site, but you have plenty of nearby options.

The advantage to staying in Orlando is that you can visit a Disney theme park, Downtown Disney, or Universal Orlando before your trip. You'll have a wide variety of entertainment options and dozens of restaurants from which to choose. Some hotels, including the **Hyatt Regency Orlando International Airport** (9300 Jeff Fuqua Blvd.; ☎ 407-825-1234; **orlandoairport.hyatt.com**), offer transportation to Port Canaveral for cruise guests. The downside to staying in Orlando is that you'll still need to allow a couple of hours in the morning for the trip to the cruise terminal. See page 43 for more details.

If You're Cruising out of Miami

You'll have many hotel options. We've spent the night before our Miami departures as far away as Orlando. Because there are so many ways to get to the Port of Miami by car, traffic and construction aren't as much of a concern as for Port Canaveral, although driving in a city as large as Miami has its own challenges (see page 43). And unlike hotels in Port

Canaveral, most in Miami charge about as much for parking—around $15 per day—as does the Port of Miami (around $20), so there's little benefit to parking off-site.

The **Holiday Inn Port of Miami–Downtown** (340 Biscayne Blvd.; ☎ 305-371-4400; **tinyurl.com/hiportofmiami**) sits within a mile of the port, with plenty of restaurants, shopping, and activities a short walk or drive away, plus an on-site fitness center and high-speed wireless Internet. Its one weakness is the small number of on-site parking spaces: If one isn't available, you'll have to find space at a nearby pay-parking lot and walk back. The **Courtyard by Marriott Miami Downtown** (200 SE 2nd Ave.; ☎ 305-374-3000; **miamicourtyard.com**) is another moderately priced hotel. Renovated at the end of 2012, the Courtyard is near restaurants, shopping, and other activities; has an on-site gym; and offers high-speed wireless Internet.

If You're Cruising out of Galveston

Wyndham offers two upscale choices, both of which we like: The **Hotel Galvez & Spa** (2024 Seawall Blvd.; ☎ 409-765-7721; **hotelgalvez.com**) is a century-old beachside hotel with modern rooms, a spa, heated pool, and free shuttle service to the port and Galveston's Strand Historic District, both less than 2 miles away. Rates are as low as $130 per night during the off-season. **The Tremont House,** in the Strand, is only a few blocks from the port (2300 Ship's Mechanic Row; ☎ 409-763-0300; **thetremonthouse.com**). Like the Galvez, the Tremont House is modern and luxurious; while it doesn't have a pool or spa, its location near downtown is better for people who want to explore the area on foot. Rates are less than $200 per night most of the year.

If You're Cruising out of San Diego

You're in luck—it's possible to stay at a Disneyland hotel before your trip! Disneyland is typically less than 3 hours (with traffic) away from the San Diego port terminal. The **Disneyland Hotel** (1150 Magic Way, Anaheim; ☎ 714-778-6600; **disneyland.disney.go.com/disneyland-hotel**) is our favorite Disney-run hotel on-property, while **Disney's Paradise Pier Hotel** (1717 S. Disneyland Drive; ☎ 714-999-0990; **disneyland.disney.go.com /paradise-pier-hotel** is usually the least expensive. **Disney's Grand Californian Hotel & Spa** (1600 S. Disneyland Dr.; ☎ 714-635-2300; **disney land.disney.go.com/grand-californian-hotel**) has the advantage of being adjacent to Disney California Adventure, making it an easy walk if you'd like to enjoy DCA's Cars Land during the evening.

In addition to Disney's hotels, many good off-site hotels are situated around the park. One of the most popular is the **Howard Johnson Anaheim** (1380 S. Harbor Blvd.; ☎ 714-776-6120; **hojoanaheim .com**), across the street from Disneyland and a shorter walk to Disneyland's entrance than Disney's own Paradise Pier Hotel.

If You're Cruising out of Vancouver

The **Pan Pacific Vancouver** (999 Canada Place, Ste. 300; ☎ 604-662-8111; **panpacificvancouver.com**) is located at Vancouver's port. It's posh and pricey, with rates between $400 and $500 US per night. Also pricey—and fabulous!—is the **Shangri-La Vancouver** (1128 W. Georgia St.; ☎ 604-689-1120; **shangri-la.com/vancouver**), with spectacular views of the ocean and mountains, huge marble bathrooms, and friendly staff. A more economical option is the Metropolitan Hotel Vancouver (645 Howe St.; ☎ 604-687-1122; **metropolitan.com/vanc**), with rates around $200 US per night.

Vancouver is a worthwhile destination in its own right, combining global sophistication and Canadian charm. The city is easily accessible by foot, taxi, and transit. Cruisers in search of international cuisine should make a point to sample the city's Asian specialties, from sushi to Indian to dim sum. For upscale dining, stick close to the downtown core around Robson Street and the cruise terminal. For an authentic experience, head to Vancouver's **Chinatown** (**vancouver-chinatown .com**) one of the largest in North America. If you're looking for something unique, try a Japanese-style hot dog sold from a food cart. It's Tokyo meets New York meets your belly.

Another must-stop for foodies is the **Granville Island Market.** We've found everything from fresh mangosteens to maple-glazed walnuts here, as well as prepared foods like salmon potpie and gooseberry tarts. Disney geeks will want to keep an eye out for the Dole Whip vendor.

Fashionistas will love hitting the high-end designer shops (**Chanel, Hermès, Louis Vuitton,** and so on), while shoppers looking for a Canadian experience should head to **Roots** (1001 Robson St.; ☎ 604-683-4305; **canada.roots.com**) or **Hudson's Bay Company** (674 Granville St.; ☎ 604-681-6211; **thebay.com**), home of the eponymous blankets. Fans of food souvenirs can pick up maple treats, British sweets and biscuits, and ketchup-flavored crisps all over the city.

If you arrive in the afternoon, walk to **Stanley Park,** along the waterfront, to see the beautiful Canadian Rockies in the distance (**vancouver.ca/parks-recreation-culture/stanley-park.aspx**). Or check out **Gastown** (**gastown.org**) and its steam-powered clock. For nightlife, check ahead before your arrival for live theater, musical concerts, or any festivals that are happening during your stay. A few good websites to try are **tourismvancouver.com, hellobc.com/vancouver,** and **timeout .com/vancouver.**

If you're a Disney-theme-park nut, you won't want to miss the **FlyOver Canada** attraction (**flyovercanada.com**) at Canada Place adjacent to the cruise terminal. The experience is nearly identical to Soarin' at Epcot and Disney California Adventure, only with footage of Canadian rather than Californian points of interest. It ain't cheap—about $18 US for adults (age 18+), $16 US for seniors (age

65+) and youth (ages 13–17), and $13 US for kids age 12 and younger for a 10-ish minute ride—but it may be worth it to see the similarity to Soarin', even in the pre-show safety video.

GET *in the* BOAT, MEN *(and Women and Kids)!*

CHOOSING A BOARDING TIME

YOU'LL BE ABLE TO CHECK IN at least 75 days in advance using DCL's online Planning Center (see page 21). This offers you a chance to verify information, ensure that you have the right credit card on file, and so on. You'll also be able to choose your boarding window—the time when you provide Disney your travel documents and board the ship.

The earliest boarding windows are usually around 10:30 a.m. We recommend choosing as early a board time as you can, or after 1:30 p.m. Here are the pros and cons to both approaches:

unofficial TIP
If you're planning to return home via the Vancouver airport, be aware that you can't check in earlier than 3 hours before your flight or later than 1 hour before for international flights—you must check in *exactly* 1–3 hours before your departure. Timing is critical.

Early Boarding Time

PROS An uncrowded ship. You'll find smaller crowds at the pools and buffet, and you'll be among the first in line for last-minute spa, restaurant, or shore-excursion availability.

CONS Most staterooms don't open to guests until at least 1:30 p.m. This means you'll be carrying everything you brought on board with you until you're able to enter your room. Guests with lots of camera equipment or big laptops may find this inconvenient.

Later Boarding Time

PROS The ability to sleep later on your boarding day and the ability to access your stateroom as soon as you board the ship. If you have children who require an afternoon nap, this may be your best option.

CONS The ship is already full of people, including lines for the pools and food. Moreover, the elevators off the atrium tend to be packed with folks and their luggage trying to get to their rooms.

CHECKING IN AT THE TERMINAL

HAVE YOUR CRUISE DOCUMENTS and government-issued ID ready as soon as you get out of the car. Many terminals, including Port Canaveral, have an initial security checkpoint outside the perimeter to ensure that only ticketed passengers enter.

Once you're past that checkpoint, you'll undergo another round of security screening just inside the terminal's entrance. You'll pass through a metal detector, and your luggage will undergo X-ray scanning. If you have bags too large to get through the security screening, use the porters at the terminal.

Disney's cruise terminals, especially those at Port Canaveral and Vancouver, are spacious, clean, and comfortable. (Miami's is a little smaller than the others, and Barcelona's and Vancouver's offer their countries' finest folding chairs for seating while you wait.) If you have to wait a few minutes for your group to be called, you'll find enough seating for your family to sit down and relax. Vending machines and bathrooms are available, and Disney provides everything from character greetings to ship models to maps on the floor to keep your kids occupied.

Once in the terminal, look for cast members handing out a mandatory (but mercifully short) health questionnaire. This questionnaire asks if anyone in your travel party has suffered from fever or nausea within the last 24 hours. Answering "yes" means you may be denied boarding, so be sure everyone is in good health. You'll return the completed form at the check-in desk.

Head for the check-in desk and have your signed cruise documents, health questionnaire, and IDs ready. If this is the first Disney cruise for anyone in your group, they'll need to accompany you to check in. Concierge has a dedicated check-in desk, and returning DCL guests can use a separate line for its Castaway Club (though given the number of return cruisers DCL sees, it's not always as fast as you'd think).

The check-in desk is where you'll receive your cabin number (if you don't already have one) and get issued your magnetic-stripe Key to the World stateroom cards. If this is your first Disney cruise, Disney will also take your photo. You may also choose to replace your photo with a current one if it's been awhile since your last cruise. The photo is used to ensure the person who gets off and back on the ship is the same person who boarded at the beginning of the cruise. The computerized systems at Disney's boarding gates display your photo when you swipe your room key to get off and on the ship.

The check-in desk will also issue your party a boarding number, usually 1–30. Rather than have everyone try to board the ship at once, Disney organizes passengers into boarding groups of about 25–30 families at a time. Loudspeakers announce every few minutes which group numbers are currently allowed to board.

If you've not yet done so, you'll have an opportunity in the cruise terminal to sign up your children for the kids' clubs before boarding. A good time to do that is while you're waiting for your boarding group to be announced.

Your Key to the World Card Explained
This card contains helpful information about your cruise.

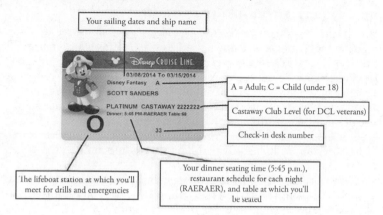

Your sailing dates and ship name

A = Adult; C = Child (under 18)

Castaway Club Level (for DCL veterans)

Check-in desk number

The lifeboat station at which you'll meet for drills and emergencies

Your dinner seating time (5:45 p.m.), restaurant schedule for each night (RAERAER), and table at which you'll be seated

Your dining schedule will be printed on your card as a series of letters. One letter will be shown for each night of your cruise. In the example above, the seven-letter code **RAERAER** indicates that this is a seven-night cruise. Each letter in the series also represents the first letter of the name of one of the ship's standard restaurants. In the example above, **R** is the *Fantasy*'s Royal Court, **A** is for Animator's Palate, and **E** signifies Enchanted Garden.

Finally, your Key to the World card also shows your transfer information, if you booked transportation through Disney to or from the port.

BOARDING THE SHIP

YOU CAN BOARD THE SHIP anytime after your boarding number is called. Have your room keys out, as they're scanned whenever you come on and off the ship.

Just before you enter the ship, photographers will offer to take a photo of your party. If this is important to you, a quick mirror check in the restroom and dressing in something you'd like recorded for posterity is a good idea. If you don't care to be photographed, breeze on past the people getting photos; they're certainly not mandatory, and lines can back up.

As you step on board, a cast member will ask your family name. Why they do this when so many parties traveling together don't necessarily have the same last name, we don't know. Either give your first names (Thurston and Lovey are our favorites) or make up a portmanteau combining your last names—no one is checking your ID—or just give a name. What doesn't work is saying you'd rather not, and it's easiest to just board as the Howells if you'd rather not announce your presence. (I mean, we all know how the paparazzi are.)

YOUR FIRST AFTERNOON ABOARD

IF YOU DIDN'T GET A *Personal Navigator* handout (see opposite page) in the terminal, pick one up at Guest Relations while you're still on Deck 3. This is also a good time to do any last-minute reservations or change your dining rotation or seating time. If this isn't your first Disney cruise and you're already familiar with the ship, you may choose to split up your group to do these tasks and meet up after you're done. It will save you time running around the ship.

Our first stop is usually Senses Spa, to book its Rainforest Room. It has even more limited availability than adult dining or a beach cabana, and you can't book it ahead of time.

Next, check for any last-minute openings at Palo or Remy if you wish to dine there and haven't booked yet. The location for this check-in desk will be noted in your *Personal Navigator.*

Recent cruises have offered special ticketed character-greeting appointments to meet the *Frozen* royals Anna and Elsa. The greetings are free, but if you want to meet the ice queen and her sis, you'll need a ticket to do so. Tickets are available for only a few hours on arrival day, so check your *Personal Navigator* for the distribution time and location.

If it's after 1:30 p.m., you can head to your room and drop any bags you carried on. You may also see your room attendant already sprucing up your cabin for the evening.

In the afternoon, people will start to swarm the Cabanas buffet (Beach Blanket Buffet on the *Wonder*) as if they've never seen food before. A nearly identical buffet is usually served in Enchanted Garden on the *Dream* and *Fantasy,* Carioca's on the *Magic,* and Parrot Cay on the *Wonder* (you'll also find far fewer people at all three restaurants). If all you're looking for is a quick bite to eat and you're all over age 18, try the quick-service Vista Café or Cove Café. We love Cabanas, but there's no shortage of food on the ship, and you've already spent enough of your day in lines.

The pool deck will be full of folks swimming and lounging. And when we say "full," we mean that it will be hectic to chaotic. If you want to relax, don't go there. But do pick up a drink at the beverage station to stay hydrated.

The chaos comes to a head with the **Sail-Away Celebration,** the kind you've seen memorialized in reruns of *The Love Boat,* with Champagne toasts, confetti, and Gavin MacLeod in shorts. It's kind of fun and a nice way to start your cruise, though this event isn't a must-do for us.

THE LIFEBOAT DRILL

THIS IS USUALLY HELD around 4 p.m. before the ship leaves port. Every member of your group will need to be present, and you'll need to bring your stateroom keys to the drill; attendance is tracked by computer, which reads your room key to validate your presence.

The lifeboat drill is the last must-do activity for the day. If you're down for an early dinner seating, it will soon be time to dress for dinner. If not, you may choose to attend the first evening show. And with that, your afternoon is done, things calm down, and you can finally relax and start your vacation.

BARE NECESSITIES

THE *PERSONAL NAVIGATOR*

YOU'LL BE GIVEN THIS HANDOUT (shown on the next page) when you board the ship. The *Personal Navigator* is a daily guide to all of the ship's activities and events, including times, locations, shop and restaurant hours, and more. You'll receive a new one every night for the following day, and extra *Navigator*s are available at Guest Services and by asking your stateroom attendant.

The format is roughly the same each day. Page 1 usually shows the date, ship's location, and sunrise–sunset times. If the ship is in port, the *Navigator* will list the time you need to be back on the ship ("All Aboard") and the ship's departure time. Also listed are the times and locations for the evening's entertainment; important announcements; games, shows, and events, including times and locations; and the dinner menu theme and "Drink of the Day."

Page 2 holds the ship's schedule for every hour of the day, separated into three sections: The top section holds the morning's activities, usually running from 8:30 a.m. until 1:30 p.m.; the middle section contains afternoon activities, from 1:45 p.m. until around 6:45 p.m.; and the bottom section lists the evening's events, from about 7 p.m. to midnight.

Each section is separated into approximately 10 rows of activities, and each row generally corresponds to an age group, location, or event. For example, you'll see rows for special events at the pool, character greetings, movies, family activities, and stuff for adults, plus the schedule for the Vibe, Edge, and Oceaneer Club/Lab kids' activities.

Page 3 has in-depth information about the daily activities described on page 2. Page 4 lists the ship's restaurant, store, and service-desk hours, plus mealtimes. Other services, such as onboard airline check-in, are also listed here. Finally, any open space on this page is usually filled with shopping advertisements.

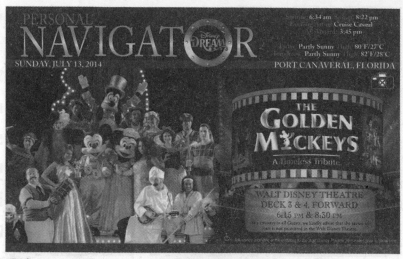

Welcome Aboard!

Your Stateroom & Luggage
Staterooms will be ready at 1:30 pm Stateroom hosts will deliver luggage throughout the day until 5:30 pm

Staterooms with Bunk Beds
Bunk beds are recessed into the ceiling and will be prepared during evening turndown service by your Stateroom Host/ess.

Stateroom Safe
Each stateroom is equipped with a secured storage safe. Instructions for use are located on the safe.

To Change Dining Assignment
Requests for a different seating will be taken today:
• 1:00 pm - 3:30 pm; Book in Royal Palace
• 3:30 pm - 4:30 pm; Please call 7-1831, 7-1832, or 7-1833

Remy & Palo Dining Reservations for Brunch & Dinner
Bookings will be taken on a first come basis today at:
• 1:00 pm - 3:30 pm, Palo; Book in Royal Palace
• 1:00 pm - 3:30 pm, Remy; Book in Royal Palace
Reservations required & cover charge applicable.
Please dial 7-9734, or 7-9735 for more information.
Openings still available for tonight!

Dinner
Please check your dining tickets for details of your dining rotation, and bring them to your specific dining location. There is no need to wait in line prior to dinner. Dining Rooms open at designated seating times and your table is reserved each night of your cruise.
• 5:45 pm - First seating
• 8:15 pm - Second seating

It's time to go Sailing Away!
Join Mickey and Minnie, along with Tinker Bell and the rest of the gang, as they welcome you aboard the Disney Dream.

4:30 pm
Deck Stage,
Deck 11, Midship

Don't Miss:

Walking Ship Tour
Preludes, Deck 3, Forward - 1:00 pm & 2:00 pm
Enjoy the beauty of the Disney Dream with your Cruise Staff in this guided tour.

Family Dance Party
Evolution, Deck 4, Aft - 7:30 pm
Bring the whole family and dance your cares away to some of your favorite hits!

Family Superstar Karaoke
D Lounge, Deck 4, Midship - 9:30 pm & 11:15 pm
Join your Cruise Staff in D Lounge tonight and sing along to your favorite song - fun for everyone.

Club New Year's Eve
D Lounge, Deck 4, Midship - 10:45 pm
Club New Year's Eve, you won't want to miss this journey of musical genres in history and performances by some of your favorite Cruise Staff. Bring your family and help us count down to a brand new year!

GET THE PICTURE!
Visit Shutters today and ask your friendly Shutters staff about the GET THE PICTURE! Digital package which includes all your stateroom photos on one photo disc. For best value, upgrade to include all printed photos, too! Visit Shutters on Deck 4, Midship for more information. Don't wait until the last day. Beat the rush and order yours now! Terms and conditions apply.

DINNER MENU	Animator's Palate: Pacific Rim Cuisine Enchanted Garden: Countries of Medici Royal Palace: French Dinner	DRINK OF THE DAY	Bahama Mama (Alcoholic) Passion Cream-Freeze (Non Alcoholic)	Fire/Security:	7-3001
				Medical Emergency:	7-3000
				Health Center:	7-1923

DISNEY CRUISE LINE NAVIGATOR APP If you prefer an electronic version of the *Personal Navigator,* there's an app for that! Available free at iTunes and Google Play, it works through the ships' onboard Wi-Fi, so you can keep your device in airplane mode while using it.

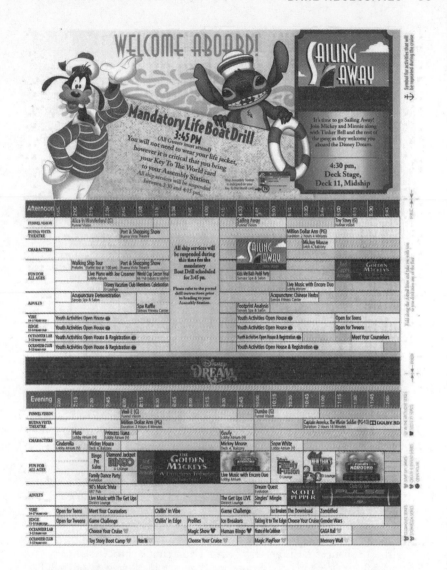

ONBOARD SERVICES

A 24-HOUR GUEST SERVICES DESK is just off the lobby on each ship to answer questions, make reservations, and provide other help. You can also contact Guest Services from your stateroom by touching the Guest Services button on your phone.

The best amenity that comes with your stateroom is likely to be your stateroom attendant, who will tidy up your cabin after you depart in the morning, deliver your *Personal Navigator,* and turn down your beds each night. You'll almost certainly see him or her more than any other crew member, and you'll be amazed at how little sleep these hardworking staff seem to need.

Given the nature of a cruise, you'll find that your stateroom attendant is in and out of your room much more often than a typical hotel housekeeper would be. This makes it particularly important to make ample use of your DO NOT DISTURB sign if you plan to sleep late, take an afternoon nap, or otherwise just don't want to be bothered for a while.

AIRLINE CHECK-IN

EVEN BEFORE YOU BOARD THE SHIP, you can request airline check-in for your flight home by making arrangements at your terminal's check-in desk. To do this, have the airline name, flight number(s), departure time and date, names of passengers as printed on their ticket(s), and the flight confirmation number(s) for each flight segment.

While on board, you can ask Guest Services to check you in to your flight if you're flying home the day your cruise returns to port. Stop by the Guest Services desk before 10 p.m. on your second night to make this request. This service is available to anyone flying out of Orlando International Airport on domestic flights (including the US Virgin Islands and Puerto Rico) on AirTran Airways, Alaska Airlines, American Airlines, Delta Air Lines, JetBlue Airways, United Airlines, and US Airways.

No matter when you register, your first flight's departure must be after 11:30 a.m. on the day your cruise ends, to ensure the ship has enough time to make it back. There's a limit of two bags per person, and each bag must weigh less than 50 pounds. (According to Disney, a few randomly selected passengers may be required to undergo additional screening at the airport, and thus are ineligible for early check-in.)

The day before your cruise ends, you'll receive printed instructions in your stateroom, along with your boarding passes and temporary luggage tags. Affix the tags to your bags and leave them in the hallway outside your stateroom between 8:30 and 10:30 p.m. The next time you see your bags will be on the baggage carousel at your destination airport. This makes for easy maneuvering at Orlando International (the airport for most DCL guests) because you simply proceed directly to the security line and on to your gate. Your airline's baggage fee will be added to your DCL bill and will appear on your checkout statement.

LAUNDRY SERVICES

SELF-SERVICE LAUNDRY FACILITIES are available on several decks on each ship, furnished with washers, dryers, and detergent for purchase. It costs around $2 to wash a load of clothes and another $2 to dry them; detergent is another $1 per load.

In addition to do-it-yourself laundry, each ship offers full-service laundry and dry cleaning on board, with pickup from and delivery to your stateroom. Simply drop your clothes in the plastic dry-cleaning bag hanging inside your closet, and complete the attached paper form with any cleaning instructions. The laundry service usually takes 24 hours, but we've had simple requests—laundering and ironing a couple of shirts—done on the same day.

PORT ADVENTURES

IN ADDITION TO GUEST SERVICES, a separate Port Adventures desk on Deck 3 (*Magic* and *Wonder*) or Deck 5 (*Dream* and *Fantasy*) handles booking for shore excursions. The staff are usually knowledgeable about the most popular excursions at each port. In addition to providing information about cost and time, they can typically answer questions regarding the appropriateness of a particular activity for the members of your family. They can also help you reschedule an activity if needed. See Part Eleven for details.

HEALTH SERVICES

EACH SHIP'S HEALTH CENTER employs a third-party doctor and nurse for medical issues. The most common reasons for visiting the Health Center are motion sickness, sunburn, and nausea, although the staff have seen their share of broken bones over the years. The Health Center (Deck 1 Forward; open 9:30–11 a.m. and 4:30–7 p.m.) can provide doses of basic over-the-counter and some prescription medicines; anything serious, such as surgery, will probably require an airlift to the nearest hospital. Also, note that use of the Health Services center isn't free, and rates are comparable to those of US hospitals—in other words, expensive—so check your insurance coverage before you leave home (see page 26 for more on that). However, just like the First Aid Centers in the Disney parks, Health Services will often provide you with a dose or two of over-the-counter medicine, such as aspirin or motion sickness tablets, for free.

TIPPING

YOU'LL ENCOUNTER CREW MEMBERS throughout your cruise, many of whom you'll see several times per day and who will have a direct impact on the quality of your trip. It's customary to give a small tip to these crew members in recognition of their service. The chart below indicates the suggested tip for these staff for each person in your cabin. Thus, if you have four people in your family and you're taking a seven-night cruise, budget $336 ($84 times four) for the personnel shown, plus any spa, bar, or other dining gratuities you'll need.

These suggested gratuity amounts are automatically added to your stateroom account based on the number of people in your cabin and your cruise length. Once on board, you can adjust these amounts or pay in cash by visiting the Guest Services desk (open 24 hours a day) on Deck 3. Lines at Guest Services get long on the last night of your cruise, so plan to make any adjustments sooner rather than later if you wish to avoid a wait.

STAFF MEMBER	Suggested Gratuity Per Day	Suggested Gratuity 3 Nights	Suggested Gratuity 4 Nights	Suggested Gratuity 7 Nights
Stateroom Attendant	$4	$12	$16	$28
Dining Room Server	$4	$12	$16	$28
Dining Room Assistant Server	$3	$9	$12	$21
Dining Room Head Server	$1	$3	$4	$7
TOTAL (Per Guest)	**$12**	**$36**	**$48**	**$84**

At Palo and Remy, a gratuity is automatically added only for alcohol; an additional gratuity for dining service is left to your discretion. It's also customary to add a gratuity for room service, again at your discretion. Finally, note that an automatic 15% gratuity is added to Cove Café and bar tabs, plus any alcohol ordered elsewhere on deck.

CHECKOUT *and* DEPARTURE

YOUR LAST NIGHT ON THE SHIP

YOU'LL RECEIVE DEBARKATION INFORMATION—including what to do with your luggage, where you'll be eating breakfast, and when you need to be off the ship—the night before your last night on board (for example night six of a seven-night cruise). This information is also available at Guest Services the last night of the cruise.

Packing

If you haven't already arranged onboard airline check-in, you'll receive luggage tags in your stateroom on your last evening aboard, along with instructions for getting breakfast before departing in the morning and gratuity envelopes. Use the luggage tags if you'd like Disney to transport your bags from the ship to the port terminal upon docking. (This enables you to walk off the ship without having to carry bags; you'll pick up your luggage before you go through Customs.) The luggage tags will be in colorful shapes of Disney characters: green Tinker Bell, orange Goofy, blue Donald Duck, and so on. Write your stateroom number, name, home address, and number of bags on each tag, and attach one tag to each piece of luggage you want Disney to transport. Place your tagged bags outside your stateroom between 8:30 and 10:30 p.m.

A few packing tips:

*un*official **TIP**
You'll need your Key to the World cards to exit the ship, so keep them handy until you're back on land.

- Don't forget to leave out clothes to wear to breakfast and off the ship the last morning.

- If you're flying home, note that any alcohol you purchased on the ship must be packed in your checked bags.

- Don't pack your passports, birth certificates, Key to the World card, or any other travel documents in your checked bags. You'll need them before you can pick up your luggage, so keep them in a bag you plan to carry by hand off the ship.

- Remove any old airline or cruise tags from your luggage before placing on a new tag.

- Keep inside your stateroom any luggage you'll carry off the ship by hand. When you've gotten off the ship, you'll find a section of the terminal dedicated to checked baggage. Checked bags will be organized by color and character, with all of the green Tinker Bell–tagged luggage together, all of the orange Goofy luggage together, and so on. Overhead signs will direct you to each section.

    Luggage will be sorted by stateroom number within each section, so look for yours by finding your stateroom number within your section. If you can't find one of your bags, check a few feet up and down the row too—sometimes the stateroom order isn't exact. Ask a cast member for help if you still can't find your luggage after checking the nearby spaces.

EXPRESS WALK-OFF

FOR GUESTS WHO WISH TO BE among the very first off the ship (those who need to get straight to the airport or who have other time-dependent plans that day), DCL offers Express Walk-Off. As soon as the ship clears Customs, guests may depart the ship. You must carry all of your own luggage to take advantage of this service; you may not leave it out the night before. Be considerate and let your cabin attendant know if you're doing this, so he or she isn't waiting for your bags to appear in the hallway the last night of the cruise.

BREAKFAST ON THE MORNING OF YOUR DEPARTURE

YOU'LL HAVE THE CHANCE FOR ONE MORE SIT-DOWN MEAL. The table-service breakfast seatings are assigned based on your seating time for dinner. Guests with the early dinner seating are scheduled for their final breakfast on board at 6:30 a.m. Guests with the later dinner seating get a last-day breakfast assignment

*un*official **TIP**
Concierge guests may order room service breakfast the last morning of the cruise.

at 8 a.m. This effectively means that any guest with a late dinner seating and an early flight will be unable to eat a table-service breakfast on their last morning. For guests in this situation, the Cabanas buffet is open beginning at 6:30 a.m. This isn't quite the gargantuan spread offered on other mornings—expect pastries, fruit, bacon, eggs, cold cereal, and not much else. Cove Café is also open beginning at 6 a.m.

PHOTO PURCHASES

IF YOU'VE PURCHASED A PHOTO CD or other photo product, it will be available for pickup on the morning of your departure. Pickup time usually starts at 7 a.m., and lines begin to form earlier than that. If you have an early flight and are using Express Walk-Off, plan to be in line to grab your CD by about 6:30 a.m. Have another member of your party grab you a banana and coffee (or one last pastry) from the buffet line for you to eat while you wait.

unofficial **TIP**
Guests with flights out of Orlando International Airport before 1 p.m. are required to leave the ship by 8 a.m.

US CUSTOMS ALLOWANCES

EACH FAMILY WILL NEED to fill out a Customs Declaration form (see next two pages). Besides the usual name and address, the form asks which countries you've visited, whether you're bringing in prohibited items such as fruits or vegetables, whether you've handled livestock, and whether you're carrying more than $10,000 in cash. (Answering "yes" to all three is probably the start of the next installment in the *Hangover* series.) See **tinyurl.com/customsdutyinfo** for more information.

U.S. Customs and Border Protection

Customs Declaration

19 CFR 122.27, 148.12, 148.13, 148.110,148.111, 1498; 31 CFR 5316

FORM APPROVED
OMB NO. 1651-0009

Each arriving traveler or responsible family member must provide the following information (only ONE written declaration per family is required):

1. Family **Name**

   First *(Given)* | Middle

2. **Birth date** Day | Month | Year

3. Number of **Family members** traveling with you

4. (a) U.S. Street **Address** (hotel name/destination)

   (b) City | (c) State

5. **Passport issued by** (country)

6. **Passport number**

7. Country of **Residence**

8. **Countries visited** on this trip prior to U.S. arrival

9. **Airline/Flight No.** or **Vessel Name**

10. The primary purpose of this trip is **business**:   Yes   No

11. I am (We are) bringing

    (a) fruits, vegetables, plants, seeds, food, insects: Yes   No

    (b) meats, animals, animal/wildlife products: Yes   No

    (c) disease agents, cell cultures, snails: Yes   No

    (d) soil or have been on a farm/ranch/pasture: Yes   No

12. I have (We have) been in close proximity of (such as touching or handling) **livestock**:   Yes   No

13. I am (We are) carrying **currency or monetary instruments** over $10,000 U.S. or foreign equivalent: Yes   No (see definition of monetary instruments on reverse)

14. I have (We have) **commercial merchandise**:   Yes   No (articles for sale, samples used for soliciting orders, or goods that are not considered personal effects)

15. **Residents** — the **total value of all goods,** including commercial merchandise I/we have purchased or acquired abroad, (including gifts for someone else, but not items mailed to the U.S.) and am/are bringing to the U.S. is: $

    Visitors — the **total value of all articles** that will remain in the U.S., including commercial merchandise is: $

Read the instructions on the back of this form. Space is provided to list all the items you must declare.

I HAVE READ THE IMPORTANT INFORMATION ON THE REVERSE SIDE OF THIS FORM AND HAVE MADE A TRUTHFUL DECLARATION.

X _____

(Signature) | Date (day/month/year)

For Official Use Only

CBP Form 6059B (10/07)

U.S. Customs and Border Protection Welcomes You to the United States

U.S. Customs and Border Protection is responsible for protecting the United States against the illegal importation of prohibited items. CBP officers have the authority to question you and to examine you and your personal property. If you are one of the travelers selected for an examination, you will be treated in a courteous, professional, and dignified manner. CBP Supervisors and Passenger Service Representatives are available to answer your questions. Comment cards are available to compliment or provide feedback.

Important Information

U.S. Residents — Declare all articles that you have acquired abroad and are bringing into the United States.

Visitors (Non-Residents) — Declare the value of all articles that will remain in the United States.

Declare all articles on this declaration form and show the value in U.S. dollars. For gifts, please indicate the retail value.

Duty — CBP officers will determine duty. U.S. residents are normally entitled to a duty-free exemption of $800 on items accompanying them. Visitors (non-residents) are normally entitled to an exemption of $100. Duty will be assessed at the current rate on the first $1,000 above the exemption.

Agricultural and Wildlife Products — To prevent the entry of dangerous agricultural pests and prohibited wildlife, the following are restricted: Fruits, vegetables, plants, plant products, soil, meat, meat products, birds, snails, and other live animals or animal products. Failure to declare such items to a Customs and Border Protection Officer/Customs and Border Protection Agriculture Specialist/Fish and Wildlife Inspector can result in penalties and the items may be subject to seizure.

Controlled substances, obscene articles, and toxic substances are generally prohibited entry.

Thank You, and Welcome to the United States.

The transportation of currency or **monetary instruments**, regardless of the amount, is legal. However, if you bring in to or take out of the United States more than $10,000 (U.S. or foreign equivalent, or a combination of both), you are required by law to file a report on FinCEN 105 (formerly Customs Form 4790) with U.S. Customs and Border Protection. Monetary instruments include coin, currency, travelers checks and bearer instruments such as personal or cashiers checks and stocks and bonds. If you have someone else carry the currency or monetary instrument for you, you must also file a report on FinCEN 105. Failure to file the required report or failure to report the *total* amount that you are carrying may lead to the seizure of *all* the currency or monetary instruments, and may subject you to civil penalties and/or criminal prosecution. SIGN ON THE OPPOSITE SIDE OF THIS FORM AFTER YOU HAVE READ THE IMPORTANT INFORMATION ABOVE AND MADE A TRUTHFUL DECLARATION.

Description of Articles (List may continue on another CBP Form 6059B)	Value	CBP Use Only
Total		

PART FIVE

SPECIAL TIPS *for* SPECIAL PEOPLE

▌ DCL *for* SINGLES

BECAUSE DISNEY CRUISE LINE (DCL) IS TARGETED TO FAMI-
LIES, roughly 90% of its guests are couples or parents and kids. That's
about 10 points higher than the cruise industry's average, and it means
that there are around 200 solo travelers per cruise on the *Magic* and
Wonder, and around 400 on the *Dream* and *Fantasy.*

Like the Disney parks, DCL is great for singles. It's safe, clean, and
low-pressure. Safety and comfort are excellent, especially for women.
If you're looking for places to relax without being hit on, Disney's
ships are perfect. The bars, lounges, and nightclubs are clean, friendly,
and interesting; the restaurants are welcoming; and the spas are excellent places for grabbing some solo time in public. One aspect that you
do have to be vigilant about when traveling alone is shore excursions
in foreign countries; more on that a bit later.

If you're interested in meeting other singles, Disney usually runs
a **Singles Mingle** session on one of the first couple of days of each
cruise. These are informal get-togethers, usually held at the Cove Café
in the adults-only part of the ship, and last about an hour. Similarly,
single and not-single guests ages 18–21 are welcome to attend a **Club
18*21 Social** during one night of their cruise. It's a meet-up attended by
guests and crew, generally during the evening after the second dinner
seating, also usually at the Cove Café.

DINING Single travelers will likely be paired with other groups for dinner at the standard restaurants. When we've cruised solo, our dinner
companions are usually one or two couples, which means we're sitting
at a table for four or six. If the cruise is especially popular, Disney may
try to squeeze in another single person to your group, too, so that everyone has a table. Our dinners with these new friends couldn't have gone
better, and we say that as pretty strong introverts. We've met interesting

people from many different places, never run out of things to talk about, and even kept in touch with a few folks when we got back home.

Solo travelers are also welcome at Palo and Remy, and we've had many fine dinners and brunches there. If you're having difficulty making a reservation for one using the DCL website before your trip, try stopping by the restaurant on the afternoon you board. We've found the staff to be exceptionally accommodating for these requests, especially if you're willing to arrive either early or late.

unofficial **TIP**
US law requires Disney to disclose most claims of crimes alleged to have taken place on board. DCL voluntarily discloses all such incidents on its website.

CRUISE FARES While some cruise lines are adding stateroom cabins designed especially for solo travelers, cabins on Disney's ships are all designed to hold at least two people. To make up for the room, bar, and shore excursion revenue lost when one person books a cabin that could hold two paying passengers, Disney adds a 100% surcharge (a single supplement, in cruise-industry lingo) to most solo-traveler fares, making the cost equivalent to two people taking the same trip. There's a small chance that you can find last-minute deals on unsold cabins without paying the full 100% supplement. Your best bet is to check the DCL website or have a travel agent research for you.

PORT ADVENTURES As with dining, there's a good chance you'll be paired with other couples for shore excursions. But unlike dinner, it's possible for a solo traveler to simply be a quiet observer during many excursions, especially those designed for groups.

unofficial **TIP**
If your port adventure involves boating, snorkeling, or any other water-based activity, you'll almost certainly be assigned another traveler or couple as a buddy for safety reasons.

We've been single travelers on everything from cooking demonstrations to snorkeling to city tours, and they've all gone well. All of the programs we've tried can accommodate single guests, and the port adventures staff makes everyone feel welcome. That said, some excursions run by third-party companies will use private taxi or shuttle services to transport guests from the ship to their activity, and it's possible for a solo traveler to be the odd man out if the vehicle doesn't have enough seats to accommodate the entire group, as Len recounts:

I was once the only solo traveler in a group of nine for an excursion in Mexico that involved a 30-minute bus ride. When we got to the departure point, we saw that not all of us were going to fit on the eight-person bus that the excursion company brought. The couples were placed together, and the Port Adventures staff hurriedly brought around an unmarked, nondescript "taxi" for me.

As I got in this random car on a random street in a random Mexican town, my last words to the others were, "Take a good look. This is what I was wearing the last time you saw me." Of course, I made it to and from the shore excursion just fine, and we all had a laugh once we were reunited. But I wouldn't recommend that others do this, especially women traveling alone.

In the (unlikely) event that you're asked to travel alone to a shore excursion, decline politely. Ask to be accompanied by a staff member or to be escorted back to the ship. Along the same lines, if you're not comfortable walking back to your stateroom at night, ask a member of the crew to escort you. And use extra caution walking to and from the parking lot at the cruise terminal.

DCL *"At Large"*

AS WITH ITS THEME PARK GUESTS, Disney realizes that its cruise guests come in all shapes and sizes and makes many accommodations to ensure that they're treated well.

Your stateroom's personal flotation devices (PFDs, also known as life jackets) are designed to fit most bodies. With PFDs, chest size, not weight, is the measurement that determines proper fit. Disney's PFDs include a nylon strap that wraps around your body to keep the PFD snug against your chest. Try on your PFD when you first get to your stateroom to ensure that the strap fits around your body. If it doesn't, mention it to your group's leader during the lifeboat drill.

The AquaDuck waterslides on the *Dream* and *Fantasy* seem able to accommodate virtually all body shapes and sizes. We've heard success stories from individuals weighing more than 300 pounds and couples weighing more than 400. The AquaDunk slide on the *Magic* has a weight limit of 300 pounds.

If an activity or port adventure has a weight limit, it will be printed in the details describing the activity; look for phrases such as "Guests must weigh" or "Weight must be" in the activity's listing. Some shore excursions, including kayaking and some scuba and snorkeling trips, have weight limits of 240 or 300 pounds per person. Segway tours generally accommodate persons of up to 250 pounds. Many Alaskan excursions involving helicopters or seaplanes have a weight limit of 250 pounds inclusive of all gear (clothing, cameras, and such); it may be possible to modify this requirement by paying an excess-weight fee for additional fuel. Other activities have weight limits of up to 350 pounds per person. Again, check the activity's details for more information, or check with the Port Adventures desk on board.

Ask for bench seating or chairs without arms at restaurants and lounges. If you don't see them, the staff should be able to provide one.

Wear comfortable shoes. You'll be surprised at the amount of walking you do on board the ship, not to mention the walking you'll do from the cruise terminal to the ship.

DCL *for* EXPECTANT MOMS

DISNEY PROHIBITS MOTHERS-TO-BE FROM SAILING if they will reach their 24th week of pregnancy at any time during the cruise. For example, a woman who is 23 weeks pregnant would not be allowed by Disney to take a 12-night transatlantic cruise. In addition, note that if you're flying to or from your cruise, airlines may have their own, different policies regarding pregnant travelers.

On board, the AquaDuck and AquaDunk waterslides are off-limits to expectant mothers, as is the waterslide at Castaway Cay. Other shore excursions, such as scuba activities, off-road driving, and parasailing, also prohibit expectant mothers from participating. In addition, some tour operators have restrictions on snorkeling and dolphin encounters.

Talk to your doctor about any shore excursions you plan to take. Also note that some excursions require lengthy drives on pothole-strewn roads, some of them dirt, gravel, or sand, in vehicles that have seen years of use. Even if all you're planning to do is relax on a beach, the drive to get there may be bumpy enough to make you reconsider going.

DCL *for* OLDER *and* YOUNGER CHILDREN

DISNEY CRUISE LINE REQUIRES that infant guests be at least 6 months of age on most sailings and at least 1 year of age on some longer voyages. Depending on how early you've booked your cruise, a surprise addition to the family may influence whether you're able to sail. If you find yourself in this situation, contact Disney as soon as possible to understand your options.

Guests with young children should think about the family's sleeping arrangements when planning their cruise. Disney does provide "pack and play"–style cribs free of charge to guests who need them. However, given the small square footage of most staterooms, the crib's footprint will have an outsized impact on the room's usable space for other family members, particularly if the child will be napping during the day. Training your young child to sleep in a bed rather than a crib might enhance your family's enjoyment of their living quarters.

On the other end of the spectrum, some 17- and 18-year-olds may encounter frustration during their trip due to Disney's strict enforcement of age restrictions on teen and adult activities. We recently traveled with a teen just days away from her 18th birthday—in fact, we booked the trip to celebrate her birthday. Even though she was a high school graduate, she was still not allowed to dine at Palo (yes, we tried bribery, and no, it didn't work), exercise in the ship's fitness center, or go to some of the cooking demonstrations. We've seen 17- and 18-year-old cousins unable to do virtually anything together because the older teen wasn't allowed into the Vibe teen club and the younger one wasn't allowed into any of the adult activities. If you have an older teen, consider whether choosing a slightly different travel date would impact his or her enjoyment of the trip.

For more on cruising with children and teens, see "Cruising with Kids" in Part One, page 13, and "Special Considerations" in Part Nine, page 142.

DCL *for* SENIORS

MOST SENIORS FIND A DISNEY CRUISE LESS TIRING than a Walt Disney World vacation. First, most seniors find considerably less walking required on the ship versus the parks. Second, the ships' adults-only areas provide a break from children (and their families) when needed. And even the most energetic onboard attraction, the AquaDuck, isn't as intense as a ride on Space Mountain or Big Thunder Mountain Railroad.

Because of their flexible schedules, retirees can often take advantage of off-peak cruise fares, especially during fall or spring, when the weather is nicest and crowds are lower because school is in session. If you're cruising to the Caribbean, the Bahamas, or Mexico, be sure to bring a jacket and sweater along with your warm-weather clothing—while temperature averages hover around 70°F in most of those locations, a cold front can drop temps into the upper 40s with little notice, and it's not uncommon to have morning temperatures in the lower 50s.

GUESTS *with* DISABILITIES

DCL STRIVES TO MAKE ITS SHIPS ACCESSIBLE TO ALL. Virtually the entire ship, from staterooms to restaurants to nightclubs and pools, is wheelchair- and ECV-friendly. More accommodations are available for other special needs too. This section describes each of those in more detail. Call DCL's Accessibility Desk at ☎ 407-566-3500 (voice) or 407-566-7455 (TTY) for specific questions.

Stateroom Furnishings

In addition to the standard amenities offered in each stateroom, Disney offers the following special equipment for guests with disabilities:

• Close-captioned TV (most stations)	• Raised toilet seat	• Shower stool
• Bed boards and rails	• Refrigerator	• Transfer benches
• Portable toilet	• Rubber bed pads	
• A Stateroom Communication Kit, including an alarm clock, door knock and phone alerts, phone amplifier, bed-shaker notification, strobe-light smoke detector, and text typewriter (TTY)		

WHEELCHAIR AND ECV USERS DCL suggests that guests using a wheelchair or ECV request a wheelchair-accessible stateroom or suite. Found on every Disney ship, wheelchair-accessible staterooms include the following features:

• Doorways at least 32 inches wide	• Fold-down shower seating and hand-held showerheads	• Open bed frame for easier entry and exit
• Bathroom and shower handrails	• Lowered towel and closet bars	• Ramped bathroom thresholds
• Emergency call buttons and additional phones in the bath and stateroom		

One advantage to having an accessible stateroom is that its wider door lets you store your wheelchair or ECV inside your cabin when it's not in use. This also makes it easier to recharge the equipment when needed. If you find yourself in a standard stateroom whose door won't fit your vehicle, you may be asked to park the vehicle in a designated area elsewhere on the ship, even at night. In practice, we've seen many ECVs parked in a corner of each deck's elevator-landing areas. Chances are that your vehicle will be stored within a short walk of your cabin.

Outside of your stateroom, special areas are set aside at most ship activities for guests in wheelchairs. At the Walt Disney Theatre, for example, Disney cast members direct guests in wheelchairs to a reserved seating area. Shops, restaurants, bars, and nightclubs are all accessible, and accessible restrooms are available throughout the ship's public areas. A limited number of sand wheelchairs are available on Castaway Cay, too, on a first-come, first-served basis.

Note that DCL's pools require a transfer from wheelchair to use. For this reason, Disney recommends that guests in wheelchairs travel with someone who can help transfer them to and from the wheelchair.

Another area to be aware of is tendering from ship to shore. Some ports, such as the one at Grand Cayman, aren't deep enough to accommodate large cruise ships such as Disney's. When DCL ships anchor at Grand Cayman, smaller boats, or tenders, pull up next to the ship, and guests board them for travel to and from Grand Cayman.

Some tenders use steps instead of ramps to get guests on board. In those cases, wheelchair passengers must use the steps. Also keep in mind that the Disney ship and tender craft both float freely in the ocean. It's not uncommon for the stairs to move 2 or 3 feet up and down during the course of a transfer. If the seas are too rough, wheelchair guests may be denied transfer.

SIGHT- AND HEARING-IMPAIRED GUESTS In addition to closed-captioning TVs, assistive listening devices and printed scripts are available for shows at the ships' main theaters and show stages. Stop by the Guest Services desk to pick those up. In addition, American Sign Language interpreters are available for live performances on some cruise dates.

unofficial **TIP**
Service animals are welcome on board, and each ship has a designated animal-relief area on an outside deck.

CHILDREN WITH DISABILITIES Disney's youth programs are open to special-needs children ages 3–17. All children must be toilet-trained and able to play well with kids who are about their same age and size.

The number of children who can participate is limited and is based on the number of available counselors, the number of other children in the programs, the number of special-needs children already enrolled, and the specific needs of the child wishing to enroll. Check with the Youth Activities team when you get on board for more details. Disney is unable to provide youth counselors for medical attention, one-on-one care, or training for a specific need.

PORT ADVENTURES Many Port Adventures have requirements concerning mobility. These are noted in the Port Adventure descriptions. You may also inquire about which activities are available to you at the Port Adventures desk while on board.

Other amenities, such as disabled parking at the cruise terminal, are also available. See DCL's Guests with Disabilities FAQ (**tinyurl .com/dclguestswithdisabilities**) for more information.

DIETARY RESTRICTIONS

WITH ENOUGH ADVANCE NOTICE, DCL's sit-down restaurants can accommodate a wide variety of special dietary needs, including low-sodium, kosher, and allergen-free requests, at no additional cost. The best way to communicate these needs to Disney is through the Special Services Information Form, available when you check in online (see page 21). Disney asks that the form be submitted by e-mail, fax, or snail mail at least 30 days before your cruise. Note that counter-service restaurants and room service usually can't accommodate special requests, although some allergies, such as gluten, are more easily accommodated. If you book through a travel agent, he or she can make a note of this on your reservation. You should also let your serving team (including the head server) know your requirements on the first night of your cruise.

Note that most port adventures are run by independent contractors, not Disney. Your food requests and accommodations will *not* be automatically transferred to excursion contractors, and some providers may not be able to work with certain dietary issues. What's more, due to legal and agricultural restrictions, in many ports you will not be able to bring certain types of food off the ship. Check with Guest Services for advice on how best to handle your dietary needs while in port.

SMOKING *on* BOARD

SMOKING, INCLUDING CIGARETTES, CIGARS, PIPES, and electronic cigarettes, is prohibited in your stateroom, on your stateroom's outdoor verandah (if it has one), and any indoor space on the ship. On the *Magic* and *Wonder,* outdoor smoking areas are available on Deck 4 starboard (right side of the ship) between 6 p.m. and 6 a.m., and on Decks 9 and 10 starboard, excluding the Mickey Pool area.

Smoking areas on the *Dream* and *Fantasy* are on the port (left) side of Deck 4 Aft, also from 6 p.m. to 6 a.m.; the port side of Deck 12 Aft, accessed by walking through the Meridian Lounge; and near the Currents Bar on Deck 13 Forward, port side.

TRAVELING *with* MEDICATION

IF YOU'RE BRINGING PRESCRIPTION MEDICINE on your cruise, your best bet is to transport it in its original containers. The problem you're trying to avoid isn't one with Disney's security staff, but the customs staffs of the countries you're visiting and US border control when you return. While it's unlikely, those folks may ask to see either the original containers (with your name on them) or a copy of a valid prescription, to ensure that you're not importing illegal or prohibited substances. We also recommend that you keep these medicines in your carry-on bag instead of checked luggage. Finally, note that Disney's onboard Health Center may not to be able to refill prescriptions (especially for controlled substances) that run out during your cruise, so get them refilled before you leave home.

FRIENDS *of* BILL W.

BEER, WINE, AND SPIRITS flow freely on cruise ships, even those run by Disney. Daily **Alcoholics Anonymous** meetings are available on each cruise. While the time and location may vary, they're generally found here:

- 8:30 a.m. at Animator's Palate on the *Magic*
- 8:30 a.m. at the Cadillac Lounge on the *Wonder*
- 8:30 a.m. at the Outlook Lounge on the *Dream* and *Fantasy*

◼◼ FRIENDS *of* DOROTHY

UNLIKE OTHER CRUISE LINES, DCL doesn't offer onboard activities specifically designed for LGBT travelers—you won't find a "gay mingle" event listed in your *Personal Navigator.* Nevertheless, DCL is very welcoming to the LGBT community. Many of our gay friends, both with and without children, offer extremely positive feedback about their Disney cruises. One friend notes:

After about the second day, you can start picking out who is "family."
We met more gay people traveling on the Disney cruise than any of
our other nongay cruises.

Single gay travelers may feel somewhat isolated, but couples or groups of friends should have no problems.

PART SIX

THE SHIPS *at a* GLANCE

OVERVIEW *and* OUR RECOMMENDATIONS

LAUNCHED IN 1998, the *Magic* holds roughly 2,700 passengers and 950 crew members. The *Wonder* has the same capacity and was launched in 1999. The *Dream* and *Fantasy,* which took their maiden voyages in 2011 and 2012, respectively, hold up to 4,000 passengers and 1,450 crew. The *Magic* and *Wonder* are the workhorses of the fleet: The *Magic* covers everything from Mexico to the Mediterranean, while the *Wonder* plies the seas from Alaska to the Caribbean.

unofficial TIP
When it comes to choosing a ship, you'll do well with either the *Dream* or the *Fantasy.* We recommend going with whichever has the price or itinerary to meet your needs.

All four ships share sleek lines, twin smokestacks, and nautical styling that calls to mind classic ocean liners, but with instantly recognizable Disney signatures. The colors—black, white, red, and yellow—and the famous face-and-ears silhouette on the stacks are clearly those of Mickey Mouse. Look closely at the *Magic*'s stern ornamentation, for example, and you'll see a 15-foot Goofy hanging by his overalls. (It's Donald on the *Wonder*'s stern, Mickey on the *Dream*'s, and Dumbo on the *Fantasy*'s.)

Interiors combine nautical themes with Art Nouveau and Art Deco inspiration. (Art Nouveau incorporates natural shapes, such as from plants and animals, into its geometric designs; Art Deco has the geometry without the nature.) Disney images are everywhere, from Mickey's profile in the wrought-iron balustrades to the bronze statue of Helmsman Mickey featured prominently in the *Magic*'s atrium, Ariel in the *Wonder*, Admiral Donald on the *Dream*, and Mademoiselle Minnie in full flapper style on the *Fantasy*. Disney art is on every wall and in every stairwell and corridor. A grand staircase on each ship sweeps from the atrium lobby to shops peddling Disney Cruise Line–themed clothing, collectibles, jewelry, sundries, and more.

Ships have two lower decks with cabins, three decks with dining rooms and showrooms, and then three or five upper decks of cabins. Two sports and sun decks offer separate pools and facilities for families and for adults without children. Signs point toward lounges and facilities, and all elevators are clearly marked as Forward, Aft, or Midship.

Our main complaint concerning the ships' design is that outdoor public areas focus inward toward the pools instead of seaward, as if Disney wants you to forget that you're on a cruise liner. On the *Magic* and the *Wonder,* there's no public place where you can curl up in the shade and watch the ocean—at least not without a Plexiglas wall between you and it. On Deck 4 of the *Dream* and the *Fantasy,* however, an open promenade, complete with comfy deck chairs, circles the ship. It's shady and fairly well protected from wind, and it offers the opportunity to sit back and enjoy the sea without your having to look through Plexiglas barriers.

Speaking of Plexiglas, a predictable but nonetheless irritating design characteristic is the extensive childproofing. There's enough Plexiglas on all four ships to build a subdivision of see-through homes. On the pool decks especially, it feels as if the ships are hermetically sealed. Plus, verandah doors have a two-part locking mechanism, with one of the two parts 6 feet off the floor—causing even adults occasional consternation in trying to operate them.

unofficial **TIP**
Disney ships have no casinos or libraries.

FEATURES FOUND ON EVERY DCL SHIP

EVERY DISNEY SHIP INCLUDES a common set of amenities, including the following:

• Adult pool and deck areas	• Movie theater
• Bars, lounges, and cafés	• Outdoor basketball court, shuffleboard, and other sports areas
• Buffet restaurant	• Outdoor LED screen for movies, concerts, and videos
• Family pools and water-play areas	• **Palo,** an upscale Italian restaurant
• Fitness center	• Photo gallery for purchasing onboard photos
• Full-service spa and salon, with sauna	• Retail shopping, including duty-free alcohol
• Guest Services desk	• Theater for live performances
• Health Center	• Video-game arcade
• Infant, child, tween, and teen clubs	

Continued on page 80

Disney Magic / Wonder DECK PLANS

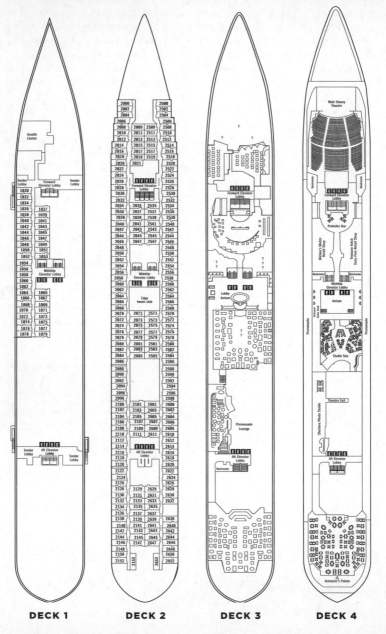

DECK 1   **DECK 2**   **DECK 3**   **DECK 4**

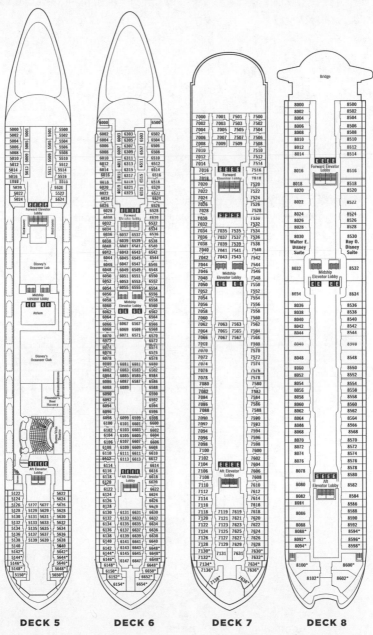

DECK 5   **DECK 6**   **DECK 7**   **DECK 8**

Continued on next page

Disney Magic / Wonder **DECK PLANS**
(continued)

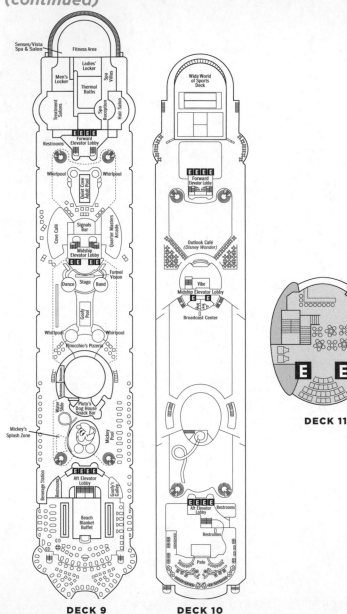

DECK 9

DECK 10

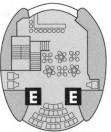

DECK 11

Disney Dream / Fantasy **DECK PLANS**

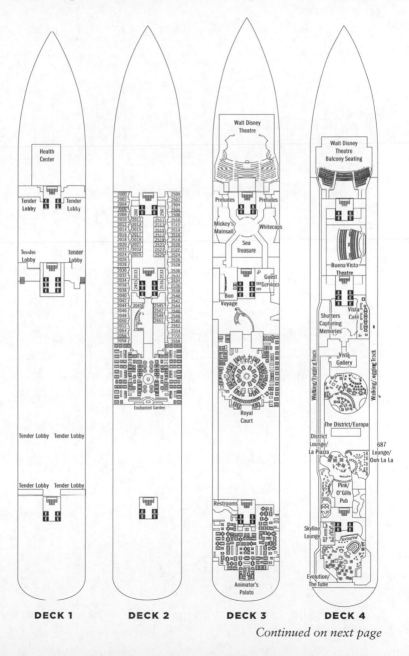

DECK 1 **DECK 2** **DECK 3** **DECK 4**

Continued on next page

Disney Dream / Fantasy DECK PLANS
(continued)

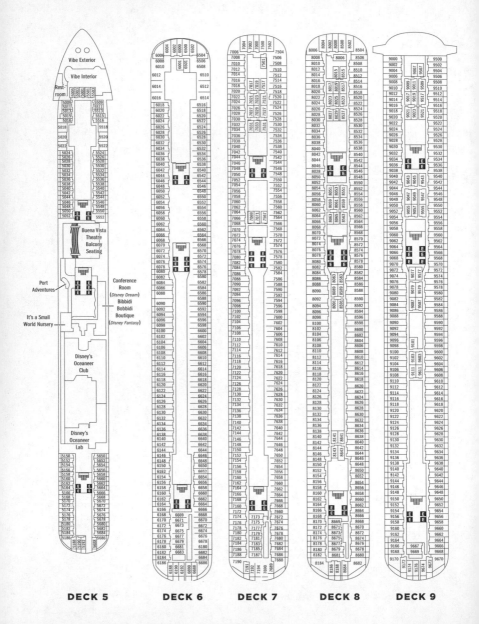

DECK 5   DECK 6   DECK 7   DECK 8   DECK 9

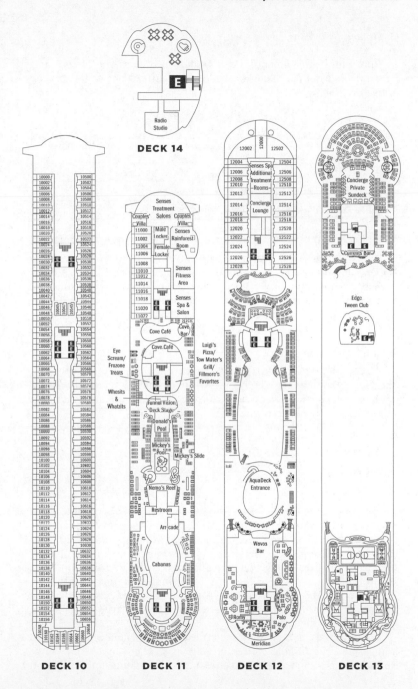

DECK 14

DECK 10

DECK 11

DECK 12

DECK 13

Continued from page 73

Some ships offer amenities not found on others. The *Dream* and *Fantasy*, for example, have the following features not found on the *Magic* or *Wonder*:

- **AquaDuck** waterslide (the *Magic* has an **AquaDunk** slide, but it's significantly different)
- **Chill Spa** for teens (the *Magic* has a couple of treatment rooms branded as Chill Spa, but the two versions are vastly different)
- Dedicated Champagne bar (**Pink** on the *Dream,* **Ooh La La** on the *Fantasy*)
- **Remy,** an upscale French restaurant • **Meridian,** a martini bar
- **Midship Detective Agency,** an interactive attraction for kids
- Miniature-golf course • Separate decks for concierge rooms • **Skyline** bar

Each ship has a few unique features too. The *Fantasy* has **Satellite Falls,** an adults-only splash pool and sun deck on Deck 13, and **Bibbidi Bobbidi Boutique** on Deck 5, providing makeovers for small children. The *Wonder* is the only ship with **Outlook Café,** a windowed indoor coffee bar–lounge on Deck 10 that's perfect for keeping warm while enjoying the views on Alaskan cruises.

RANKING THE SHIPS

IF YOUR CRUISE DESTINATION is the Bahamas or the Caribbean, one choice you'll have is whether to sail on either the *Magic* and *Wonder* or on the *Dream* and *Fantasy.* Ignoring the different itineraries each ship serves, here's how we rank the Disney ships:

1. *Fantasy*

2. *Dream*

3. *Magic*

4. *Wonder*

The *Fantasy* and *Dream* have better restaurants, bars, and pools than the older ships, plus more on-deck activities, more space for children's activities, more deck space for tanning, better spas, and more interactive games. These advantages make up for the slightly smaller cabin sizes on the *Dream* and *Fantasy,* whose nonconcierge staterooms are 2–9% (5–22 square feet) smaller than corresponding cabins on the *Magic* and *Wonder.* Another minor downside: Because the newer ships carry more passengers, Castaway Cay is more crowded when they're in port.

We rank the *Fantasy* highest because of its **Skyline** bar, **The Tube** lounge, and the onboard interactive games. The *Magic*'s new **After Hours** lounge area replaces Beat Street, which in theme and execution was one of the ship's weak spots; in particular, the transformation of Rockin' Bar D into **Fathoms** improved both the theming and the bar menu. Minor changes to **Keys,** the piano bar formerly known as Sessions, and to **O'Gills Pub,** formerly Diversions, are welcome, albeit more cosmetic. The *Wonder,* though ranked last, does have the **Outlook Café** on Deck 10, which the *Magic* does not. It's wonderful for reading, lounging, or sightseeing in cold weather. Stake out your spot early on the Tracy Arm glacier day of Alaskan voyages—it's one of the few warm indoor spots with panoramic views.

◼◼ *The* **Disney Magic**

THE FIRST DCL SHIP, the *Magic* was launched in 1998 and underwent an extensive renovation (or reimagining, in Disney-speak) during a two-month dry dock in Cadiz, Spain, during the summer of 2013. Major changes included the following:

* **After Hours,** a retheming of the *Magic*'s nightlife area, formerly known as Beat Street and one of the ship's weakest areas

* The new **AquaDunk** vertical-start waterslide. You begin by standing on top of a trapdoor, and then plunge down almost vertically before spinning through a couple of turns and sliding to a stop on the main deck.

* A rethemed buffet, **Cabanas,** on Deck 9

* **Carioca's,** a new Brazilian-themed restaurant—a big improvement over the dismal Parrot Cay

* A rethemed **Nephews' Pool,** the **Twist 'n' Spout** waterslide, the **AquaLab** water-play area for older kids, and the **Nephews' Splash Zone** water-play area for toddlers

* Newly rethemed **Oceaneer Club** and **Oceaneer Lab** kids' clubs, including the new Marvel Avengers Academy in the Oceaneer Lab

* A new Irish-themed sports bar, **O'Gills,** replacing the generic Diversions sports bar

* Newly refurbished retail shops

* A new stage show, *Walt Disney: The Dream Goes On*

The makeover also includes cosmetic updates to the *Magic*'s lobby atrium; Keys (formerly Sessions), the piano bar; Palo, an adults-only, fine-dining Italian restaurant; and Fathoms (formerly Rockin' Bar D), the dance club. In addition, Vista Spa was changed to Senses Spa.

The *Disney Wonder*

LAUNCHED IN 1999, the second of Disney's four ships is in a bad situation for 2014 and beyond. With the *Magic* out of dry dock and with the *Dream* and *Fantasy* having launched in 2011 and 2012, respectively, the *Wonder* is now the "oldest" ship in the fleet, and it shows. By no means is the ship falling apart, but the wear and tear are especially evident compared with the condition of the other three ships. That said, there are deals to be found on the *Wonder,* and it's the only Disney ship serving Alaska and the California coast.

We expect the *Wonder* to undergo an extended refurbishment in the fall of 2016, to bring its entertainment and amenities in line with the *Dream, Fantasy,* and *Magic.* The timing of this is more dependent on the expansion work being done on the Panama Canal than on Disney's schedules—increasing the size of the ship would make it too large to fit through the canal's current locks, making it impossible for the ship to return to Alaska. The Panama Canal expansion project is slated to finish in late 2015.

For now, the *Wonder* is nearly identical to the pre-2013 version of the *Magic,* with slightly different theming for the restaurants and lounges. When you board the ship at Deck 3, you're greeted by Ariel instead of Mickey and an Art Nouveau–style atrium rather than Art Deco. Following the *Little Mermaid* theme, one of the standard rotational-dining restaurants on the *Wonder* is **Triton's** (on the *Magic,* its counterpart is the *Beauty and the Beast*–themed **Lumiere's**).

From a technological standpoint, the *Wonder* is missing many of the features of the newer ships. There's no waterslide like the **Aqua-Duck** (*Dream* and *Fantasy*) or **AquaDunk** (*Magic*) on the pool deck. Though each ship has a restaurant called Animator's Palate, the version on the *Wonder* doesn't have the interactive show as do the restaurants on the other ships. Inside staterooms are missing the virtual portholes found on the *Dream* and *Fantasy,* and there is no interactive artwork or Midship Detective Agency in the corridors.

There is little to differentiate the restaurants on the *Wonder* from those on the *Magic,* though it does still have our two least favorite dining venues on any Disney ship: **Beach Blanket Buffet** and **Parrot Cay. Palo** remains a great choice for adults. We would choose (and have chosen) to dine there every night if there's availability.

Like all the ships in the fleet, the *Wonder* has impeccably themed kids' areas. We know your brood will have a great time no matter what their ages.

The *Wonder* splits its time among Alaska, the California coast, and the Caribbean, and Hawaii; repositioning cruises also take it through the Panama Canal. It sets sail from Galveston, Miami, San Diego, and Vancouver.

Our favorite spot on the *Wonder* is the **Outlook Café,** just up the stairs from the Cove Café.

The **Disney Dream**

FOLLOWING THE SUCCESSES OF THE *MAGIC* AND *WONDER*, DCL ordered two new ships that would more than double the number of guests they could serve, allow them to expand the number of itineraries offered, and bring several first-evers to a cruise ship. The new *Dream*-class vessels were built by Meyer Werft in Germany rather than Italy's Fincantieri, which created the *Magic* and *Wonder*.

The *Disney Dream,* the first of these new ships, set sail in 2011. It's 151 feet longer, 35 feet taller, and 15 feet wider than the *Magic* or *Wonder*. With three additional passenger decks, the ship can hold 50% more passengers and crew than its predecessors, yet it still has the classic lines of the smaller ships.

Disney Imagineering had great fun designing the second-generation ships. Inside cabins were given virtual portholes, which show the view from the bridge on a round screen. This feature proved so popular with kids that on many cruises, interior cabins had fares higher than those of ocean-view cabins. On the top deck, the **AquaDuck**, a waterslide that circles the ship, was added to the usual pools. Between the pool deck and your cabin, you'll find interactive art that reacts when you pass by it, along with the **Midship Detective Agency,** a scavenger hunt–type game that sends families all over the ship collecting clues.

Restaurants were given a huge makeover. The dreadful Topsiders (formerly on the *Magic*) and Beach Blanket Buffet (on the *Wonder*) were replaced with **Cabanas,** a new buffet that improved on both traffic flow and food quality. **Animator's Palate** remained on board but was plussed up with new technology as part of the dinner show. The mediocre Parrot Cay became **Enchanted Garden,** the prettiest of the main dining rooms on board. Finally, Lumiere's (*Magic*) and Triton's (*Wonder*) were reimagined as **Royal Palace,** a tribute to all things Disney princess, but mostly Cinderella.

Both adults and kids scored big with improvements to the new ship. In addition to the adults-only Palo, **Remy** was added as another upscale-dining option for the 18-and-up crowd. With a subtle *Ratatouille* theme, and not one, but two celebrated chefs creating the menus, Remy initially shocked cruisers with its surcharge—$75 plus wine per diner, the highest in the industry—but diners were pleased nonetheless. The adult lounges, in the area called **The District** on Deck 4, provide more-intimate, better-themed spaces to take the edge off than the old Beat Street on the *Magic* and Route 66 on the *Wonder*. **Skyline,** one of The District's bars, showcases a great use of technology, with a cityscape behind the bar that changes every 15 minutes. It's mesmerizing.

*un**official* TIP
We recommend the *Dream* or *Fantasy* over the *Magic* and *Wonder* to travelers who are more concerned with the ships and dining than the itineraries of their cruises.

Senses Spa replaced the Vista Spa and outdid it in every way.

Kids got greatly expanded club areas with a Pixar theme. The teen area got a makeover that left it one of the most stylish spaces on board and gave it its own pool (the cast-member pool area from the older ships). Teens also got their own pampering spot, **Chill Spa**.

Some categories of cabins are a few square feet larger or smaller than their equivalents on the *Magic* and *Wonder*, but all (as does the *Magic* after its refurbishment) have nicer furnishings and linens than the *Wonder*.

In spite of all this, the *Dream* feels different yet very familiar to people coming to it from the *Magic* or *Wonder*—kind of like seeing Walt Disney World after going to Disneyland. The theme is still Art Deco. The Cove Café still serves great coffee. Most of the shows are still not worth your time.

The **Disney Fantasy**

THE *FANTASY* SAILED ITS MAIDEN VOYAGE in 2012, one year after the *Dream* came into service. The ship is nearly identical to its sister but has some tweaks as a result of guest and cast-member feedback. Both the *Dream* and the *Fantasy* are based out of Port Canaveral and sail the Caribbean. While the *Dream* has mostly three- and four-night itineraries, the *Fantasy* is almost exclusively seven-night sailings.

Walking into the atrium of the *Fantasy*, you see a bronze statue of Minnie Mouse and a striking peacock-inspired carpet—an indication of the Art Nouveau style of the *Fantasy* as opposed to the *Dream*'s Deco look. A glance up to Deck 5 reveals one of the Fantasy's "improvements" over the *Dream*—the **Bibbidi Bobbidi Boutique**—that came in response to parents' desires to spend more money on board.

The *Dream*'s technology package got some enhancements on the *Fantasy*. The **Midship Detective Agency** has three different story lines (including the Muppets) for folks to experience, and the show at **Animator's Palate** got a very cool audience-interaction element that we won't spoil here. Other than this addition, the restaurants are identical to the *Dream*'s, with one subtle name change: Royal Palace is **Royal Court** and includes even more princess-y goodness. **Cabanas, Enchanted Garden, Palo,** and **Remy** are the same.

On the pool deck, the **AquaDuck** adds the **AquaLab** splash area, and adults get **Satellite Falls**, a quiet water feature on Deck 13 Forward.

The *Fantasy*'s nightlife area is **Europa**. **Skyline** is the one constant between the two bar-nightclub areas on the ships, though it displays different cityscapes in this rendition. **The Tube**'s *Austin Powers*–style decor makes it a very fun place to hang out, but **Ooh La La** is either too high-concept or low-concept for our tastes; we prefer the whimsical look of the *Dream*'s **Pink** for our Champagne needs. **O'Gills** doesn't feel particularly Irish, though it has the same big-screen TVs as **687,** the sports bar on the *Dream*.

PART SEVEN

DINING

NOSHES, NOSHES EVERYWHERE

THE FIRST THING MANY FOLKS DISCOVER when exploring the ships on embarkation day is the buffet. In the way that some people remember the birth of their first child, we remember our first look at the spread at Cabanas. (Sorry, Hannah. Love, Dad.) On one table sat a pile of crab legs that almost reached eye level. Next to this sat a trawler's worth of peel-and-eat shrimp. Surrounding these were tubs of melted butter and enough cocktail sauce to float the ship itself. On the other side of the aisle, a chef was flash-cooking a steak, the spices, sizzle, and flame making the air smell savory. It was glorious.

You'll never go hungry on a Disney cruise. The variety of dining options is staggering, including everything from coffee shops and pizza stands to Vegas-size buffets to ritzy French and Italian restaurants. That said, we've learned a few ways to increase your chances of enjoying memorable meals on board. This section describes your dining options in detail and includes our advice on how to make the most of them.

ROTATIONAL DINING

ONE OF THE INNOVATIONS that Disney Cruise Line (DCL) brought to the cruise industry is the concept of rotational dining, in which you visit one of three standard restaurants on each different night of your cruise. As you change from restaurant to restaurant, your server team—your waiter, beverage person, head waiter, and maître d'—all move with you. Your team will quickly learn your dining proclivities, including preferred drinks and favorite desserts, and make menu suggestions. Along with your stateroom attendant, you'll almost certainly rely on your dining team more than any other members of the crew during your trip.

The rotational restaurants have two dinner seatings, typically 5:45 p.m. and 8:15 p.m. Because Disney sets the schedule, there's no need to make reservations each night. You can request either the earlier or later seating when booking your trip or once aboard the ship. You can also request changes to your rotation, specifying which restaurants you visit each night.

unofficial **TIP**
DCL restaurants (except Palo and Remy, naturally) have kids' menus for breakfast, lunch, and dinner. Kids (except for infants in the nursery) may also dine in their club areas free of charge.

Unlike other cruise lines, which may seat several families or groups together, Disney generally keeps families at their own tables. The exception to this would be singles or couples, who are routinely seated with other groups. If you're traveling alone or in a group of two or three and you prefer not to be seated with others during your rotational dining, call DCL in advance to make this request, which is not guaranteed but almost always honored.

You'll repeat at least one of the three standard restaurants on cruises of four nights and longer. Rather than visit the same restaurant twice on a four-night cruise, we recommend using one of those nights to visit Palo (on any ship) or Remy (on the *Dream* and *Fantasy*). You must pay an additional charge to dine at these restaurants, but the food is stellar, the crowds are small, and the service is impeccable.

unofficial **TIP**
If you're honeymooning or doing something similarly special, be sure to point this out—it may help you with your request for a private table, as well as possibly result in other surprises.

Another, less formal (and less expensive) option to rotational dining is the dinner buffet on each ship. Finally, at least one of the rotational restaurants is open for breakfast and lunch each day. Check your *Personal Navigator* for details.

DCL RESTAURANT CATEGORIES

IN GENERAL, FOOD OFFERINGS on Disney Cruise Line are differentiated by freshness, quality, and service:

COUNTER SERVICE Available on each ship's pool deck, fast food includes staples such as burgers, chicken strips, pizza, and sandwiches. In *The Unofficial Guide to Walt Disney World,* we equate the quality of the counter-service restaurants in the theme parks with that of McDonald's and Taco Bell. With a few exceptions, the food quality at DCL's counter-service restaurants is more like what you'd find in your local supermarket's frozen-food aisle: edible but not as good as something made from scratch (or even at McDonald's). The best items on board are the fresh sandwiches and wraps and, if your timing is right, pizza straight from the oven. A complete list of counter-service restaurants by ship begins on page 90.

CAFÉS AND LOUNGES Each ship has a dedicated coffee bar called **Cove Café** that serves espresso, cappuccino, teas, and smoothies, plus wine, mixed drinks, and spirits. A good alternative to a big dinner is Cove Café's small selection of complimentary cold appetizers, available each evening. Besides Cove Café, a few of the ships' bars and lounges serve appetizers too. These are described in detail in Part Eight, Entertainment and Nightlife.

BUFFETS Each ship has at least one large buffet, usually open for breakfast and lunch. Buffets tend to serve a bit of everything at each meal and are the easiest way to satisfy disparate appetites. The buffets at **Cabanas** on the *Magic, Dream,* and *Fantasy* are as large and diverse as those at many Las Vegas hotels. Besides offering variety, buffets let picky kids see exactly what food they're getting. They also offer plenty of seating with ocean views, indoors and out.

FULL-SERVICE RESTAURANTS Each Disney ship has four or five full-service restaurants. Three of these are part of the standard rotational-dinner schedule available to every guest on the ship.

ADULT DINING The upscale Italian restaurant **Palo,** found on each ship and for which Disney charges an additional fee of $25, serves dinner to cruisers 18 and older. The *Dream* and *Fantasy* have a fifth restaurant, **Remy,** which serves high-end French cuisine and levies a $75 surcharge. Both Palo and Remy serve brunch on selected sea days (still adults-only). Both are also difficult to get into, so book a table at **disneycruise.com** at least 75 days before you sail. See the next page for more information.

Along with dinner, one sit-down restaurant is usually open for breakfast and lunch each day, even when the ship is in port. Breakfast and lunch may include both a buffet and the option to order from a menu.

Virtually all of the food served at the rotational restaurants will be familiar to American palates. Most dishes, especially at dinner, feature cuts of steak, chicken, and fish no different from those you'd find at a chain eatery. DCL's chefs will add some sort of flavor twist to these, such as soy and sesame if it's an Asian-themed restaurant, but the basic ingredients will be recognizable to almost everyone.

Although fresher and of higher quality than the counter-service restaurants, most of the food served at the full-service restaurants is prepared well ahead of time. You get your order faster this way, but it's also well-nigh impossible to customize that order. We've been told, for instance, that we couldn't order a roast-beef-and-mayo sandwich without the mayo. If you're a moderately finicky eater, you can do the customizing yourself, provided your dish consists of discrete ingredients that you can subtract easily. A BLT without lettuce is probably doable; tomato-and-basil soup sans the basil probably isn't.

THEME NIGHTS

ON CRUISES OF LONGER THAN THREE NIGHTS, DCL adds themed dinners. These include a Pirates' menu (somewhat Caribbean-influenced, on Pirate Night), Till We Meet Again (the last night of your cruise), the Captain's Gala, and Prince and Princess menus. The menus available on your cruise will depend on your itinerary—for example, Alaskan voyages typically add a seafood-focused night featuring local salmon and king crab. On these nights, each main dining area serves the same menu.

*un***official TIP**
Remy's dress code requires a tuxedo or jacket for men, along with dress pants. Ties are optional. Acceptable women's attire includes evening gowns, cocktail dresses, blouses and skirts, and pantsuits.

DRESS CODE

SHORTS AND T-SHIRTS are acceptable at all meals at the standard restaurants, even for adults. We think most adults will feel more appropriately dressed in pants or dresses at dinner; Bermuda shorts paired with a nice button-down shirt and shoes would probably also work.

A mother of four from Midland, Texas, is happy for this shorts-tolerant policy:

> There was no way I was going to pack 8–10 pairs of pants—minimum!—for my kids and my husband for our seven-night cruise. Shorts take up less luggage space and can be worn all day. It's less laundry for me to do when we get home too.

Swimwear and tank tops are prohibited at any time, and frankly you'd be freezing for most of your meal.

The dress code at Palo is more upscale: dress pants and long-sleeved shirt or jacket for men; dress, blouse and skirt, or pantsuit for women. Athletic shoes, flip-flops, blue jeans, shorts, and capris aren't permitted, though we've seen women in black jeans paired with a smashing jacket and fabulous shoes.

MAKING RESERVATIONS

NO RESERVATIONS ARE REQUIRED for any night at any of the three standard rotational-dining restaurants. Reservations are required for Palo and Remy and can be made up to 120 days in advance in some circumstances. Reserve online at the DCL Planning Center (see page 21).

CATEGORY	DAYS IN ADVANCE RESERVATIONS CAN BE MADE
Guests in suites or concierge staterooms	**120 DAYS**
Platinum Castaway Club members	**120 DAYS**
Gold Castaway Club members	**105 DAYS**
Silver Castaway Club members	**90 DAYS**
All other guests	**75 DAYS**

FULL-SERVICE RESTAURANTS: RATED AND RANKED

TO HELP YOU MAKE YOUR DINING CHOICES, we've developed profiles of DCL's sit-down restaurants, listed alphabetically by restaurant following each ship's counter-service-dining coverage. The profiles allow you to quickly check a given restaurant's cuisine, star rating, quality rating, and specialties.

STAR RATING The star rating represents the entire dining experience: style, service, and ambiance, in addition to the taste, presentation, and quality of the food. Five stars is the highest rating and indicates that the restaurant offers the best of everything. Four-star restaurants are above average; three-star restaurants offer good, though not necessarily memorable, meals. Two-star restaurants serve mediocre fare. (No DCL restaurants merit one star.) Our star ratings don't correspond to ratings awarded by AAA, Mobil, Zagat, or other restaurant reviewers.

QUALITY RATING The food quality is rated on a scale of one to five stars, five being the best rating attainable. The quality rating is based on the taste, freshness of ingredients, preparation, presentation, and creativity of the food served. Price is not a consideration. If you want the best food available and cost is not an issue, you need look no further than the quality ratings.

DCL ROTATIONAL RESTAURANTS BY CUISINE			
RESTAURANT	**SHIP**	**OVERALL RATING**	**QUALITY RATING**
AMERICAN/ASIAN			
Animator's Palate	All	★★★	★★★
AMERICAN/BRAZILIAN			
Carioca's	Magic	★★★	★★★
AMERICAN/CARIBBEAN			
Parrot Cay	Wonder	★★	★★
AMERICAN/CONTINENTAL			
Enchanted Garden	Dream, Fantasy	★★★	★★★
AMERICAN/FRENCH			
Lumiere's	Magic	★★★	★★★
Royal Court	Fantasy	★★★	★★★
Royal Palace	Dream	★★★	★★★
Triton's	Wonder	★★★	★★★
BUFFET			
Cabanas	Dream, Fantasy, Magic	★★★	★★★
Beach Blanket Buffet	Wonder	★★½	★★½

DCL ADULT-ONLY RESTAURANTS BY CUISINE		
SHIP *Dream, Fantasy* **CUISINE** French **RESTAURANT** Remy		
OVERALL RATING	QUALITY RATING	VALUE RATING
★★★★½	★★★★½	★★★★½
SHIPS All **CUISINE** Italian **RESTAURANT** Palo		
OVERALL RATING	QUALITY RATING	VALUE RATING
★★★½ *Magic, Wonder* ★★★★ *Dream, Fantasy*	★★★½ *Magic, Wonder* ★★★★ *Dream, Fantasy*	★★★½ *Magic, Wonder* ★★★★ *Dream, Fantasy*

Disney Magic DINING

COUNTER-SERVICE RESTAURANTS

Daisy's De-Lites

QUALITY B   PORTION Small–Medium   LOCATION Deck 9 Aft

WHEN TO GO Typical hours: breakfast, 6:30 a.m.–9 a.m.; lunch, 11 a.m.–6:30 p.m. Check your *Personal Navigator* for exact schedule.

SELECTIONS Breakfast includes pastries, croissants, muffins, and yogurt; lunch offerings include sandwiches, wraps, salads, fruit, and cookies.

COMMENTS A good alternative to the breakfast buffet if all you're looking for is a few croissants and some coffee. The wraps are small and tasty and make an excellent snack between lunch and dinner. *Note:* Daisy's De-Lites was named Goofy's Galley before the *Magic*'s 2013 dry dock.

Pete's Boiler Bites

QUALITY B   PORTION Medium   LOCATION Deck 9 Aft

WHEN TO GO Typical hours: 11 a.m.–6 p.m. Check your *Personal Navigator* for exact schedule.

SELECTIONS Grilled hot dogs and sausages; hamburgers and veggie burgers; chicken strips; chicken sandwiches; tacos; fries.

COMMENTS The tacos are a surprise find here. A nearby fixin's bar provides toppings for your order.

Pinocchio's Pizzeria

QUALITY C   PORTION Medium   LOCATION Deck 9 Aft

WHEN TO GO Typical hours: 11 a.m.–6 p.m. Check your *Personal Navigator* for exact schedule.

SELECTIONS Cheese, pepperoni, barbecue-chicken, and veggie pizza slices, plus a specialty pizza every day.

COMMENTS About the same quality as frozen pizza . . . but there are plenty of times when that's exactly what you want.

FULL-SERVICE RESTAURANTS

Animator's Palate   ★★★   Deck 4 Aft

AMERICAN/ASIAN   QUALITY ★★★   SERVICE ★★★★   FRIENDLINESS ★★★★

Reservations Not accepted. **When to go** Dinner. **Bar** Yes. **Alcohol** Red, white, and sparkling wines, plus mixed drinks and spirits. All alcohol costs extra. **Dress** Casual;

no tank tops or swimwear. **Hours** Nightly dinner seatings usually at 5:45 and 8:15 p.m.; check your *Personal Navigator* for the exact schedule.

SETTING AND ATMOSPHERE The idea behind Animator's Palate is that you begin dining inside an old-fashioned black-and-white animated film that is slowly colorized as dinner goes along. The entrance's walls are decorated with black charcoal sketches of various Disney characters. Inside, the entire color scheme starts out in black, white, and gray from floor to ceiling, including checkerboard-tile floor, black chairs, white tablecloths with black napkins, and black-and-white uniforms for the waitstaff. Even the ship's support columns are dressed up, in this case as white artist's brushes pointed to the ceiling.

Along the outside wall are video monitors that display images and "how to draw" sketches from Disney films. As the evening progresses, you'll notice bits of color being added to the walls and artwork, eventually becoming fully saturated by the end of your meal.

Animator's Palate on the *Magic* will receive an upgrade during summer 2014, adding the *Animation Magic* dinner show that debuted on the *Fantasy*. At the beginning of your second night's dinner at Animator's Palate, you're given a sheet of paper and crayon and told to draw a self-portrait. At the end of the evening, all of the diners' self-portraits are shown in an animated cartoon similar to Disney's 1929 short cartoon *The Skeleton Dance*.

HOUSE SPECIALTIES Vegetable stir-fry; roasted-garlic or red-pepper dip with bread.

COMMENTS Disney characterizes the cuisine at Animator's Palate as Pacific Rim/American, but it's really just standard chain-restaurant fare. There are probably as many Italian selections—pasta, risotto, focaccia—as Asian. A handful of dishes, such as the vegetable stir fry, have origins in the East; others are American dishes enrobed in a culinary kimono of sesame, ginger, or teriyaki sauce to make them "Pacific Rim." The food isn't *bad* . . . but neither is it Asian.

Cabanas ★★★   Deck 9 Aft

AMERICAN/BUFFET   QUALITY ★★★   SERVICE ★★★★   FRIENDLINESS ★★★★

Reservations Not accepted. **When to go** Breakfast, lunch, and dinner. **Bar** Yes. **Alcohol** Red, white, and sparkling wines, plus mixed drinks and spirits. All alcohol costs extra. **Dress** Casual; no tank tops or swimwear at dinner. **Hours** Daily breakfast buffet, 7–10:45 a.m.; daily lunch buffet, noon–1:30 p.m.; nightly sit-down dinner, 6:30–8:30 p.m. Hours are subject to change, so check your *Personal Navigator* for the exact schedule.

SETTING AND ATMOSPHERE Recently renovated and rethemed, Cabanas is entered from either side of Deck 9 Aft. On either side is a line of buffet tables that run the length of the restaurant. Indoor and outdoor seating are arranged around the buffet. The indoor seating is air-conditioned and features floor-to-ceiling windows, affording excellent ocean views. Outdoor seating is great on mornings when the ship is docking because you're sometimes able to watch the port come into view. Large murals lining the walls display pirate and fish imagery. Coffee, soft drinks, juices, and water are served from dispensers placed at regular intervals throughout the restaurant.

HOUSE SPECIALTIES Made-to-order omelets for breakfast; lunch seafood bar including oysters, clams, crab legs, and peel-and-eat shrimp.

COMMENTS The breakfast and lunch buffets would be competitive with those at many Las Vegas resorts and serve about as wide a variety of items as you'll find anywhere. Breakfast includes everything from fruit, yogurt, and oatmeal to doughnuts, lox, and custom-made omelets. Even cold cereal has options: Besides the usual cornflakes and granola, there's a "build your own" muesli bar where you can add ingredients ranging from brown sugar to exotic dried fruits. Don't worry if you skipped dessert last night—you can get several at breakfast here. We haven't asked, but we'd bet hard cash that the staff would make you filet mignon if you requested nicely.

Lunch is a similarly lavish spread, with everything from chicken tenders, sandwiches, and burgers to salmon steaks and pasta. A big draw at lunch is the peel-and-eat shrimp, usually complemented by clams, oysters, and crab legs.

Cabanas switches from buffet to sit-down service for dinner. The menu changes frequently, usually along with the menus at the other main restaurants. Appetizers typically include soups and salads, along with meat- and fish-based dishes. Entrées usually include chicken, fish, steak, and vegetarian options. We recommend Cabanas for dinner at sunset on longer cruises, as an alternative to dining a second time at one of the main restaurants, especially Lumiere's.

Carioca's ★★★ Deck 3 Aft

AMERICAN/BRAZILIAN QUALITY ★★★ SERVICE ★★★★ FRIENDLINESS ★★★★

Reservations Not accepted. **When to go** Dinner. **Bar** Yes. **Alcohol** A decent selection of reds, whites, and sparkling wines. If you're in the mood for a cocktail, try the berry-flavored Caipirosa. All alcohol costs extra. **Dress** Casual; no tank tops or swimwear at dinner. **Hours** Breakfast buffet on select days, 8:30–10:45 a.m.; lunch buffet on select days (hours vary); nightly dinner seatings usually at 5:30 and 8 p.m. Hours are subject to change, so check your *Personal Navigator* for the exact schedule.

SETTING AND ATMOSPHERE The *Magic*'s newest restaurant, Carioca's is named for José Carioca, one of the three birds in Disney's animated 1944 film *The Three Caballeros.* The word *carioca* is slang for a native of Rio de Janeiro, and so Carioca's theme is Brazilian festival. The restaurant uses lighting effects to transform the setting: When the lighting effects are off at breakfast and lunch, Carioca's interior has a cool white-and-gray floor, white walls, and white tablecloths. Round white lanterns hang from the ceiling, accented by a handful of colorful red, orange, and yellow lights. For dinner, rich yellow and brown lighting transforms the restaurant into a cinnamon-and-gold nightspot. It's a little darker than you'd expect at night, but still way nicer than when it was Parrot Cay.

HOUSE SPECIALTIES The menu also got an overhaul, and it's much improved. Lunch and breakfast are unremarkable American fare—dinner is when Carioca's really shines. The signature dish is the José Carioca's: three grilled skewers of Brazilian sausage, chili-crusted lamb, and beef tenderloin, with a side of tomato-flavored rice and a delicious *chimichurri* sauce (think a South American pesto). The tenderloin and lamb can be a bit dry, but the chimichurri sauce balances it out. At least one person at your table should try this.

The other entrée we really liked—in small bites—was the slow-roasted pork belly, with sides of mashed sweet potato, grits, and collard greens. The pork's skin was incredibly crispy, almost to the point where you'd think it was fried, yet the meat underneath was tender and juicy. Combined with the grits and sweet potatoes, it's almost *too* rich, which is why we suggest ordering this as an entrée for the table to share, with each person also ordering another entrée.

Vegetarian options include corn tortillas with Veracruzan refried-bean dip and a relish of green tomatillo, chile, and shredded white cabbage and carrot. It's not as spicy as the black-bean soup appetizer, which has a touch of habanero pepper, but the tortillas are a filling dish.

Beyond the vegetarian black-bean soup, the other appetizers we like are salads: the tiger shrimp ceviche, with cucumber, cilantro, and tomato-citrus dressing; and the Cuban salad, with avocado, pineapple, toasted Cuban bread, and a tangy cider-vinegar dressing. We'd avoid the ahi-tuna-and-avocado tower—the tuna at Palo is much better.

OTHER RECOMMENDATIONS If you subscribe to the "everything tastes better on a stick" philosophy and you're also in the mood for seafood, try the lobster, shrimp, and mahimahi skewers. These are served on a salad of quinoa (the grain of the moment, judging from how many recipes in which Disney uses it) with dried-mango, pineapple, and toasted-coconut salsa.

COMMENTS We're glad to see the menu improve, and we'd be happy to dine at Carioca's twice on longer sailings.

Lumiere's ★★★   Deck 3 Midship

AMERICAN/FRENCH   QUALITY ★★★   SERVICE ★★★★   FRIENDLINESS ★★★★

Reservations Not accepted. **When to go** Breakfast. **Bar** Yes. **Alcohol** Limited selection of red, white, and sparkling wines, plus mixed drinks and spirits. All alcohol costs extra. **Dress** Casual; no tank tops or swimwear at dinner. **Hours** À la carte breakfast on select days, 8–9:30 a.m.; à la carte lunch on select days, 11:45 a.m.–1:30 p.m.; nightly dinner seatings usually at 5:45 and 8:15 p.m. Hours are subject to change, so check your *Personal Navigator* for the exact schedule.

SETTING AND ATMOSPHERE Despite the name, there are only a few references to *Beauty and the Beast* inside the restaurant. The most notable are the light fixtures, which contain a single red rose. There's also a mural on the back wall that depicts characters from the movie. Besides these, most of Lumiere's decor is Art Deco, which makes sense given the restaurant's location, just off the ship's atrium.

HOUSE SPECIALTIES Lobster mac and cheese; crispy roasted duck breast.

COMMENTS Disney puts escargot and French onion soup on the menu of each French-themed standard dining room in the cruise line. Besides these, however, most of the rest of the menu is decidedly un-French and would be equally at home at your neighborhood TGI Friday's: grilled meats and chicken, a vegetarian tofu selection, and pasta. A couple of entrées, such as the lamb shank and crispy duck breast, stand out. The Grand Marnier soufflé is the most popular dessert, but the brioche bread pudding with toffee sauce is better.

Palo ★★★½ Deck 10 Aft

ITALIAN QUALITY ★★★½ VALUE ★★★½ SERVICE ★★★★½ FRIENDLINESS ★★★★

Reservations Required. **When to go** Brunch on sea days; dinner nightly. **Bar** Yes. **Alcohol** Large list of Italian wines, listed by region, plus select wines from around the world; mixed drinks and spirits; *limoncello;* grappa; ice wine. All alcohol costs extra. **Dress** Pants and dress shirt or jacket for men; dress, skirt and blouse, or pantsuit for women. No blue jeans, shorts, capris, flip-flops, or athletic shoes. **Hours** Brunch on sea days on cruises of 4 nights or longer, 10 a.m.–12:30 p.m.; nightly dinner, 6–8:30 p.m. Hours are subject to change, so check your *Personal Navigator* for the exact schedule. **Special comments** An additional $25/person charge will be added to your cruise bill for each meal at Palo. If you need to cancel a reservation, you must do so by 2 p.m. on the day of your reservation, or the full per-person charge will be applied to your bill. Guests must be age 18 and up to dine.

SETTING AND ATMOSPHERE Palo sits across the entire Aft section of Deck 10, which means that almost every seat has a spectacular view of the ocean sunset during dinner. On the *Magic,* Palo has contemporary decor, with tan-wood panels, round leather benches, and deep-purple fabric on the wood chairs. A small bar is available for guests waiting for their tables to become available; part of the kitchen is open to the view of guests sitting in the middle of the restaurant. Red-and-white-striped poles near the bar, evocative of those used to steer gondolas, call to mind Palo's roots in Venice (*palo* means "pole").

Because Palo has an adults-only policy, the restaurant is much quieter than DCL's main dining rooms. The quietest tables are those on the port side, aft (left and forward), tucked away behind the curve of the restaurant. If you're looking to do some people-watching with dinner, request a table on the starboard (left) side of the ship, near Palo's entrance. Brunch offers open seating, so sit wherever the view is best. Background music is mostly Italian and ranges from Vivaldi to Sinatra, as God intended.

HOUSE SPECIALTIES For a first course at dinner, try the fish-and-seafood soup, laden with mussels, clams, and lobster. The *antipasto freddo,* which comprises a selection of familiar cheeses and cured meats, could be a little more adventurous. Our favorite entrées are the lobster ravioli in truffle-butter sauce; the spicy penne *arrabbiata;* and the rack of lamb, roasted with garlic and shallots. The chocolate soufflé, by far the most popular dessert, is served with both dark- and white-chocolate sauces.

Palo's brunch menu is the best on board. One large table is dedicated to breads, muffins, and pastries, along with sliced fruits and fresh vegetables (the roasted asparagus is tasty). An entire aquarium's worth of fish is available in another section, including shrimp cocktail, cured salmon, smoked-trout mousse, seared tuna, scallops, crab legs, crawfish, and mussels. Eggs cooked in every conceivable way, including Benedict, Florentine, Julia, and customized omelets, are on the menu too. Not enough? Try the selection of made-to-order pizzas.

COMMENTS Palo, the *Magic*'s one upscale restaurant, is its own little island of adult serenity and food. Service is very good, and don't be surprised if the maître 'd and your server are from Italy.

Dinners at Palo are tasty and relaxing, especially with a glass or two of wine. That being said, we think Palo is better for brunch— besides the best selection of midday food anywhere on the ship, the view out of Palo's windows is much better during the day; once the sun sets at dinner, Palo's spectacular windows just reflect the inside of the restaurant. If we could improve one thing at Palo, it would be the coffee served, which is Illy. A restaurant this good should offer better.

Finally, note that we rate Palo on the *Dream* and *Fantasy* higher overall, as well as for quality and value. It's undeniably very good on both the *Magic* and the *Wonder,* but the decor on the *Dream*-class ships is more sophisticated, and the kitchens are larger, allowing for better food preparation.

Disney Wonder DINING

COUNTER-SERVICE RESTAURANTS

Goofy's Galley

QUALITY B   PORTION Small–Medium   LOCATION Deck 9 Aft

COMMENTS Menu selections and hours are the same as for Daisy's De-Lites on the *Magic;* see page 90 for details.

Pinocchio's Pizzeria

QUALITY C   PORTION Medium   LOCATION Deck 9 Aft

COMMENTS See profile of Pinocchio's Pizzeria on the *Magic* (page 90) for details.

Pluto's Dog House

QUALITY B   PORTION Medium   LOCATION Deck 9 Aft

COMMENTS Menu selections and hours are the same as for Pete's Boiler Bites on the *Magic;* see page 90 for details.

FULL-SERVICE RESTAURANTS

Animator's Palate ★★★ Deck 4 Aft

AMERICAN/ASIAN   QUALITY ★★★   SERVICE ★★★★   FRIENDLINESS ★★★★

COMMENTS See profile of Animator's Palate on the *Magic* (page 90) for details.

Beach Blanket Buffet ★★½ Deck 9 Aft

AMERICAN/BUFFET QUALITY ★★½ SERVICE ★★★★ FRIENDLINESS ★★★★

Reservations Not accepted. **When to go** Lunch. **Bar** Yes. **Alcohol** Limited selection of red, white, and sparkling wines, plus mixed drinks and spirits. All alcohol costs extra. **Dress** Casual; no tank tops or swimwear at dinner. **Hours** Daily breakfast, as early as 6:45 a.m. on port days and 7:45 a.m. on sea days, until 10:45 a.m.; daily lunch, noon–2 p.m.; nightly dinner, 6:30–8:30 p.m. Hours are subject to change, so check your *Personal Navigator* for exact times.

SETTING AND ATMOSPHERE A beach-themed cafeteria on Deck 9 Aft, with both indoor and outdoor seating. The inside area gets busy and noisy starting around 8:30 a.m., with lines developing even for coffee refills. We prefer having breakfast at the outdoor tables on the starboard side, with less-trafficked walkways, better views, and fresh air.

HOUSE SPECIALTIES Breakfast features the usual buffet staples: fruit, cereal, eggs, waffles, bacon, sausage, and pastries. Lunch includes soups, salads, sandwiches, and burgers, plus a couple of alternative offerings such as pasta or fish. Beach Blanket Buffet's lunches are loosely themed each day, with Italian, Asian, and seafood as examples of the offerings. The fact that you can make it through a meal and not realize the cuisine until well into it—"Hey, this seems to be Italian!"—gives you an example of how loosey-goosey the theming is. The dinner menu features selections from the main dining rooms, so there will be something to everyone's liking available.

COMMENTS Beach Blanket Buffet has two separate and identical buffet setups, on either side of the main entrance. There's not enough space, however, to pop back to one station just to grab another croissant—you've got to either excuse your way up the line or start at the beginning. The coffee situation is similar, with the only dispensers placed at the end of the buffet.

Because you're issued a tray and flatware as soon as you enter BBB, it gives off a distinct cafeteria vibe, but if you're feeling a little overfed after your dinners (and maybe late-night buffets), Beach Blanket Buffet is a good option for those who wish to control portions and load up on fruit and vegetables for breakfast and lunch.

Palo ★★★½ Deck 10 Aft

ITALIAN QUALITY ★★★½ VALUE ★★★½ SERVICE ★★★★½ FRIENDLINESS ★★★★

COMMENTS See profile of Palo on the *Magic* (page 94) for details. A slight difference is the coffee, which is Nescafé instead of Illy—again, though, a restaurant this good should serve better.

Parrot Cay ★★ Deck 3 Aft

AMERICAN/CARIBBEAN QUALITY ★★ SERVICE ★★★★ FRIENDLINESS ★★★★

Reservations Not accepted. **When to go** Breakfast; avoid otherwise if you can. **Bar** Yes. **Alcohol** Limited selection of red, white, and sparkling wines, plus mixed drinks and spirits. All alcohol costs extra. **Dress** Casual; no tank tops or swimwear at dinner.

Hours Breakfast buffet on select days, 7:30–10:45 a.m.; lunch buffet on select days, noon–1:30 p.m.; nightly dinner seatings at 5:45 p.m. and 8:15 p.m. Hours are subject to change, so check your *Personal Navigator* for exact times.

SETTING AND ATMOSPHERE This is possibly the least attractive restaurant on the entire ship, if not the entire cruise line. Parrot Cay is supposed to evoke images of Caribbean-island architecture, with shades of blue, green, and teal. Unfortunately, the low ceiling and poor lighting make it feel more like a "Jamaica Me Crazy" party at a fraternity house.

HOUSE SPECIALTIES None worth recommending.

COMMENTS Parrot Cay tries to Caribbean-ize standard-issue DCL dishes by adding jerk seasoning, plantains, and tropical fruits as garnishes, but it's essentially the same food you can get anywhere on the ship. Need to turn an Italian mozzarella-and-tomato plate into an island-themed appetizer? Add a bit of grilled gourd and it becomes the St. Maarten Stack! You'll be much happier if you can swing reservations at Palo on the night you're supposed to eat at Parrot Cay. If that doesn't work, try the Cove Café's antipasto sampler or room service.

Triton's ★★★ Deck 3 Midship

AMERICAN/FRENCH QUALITY ★★★ SERVICE ★★★★ FRIENDLINESS ★★★★

Reservations Not accepted. **When to go** Lunch. **Bar** Yes. **Alcohol** Limited selection of red, white, and sparkling wines, plus mixed drinks and spirits. All alcohol costs extra. **Dress** Casual; no tank tops or swimwear at dinner. **Hours** Daily breakfast, 8–9:30 a.m.; daily lunch, noon–1:30 p.m.; nightly dinner seatings at 5:45 and 8:15 p.m. Hours are subject to change, so check your *Personal Navigator* for details.

SETTING AND ATMOSPHERE In case you've forgotten that King Triton is Ariel's father in *The Little Mermaid*, a large tile mosaic of Triton and Ariel sits at the back of this restaurant as a reminder. Besides the art, Triton's blue, beige, and gray colors lend a vague sea theme to the inside, but if you've visited any of the other restaurants, you'll be inclined to think that any of them could be switched out just by changing the paint and light fixtures.

HOUSE SPECIALTIES Breakfast features the usual suspects: fruit, cereal, eggs, waffles, bacon, sausage, and pastries. Lunch includes soups, salads, sandwiches, and burgers, plus a couple of alternative offerings such as pasta or fish. Dinner appetizers include escargots and French onion soup; order one of the crispy duck breast for the table if no one is adventurous enough to try it themselves. The Grand Marnier soufflé is probably the most popular dessert.

COMMENTS You know Disney is serious about the French theme when they put snails on the appetizer menu. *C'est si bon!* There are other Gallic influences on the menu—many of the entrées have sauces made with butter, wine, or spirits—plus enough standard vegetarian, chicken, beef, and pork dishes to make anyone happy.

Disney Dream DINING

COUNTER-SERVICE RESTAURANTS

Fillmore's Favorites

QUALITY C   PORTION Small–Medium   LOCATION Deck 11 Midship

WHEN TO GO Typical hours: 10:30 a.m.–6 p.m. Check your *Personal Navigator* for the exact schedule.

SELECTIONS Sandwiches, wraps, salads, fruit, cookies.

COMMENTS While the lineup can change, it usually includes a roast-beef-and-Cheddar sandwich, a "Greek salad" veggie wrap, and a chicken Caesar wrap. Fresh fruit, such as whole bananas, grapes, and oranges, is also available.

Luigi's Pizza

QUALITY C   PORTION Medium   LOCATION Deck 11 Midship

WHEN TO GO Typical hours: 10:30 a.m.–6:30 p.m. Check your *Personal Navigator* for the exact schedule.

SELECTIONS Cheese, pepperoni, barbecue-chicken, and veggie pizza slices.

COMMENTS As with the pizza joints on the *Magic* and *Wonder,* no one will mistake Luigi's for authentic pizza, but it's fine in a pinch. Occasionally open after dinner, when ordering a whole pie is a convenient alternative to room service or restaurant dining.

Tow Mater's Grill

QUALITY C   PORTION Large   LOCATION Deck 11 Midship

WHEN TO GO Typical hours: 10:30 a.m.–11 p.m. most days. Check your *Personal Navigator* for the exact schedule.

SELECTIONS Grilled hot dogs, sausages, burgers, and chicken sandwiches; fried-chicken strips; fries.

COMMENTS The fries and burgers aren't anything special—they serve primarily as sustenance for chlorine-addled kids (that is, if they can be pried out of the nearby pool long enough to eat). The chicken strips and hot dogs are the best things on the menu. A nearby fixin's bar provides toppings for burgers and sandwiches.

FULL-SERVICE RESTAURANTS

Animator's Palate ★★★   Deck 3 Aft

AMERICAN/ASIAN   QUALITY ★★★   SERVICE ★★★★   FRIENDLINESS ★★★★

Reservations Not accepted. **When to go** Dinner. **Bar** Yes. **Alcohol** Red, white, and sparkling wines, plus mixed drinks and spirits. All alcohol costs extra. **Dress** Casual; no tank tops or swimwear. **Hours** Nightly dinner seatings usually at 5:45 and 8:15 p.m.; check your *Personal Navigator* for the exact schedule.

SETTING AND ATMOSPHERE Each DCL ship has a restaurant called Animator's Palate, and all four pay tribute to Disney's (and Pixar's) animation processes. And although all Disney ships have a restaurant called Animator's Palate, there are three different implementations. Unlike the black-and-white decor on the *Magic* and *Wonder,* that of Animator's Palate on the *Fantasy* (and the *Dream*) features vivid colors: The floor has red carpet with stars of silver, gold, and blue, and the walls are the color of caramel. The backs of the dining-room chairs are patterned after Mickey Mouse's pants, with red backs, yellow buttons, and a black "belt" at the top.

Shelves along the walls hold small toy versions of Disney and Pixar icons, in between video screens displaying animation sketches from popular Disney movies. The more interesting ones will show on one screen how one complete animated cel is drawn, starting from sketches of the main characters to how key background elements are drawn, color samples for walls and floors, and the finished art. The art changes throughout the evening, keeping the view fresh for everyone.

At certain points during your dinner, some of the screens will switch from sketches to an interactive video featuring the surfer-dude turtle Crush from *Finding Nemo.* When we say "interactive," we mean it—Crush will ask you questions and react to your responses, allowing you to have an actual conversation with the animated turtle. Based on the same real-time computer graphics found in Epcot's *Turtle Talk with Crush* attraction (also found at other Disney parks), the technology behind this minishow allows Crush's mouth to move in the appropriate way as his words are spoken. Parents may be more amazed than children.

HOUSE SPECIALTIES Vegetable stir-fry; roasted-garlic or red-pepper dip with bread.

COMMENTS The "wow" factor doesn't extend to the food—as is the case at the other Animator's Palates, the cuisine isn't much different from what you might get at Applebee's or Chili's, despite the Pacific Rim/American designation.

Cabanas ★★★ Deck 11 Aft

AMERICAN/BUFFET   QUALITY ★★★   SERVICE ★★★★   FRIENDLINESS ★★★★

COMMENTS See profile of Cabanas on the *Magic* (page 91) for details.

Enchanted Garden ★★★ Deck 2 Midship

AMERICAN/CONTINENTAL   QUALITY ★★★   SERVICE ★★★★   FRIENDLINESS ★★★★

Reservations Not accepted. **When to go** Lunch, especially on your embarkation day, when the crowds are headed to Cabanas. **Bar** Yes. **Alcohol** Limited selection of red, white, and sparkling wines, plus mixed drinks and spirits. All alcohol costs extra. **Hours** Breakfast buffet on select days, 8–10 a.m.; lunch on select days, noon–1:30 p.m.; nightly dinner seatings at 5:45 and 8:15 p.m. Hours are subject to change, so check your *Personal Navigator* for the exact schedule.

SETTING AND ATMOSPHERE Designed to evoke a 19th-century French greenhouse, with patinaed cast-iron arches supporting a spectacular ceiling display of plants, sun, and sky, Enchanted Garden is surely the prettiest of the *Dream*'s three main rotational restaurants.

During lunch, lights in the ceiling simulate the midday sun, and diners see what appears to be ivy climbing up the side of the ironworks; as the sun sets, the "sky" turns to dusk and eventually to dark. Lights, in the shape of flowers and hung from the ceiling, open their "petals" as night falls.

The centerpiece of Enchanted Garden is a burbling concrete fountain, 7 feet tall, topped by Mickey Mouse. The best seats are the round, raised, high-backed booths along the center walk, which allow you to see all the action in one half of the restaurant. Look for framed Hermès scarves outside the restaurant—a nice (and expensive) touch of France. Disney says Enchanted Garden is inspired by the gardens at Versailles, but we think it looks more like the hothouse at Paris's Les Jardin des Plantes. We could be wrong.

HOUSE SPECIALTIES Roast pork tenderloin seasoned with smoked salt; scallops with roasted asparagus; seared-tuna salad on field greens; and seaweed with squid.

COMMENTS The menu is more American bistro than Paris brasserie, despite the French setting. Besides substituting brioche for bread, the most French thing on the menu is usually the use of the words *julienne* to describe how the vegetables are cut and *consommé* to describe the soup.

There's usually at least one pork dish, such as roast pork tenderloin, one chicken dish (baked or roasted), and a steak or prime rib available, along with several seafood and vegetarian options. Honestly, you could serve these dishes at Animator's Palate or Royal Court without anyone noticing, but maybe the scenery here makes the food taste a little bit better.

Palo ★★★★ Deck 12 Aft and Starboard

ITALIAN QUALITY ★★★★ VALUE ★★★★ SERVICE ★★★★½ FRIENDLINESS ★★★★

Reservations Required. **When to go** Brunch on sea days; dinner nightly. **Bar** Yes. **Alcohol** Large list of Italian wines, listed by region, plus select wines from around the world; mixed drinks and spirits; *limoncello*; grappa; ice wine. All alcohol costs extra. **Dress** Pants and dress shirt or jacket for men; dress, skirt and blouse, or pantsuit for women. No jeans, shorts, capris, flip-flops, or athletic shoes. **Hours** Brunch, 10 a.m.–12:30 p.m. on sea days on cruises of 4 nights or longer; nightly dinner, 6–8:30 p.m. Hours are subject to change, so check your *Personal Navigator* for the exact schedule. **Special comments** An additional $25/person charge will be added to your cruise bill for each meal at Palo. If you need to cancel a reservation, you must do so by 2 p.m. on the day of your reservation, or the full per-person charge will be applied to your bill. Guests must be age 18 and up to dine.

SETTING AND ATMOSPHERE Palo is on the starboard side at the back of Deck 12, opposite the adults-only French restaurant Remy (see next profile) and adjacent to the Meridian bar. Although all four Disney ships have a restaurant named Palo, the restaurants on the *Dream* and *Fantasy* have the nicest furnishings.

The entrance to Palo on the *Dream* has a pretty gold-and-ruby-colored glass chandelier, surely one of the most photographed parts of the restaurant. Guests entering Palo walk past a glass-enclosed wine closet and see the main dining room, decorated with deep mahogany wood–paneled walls and columns, and rich burgundy carpet. One half of the room features deep-green patterned fabric on the booths and chairs, with paintings of the Italian countryside and seashore along the walls. The other half of Palo uses a saturated red fabric for its seating; illustrations of Italian villas hang on the walls. Also within the *Dream*'s Palo, and unique to Disney's larger ships, are small private dining rooms with custom fabrics, wallpaper, and lighting. Stick your head inside if one is empty, and you'll see how the wealthy merchants of Venice might have lived.

Naturally, tables next to Palo's floor-to-ceiling windows afford the best views, but tables near the back wall sit on an elevated platform, allowing diners there to see over the tables nearest the windows. Our favorite table is to the left of the entrance, tucked by itself in a rounded corner along the inside wall and surrounded by a mural depicting Venice from the water. It's a bit high profile, though; quieter seats are available at the far ends of either side of the restaurant. Brunch offers open seating, so sit wherever the view is best.

HOUSE SPECIALTIES Start your dinner with the cioppino, a tomato-based fish stew with squid, clams, and shrimp, or the white-bean soup, with prosciutto and perfectly al dente beans. A complete selection of pasta is available, either as a separate course or as an entrée. One of these, the vegetarian mushroom risotto, is so rich you'd swear it had beef in it. Our favorite meat entrée is the rack of lamb, which comes in a crispy crust of Parmesan cheese and oregano. For seafood, we like the grilled tuna with potato risotto a bit more than the grilled scallops. The chocolate soufflé, by far the most popular dessert, comes with both dark- and white-chocolate sauces.

As on the other ships, Palo's brunch menu is very good. One large table is dedicated to breads, muffins, and pastries, along with sliced fruits and fresh vegetables (the roasted asparagus is tasty). An entire aquarium's worth of fish is available in another section, including shrimp cocktail, cured salmon, smoked-trout mousse, seared tuna, scallops, crab legs, crawfish, and mussels. Eggs cooked in every conceivable way, including Benedict, Florentine, Julia, and customized omelets, are on the menu too. Not enough? Try the selection of made-to-order pizzas. If there's any room left for dessert, small cups of tiramisu will take care of your sweet tooth.

COMMENTS Given what you've already spent on the cruise, dropping another $25 to dine at Palo requires no thought whatsoever. Because the food is cooked to order, it tastes substantially better than anything coming from the main dining rooms. The menu offers a wide selection, and many dishes—especially the soups—are done very well. It's no wonder that DCL allows guests to make only one reservation before boarding.

Remy ★★★★½ Deck 12 Aft

FRENCH QUALITY ★★★★½ VALUE ★★★★½ SERVICE ★★★★½ FRIENDLINESS ★★★★

Reservations Required. **When to go** Dinner. **Bar** Yes. **Alcohol** An extensive selection of French wines and Champagnes. **Dress** Jackets and dress shirts for men; dresses, blouses and skirts, or pantsuits for women. **Hours** Brunch on sea days on cruises of 4 nights or longer, 10 a.m.–12:30 p.m.; nightly dinner, 6–9 p.m. Hours are subject to change, so check your *Personal Navigator* for the exact schedule. **Special comments** An additional $50/person charge will be added to your cruise bill for each brunch at Remy, $75/person for each dinner. The wine pairing for dinner is $99/person. If you need to cancel a reservation, you must do so by 2 p.m. on the day of your reservation, or the full per-person charge will be applied to your bill. Guests must be age 18 and up to dine.

SETTING AND ATMOSPHERE Remarkably understated for a Disney restaurant, and one named after a cartoon rat at that. The most prominent features at Remy are the floor-to-ceiling windows, which look out over the ocean on the port side of the ship from high on Deck 12; and the Art Nouveau lights, which seem to spring from the floor as thick vines, branching out into yellow lights as they reach the ceiling. Besides those touches, and perhaps the oval mirrors along the wall opposite the windows, the rest is simple and elegant: oval, round, and square tables, all with white-linen tablecloths, and round-backed wood chairs with white upholstery. The olive-green carpet pattern matches the Art Nouveau decor without being distracting. A small teak deck wraps around Remy, allowing you to walk out for a quick breath of fresh air between courses.

HOUSE SPECIALTIES The tasting menu may be one of the best 3-hour dining experiences you'll ever have. Splurge on the wine pairing. If the tasting menu sounds like too much food, Remy's meat entrées usually include Australian Wagyu beef and pork from central France.

Remy also offers an extensive brunch on days when the ship is at sea. Like the brunch at Palo, Remy's has an extensive selection, including fruit, pastries, seafood, beef, pork, pasta, and fish. A Champagne pairing is available for an additional $25 per person. We prefer the dinner experience, but spending the morning at Remy is a lovely way to start a day at sea.

COMMENTS What makes a great restaurant such as Remy different from restaurants that are simply very good is that, while the latter usually have a few signature dishes that they do very well, virtually *everything* at Remy is nothing short of exceptional. An appetizer of carrots—yes, the root vegetable—will be the most extraordinary carrots you've ever had, probably in varieties and colors you didn't know existed, and with a flavor that is the pure essence of carrot-ness. Now imagine a meal of three to eight courses, all equally as good, ranging from soups, seafood, and beef, to sides, cheese courses, and desserts. That's an average evening at Remy.

Remy offers both a standard dinner menu and a chef's tasting menu. If you have the time or the inclination, order the latter—it allows you to savor every bit of creativity and technical mastery the kitchen can muster.

A couple of examples from our meals: One course early in the tasting menu was billed as the chef's interpretation of a grilled-cheese sandwich with tomato soup. The entire serving consisted of one small, golden-brown cube, about the size of a postage stamp on each side, designed to be eaten in one bite. The outside of the cube was a Cheddar cheese, coated with seasoned bread crumbs and fried lightly. Inside was a tomato sauce, barely seasoned and reduced to concentrate the flavor. The first bite—it took maybe two to finish the entire thing—tasted of crispy, butter-fried bread and melted cheese. The second was all tomato: bright, slightly acidic, and sweet at the same time, balancing out the butter and cheese from the outside coating. Remy's chefs had both amplified the flavors to their essence and reduced the size of the dish to its bare minimum.

Another appetizer was the chef's take on cheese pizza. Its base was a small, crispy wafer of baked bread, barely thicker than a sheet of paper. On top of that was a half-inch layer of white foam, about the consistency of whipped cream but made from Parmesan cheese. And on top of that were three small basil leaves.

The pizza's tomato "sauce" was presented in a Champagne flute as a clear, intensely flavored liquid. The kitchen had achieved this transparency by repeatedly filtering juice from ripe tomatoes through layers of fine cheesecloth, trapping the red bits and letting the clear juice through. We were instructed to follow a bit of the crust and cheese foam with a sip from the flute, and the flavors combined beautifully.

One last tip on the tasting menu: Remy offers a wine pairing for most courses. The selections are very good, but it's a *lot* of wine that could easily be split between two people. Len's first evening at Remy began with a martini at Meridian and continued with the wine pairing for dinner. The first few courses were memorable, but by the time he realized how much alcohol was involved, it was too late. The last quarter of the meal is a hazy memory that apparently involved Len applauding someone else's cheese cart as it rolled by for dessert. That called for another, alcohol-free, dinner at Remy. Pity his suffering.

Royal Palace ★★★ Deck 3 Midship

AMERICAN/FRENCH QUALITY ★★★ SERVICE ★★★★ FRIENDLINESS ★★★★

Reservations Not accepted. When to go Lunch. Bar Yes. Alcohol Limited selection of red, white, and sparkling wines, plus mixed drinks and spirits. Dress Casual; no tank tops or swimwear at dinner. Hours Daily breakfast, 8–9:30 a.m.; daily lunch, noon–1:30 p.m.; nightly dinner seatings at 5:45 and 8:15 p.m. Hours are subject to change, so check your *Personal Navigator* for the exact schedule.

SETTING AND ATMOSPHERE The most attractive part of Royal Palace may be its entrance, done in gold-and-white-marble tile below a pretty flower-shaped chandelier accented with blue-glass "diamonds" and red "rubies." Inside the doors, gold-and-white faux-marble columns form a circle just inside one ring of tables; royal-blue carpet with gold trim lines the inner part of the restaurant. Drapes cover the windows lining one side of the room, and mosaic-tile pictures of Disney princesses line another.

HOUSE SPECIALTIES Breakfast is standard buffet fare: fruit, cereal, eggs, waffles, bacon, sausage, and pastries. Lunch includes soups, salads, sandwiches, and burgers, plus a couple of alternative offerings such as pasta or fish. Dinner appetizers include escargots and French onion soup; the wild-boar tenderloin entrée is tasty. The Grand Marnier soufflé is probably the most popular dessert.

COMMENTS You know Disney is serious about the French theme when they put snails on the appetizer menu. There are other Gallic influences on the menu—many of the entrées have sauces made with butter, wine, or spirits—plus enough standard vegetarian, chicken, beef, and pork dishes to make anyone happy.

Disney Fantasy DINING

COUNTER-SERVICE RESTAURANTS

Fillmore's Favorites

QUALITY C   PORTION Small–Medium   LOCATION Deck 11 Midship

COMMENTS See profile of Fillmore's Favorites on the *Dream* (page 98) for details.

Luigi's Pizza

QUALITY C   PORTION Medium   LOCATION Deck 11 Midship

COMMENTS See profile of Luigi's Pizza on the *Dream* (page 98) for details.

Tow Mater's Grill

QUALITY C   PORTION Large   LOCATION Deck 11 Midship

COMMENTS See profile of Tow Mater's Grill on the *Dream* (page 98) for details.

FULL-SERVICE RESTAURANTS

Animator's Palate ★★★ Deck 3 Aft

AMERICAN/ASIAN QUALITY ★★★ SERVICE ★★★★ FRIENDLINESS ★★★★

Reservations Not accepted. When to go Dinner. Bar Yes. Alcohol Red, white, and sparkling wines, plus mixed drinks and spirits. All alcohol costs extra. Dress Casual; no tank tops or swimwear. Hours Nightly dinner seatings usually at 5:45 and 8:15 p.m.; check your *Personal Navigator* for the exact schedule.

SETTING AND ATMOSPHERE Each DCL ship has a restaurant called Animator's Palate, and all four pay tribute to Disney's (and Pixar's) animation processes. And although all Disney ships have a restaurant called Animator's Palate, there are three different implementations. Unlike the black-and-white decor on the *Magic* and *Wonder,* that of Animator's Palate on the *Fantasy* (and the *Dream*) features vivid colors: The floor has red carpet

ROYAL COURT ROYAL TEA   ROYAL COURT, DECK 3 MIDSHIP

EXCLUSIVE TO THE *Fantasy,* this event combines afternoon tea with Disney-princess meet-and-greet opportunities, including music, singing, and dancing. It's very expensive—prices start at $279 and can reach $500 pretty quickly—but the prices hold down the crowds, so you're likely to get lots of personal princess attention.

You'll be served a selection of teas, plus small sandwiches, cookies, cakes, and other finger food. Children also receive a few souvenirs: Girls get a tiara, necklace, jewelry box, friendship bracelet, necklace, and Cinderella doll; boys receive a Duffy teddy bear doll, autograph book, sword and shield, and Disney pins.

The Royal Court Royal Tea is for guests ages 3 and up. Prices start at $279 for one adult and one child; each additional child is $210 and each additional adult is $69. Space is very limited. Reservations can't yet be made online, so stop by Guest Services to make arrangements.

with stars of silver, gold, and blue, and the walls are the color of caramel. The backs of the dining-room chairs are patterned after Mickey Mouse's pants, with red backs, yellow buttons, and a black "belt" at the top.

Shelves along the walls hold small toy versions of Disney and Pixar icons, in between video screens displaying animation sketches from popular Disney movies. The more interesting ones will show on one screen how one complete animated cel is drawn, starting from sketches of the main characters to how key background elements are drawn, color samples for walls and floors, and the finished art. The art changes throughout the evening, keeping the view fresh for everyone.

The version of Animator's Palate on the *Fantasy* includes *Animation Magic,* an impressive special effect. At the beginning of the second night you dine there, you're given a sheet of paper and crayon and told to draw a self-portrait. At the end of the evening, all of the diners' self-portraits are shown in an animated cartoon similar to Disney's 1929 short cartoon *The Skeleton Dance.*

At your first scheduled dinner at Animator's Palate, you get a different show. At certain points during your second dinner, some of the screens will switch from sketches to an interactive video featuring the surfer-dude turtle Crush from *Finding Nemo.* When we say *interactive,* we mean it—Crush will ask you questions and react to your responses, allowing you to have an actual conversation with the animated turtle. Based on the same real-time computer graphics found in Epcot's *Turtle Talk with Crush* attraction (also at other Disney parks), the technology behind this minishow allows Crush's mouth to move in the appropriate way as his words are spoken. Parents may be more amazed than children.

HOUSE SPECIALTIES Vegetable stir-fry; roasted-garlic or red-pepper dip with bread.

COMMENTS When it comes to the food, it's the same old story—as is the case at the other three Animator's Palates, the dishes are pedestrian chain-restaurant fare, despite the Pacific Rim/American designation. On the *Fantasy,* anyway, the entertainment makes up for whatever the food lacks.

Cabanas ★★★   Deck 11 Aft

AMERICAN/BUFFET QUALITY ★★★★ SERVICE ★★★★ FRIENDLINESS ★★★★

COMMENTS See profile of Cabanas on the *Magic* (page 91) for details.

Enchanted Garden ★★★   Deck 2 Midship

AMERICAN/CONTINENTAL QUALITY ★★★ SERVICE ★★★★ FRIENDLINESS ★★★★

COMMENTS See profile of Enchanted Garden on the *Dream* (page 99) for details.

Palo ★★★★   Deck 12 Aft and Starboard

ITALIAN QUALITY ★★★★ VALUE ★★★★ SERVICE ★★★★½ FRIENDLINESS ★★★★

COMMENTS See profile of Palo on the *Dream* (page 100) for details.

Remy ★★★★½ Deck 12 Aft

FRENCH QUALITY ★★★★½ VALUE ★★★★½ SERVICE ★★★★½ FRIENDLINESS ★★★★

COMMENTS See profile of Remy on the *Dream* (page 102) for details.

Royal Court ★★★   Deck 3 Midship

AMERICAN/FRENCH QUALITY ★★★ SERVICE ★★★★ FRIENDLINESS ★★★★

Reservations Not accepted. **When to go** Lunch. **Bar** Yes. **Alcohol** Limited selection of red, white, and sparkling wines, plus mixed drinks and spirits. **Dress** Casual; no tank tops or swimwear at dinner. **Hours** Breakfast, 8–9:30 a.m.; lunch, noon–1:30 p.m.; nightly dinner seatings at 5:45 and 8:15 p.m. Hours are subject to change, so check your *Personal Navigator* for the exact schedule.

SETTING AND ATMOSPHERE The most distinctive design elements of Royal Court are the gold-colored wood columns on the floor, which rise to attach to the ceiling through flared white glass decorated with plant stems and shaped like flower petals. Along with these, white-marble columns and carpet patterned to look like fancy rugs give Royal Court a formal feel, even when it's half-full of kids. Small, round lamps placed around the room are designed to look like Cinderella's pumpkin coach, and some of the walls feature tile murals depicting scenes from *Cinderella* and other Disney princess films. Tables near the starboard wall sit under portholes that offer ocean views, although these are partially blocked by a privacy wall running along the inside perimeter of the restaurant.

HOUSE SPECIALTIES Breakfast is standard buffet fare: fruit, cereal, eggs, waffles, bacon, sausage, and pastries. Lunch includes soups, salads, sandwiches, and burgers, plus a couple of alternative offerings such as pasta or fish. Dinner appetizers include escargots and French onion soup; the wild-boar tenderloin entrée is tasty. The Grand Marnier soufflé is probably the most popular dessert.

COMMENTS Only differences in decor distinguish Royal Court from Royal Palace on the *Dream* (see page 103).

PART EIGHT

ENTERTAINMENT *and* NIGHTLIFE

■ LIVE THEATER *on the* SHIPS

LIVE ENTERTAINMENT IS PRESENTED at the **Walt Disney Theatre** most nights, on most itineraries. Shows are typically either Disney-themed theatrical productions (typically musicals) or variety acts, including comedians, magicians, or ventriloquists. The theatrical shows are usually of two types: retellings of familiar stories, and "jukebox" musicals.

Disney's Aladdin: A Musical Spectacular, on the *Fantasy,* is an example of the retelling genre. The cruise version features live actors and multiple Arabian-themed sets reprising key scenes from the animated film, including the most popular songs, in about half the time of the original movie. The *Magic*'s *Twice Charmed: A Twist on the Original Cinderella Story,* is probably the best show in this category; the *Fantasy*'s *Aladdin* is a distant second; and the *Wonder*'s *Toy Story: The Musical* is third.

Examples of jukebox musicals include *Disney Dreams, Disney Wishes, Disney's Believe, The Golden Mickeys,* and *Villains Tonight!* Each features songs and characters from many different Disney films, the numbers linked by an original story. We're generally not fans of these shows, especially *Villains Tonight!* The story lines are threadbare, serving to string together the musical numbers rather than provide interesting narrative. Lack of plot, however, isn't our primary objection to these shows—we realize it's a Disney cruise. Rather, they recycle the same handful of characters and songs played in every entertainment venue throughout the ship. If you haven't heard "Be Our Guest" from *Beauty and the Beast* performed a dozen times on board, have your hearing checked when you get home.

Finally, the *Magic* puts on a welcome-aboard show on the first night of its seven-nights-and-up itineraries and a farewell show on the last night. The welcome show commingles a few musical numbers with a review of the ship's major features and schedule. The farewell show is a recap of the same, with guest photos from throughout the cruise thrown in. These are good times to go to the spa.

A BIT OF ADVICE You'll probably see at least one musical if you're taking small children on your cruise. Along with reading the show profiles that follow, we recommend watching a few minutes of each show on YouTube before you leave for the cruise. This will not only help you decide which show is worth your time, but it will also let you know what you're missing in case another entertainment option is available.

Disney often uses the term "Broadway-style" to describe its theater offerings. This should not be taken to mean that you will see the national-touring-company equivalent of a Broadway hit (like the version of *Rock of Ages* staged on some Norwegian Cruise Line sailings), nor should you expect to see as much nuance or complexity in the storylines of DCL shows as you might in legitimate theater. Frankly, as frequent patrons of actual New York City theater, we had long bristled at the "Broadway-style" descriptor, thinking it laughable to compare the simplified storytelling onboard with current New York productions marketed to families, such as *Matilda,* or even with Disney's own Broadway version of *The Lion King.*

After speaking with cast members about our concerns, we learned that from a technical standpoint, DCL performances do have much more in common with Times Square than Topeka: The stage mechanics, costuming, special effects, and lighting are all as close to state-of-the-art as is practicable at sea. If you find your eyes glazing over when you take your children to the show, try paying attention to the technological aspects of the programming—they'd be top-notch in most locales and are nothing less than remarkable given the constraints of an ocean liner.

And if that fails, consider that the DCL theaters, like most Broadway theaters, allow you to bring a glass of wine with you to your seat.

THE *MAGIC'S* SHOWS

WE HEAR THAT THE MAGIC is supposed to get a new stage show in May 2015, based on the Disney animated film *Tangled.* At press time, it wasn't clear whether this show would replace an existing production such as *Twice Charmed* or be worked in alongside the other shows on the *Magic's* longer voyages.

All Aboard: Let the Magic Begin ★★
Walt Disney Theatre, Deck 4 Forward

Welcome-aboard show with a few songs and a lot of talk about the cruise

When to go Typical showtimes are 6:15 and 8:30 p.m. on your embarkation day. Presented on cruises of 7 nights and longer. **Duration** 50 minutes. **Our rating** Skip it and tour the ship instead; ★★.

DESCRIPTION AND COMMENTS More than half of *All Aboard*'s 50-minute showtime consists of the *Magic*'s cruise director explaining the ship's dining, entertainment, and shopping options, plus port logistics. The rest is a handful of song-and-dance numbers featuring Disney characters and involving a young boy who dreams of becoming the ship's captain. Featuring a couple of original songs, the show serves as an introduction to the Walt Disney Theatre. It's a shame they can't put all the songs at the beginning of the show, because we'd skip the rest of it.

Disney Dreams: An Enchanted Classic ★★★½
Walt Disney Theatre, Deck 4 Forward

Peter Pan saves the day

When to go Typical showtimes are 6:15 and 8:30 p.m. Check your *Personal Navigator* for specific dates. **Duration** 55 minutes. **Our rating** Not to be missed; ★★★½.

DESCRIPTION AND COMMENTS *Disney Dreams* is one of the better stage shows on any Disney ship. Peter Pan must help a young girl named Anne Marie "find her own magic" before sunrise. Peter does this by whisking her through scenes from *Aladdin, Beauty and the Beast, Cinderella, The Little Mermaid,* and *The Lion King,* with each story's main characters appearing in key scenes from their respective movie and singing their signature songs. The sets are attractive, the special effects are good, and the script is fast-paced and entertaining. The cast seems to enjoy it, too, and it shows. We rate *Disney Dreams* as not to be missed.

Remember the Magic: A Final Farewell ★★
Walt Disney Theatre, Deck 4 Forward

Recap of your *Magic* cruise

When to go Typical showtimes are 6:15 and 8:30 p.m. on the night before your cruise concludes. Presented on cruises of 7 nights and longer. **Duration** 25 minutes. **Our rating** Not worth seeing; ★★.

DESCRIPTION AND COMMENTS *Remember the Magic* uses sets and characters from the ship's other shows, including *All Aboard* and *Disney Dreams,* to recap the cruise's highlights. Photographs and video clips of families at play, taken by Disney photographers during the itinerary, are shown on video screens during the songs. Expect songs and dances by Disney princesses and jokes about eating too much at the buffet. We recommend skipping this show and spending your last night revisiting your favorite activities on board.

Twice Charmed: An Original Twist on the Cinderella Story
★★★½   **Walt Disney Theatre, Deck 4 Forward**

A fresh take on a classic tale

When to go Typical showtimes are 6:15 and 8:30 p.m. Check your *Personal Navigator* for specific days. **Duration** 55 minutes. **Our rating** A new narrative for a familiar story; ★★★½.

DESCRIPTION AND COMMENTS If you recall from the original *Cinderella* movie, the stepmother breaks the first glass slipper just as it's about to be fit on Cinderella's foot. Cinderella, however, produces the second glass slipper, shows that it fits, and goes on to marry the prince.

Twice Charmed begins where that story ends. As the show opens, Cinderella's evil stepmother and stepsisters are lamenting the fact that they didn't know Cinderella had the second slipper. A wicked fairy godfather appears to send the evil stepfamily back in time and destroy Cindy's slipper before the prince's foot-fitting team ever arrives. Cinderella must then find a new way to convince the prince that they're meant to be together. As is the case with any Disney film, you can guess in the first 5 minutes how it's all going to end, but *Twice Charmed* is interesting anyway because it has a new narrative. The sets are pretty, the songs aren't bad, and it's an enjoyable way to spend an evening.

Villains Tonight!   ★★   Walt Disney Theatre, Deck 4 Forward

Disney heels do comedy

When to go Typical showtimes are 6:15 and 8:30 p.m. Check your *Personal Navigator* for specific days. **Duration** 55 minutes. **Our rating** The villain here is the show itself; ★★.

DESCRIPTION AND COMMENTS In *Villains Tonight!*, Hades, ruler of the underworld, has lost his edge after being defeated by Hercules. He's visited by the Fates, who tell Hades he must prove he's still truly evil or give up his throne. Hades dispatches his two sidekicks, Pain and Panic, to bring every Disney villain they can find back to the underworld. Musical numbers pop up every time Pain and Panic make contact with a villain, including *The Little Mermaid*'s Ursula the Sea Witch in a burlesque number, the evil queen from *Snow White,* Maleficent from *Sleeping Beauty,* and *The Lion King*'s Scar, in what, judging by the costumes, is a *Mad Max Beyond Africa* musical number.

Disney villains *should* be comedy gold. They don't have to follow the same rules as Disney's good guys—they can hurl insults and petty criticisms and express self-centered opinions. There's some of that in this script, but it's done at such a glacial pace that you wonder whether the long pauses are intended solely to extend the show's run time. A tighter, more up-tempo script would make better use of the performer's talents.

Every *Villains* show includes a painful effort to make the show hip and contemporary. On one recent sailing, there were three separate references to the Kardashians, including making fun of Kim's baby. And on each occasion the joke fell flat and the character responded with "Too soon?" We were embarrassed for the performers.

Walt Disney: The Dream Goes On   ★★★
Walt Disney Theatre, Deck 4 Forward

Retrospective of Walt's life and art

When to go Typical showtimes are 6:15 and 8:30 p.m. Check your *Personal Navigator* for specific days. **Duration** 45 minutes. **Our rating** An improvement over *All Aboard,* it has potential; ★★★.

DESCRIPTION AND COMMENTS A new show for the *Magic,* the show uses film clips, audio, and stage reenactments to trace Walt's life from the creation of Mickey Mouse through the theme parks. The show's highlights include songs from Disney-theme-park attractions, such as Main Street, U.S.A.; The Haunted Mansion; and *Country Bear Jamboree.* The show also benefits from not drawing heavily from *Beauty and the Beast, The Little Mermaid,* or *The Lion King.* The pacing is a little uneven—it could be improved with better dialogue to link the segments—but overall the show is a nice tribute to the guy who started it all.

THE *WONDER'S* SHOWS

Disney Dreams: An Enchanted Classic ★★★½
Walt Disney Theatre, Deck 4 Forward

Peter Pan saves the day

COMMENTS See profile of this show on the *Magic* (page 109) for details.

The Golden Mickeys ★★ Walt Disney Theatre, Deck 4 Forward

Disney spin on an awards show

When to go Typical showtimes are 6:15 and 8:30 p.m. Check your *Personal Navigator* for specific days. **Duration** 45 minutes. **Our rating** There are better uses of your time; ★★.

DESCRIPTION AND COMMENTS One of the least coherent live shows on any Disney cruise ship, *The Golden Mickeys* starts out as an Oscar-style awards show, except it's the Disney gang giving themselves awards for their own movies in different, made-up categories. As each award winner is announced, live performers reenact the movie's key scenes on stage, including songs, as clips from the movies play on the stage's screen backdrop.

There are many problems with the show. For one, the "awards" stop making sense almost as soon as they're presented: The "Best Heroes" award is simply a montage of main characters from Disney films, and one of the last awards, "A Salute to Friendship," is apparently the only way the show's writers could think of getting Woody, Buzz, and Jesse together on stage. Unless you have a pressing need to see another rendition of songs from *The Lion King* and *Beauty and the Beast,* this show isn't worth your time.

Toy Story: The Musical ★★★½ Walt Disney Theatre, Deck 4

Retelling of the original film

When to go Typical showtimes are 6:15 and 8:30 p.m. Check your *Personal Navigator* for specific days. **Duration** 55 minutes. **Our rating** Worth seeing; ★★★½.

DESCRIPTION AND COMMENTS This is a stage adaptation of the first *Toy Story* movie, with a new soundtrack not heard in the original film. Besides Buzz and Woody, all of the film's major characters make appearances in the show, including Rex, Hamm, and Mr. Potato Head. The show's sets are complemented by video projections displayed on the stage's back screen.

Virtually everyone taking a Disney cruise will already have seen the movie, so the stage version won't hold any surprises. Still, the songs and lyrics are interesting enough to make the show worth watching.

THE *DREAM'S* SHOWS

Disney's Believe ★★★ Walt Disney Theatre, Deck 3 Forward

Magic triumphs over cynicism

When to go Typical showtimes are 6:15 and 8:30 p.m. Check your *Personal Navigator* for specific days. **Duration** 50 minutes. **Our rating** Nice change of pace; ★★★.

DESCRIPTION AND COMMENTS A botanist father who doesn't believe in magic must learn to believe in order to reconnect with his daughter on her birthday. The father's guide is *Aladdin*'s wisecracking Genie, who takes Dad through time, space, and Disney music on his journey to acceptance.

Believe has one of the most sophisticated sets of any Disney stage show at sea, and there are enough visual elements to entertain almost any kid. Although it's not a holiday show, the plot seems like a loose adaptation of Charles Dickens's *A Christmas Carol,* with a committee of ghosts, including Mary Poppins, Peter Pan, Baloo from *The Jungle Book,* Rafiki from *The Lion King,* and Pocahontas from Scarsdale, judging by her accent. (Erin begs to differ: "No princess from Scarsdale would be caught dead in that *shmata.*")

Many other Disney stars appear throughout the show, but, thankfully, *Believe* includes some less familiar characters and songs. The final stretch has a hit parade of other princesses and ends with performances by Mickey and Minnie.

The Golden Mickeys ★★ Walt Disney Theatre, Deck 3 Forward

Disney spin on an awards show

COMMENTS See profile of this show on the *Wonder* (page 111) for details.

Villains Tonight! ★★ Walt Disney Theatre, Deck 3 Forward

Disney heels do comedy

COMMENTS See profile of this show on the *Magic* (page 110) for details.

THE *FANTASY'S* SHOWS

Disney's Aladdin: A Musical Spectacular ★★★
Walt Disney Theatre, Deck 3 Forward

Song-filled extravaganza

When to go Typical showtimes are 6:15 and 8:30 p.m. Check your *Personal Navigator* for specific days. **Duration** 45 minutes. **Our rating** Needs more Genie; ★★★.

DESCRIPTION AND COMMENTS A song-filled retelling of Disney's *Aladdin,* this live show features stage sets of Agrabah, the Cave of Wonders, and the Sultan's palace, along with the film's main characters: Aladdin, Princess Jasmine, Jafar, Iago, and the Genie. All of the major numbers are performed, including "Friend Like Me" and "A Whole New World." Because it's an adaptation of an existing film, *Aladdin* has less saccharine Disney sweetness than, say, *Believe*.

Having seen the film in theaters and the live stage show at Disney California Adventure, we were disappointed in the *Fantasy*'s production of *Aladdin*. The actors' performances and singing were fine, but the set design and script aren't quite as good as we'd expected. For example, in the movie and the theme park show, Genie has the most important role in the production: Besides providing narrative and background, he tells jokes to keep the script moving. In live performances at DCA, Genie often ad-libs topical humor into the act, and so many one-liners come so fast that he's virtually guaranteed the biggest ovation at the end.

For some reason, though, Genie's onboard humor has been diluted so much that it doesn't provide the spark the rest of the script needs. He tells fewer jokes, and with less bite, than in either the DCA show or the film. (Perhaps the ship's flaky onboard Internet keeps the Genie from regular access to TMZ.com.) Also, we're surprised that the stage sets on a $900 million cruise ship aren't as detailed as those made for a theme park more than 10 years ago.

Disney's Believe ★★★   Walt Disney Theatre, Deck 3 Forward
Magic triumphs over cynicism

COMMENTS See profile of this show on the *Dream* (on the previous page) for details.

Disney Wishes ★★★½   Walt Disney Theatre, Deck 3 Forward
Teen-focused song and dance

When to go Typical showtimes are 6:15 and 8:30 p.m. Check your *Personal Navigator* for specific days. Duration 50 minutes. Our rating Entertaining; ★★★½.

DESCRIPTION AND COMMENTS In *Disney Wishes*, graduating high-schoolers Kayla, Nicole, and Brandon are visiting Disneyland Park in search of the ride of their lives. This search is complicated by the trio's imminent split for college, as well as Brandon's hush-hush crush on Kayla. Nicole, Brandon's sister, has her own dark secret: She wants to be an artist.

Wishes has young actors, fast-moving dance numbers, and lots of visual razzle-dazzle, so it's entertaining for tweens and teens. It's not bad for parents, either, especially if they can recognize the bits of Magic Kingdom park trivia interspersed in the dialogue. According to maritime law, which requires that Disney stage shows must include at least one song from *Aladdin, Beauty and the Beast, The Lion King,* or *The Little Mermaid,* there's also a rendition of "Under the Sea." But most of the show's songs come from less-familiar Disney films, such as *Hercules, The Jungle Book, Mulan, Pinocchio,* and *Tangled,* making it easier to sit through than most other shows of this type.

OTHER LIVE PERFORMANCES

BESIDES LIVE STAGE SHOWS, THE WALT DISNEY THEATRE hosts variety acts, including everything from magicians and comedians to ventriloquists, jugglers, hypnotists, and musicians. Repositioning cruises, with their many sea days, may have guest Broadway artists or other niche celebrities. Many of these acts will do preview shows or short sets at various venues throughout the ship before their major engagement at the theater. We've seen some incredible onboard acts, and also a few for whom *mediocre* would be a kind description. If there are previews, we suggest catching a few minutes (or asking other guests who've seen them) to decide whether the act is worth your time.

In our experience, the best live acts tend to be the magicians and comedians, who can adapt their material to the audience as the show is happening, and revamp parts of their act between shows.

 # MOVIES

RECENT DISNEY MOVIES, including films released during the cruise, are shown at the **Buena Vista Theatre** on each Disney ship. Each theater is equipped with digital film projectors, state-of-the-art sound systems, and the capability to show 3-D films (complete with 3-D glasses for guests). Padded, upholstered seats are arranged stairlike behind the screen, allowing good views from almost anywhere in the theater. About half a dozen films are shown on any cruise, typically two or three per day beginning around 9:30 a.m. and running through midnight. Admission is free. Popcorn and drinks are sold outside the theater before and during each presentation; you can also bring your own snacks and drinks.

Classic Disney films are also shown on a giant 24-by-14-foot LED screen perched high above each ship's family pool (**Goofy's Pool** on Deck 9 of the *Magic* and *Wonder;* **Donald's Pool** on Deck 11 of the *Dream* and *Fantasy*).

 # LIVE SPORTS

ON THE WONDER, the main sports bar is **Diversions;** it's **687** on the *Dream* and **O'Gills** on the *Magic* and *Fantasy*. These are your primary venues for viewing baseball, basketball, and soccer. NFL football games are usually shown here, too, and some games are also shown on the ships' **Funnel Vision** big screen on the pool deck. Keep in mind that the ship gets its TV broadcasts from satellite transmissions, which can be affected by weather. If you want to watch a specific game, show up at least 30 minutes beforehand and ask a crew member to find the right station—there are hundreds of channels, and it sometimes takes a while to find your game.

If you happen to be sailing during a sporting event of national or worldwide interest, expect that it will be available for viewing in nearly every public space with seating, even if it's not immediately apparent that screens are present. We sailed on the *Wonder* during the

2014 World Cup soccer finals; the *Personal Navigator* listed only two viewing venues, but we found screens pulled down from the ceiling in every bar, lounge, and café to show the big game.

THEME NIGHTS *and* HOLIDAY ENTERTAINMENT

PIRATE NIGHT

THIS IS HELD ON ONE NIGHT on virtually every cruise. The crew, restaurants, and entertainment take on a pirate theme. The ship's transformation begins early in the day, when the usual background music is replaced by songs and audio from the theme parks' Pirates of the Caribbean ride and the spinoff film series. Afternoon craft sessions and family activities are pirate-themed as well. Sometime in the afternoon, your stateroom attendant will drop off in your cabin a pirate bandana for each member of your group to wear, as well as booty, such as chocolate "coins" covered in gold foil.

On cruises of four-plus nights, each ship's main restaurant will have a special menu for the evening, designed to look like a treasure map. Virtually all of the crew, as well as the ship's officers, will wear special pirate outfits, and families have an opportunity to pose for photos with them before dinner. Many guests pack special outfits just for Pirate Night, including black knee-high boots, capri pants, white puffy shirts, and eyeliner. (The women dress up too.)

Pirate Night concludes with a stage show and video on the family pool's Funnel Vision screen, accompanied by a short fireworks display. The fireworks are usually shot from the starboard side, so you'll have a better view from there. The best viewing spots are as follows:

- *Magic* and *Wonder:* Deck 10 Starboard, looking over Goofy's Pool
- *Dream* and *Fantasy:* Deck 12 Forward, near Currents bar

PIXAR NIGHT On Alaskan cruises, Pirate Night is replaced by Pixar Night. This consists of a lobby-atrium dance party with Pixar characters, such as Dug and Russell from *Up;* Mr. and Mrs. Incredible; Mike and Sulley from *Monsters, Inc.;* and several others. If you've never had an opportunity to get photos with *Ratatouille's* Remy and Emile, here's your chance. Additional events include a showing of *Toy Story: The Musical* (see page 111) as well as a Pixar-themed dinner menu, complete with 3-D viewing glasses. If you want your Pixar Night to end in a sugar coma, try the Buzz Lightyear ice-cream sundae for dessert: bubble gum–flavored ice cream and marshmallows topped with fudge sauce, whipped cream, and a cherry. It's a shade of blue you didn't even know existed in animation. Note that far fewer guests dress up for Pixar Night than for Pirate

Night—you may find a few pint-size Woodys walking around, but there's no implied pressure to make costuming part of your evening.

FORMAL NIGHT

THIS IS A CHANCE FOR FAMILIES to put on the ritz. The crew and officers also get into the act by wearing their dress whites. While there are no special meals or activities, you'll see many families getting their photos taken in the ship's atrium before or after dinner.

If you're the kind of person for whom the words "Formal Night" cause a near-allergic reaction, not to worry: You can always eat at the upper-deck buffet or get room service to avoid the whole business altogether.

*un*official **TIP**

Formal Night is very popular for reservations at **Palo** and **Remy**.

As for what *formal* or *dress-up* means, you'll see a wide range of interpretations. Many men, if not most, will wear a long-sleeved dress shirt, usually with a jacket; ties are optional. Most women will wear dresses or skirts, or pants with dressy tops. A nice shirt and pants are appropriate for teen boys, and teen girls usually dress as if they're going to a high school dance. Small children are not expected to dress up, but young girls frequently take this opportunity to don the outfit of their favorite princess. Frequently, you'll see a family decked to the nines, with the gentlemen in tuxes and the ladies in gowns.

If you don't have any fancy duds handy, you can rent them before you leave home by visiting **Cruiseline Formalwear** (**cruiselineformal wear.com**). Your garments will be delivered directly to your stateroom, and you'll return them to your stateroom attendant at the end of your cruise.

HALLOWEEN

ONE OF THE BEST PLACES TO CELEBRATE HALLOWEEN is on a Disney cruise. The crew and officers dress up, and many families bring special costumes to wear for this one night on board. Even the Disney characters dress up—one of our favorite memories is being "attacked" by Zombie Goofy one Halloween on board the *Magic,* while his guide murmured "Brains!" as they shuffled along.

Most of the family activities have a Halloween theme: Animation classes feature scary characters, the crafts sessions may be villain-themed, and even the karaoke is spooky. As darkness falls, photographers are stationed in each ship's atrium before and after dinner, so families can get photos of themselves dressed up. Kids can visit various areas of the ship to trick-or-treat.

DCL ships begin celebrating Halloween in September, just as at the theme parks. Expect to see pumpkins, black cats, and other decor starting around the last week of September and running through

October 31. Every ship offers Halloween-themed movies, deck parties, craft-making, and more.

Introduce your kids to the audience-participation legacy of *The Rocky Horror Picture Show* at the **Nightmare Before Christmas Sing and Scream.** Sing along with the movie, and then meet Jack and Sally after the show. There's also a new Halloween-themed deck party, *Mickey's Calling All the Monsters Mouse-Querade,* along with storytelling sessions for kids. For the grown-ups, the ship's dance club hosts a costume party.

THANKSGIVING

IF YOUR CRUISE DATES INCLUDE THE FOURTH THURSDAY in November, you'll be celebrating Thanksgiving aboard your ship. Expect to see Mickey, Minnie, Goofy, and Donald in their Pilgrim costumes, plus many other Disney characters in seasonal outfits. However, don't be surprised to see the rest of the ship already decked out for Christmas. The main dining rooms on each ship will serve a traditional Thanksgiving menu. And it wouldn't be Turkey Day without (American) football, even on DCL. Games are broadcast on each ship's big Funnel Vision LED screen near the family pool, as well as at the sports bars.

CHRISTMAS, HANUKKAH, AND KWANZAA

DISNEY BEGINS DECORATING ITS SHIPS FOR THE WINTER holidays around the middle of November. Holiday-themed activities, events, and entertainment usually start around December 1 each year, including a Christmas tree, Hanukkah menorah, and Kwanzaa kinara placed in each ship's atrium. A tree-lighting ceremony typically takes place on the first night of each cruise in December.

Family activities include making holiday greeting cards, drawing Disney characters in holiday outfits, building gingerbread houses, and so on. As at Epcot theme park, each ship will have storytellers scheduled throughout the day, along with special holiday-themed merchandise. Expect to see Mickey, Minnie, Goofy, and other characters dressed in winter finery, and lots of holiday movies on your stateroom television.

The most interesting decorations, however, are on **Castaway Cay,** where palm trees are decorated with garland, lights, and bulbs, and plastic snowmen sit on the sand. Disney characters wear holiday-themed island outfits, and even the shuttle bus from the dock is decorated with reindeer antlers.

Religious services are typically offered during each night of Hanukkah. A Catholic Mass is held at midnight on December 24, and a Mass and interdenominational service are held on December 25. Santa Claus distributes small gifts to children in the atrium on Christmas morning, along with milk and cookies. Should you need a little gift-wrapping help, that service is available on board at no extra charge. Check your *Personal Navigator* for the location, or ask at Guest Services.

Finally, the ship's onboard music, piped into the hallways and public areas, switches from standard Disney tunes to Christmas-themed tracks. Some people enjoy it; others prefer the standard Disney music.

NEW YEAR'S EVE

DURING THE DAY, video screens on each ship's pool deck display a clock counting down the hours, minutes, and seconds until midnight. The pool deck is also the site for a big family-themed party in the evening, with DJs and live entertainment continuing through midnight. Each ship's dance club also hosts a party, complete with DJ, hats, noisemakers, confetti, and bubbly drinks at midnight. Families will want to see the special fireworks display and the atrium's balloon drop at midnight. The ships' kids' clubs host parties early in the evening, allowing the little ones to get to bed at a reasonable hour.

NIGHTCLUBS, BARS, CAFÉS, *and* LOUNGES

*un*official **TIP**
The drinking age on all DCL itineraries is 21. The exception is round-trip sailings from a European port, in which case guests ages 18–20 traveling with a parent or guardian may drink with the parent's written consent. (That means under-21 honeymooners cruising in Europe without their parents can't imbibe.)

DISNEY CRUISE LINE'S SHIPS and entertainment are targeted primarily to families, but each ship has a collection of adult-oriented nightclubs and lounges to visit. All serve alcohol. Nightclubs typically offer dancing and live acts, such as magicians; lounges are oriented to conversation, with smaller spaces and comfortable seating.

This section lists the nightclubs and lounges found across all four ships; we've included the **Cove Café** coffee bar as well, since it also serves alcoholic drinks. Club hours vary, so check your *Personal Navigator* for exact schedules.

ON THE *MAGIC*

Cove Café   LOCATION: **Deck 9 Midship**

SETTING AND ATMOSPHERE Cove Café is the *Magic*'s adults-only coffee bar and one of our favorite places on the ship. The walls are covered in a combination of light-cherry-colored wood paneling and upholstered fabric, while the floor is a mixture of honey-tinted hardwoods. What we like best is the way Disney has arranged seating along the curved, L-shaped bar: At one end is a private rounded corner cutout with a couple of comfortable stuffed chairs. At the opposite end is an open area with satellite TV, couches, and armchairs. Depending on how social you're feeling, you can sit by yourself at one end or be among a group at the other.

SELECTIONS Cove serves just about every java you can think of: espresso, cappuccino, latte, Americano, and flavored variations. The Cove serves Illy espresso and has excellent service. Cove also serves hot teas and has a good selection of wines, Champagnes, spirits, and mixed drinks. Prices for these are the same as throughout the rest of the ship.

Besides beverages, the Cove Café has a self-serve refrigerated case stocked with small bites to eat throughout the day. Breakfast items usually include plain and chocolate croissants, Danish, and fruit. Afternoon and evening service usually consists of cookies, brownies, cakes, crackers, and fruit. Dinner, though, is our favorite because, for a couple of hours, Cove Café brings out a selection of prosciutto, dried sausages, marinated olives, cheeses, and bread. You can make a light supper out of these and a drink; because most families are either at dinner or preparing for it, there's a chance you'll have the café all to yourself.

unofficial **TIP**
If you're one of those people who needs a coffee or six every day, ask your server for a **Café Fanatic** rewards card; you'll get every sixth specialty coffee free.

COMMENTS The Wi-Fi signal here is fairly strong, making it a good spot to catch up on e-mail or the latest news. You'll also find here a small selection of current magazines and periodicals, and this is part of the real attraction at the Cove: the ability to sit in a comfy chair, surrounded by $350 million of luxury cruise ship, sip coffee, and flip through the pages of *The New Yorker* in blessed silence.

ACROSS THE SHIPS All four DCL ships have a Cove Café. Those on the *Magic* and *Wonder* are more or less identical, and they're a little larger than the Cove Cafés on the *Dream* and *Fantasy*. The Cove on the *Wonder,* however, connects to the **Outlook Café** (see page 123), which is unique to that ship. The Coves on the *Dream* and *Fantasy* are likewise almost identical twins, but they don't have the televisions found in the cafés on the *Magic* and *Wonder*. Guests at all Cove Cafés must be at least age 18 to enter, at least 21 to drink.

Promenade Lounge   LOCATION: Deck 3 Aft

SETTING AND ATMOSPHERE The Promenade Lounge hosts family activities during the day and live music at night. It's done in the same Art Deco style as the rest of the *Magic,* with cherrywood finishes, creamy lighting, and brass accents. Sixteen computers line one wall, providing 24-hour Internet access . . . because nothing goes together like alcohol and the web.

SELECTIONS Beer and wine by the glass, spirits, mixed drinks, and coffee. Free snacks are served, starting in the afternoon—mostly chips, salsa, and the like.

COMMENTS Though one of the most attractive nightspots on the ship, the Promenade Lounge sits adjacent and open to pedestrian traffic from one of the *Magic*'s main inside walkways, making it louder and less relaxing than it could be. Nighttime entertainment is usually provided by a singing duo, such as a pianist and vocalist, making for an enjoyable way to spend half an hour after a meal. (For the performers, though, it's got to be like singing in a bus station due to the outside noise. Some glass and wood partitions would work wonders here.) We recommend using the Promenade as a meeting place for groups to get a drink before dinner at Carioca's or Lumiere's (see Part Seven, Dining) or to listen to the live music with a nightcap.

ACROSS THE SHIPS There's also a Promenade Lounge on the *Wonder*. Like the Promenade on the *Magic,* it's a nice place to have a before- or after-dinner cocktail, as long as you can deal with all the people promenading past on their way to other parts of the ship. The comparable bar on the *Dream* and *Fantasy* is **Bon Voyage** (see page 126).

Signals   LOCATION: Deck 9 Midship

SETTING AND ATMOSPHERE Signals is an adults-only outdoor bar next to the adult pool. It has a few seats for those looking to get some shade, but most patrons take their drinks back to their deck chairs to sip in the sun.

SELECTIONS Much of Signals' menu is devoted to popular beers and frozen drinks, but they can whip up almost anything you can think of. Signals also serves coffee, juices, and bottled water. Soda machines are nearby.

COMMENTS It doesn't have much atmosphere to speak of, but due to its location near the Quiet Cove Pool, it is a little quieter than most bars.

ACROSS THE SHIPS Only the *Magic* and *Wonder* have Signals bars. The *Dream* and *Fantasy* have a total of four outdoor bars: one on each ship called **Currents** and another on each ship called **Waves** (see pages 126 and 128, respectively). Drinks and service are comparable at all of these, but we think Currents has the best views and the nicest decor. Also, Signals serves guests age 21 and older only, while Currents and Waves welcome kids.

After Hours

This is Disney's name for the collection of bars on the *Magic*'s Deck 3 Forward. It includes **Fathoms,** a venue for live entertainment and dancing; **Keys,** a piano bar; and **O'Gills Pub,** a sports bar. Newly rethemed after the ship's fall 2013 dry dock, After Hours has a contemporary urban nightclub theme, pulled together by a new white-and-silver color scheme, accented by chrome light fixtures. It's a welcome improvement over the former club space, Beat Street, which consisted of two-dimensional plywood shapes painted to look like a cityscape at night.

Some After Hours lounges, such as Fathoms, are home to family-oriented entertainment during the day, but all usually have an adults-only policy (age 18 and up to enter, 21 and up to drink) after 9 p.m.

After Hours' bars generally carry the same selection of wine and beer, although each serves its own unique line of cocktails. O'Gills Pub, the sports bar, also has a collection of Irish beers not found elsewhere.

Fathoms LOCATION: Deck 3 Forward

SETTING AND ATMOSPHERE Formerly Rockin' Bar D, Fathoms has an undersea theme: fiber-optic light fixtures shaped like jellyfish, sand-art murals along the bar, and silver-and-black bench seating that undulates like ocean waves. Six sets of couches are built into Fathoms' back wall, providing an excellent semiprivate view of the entertainment stage.

The middle of the club holds a dance floor and a raised stage with a professional sound system and lighting. Armchairs upholstered in silver fabric are arranged in groups of two or three around circular cocktail tables. These help control the echo in Fathoms' large, open floor plan.

SELECTIONS Sea-themed cocktails make up most of Fathoms' bar menu, although beer, wine, and spirits are also available. Drinks range in price from $8.75 for a **Black Pearl** (Crown Royal, Drambuie, and Coke) to $10.75 for a **Blue Tang** (Grey Goose citrus vodka, peach schnapps, blue curaçao, pineapple juice, and sugared rum). Our favorite is the $9.75 **Anemone,** with gin, mango puree, and muddled lemon, orange, and lime, topped with Champagne.

COMMENTS Like other DCL nightclubs, Fathoms does double-duty during the day by hosting family-oriented activities, such as scavenger hunts, bingo, and talent shows. At night the stage hosts everything from game shows to live music, dancing, DJs, karaoke, comedians, magicians, and other performers. The game shows' setups follow well-known television models: There's one similar to *The Newlywed Game,* for example, where contestants try to guess how their partner will answer some random set of questions. This being Disney, though, you probably won't hear any questions about "making whoopee."

ACROSS THE SHIPS Fathoms doesn't have an identical sibling on the other ships, but it's most similar to **WaveBands** on the *Wonder* (see page 125), **Evolution** on the *Dream* (see page 129), and **The Tube** on the *Fantasy* (see page 138).

Keys LOCATION: Deck 3 Forward

SETTING AND ATMOSPHERE Keys features live piano music nightly. Six large porthole windows run along one of the rectangular room's long walls. The bar is in the middle of the opposite wall, and the piano player is between the two, at the far end of the room from the entrance doors.

Keys' theming got an overhaul during the *Magic*'s 2013 dry dock, and it's now supposed to evoke a Chicago-style lounge from the 1960s. The new furnishings include modern sofas and chairs whose curved, radius-style arms and backs are in marked contrast to the formless oversize chairs of the previous decor. Gone also is the pastel carpet, in favor of a crisp silver with geometric sunbursts. The live entertainment's audio levels tend to be a bit loud for such a small space, but it's a pleasant enough experience.

SELECTIONS The bar menu includes specialty drinks with music-themed names, such as the **Moji-Do,** a mojito; **Bloody Mi-Re,** a Bloody Mary with vodka, yellow-tomato juice, lime, and whiskey-flavored Worcestershire sauce; and **Rob Roy,** made the typical way (Scotch, vermouth, and bitters), only *Rob* is spelled with the musical symbol for a flat note. Most of these cocktails are about $10.75, about $5 more per drink than at O'Gills Pub (see next profile). The most expensive drink is a $15 Manhattan, made with Jack Daniel's Sinatra Select whiskey, Antica Formula vermouth, and Cointreau. Coffee, cappuccino, and espresso are available, too, but we recommend the Cove Café if you're looking for those.

COMMENTS Live entertainment usually begins with a show around 7:30 p.m.; a typical night's schedule will have more performances around 9:30, 10:30, and 11:30 p.m. The pianists are acceptable, if nondescript, and play medleys of well-known songs by familiar artists. Some nights have themes, such as '50s and '60s hits, Elvis, or Simon and Garfunkel, and you can always make requests.

During the day, Keys is often used for group seminars on everything from wine and spirits to acupuncture, Chinese herbs, and back-pain treatments. (We sense a "feel better one way or another" theme here.) Check your *Personal Navigator* for details. The bar typically opens anywhere from 5:30 to 6:30 p.m. Children are admitted to Keys until 9 p.m., when it becomes an adults-only venue until its midnight closing.

ACROSS THE SHIPS The *Magic*'s Keys is most similar to the *Wonder*'s **Cadillac Lounge** (see next page). The entertainment is interchangeable between the two, and the retro decor is a toss-up.

O'Gills Pub   LOCATION: Deck 3 Forward

SETTING AND ATMOSPHERE The former Diversions has been rechristened as an Irish bar—the name is a nod to the Disney classic *Darby O'Gill and the Little People*—although it's an "Irish bar" in the same way that Lucky Charms is an "Irish breakfast," which is to say not very. Sure, there's a clover pattern woven into the green carpet and background music that features a lot of fiddle-and-flute and U2, but if you've come expecting Raglan Road at Walt Disney World, you're in for a disappointment.

Nine wall-mounted televisions provide live satellite coverage of whatever sports are being played around the world. Comfortable burgundy-leather banquettes are built into the wall, and padded leather armchairs surround the tables set within the banquettes. In the middle of the room, about a dozen bar-height tables and stools provide the best views of the most TVs.

SELECTIONS The bar menu includes a beer flight of five (5-ounce) Irish brews ($9.75). There's also a selection of Irish whiskeys: Tullamore Dew ($9.25), Kilbeggan ($9.25), Middleton ($11.50), and Connemara ($12.50). Beyond these are standard drinks you'll find throughout the ships, including cocktails; red, white, and sparkling wines; and Scotch and other whiskeys. The cocktails are reasonably priced at $5.75 each. Try the **Royal Velvet,** a mix of Guinness stout and sparkling wine.

COMMENTS A comfy spot to sit, sip, and watch the game.

ACROSS THE SHIPS O'Gills Pub on the *Magic* joins the *Fantasy*'s bar of the same name (see page 134). Along with the *Dream*'s **687** (see page 131), these are the DCL fleet's upscale sports bars. The bigger televisions at the *Magic*'s O'Gills make it easier to watch events from across the room. The open seating at **Diversions** on the *Wonder* (see page 124) means that you're more likely to interact with other guests, whereas you can more easily keep to yourself at 687 and both O'Gills.

ON THE *WONDER*

Cove Café LOCATION: Deck 9 Forward

COMMENTS See profile of Cove Café on the *Magic* (page 118) for details.

Outlook Café LOCATION: Deck 10 Forward

SETTING AND ATMOSPHERE What makes the Outlook Café special is that its seating area is surrounded by large glass windows, making it the perfect venue in which to get some sun in a climate-controlled environment. This means air-conditioning when the *Wonder* is in the Caribbean and heat when it's plying the waters off Alaska.

SELECTIONS Coffees, teas, wine, beer, mixed drinks, and Champagne by the glass. Complimentary snacks are also offered.

COMMENTS An extension of the Cove Café, the Outlook Café, found upstairs via a spiral staircase, is a lovely place to while away some time.

ACROSS THE SHIPS The Outlook Café is unique to the *Wonder*. As at the Cove Cafés, guests must be age 18 to enter, 21 to drink.

Promenade Lounge LOCATION: Deck 3 Aft

COMMENTS See profile of Promenade Lounge on the *Magic* (page 119) for details.

Signals LOCATION: Deck 9 Midship

COMMENTS See profile of Signals on the *Magic* (page 120) for details.

Route 66

This is the designation for the bars and lounges found on the *Wonder*'s Deck 3 Forward. As you might guess from the name, the theming is a nostalgic tribute to what was once America's premier highway: road signs, old-timey gas pumps, and murals depicting billboards and postcards from the days before the Jet Age.

Route 66 has a dance club, **WaveBands,** that also hosts games and entertainers, such as magicians, at night. A piano bar, the **Cadillac Lounge,** and a sports bar, **Diversions,** round out the area. Of these, we like Cadillac Lounge the most, but we find all the clubs far too large and impersonal to be truly enjoyable. Some Route 66 lounges, such as WaveBands, are home to family-oriented entertainment during the day, but all usually have an adults-only policy after 9 p.m.

Route 66's bars have substantially the same drink menus, but the Cadillac Lounge is the only club of the three that serves Champagne by the glass.

Cadillac Lounge　LOCATION: Deck 3 Forward

SETTING AND ATMOSPHERE This is the *Wonder*'s piano bar. The decor pays tribute to 1950s-era Cadillac cars by way of leather-upholstered bar-stools and chairs, couches made to look like automobile rear seats, and a bar built into a replica of the front of a Cadillac Coupe de Ville, complete with working headlights.

"Designed by General Motors" isn't something we normally listen for when discussing bar theming, but it works here. The furnishings—with dark woods; carpets in burgundy, gold, and fuchsia; leather-covered walls; chrome accents; and those butter-and-chocolate-colored leather barstools—clearly indicate that this is a bar meant to evoke a very specific time and place.

The best seats in the house are in the far corner, opposite the main entrance and to the right of the piano player. These include a comfortable leather couch and two leather armchairs, plus a side table to hold drinks. From here you can listen to the music and watch some of the action at the bar, tucked away in your own discreet corner of the lounge.

SELECTIONS The Cadillac Lounge serves beer, wine, spirits, and cocktails, and it's the only bar in Route 66 that serves Champagne by the glass (outside Route 66, the **Outlook Café** also serves Champagne; see previous page). Coffee, cappuccino, and espresso are available as well, but we'd recommend the Cove Café if you're looking for those. Free snacks and appetizers, including caviar, are available all evening.

COMMENTS Live entertainment usually begins with a show around 7:30 p.m.; a typical night's schedule will have more performances around 9:30, 10:30, and 11:30 p.m. The pianists are acceptable, if nondescript, and play medleys of well-known songs by familiar artists. Some nights have themes, such as '50s and '60s hits, Elvis, or Simon and Garfunkel, and you can always make requests.

During the day, the Cadillac Lounge is often used for group seminars on everything from wine and spirits to homeopathic treatments like acupuncture. Check your *Personal Navigator* for details. The bar typically opens anywhere from 5:30 to 6:30 p.m. Children are admitted to the Cadillac Lounge until 9 p.m., when it becomes an adults-only venue until its midnight closing.

ACROSS THE SHIPS The Cadillac Lounge is most similar to the *Magic*'s **Keys** (see page 121). The entertainment is interchangeable between the two, and the retro decor is a toss-up.

Diversions　LOCATION: Deck 3 Forward

SETTING AND ATMOSPHERE Diversions is the *Wonder*'s sports bar. Large LCD screens are mounted on walls and columns all around the room, allowing you to watch multiple games in progress at the same time. There's plenty of seating—mostly large fabric-covered and upholstered chairs, plus a handful of semicircular booths in the back—to accommodate large crowds. If you're interested in playing a few games, Diversions has tables for checkers, chess, and backgammon too.

SELECTIONS Diversions usually has a hot-appetizer bar available during games, with nachos, hot dogs, wings, and other bar food. A full drink menu is available, and waitstaff serve you at your seat so you don't have to miss any of the game.

COMMENTS We've had a good time watching basketball at Diversions. Given the size of the ship, the odds are good that you'll be able to find other fans of your favorite teams too. And because Diversions' satellite feed pulls in sporting events from around the world, there's always something to watch. If there's a specific game that you want to see, show up at least 30 minutes before the game and ask a member of the crew to find the right station—with literally hundreds of channels, it sometimes takes a while to find the right one.

Besides televised sports, Diversions hosts family-oriented and adult activities throughout the day, ranging from Disney-character-drawing classes for kids to trivia contests and afternoon beer tastings. Check your *Personal Navigator* for the schedule.

ACROSS THE SHIPS Diversions is the least interesting sports bar in the DCL fleet, with decor more likely to be found in an Omaha Marriott than on a billion-dollar cruise ship. **687** on the *Dream* (see page 131) and the Irish-themed **O'Gills** on the *Magic* and *Fantasy* (see pages 122 and 134, respectively) are a little more upscale. Diversions' open floor plan means that you're more likely to interact with other guests, whereas you can keep to yourself more easily at 687 and O'Gills.

WaveBands   LOCATION: Deck 3 Forward

SETTING AND ATMOSPHERE This is the *Wonder's* dance club. The idea behind the theming is that you're supposed to be inside a radio. Lightning bolts line the ceiling, representing the flow of electricity, and illuminated green photographs of computer circuit boards line the bar and railings. Padded chairs surround small, round tables, and, because WaveBands doubles as an activity space for families during the day, there's plenty of room to sit.

SELECTIONS The usual wine, beer, spirits, and mixed drinks. Free hors d'oeuvres and snacks are available all evening.

COMMENTS The ship's crew sometimes dons costumes and leads dances on WaveBands' dance floor. Thus, you may see crew members barely old enough to drink doing their best imitation of John Travolta in his white polyester suit from *Saturday Night Fever*. Depending on how much the people around you are participating—which is probably linked to how much the people around you are drinking—this is either funny or sad. Do the young 'uns a favor and jump out on the dance floor.

ACROSS THE SHIPS WaveBands doesn't have an identical sibling on the other ships, but it's most similar to **Fathoms** on the *Magic* (see page 121), **Evolution** on the *Dream* (see page 129), and **The Tube** on the *Fantasy* (see page 138). WaveBands' theming is the oldest and least sophisticated, which makes sense because the *Wonder* is the second-oldest ship and hasn't undergone refurbishment as the *Magic* has.

ON THE *DREAM*

Bon Voyage LOCATION: Deck 3 Midship

SETTING AND ATMOSPHERE Sitting just off the atrium, Bon Voyage is one of the prettiest, if not smallest, of the *Dream*'s bars, with just 10 seats at the counter plus 4 covered armchairs a few feet away. The two highlights here are the gorgeous Art Deco mural behind the bar—which shows well-heeled passengers in 1920s formal wear departing their touring cars to board the *Dream*—and the swirled, maize-yellow illuminated bar face, which reflects gold light off the beige-marble floors.

SELECTIONS Bon Voyage's bar menu is similar to that in The District (see page 128) and includes draft and bottled beer, wines by the glass and bottle, spirits, and mixed drinks, including a few special fruit-flavored martinis. Service is excellent.

COMMENTS Open from around noon to 11 p.m. daily, Bon Voyage is a good spot for groups to meet before dinner or to have a nightcap before departing for the elevators. Because it's in a heavily trafficked area, there's no live entertainment, and it isn't our first choice for a quiet drink or conversation, but it is a good place to fortify yourself while standing in those character-greeting lines. Sometimes you need a little liquid courage to face Chip 'n' Dale.

ACROSS THE SHIPS The *Fantasy* also has a Bon Voyage just off the Deck 3 atrium; the *Dream*'s Bon Voyage is more appealing, even without live entertainment. The **Promenade Lounge** is the comparable bar on the *Magic* and *Wonder* (see page 119).

Cove Café LOCATION: Deck 11 Forward

COMMENTS See profile of Cove Café on the *Magic* (page 118) for details.

Currents LOCATION: Deck 13 Forward

SETTING AND ATMOSPHERE This outdoor area has the best views of any bar on the *Dream.* Built behind and into the structure supporting the forward stairs and elevators, the curved, glossy white face of the bar mirrors the curve along the opposite deck rail and provides some shade during the day. Currents is beautiful at night, when a royal-blue neon sign (which calls to mind the nameplate on a 1950s car) lights up the bar and bar shelves, accented with matching blue tile.

Ten stationary barstools are spaced far enough apart for easy access to walk-up traffic. Most guests take drinks back to their lounge chairs, but there's also plenty of (unshaded) armchair seating around Currents.

SELECTIONS Currents serves bottled and draft beer, cocktails, and frozen drinks.

COMMENTS The one downside to Currents is that it's next to a smoking section. Depending on the prevailing winds, this is either not an issue at all or a mild annoyance.

ACROSS THE SHIPS Currents is the same on the *Dream* and the *Fantasy*. **Signals** on the *Magic* and *Wonder* is similar (see page 123), but Currents' layout is much more open, with much better views and nicer decor. Also, where Signals is adults-only, Currents welcomes kids and serves nonalcoholic concoctions just for them.

Meridian   LOCATION: Deck 12 Aft

SETTING AND ATMOSPHERE Situated between the restaurants Palo and Remy, Meridian is the *Dream*'s martini bar. It's also one of our favorite bars on the ship.

Sitting high up on Deck 12 Aft, Meridian has windows on three sides of its relatively small, square room. Panoramic views of the sunset await early diners who stop in around dusk. Antique ship-navigation maps and instruments adorn the walls and shelves. Meridian's furnishings include rich brown-leather couches and armchairs, as well as cocoa-colored teak floors with brass inlays. Meridian also has outdoor seating on a teak deck that runs along one wall of Remy. It's lovely on warm summer evenings—and in demand around dusk, so don't be surprised if it's standing room only.

SELECTIONS Meridian's bar menu emphasizes mixed drinks and spirits over beer and wine, although those are also available, as are coffees. The best thing about Meridian is the bartending staff, who will often offer to make a custom martini for you on the spot. This usually starts with the bartender inquiring whether you like fruit- or herb-based drinks and what kinds of liquors you usually prefer. A couple of minutes of muddling, shaking, and stirring, and you have the first draft of your new drink. And if it's not quite what you expected, they'll be happy to start over.

COMMENTS We recommend stopping by Meridian for its martini experience alone, even if you don't have reservations for Remy or Palo (see Part Seven). If you're dining at Remy, though, beware of the combined effect of Meridian's martinis and Remy's wine pairings—as Len found out, it may be more than you bargained for.

Meridian usually opens around 5 p.m. and stays open until midnight. It's one of the few DCL nightspots with a dress code: Inside the lounge, men should wear dress shirts and pants, and women should wear dresses, skirts and blouses, or pantsuits. If you're just visiting the outdoor area, jeans and shorts are allowed, but swimwear, T-shirts, or tank tops are verboten.

ACROSS THE SHIPS Both the *Dream* and the *Fantasy* have nearly identical Meridian lounges; the *Magic* and *Wonder* do not.

Vista Café   LOCATION: Deck 4 Midship

SETTING AND ATMOSPHERE A small, Art Deco–themed nook in a corner of Deck 4.

SELECTIONS Vista Café serves everything from coffee and complimentary pastries in the morning to beer, wine, cocktails, and light snacks at night.

COMMENTS With only four seats at the bar, this isn't the place for large groups. It's most useful as a place for a family to get a drink and a bite to eat on their way to one of the day's activities on Decks 3 or 4.

ACROSS THE SHIPS Vista Cafés can be found on both the *Dream* and the *Fantasy* but not the *Magic* or *Wonder*. Both cafés offer the same food and drink and are about the same size; the only significant difference is the decor—the Vista on the *Fantasy* has that ship's Art Nouveau theme rather than the Art Deco styling of the *Dream*. The marble floor of the *Fantasy*'s version is a bit bigger than the *Dream*'s, making the former Vista Café seem more of an intentionally designed space versus one carved out of an underutilized corner.

Waves   LOCATION: Deck 12 Aft

SETTING AND ATMOSPHERE Tucked behind the rear smokestack, Waves is an outdoor bar catering primarily to sunbathers on Deck 12. Waves' eight fixed barstools are arranged around an attractive white tile face, and the back of the bar is decorated with small tiles in varying shades of blue. An overhang above the bar provides shade for guests seated or standing at the bar, but most of the seating—upholstered blue cushions on glossy, curved-back teak booths, plus various sets of tables and chairs—is directly in the sun.

SELECTIONS The most popular drinks at Waves are bottled beers, frozen cocktails, and mixed drinks. Nonalcoholic smoothies and fruit juices are available for children and teetotalers.

COMMENTS Waves' hours vary, but it's usually open from late morning to late evening. Most visitors are coming from the lounge chairs or sports activities on Deck 13; some are just looking for a quiet spot away from the crowds.

ACROSS THE SHIPS Both the *Dream* and the *Fantasy* have Waves bars, and they're essentially identical. **Signals** is the outdoor bar on the *Magic* and *Wonder* (see page 123); Waves, however, is quieter, has nicer decor, and welcomes kids (Signals is 21-and-up only).

The District

This is the designation for the five bars and lounges on the *Dream*'s Deck 4 Aft: **District Lounge,** in a hallway connecting the different venues; **Evolution,** a dance club; **Pink,** a Champagne bar; **687,** an upscale sports bar; and **Skyline,** a cosmopolitan watering hole.

The theming is meant to evoke images of exclusive urban nightlife. Along the faux-brick walls and behind velvet ropes are black-plastic silhouettes of couples "waiting" to get in. Other walls have black-plastic images of paparazzi or simply the logos of the clubs illuminated in a repeating pattern.

Most of The District's bars open between 5 and 5:30 p.m. and stay open until midnight. District Lounge usually opens a little earlier;

Evolution operates from around 10 p.m. to 2 a.m. Hot snacks are usually provided throughout the evening in one of The District's circular pedestrian walkways.

Evolution, Pink, and Skyline only admit guests age 18 and up. Families are welcome at District Lounge and 687 until 9 p.m., when the bars become adults-only.

District Lounge   LOCATION: Deck 4 Aft

SETTING AND ATMOSPHERE An attractive, contemporary bar and seating area are bisected by a walkway connecting The District's bars. The bar seats six along its curving, white-stone front. Lights hidden beneath the black-marble top point down, creating smoky gray shadows in the stone. Behind the bar is a bronze-colored wall; orange lighting illuminates the bottles and provides this side of District Lounge with its most prominent color.

A lounge with couches and armchairs sits across the walkway opposite the bar; although it's not perfect, it's one of the more stylish places on the *Dream*. While the lounge is completely open to (and exposed to noise from) guests going from club to club, off-white leather couches, champagne-colored metal poles, and cocoa-colored carpeting provide a visual boundary marking its border. Deeper inside are U-shaped armchairs, covered outside in the same white leather and inside in deep-brown leather, arranged in groups of four around small tables. A curving, chocolate-colored, illuminated wall provides a backdrop.

SELECTIONS The bar menu has a bit of everything: draft and bottled beer, cocktails, frozen drinks, whiskeys and tequilas, and wine and Champagne by the glass and bottle. There's also a special martini menu ($8.50–$9.50) not found at other clubs in The District. A few nonalcoholic drinks and coffee are available as well.

COMMENTS The best seats are along the lounge's inside wall, where you can relax in those deep armchairs while watching everyone else shuttle between clubs. This is also the best vantage point from which to watch the District Lounge's entertainment, which includes live singers and pianists later at night. The lounge is also a good meeting place to start out the evening, especially for groups who haven't decided which of The District's bars to visit.

ACROSS THE SHIPS The District Lounge roughly corresponds to the Venice-themed **La Piazza** lounge on the *Fantasy* (see page 136) but has no relative on the *Magic* or *Wonder*. We like the District Lounge more than La Piazza: Its recessed seating allows you to enjoy a drink away from the bustle of clubgoers walking to their next destination.

Evolution   LOCATION: Deck 4 Aft

SETTING AND ATMOSPHERE The *Dream*'s dance club, Evolution is, according to Disney, designed as "an artistic interpretation of the transformation of a butterfly . . . emerging from a chrysalis." What this entails is a lot of yellow, orange, and red lights arranged in the shape of butterfly wings and hung around the club. Pairs of wings hang above the dance floor, and we'll forgive you for comparing the slightly tipsy, dancing tourists to wriggling pupae. A couple of the walls are wing-patterned, too, bathing guests seated at the leather couches alongside in hues of ginger and crimson.

Fortunately, most of the butterfly theming is concentrated around the dance floor and along a couple of back walls. Between the two, it's not as noticeable; plastic-shell chairs sit in the dimly lit sections, occasionally alongside high-backed couches. Short bar-stools line the outside edge of the room, surrounding small, round tables. The circular bar has gold-leather seats on one side, allowing guests a view of the dance floor while they drink; the other half of the bar is for walk-up traffic.

SELECTIONS Evolution's drink menu is similar to District Lounge's, offering draft and bottled beer, cocktails, spirits, and wine and Champagne by the glass and bottle.

COMMENTS Because it's one of the largest venues on the *Dream,* Evolution is the site of family activities throughout the day, holding everything from hands-on craft-making seminars to tequila tastings to time-share presentations. Evolution's adults-only entertainment usually starts later than at other bars in The District, around 10 or 10:30 p.m.; check your *Personal Navigator* for details.

unofficial **TIP**

Look carefully inside a few of the bubble lights on the wall, and you'll see a tiny pink elephant from Disney's *Dumbo.* It's a little odd because Dumbo is the mascot of the *Fantasy,* which has its own Champagne bar, the French-themed **Ooh La La** (no elephants).

Live entertainment includes magicians, comics, singers, and more. In addition to live acts, Evolution's DJs sometimes dedicate an entire night's music to a specific genre. Common themes include classic rock, disco, and something called urban country. Evolution also hosts get-togethers for adults ages 18–21, in an event helpfully called Club 18*21.

ACROSS THE SHIPS Evolution is most similar to **The Tube** dance club on the *Fantasy* (see page 138), **Fathoms** on the *Magic* (see page 121), and **WaveBands** on the *Wonder* (see page 125). We rate Evolution as the second-best dance club on Disney Cruise Line, behind The Tube. Theming, lighting, and seating are nicer than at Fathoms and WaveBands, while The Tube's London Underground ambience is better executed than Evolution's more-conceptual "caterpillar to butterfly" idea.

Pink LOCATION: Deck 4 Aft

SETTING AND ATMOSPHERE Pink, the *Dream*'s Champagne bar, is our favorite nightspot on the ship. Decorated in silvers, whites, and golds, the space is intended to make you think you're sitting inside a glass of Champagne. In the walls are embedded round lights of white and pink, tiny near the floor and larger near the ceiling, imitating the carbon dioxide fizz inside a flute of bubbly. The silver carpet's starburst pattern calls to mind bubbles rising from below, and the rounded, glossy white ceiling is meant to represent the top of the glass. The light fixtures are upside-down Champagne flutes. Behind the bar are a multitude of glass "bubbles," expanding as they rise from the bar shelf to the ceiling.

Around the bar are half a dozen stools, with silver legs and clear, oval plastic backs that continue the bubble theme. Beyond the bar, a couple of burgundy chairs sit among their silver-velvet sisters. After a few drinks, we're pretty sure these are supposed to represent rosé Champagne, of which several are served at the bar. The best seats in the house, though, are on the padded couch inside a dome-shaped cubby in the wall at one end of the lounge. Move a couple of those big chairs in front and you have a private little cocoon, or slide them away for a view of the entire room.

SELECTIONS Pink's Champagne menu includes many recognizable names: Cristal, Moët et Chandon, Taittinger, Veuve Clicquot, and the requisite Dom Pérignon. Champagne-based cocktails are also available; most include fruit juices, such as mango, pomegranate, and peach, while a few include other liquors—the **Elderbubble** ($10.50), for example, contains raspberry vodka along with Champagne and elderflower syrup. A small selection of white, red, and dessert wines is available by the glass (more by the bottle), along with a dozen or so whiskeys and Cognacs.

COMMENTS If you love Champagne, Pink is a relative bargain. Its markup is generally less than twice the average retail price—usually considerably less than what Disney charges at its theme park resorts. For example, a bottle of Taittinger La Française sells for about $35 plus tax at your local wine store. The same bottle costs $69 at Pink: a fairly standard double bar markup, but a far cry from the $108 per bottle (a triple markup) charged on Disney property. Similarly, Pink's Dom Pérignon, at $225 per bottle, is marked up a little more than one-and-a-half times over retail—at Walt Disney World's Grand Floridian Resort, it's nearly $300 a bottle.

ACROSS THE SHIPS Only the *Dream* and the *Fantasy* have Champagne bars, and this is one of the main reasons we prefer these ships over the *Magic* and the *Wonder*. However, we like Pink's relatively understated theming better than the *très feminine* French-boudoir decor of **Ooh La La** on the *Fantasy* (see page 135).

687   LOCATION: Deck 4 Aft

SETTING AND ATMOSPHERE Anytime you see a venue with a dozen flat-panel TVs, there's a good chance that it's a sports bar. On the *Dream* it's called 687, and the screens are set in rows above the bar, in a cluster at a far end of the room, and individually in some seating areas.

The bar is set in the middle of 687's rectangular floor. Four port-hole windows across from the bar provide light during the day, and moss-colored couches beneath them work to separate the wall into group-size partitions. The scarlet, green, and gold carpet and bur-gundy-painted, wood-paneled walls give 687 a more masculine feel than the sports bars on the *Fantasy, Magic,* and *Wonder.*

Besides the couches, barstools and tables are arranged around the room to provide good views of either set of televisions. A few leather-covered armchairs are also arranged around the screens and across from the couches. There's plenty of room to stand between these, too, in case you want to just catch up on some scores. Couches arranged in some of the corners provide quieter spots to unwind.

SELECTIONS Bar and table service are excellent. The menu is similar to District Lounge's and includes both draft and bottled beer, cocktails, spirits, and wine and Champagne by the glass, plus coffees and non-alcoholic drinks. Unique to 687 is a selection of "Beercktails" (a word that no self-respecting adult would ever use): cocktails of beer, spirits, and fruit juice. The most popular of these is the **Baha Fog** ($5.75), which adds a shot of tequila to a glass of Corona with lime.

COMMENTS We've spent a few evenings watching games at 687. The seating is comfortable, and it's easy to see and hear the action on the screens. Because of the way the seating is arranged, however, we've found it difficult to start conversations with other patrons. Try sitting at the bar if that's important to you.

Besides sporting events, 687 hosts family activities during the day, including movie, music, and sports trivia. A selection of board games is available in case you want to play rather than watch. Finally, this is usually where runners meet before debarking for the start of the Castaway Cay 5K run when the *Dream* is docked there.

ACROSS THE SHIPS We find 687 more upscale than **Diversions** on the *Wonder* (see page 124) or **O'Gills** on the *Magic* and *Fantasy* (see pages 122 and 134, respectively). While its seating isn't as open, it's a posh place to catch up on the day's highlights in relative quiet.

Skyline   LOCATION: Deck 4 Aft

SETTING AND ATMOSPHERE Along with Pink, Skyline is one of our two favorite bars on the *Dream*. The concept is that you're in a lounge high on the edge of some of the world's most famous cities. Behind the bar are seven "windows"—large high-definition television screens—affording panoramic views of New York City, Chicago, Rio de Janeiro, Paris, and Hong Kong.

Each city is shown for about 15 minutes across all seven screens; then the scene changes to another locale. The foreground of each view includes close-up views of apartments and offices, while the middle and background show each city's iconic architecture and landscape.

That would be mildly interesting scenery on its own, but Disney has added special effects that make Skyline beautiful. Each view shows the city in motion: Cars move along streets, neon signs blink to illuminate sidewalks, and apartment lights go on and off as their residents come and go. (Look closely and you can even see Mickey Mouse waving to you from inside a tiny apartment in Paris.) A second effect is that the scenery changes depending on the time of day you're inside. If you get here in late afternoon, you'll see the sun setting on these towns. Stay long enough—and we have—and dusk turns to evening, then evening to night.

Last, Skyline has mirrors on the walls perpendicular to the video screens. Because the mirrors are set at right angles to the screens, they reflect the videos and make the bar look longer than it is. It's a well-known decorating trick for making a small room seem larger, but it's still nice to see it included here.

The rest of the decor is natural surfaces: wood panels, ceiling, and floors, in colors ranging from honey to mahogany; dark marble countertops; and leather chairs.

SELECTIONS The specialty is "around the world" cocktails themed to the featured cities. For example, the **1914** ($8.50), representing Chicago, pairs Absolut Vanilla and Absolut Kurant vodkas with fresh blackberries and raspberries; the **Zen-Chanted** ($10.50), representing Hong Kong, is made with 3Vodka (distilled from soybeans), Zen green-tea liqueur, Cointreau, and guava and lime juices.

COMMENTS Adding movement to the scenery means the view at Skyline doesn't get boring. It also means that the club doesn't need a television to hold its patrons' attention. And the cityscapes are a great way to break the ice with fellow cruisers.

ACROSS THE SHIPS Although there are Skylines on both the *Dream* and the *Fantasy*, their drink menus are mostly different. Drinks at the *Dream*'s Skyline tend toward the fruity, whereas drinks at the *Fantasy*'s Skyline make more use of herbs and spices, such as basil, thyme, coriander, cilantro, and paprika.

ON THE *FANTASY*

Bon Voyage   LOCATION: Deck 3 Midship

SETTING AND ATMOSPHERE Just off the atrium and done in the same Art Nouveau style as the rest of the ship, Bon Voyage is one of the prettiest bars on the *Fantasy*. Behind the bar are two gold-and-white peacocks etched in glass, while the bar's face is a translucent gold marble. Cinnamon-colored wood accents complete the look. Bon Voyage has just 10 seats at the counter, plus 2 fabric-covered couches and 6 armchairs a few feet away.

SELECTIONS The bar menu is similar to that at La Piazza (see page 136) and includes draft and bottled beer, wines by the glass and bottle, spirits, and mixed drinks, including a few special fruit-flavored martinis.

COMMENTS Near the atrium and open from around noon to 11 p.m. daily, Bon Voyage is a good spot for groups to meet before dinner or have a nightcap before departing for the elevators. Because it's in a heavily trafficked area, there's no live entertainment at the bar, and it's not our first choice for a quiet drink or conversation.

ACROSS THE SHIPS The *Dream*'s Bon Voyage is done in Art Deco rather than the *Fantasy*'s Art Nouveau version and is more appealing, even without live entertainment. The **Promenade Lounge** is the comparable bar on the *Magic* and *Wonder* (see page 119).

Cove Café   LOCATION: Deck 11 Forward

COMMENTS See profile of Cove Café on the *Magic* (page 118) for details.

Currents   LOCATION: Deck 13 Forward

COMMENTS See profile of Currents on the *Dream* (page 126) for details.

Meridian   LOCATION: Deck 12 Aft

COMMENTS See profile of Meridian on the *Dream* (page 127) for details.

Vista Café   LOCATION: Deck 4 Midship

COMMENTS See profile of Vista Café on the *Dream* (page 127) for details.

Waves   LOCATION: Deck 12 Aft

COMMENTS See profile of Waves on the *Dream* (page 128) for details.

Europa

This is the designation for the five nightspots on the *Fantasy*'s Deck 4 Aft: **O'Gills Pub,** a sports bar; **Ooh La La,** a Champagne bar; **La Piazza,** an Italian-inspired lounge; **Skyline,** a cosmopolitan watering hole; and **The Tube,** a London subway–themed dance club.

While the nightlife districts on the other three ships have distinctive theming, Europa has next to none. The ostensible theme is Europe, but the decor consists mostly of just shiny gold walls, with each club's name illuminated and repeated in a pattern. That said, one nice touch found only at Europa lies in the round black-and-white photos on the walls: The images, which feature European icons, including the Eiffel Tower, London's Big Ben, and the Leaning Tower of Pisa, turn into short animated videos. Also, for what it's worth, the bathrooms here are decorated fabulously and worth a special trip.

Most of Europa's bars open between 5 and 5:30 p.m. and stay open until midnight. La Piazza usually opens a little earlier than that; The Tube operates from around 10 p.m. to 2 a.m. Hot appetizers are usually provided throughout the evening in one of La Piazza's circular pedestrian walkways.

Ooh La La, Skyline, and The Tube only admit guests age 18 and up. Families are welcome at La Piazza and O'Gills Pub until 9 p.m., when they become adults-only.

O'Gills Pub   LOCATION: Deck 4 Aft

SETTING AND ATMOSPHERE The *Fantasy*'s sports bar, O'Gills lies just off one side of La Piazza (see next page). It's ostensibly an Irish pub, but it's the least visually interesting bar in Europa. The attempts at theming—Irish music and liberal use of four-leaf clovers—are halfhearted at best; with some paint, antiques-store scavenging, and the right "beer of the month" subscription, O'Gills could pass as a Chicago-, Dallas-, or Green Bay–themed bar.

The centerpiece is a huge high-def video screen in the back corner, which shows sporting events and sports news all day long. Several other smaller screens are distributed throughout the room, and there's plenty of seating and standing room.

SELECTIONS The bar menu includes bottled and draft beer, including a house draft lager and several Irish brews. Wine is available by the glass and bottle, and the friendly bartenders can mix up any cocktail you want. The specialty is Irish whiskey and Scotch; a private-label Irish cream liqueur is on the menu too. The mixed drinks are reasonably priced at $5.75 each. Try the **Royal Velvet,** a mix of Guinness stout and sparkling wine.

COMMENTS You wouldn't come here for the Irish ambience, but as a generic sports bar, O'Gills isn't bad.

ACROSS THE SHIPS There's another O'Gills on the *Magic* (see page 122). As a sports bar, however, it's similar to **687** on the *Dream* (see page 131) and **Diversions** on the *Wonder* (see page 124). We prefer 687, O'Gills on the *Magic,* and Diversions because they have better sight lines to the TV screens from the seats.

Ooh La La LOCATION: Deck 4 Aft

SETTING AND ATMOSPHERE This is the *Fantasy*'s Champagne bar. The French-boudoir theme is enough to make you break out in "Lady Marmalade" from *Moulin Rouge:* rose-colored upholstery on the walls, purple carpet, and chairs lined with gold fabric. Along one wall are a series of padded couches in ivory and green. Gold-edged mirrors and fleurs-de-lis line the walls. A single red chair and a couple of small, red-topped side tables provide a touch of bold color.

The bar, at the far end of the lounge, seats six around its black marble top. In keeping with the boudoir theme, the mirror behind the bar looks like an oversize version of one you'd find on the dressing table of a fashionable Frenchwoman at the *fin de siècle.* And because it's a Champagne bar, hundreds of small glass bubbles fill the mirrors.

SELECTIONS Ooh La La serves reasonably priced Champagnes by the glass and bottle. A couple of these, such as Pommery Rosé Brut and Bollinger La Grande Année, aren't found at Pink, the Champagne bar on the *Dream.* Available along with these are such familiar names as Taittinger and Dom Pérignon. A glass of bubbly starts at around $6 and goes up to $18; bottles cost anywhere from around $50 to $500.

Champagne cocktails, with fruit juices and other liquors, cost around $11, but remember the Second Law of Champagne: If it needs another ingredient, you're drinking the wrong Champagne. (The First Law: Champagne goes with everything!) Sparkling wines, along with reds and whites, are available by the glass and bottle, and the fully stocked bar can furnish virtually any cocktail you like.

COMMENTS The best seats in Ooh La La are on the L-shaped silver couch near the main entrance. It's the perfect private place to do some people-watching. Another nice touch is the use of area rugs to mark off sections of seats—it's possible to mingle within that small area, having individual conversations while still being part of the group. The club has three porthole windows—which we didn't expect—with ocean views and seating below. If you visit during the late afternoon, the light from outside provides a gentle transition from day to dusk. One of our favorite bartenders, Lindsay, can be found pouring bubbly and mixing cocktails at Ooh La La.

ACROSS THE SHIPS Only the *Dream* and the *Fantasy* have Champagne bars, and this is one of the main reasons we prefer these ships over the *Magic* and the *Wonder*. However, we like the relatively understated theming of **Pink** on the *Dream* (see page 130) better than the over-the-top decor of Ooh La La.

La Piazza   LOCATION: Deck 4 Aft

SETTING AND ATMOSPHERE This Venetian-themed lounge sits near the front of Europa. Appropriately, La Piazza ("The Plaza") serves as the walkway to O'Gills and Ooh La La, whose entrances sit just off this venue; farther beyond are Skyline and The Tube, so you'll walk by La Piazza on the way.

The bar sits in the middle of a bright circular room. It's themed to look like an Italian carousel, its ceiling decorated with hundreds of carousel lights. Around the bar are rose-colored barstools; lining the wall are golden, high-backed, upholstered couches with small tables for drinks. The couches are separated, elevated, and set into niches in the walls, making them good vantages from which to watch people walk between the clubs.

SELECTIONS La Piazza's bar menu features Peroni and Moretti, two Italian beers, as well as Prosecco (Italian sparkling wine) and *limoncello* (an Italian lemon-flavored liqueur). These ingredients also make their way into La Piazza's five signature cocktails—the **Mercutio** ($5.75), for example, features Absolut Pears vodka, limoncello, grappa, and fresh lemon juice, with the sweetness of the pear and grappa balancing out the tartness of the citrus.

COMMENTS The couches are good spots for watching La Piazza's live entertainment, which has been an up-tempo jazz trio on each of our cruises. If you're not into music, our favorite pastime at La Piazza takes place starting at 11 p.m., when we start to wager a round of drinks on the number of couples who will stop to take photos on La Piazza's Vespa motorcycle-and-sidecar prop in the next 10 minutes. The over–under on that bet is usually 2.5, and the rules prohibit shouting encouragement to the *ubriachi*.

ACROSS THE SHIPS Somewhat similar to **District Lounge** on the *Dream* (see page 129), La Piazza has a better drink menu, while District Lounge has a better layout. Neither the *Magic* nor the *Wonder* has a comparable bar.

Skyline   LOCATION: Deck 4 Aft

SETTING AND ATMOSPHERE Skyline is our favorite bar on the *Fantasy*. The concept is that you're in a lounge high on the edge of some of the world's most famous cities. Behind the bar are seven "windows"—large high-definition television screens—affording panoramic views of seven cities: Athens, Barcelona, Budapest, Florence, London, Paris, and St. Petersburg.

Each city is shown for about 15 minutes across all seven screens; then the scene changes to another locale. The foreground of each view includes close-up views of apartments and offices, while the middle and background show each city's iconic architecture and landscape.

That would be mildly interesting scenery on its own, but Disney has added special effects that make Skyline beautiful. Each view shows the city in motion: Cars move along streets, neon signs blink to illuminate sidewalks, and apartment lights go on and off as their residents come and go. (Look closely and you can even see Mickey Mouse waving to you from inside a tiny apartment in Paris.) A second effect is that the scenery changes depending on the time of day you're inside. If you get here in late afternoon, you'll see the sun setting on these towns. Stay long enough—and we have—and dusk turns to evening, then evening to night.

Last, Skyline has mirrors on the walls perpendicular to the video screens. Because the mirrors are set at right angles to the screens, they reflect the videos and make the bar look longer than it is. It's a well-known decorating trick for making a small room seem larger, but it's still nice to see it included here.

The rest of the decor is natural surfaces: wood panels, ceiling, and floors, in colors ranging from honey to mahogany; dark marble countertops; and leather chairs.

SELECTIONS The specialty is "around the world" cocktails themed to the featured cities. For example, **El Conquistador** ($8.50), representing Barcelona, pairs Tanqueray gin and Absolut Peppar vodka with fresh muddled strawberries, basil, and cracked black pepper; the **Aquincum** ($10.50), representing Budapest, is made with 901 Tequila, Grand Marnier, paprika, and freshly squeezed lime juice.

COMMENTS Adding movement to the scenery means the view at Skyline doesn't get boring. It also means that the club doesn't need a television to hold its patrons' attention. And the cityscapes are a great way to break the ice with fellow cruisers.

ACROSS THE SHIPS Although there are Skylines on both the *Dream* and the *Fantasy,* the latter one features two more cities in its "windows" than the one on the *Dream.* Also, their drink menus are mostly different. Drinks at the *Dream*'s Skyline tend to be flavored with fruits and fruit juices, such as cranberry, pomegranate, lemon, and lime; drinks on the *Fantasy*'s Skyline are made with fruits, too, but also with herbs and spices, such as basil, thyme, coriander, cilantro, and paprika. We find that these extra ingredients add another layer of flavor and cut some of the fruits' sweetness. If you're unsure about ordering one of these cocktails, ask the bartender to make the drink without the herbs or spices, and take a sip. Then have the remaining ingredients added and sip again.

The Tube LOCATION: Deck 4 Aft

SETTING AND ATMOSPHERE With a London subway–meets–*Austin Powers* theme, The Tube is the *Fantasy*'s dance club. Its decor includes leather couches with prints that look like Underground tickets, 1960s-mod egg-shaped chairs, and a floor painted like a London subway map. We especially like the upholstered leather couch set deep inside the lounge because it's under a set of lights in the shape of a crown and across from two shiny silver armchairs designed to look like thrones. A couple of red phone booths are set on either side of the dance floor. *Yeah, baby!*

SELECTIONS The Tube's circular bar, set under Big Ben's clock face, serves a typical menu of bottled beer, mixed drinks, spirits, and wine and Champagne by the glass. The Tube also serves six signature drinks, several of which are made with sodas or sparkling wines. Our favorite is **Mind the Gap** ($8.50), a mix of whiskey, Drambuie, and Coke.

COMMENTS The Tube usually opens around 10 p.m. and sometimes gets things going with a quick game of Match Your Mate (think *The Newlywed Game,* only groovier). Dancing usually gets started around 10:30 or 11 p.m. Most of the music is contemporary dance, but there are themed nights with disco and, of course, British hits.

ACROSS THE SHIPS The club's closest counterparts are **Fathoms** on the *Magic* (see page 121), **WaveBands** on the *Wonder* (see page 125), and **Evolution** on the *Dream* (see page 129). The Tube, though, is our favorite dance club on any of the ships.

PART NINE

ACTIVITIES, RECREATION, *and* SHOPPING

BESIDES EAT, DRINK, BE ENTERTAINED, and explore ports, there's lots to do on every Disney Cruise Line (DCL) itinerary:

- **Family activities** are held throughout the day and include trivia contests, bingo, deck parties, and more.
- **Children's programs,** the strength of Disney Cruise Line, begin as early as 7 a.m.
- It wouldn't be a Disney cruise without **character greetings,** including Mickey, Minnie, and the Disney princesses.
- Each ship's **pools and water-play areas** are the center of activity during the day on most cruises.
- **Onboard seminars** are inexpensive (some are free) and cover everything from cooking demonstrations to wine tastings.
- Runners and sports fans will find a **measured track** on each ship, plus **basketball, volleyball, miniature golf,** and more.
- After a tough day on shore, you can relax at the **spa.**
- **Shopping opportunities** are available on board and in port.

FAMILY ACTIVITIES

BINGO

DCL IS ONE OF THE FEW CRUISE LINES that have no casino gambling on board. What it does have is bingo, played most days on most ships, with at least two 90-minute sessions per day. The cost to play is about $10 per paper card per game, with four to six games played per hour. Prizes range from duffel bags filled with DCL swag to actual cash jackpots of several thousand dollars.

With that much money at stake, it's no surprise that many people take these games seriously. Games are fast-paced, and players are expected to keep up. If you're bringing along your family, consider renting an electronic bingo machine for about $20 (plus the cost of the cards). These machines receive signals from the bingo console, telling them which numbers have been called. Because the machines keep track of the state of the game, there's no need to be hypervigilant every second.

DECK PARTIES

FEATURING DISNEY CHARACTERS, deck parties are usually held several times per cruise, usually near the family pool or in the ship's main lobby. The first party, known as the **Sail-Away Celebration,** happens as you leave port on embarkation day. Expect to hear every Black Eyed Peas song ever recorded over the rest of your cruise.

All outdoor parties are high-energy affairs, with loud music, dancing, games, and other activities, plus videos displayed on the ship's giant LED screen. The indoor versions omit only the giant video screens. Check your *Personal Navigator* for dates and times.

FAMILY NIGHTCLUBS

IN ADDITION TO ITS MYRIAD adult-entertainment offerings (see Part Eight), DCL has what would be an oxymoron in any other context: the family nightclub. Set up like grown-up nightspots, with snazzy decor and their own bars, tables and chairs, and dance floors, these lounges offer daytime and nighttime entertainment, including comedy shows, trivia contests, cooking demos, karaoke, line dancing, and more. (Many of the same activities are also offered during the day at some adult lounges.) Refreshments are served, including cocktails for Mom and Dad and smoothies and sodas for the kids (all at an extra charge).

Family nightclubs are found on each ship's Deck 4 Midship. On the *Wonder,* it's **Studio Sea;** on the other three ships, it's **D Lounge.** Hours vary, so check your *Personal Navigator* for details.

On some cruises of seven nights or longer, a guest-participation talent show will be on the activity list. We've seen some amazingly talented child gymnasts, dancers, and magicians on board, as well as charming parent–child duets, a few little kids being randomly cute, and a 15-year-old singer who could give Beyoncé a run for her money. If this is something you think you might like to participate in, be sure to pack whatever shoes, costumes, karaoke tracks, or sheet music you might need to perform. DCL prohibits guests from bringing their own musical instruments on board, but if you need a piano or guitar for your performance, that can probably be arranged.

SPORTS AND FITNESS

THE DISNEY SHIPS have several sports options available for families, covered later in this chapter, beginning on page 164.

CHILDREN'S PROGRAMS *and* ACTIVITIES

DCL YOUTH CLUBS IN BRIEF

FLOUNDER'S REEF NURSERY   *Wonder*

LOCATION Deck 5 Aft   AGES 6 or 12 months (depending on itinerary)–3 years
OPENS Varies   CLOSES 11 p.m.
FEE $9/hour for first child, $8/hour for each additional child
MEALS Bring your own food, milk, and formula

IT'S A SMALL WORLD NURSERY   *Magic, Dream, Fantasy*

LOCATION Deck 5 Aft   AGES 6 or 12 months (depending on itinerary)–3 years
OPENS Varies   CLOSES 11 p.m.
FEE $9/hour for first child, $8/hour for each additional child
MEALS Bring your own food, milk, and formula

OCEANEER CLUB/OCEANEER LAB   *All ships*

LOCATION Deck 5 Midship   AGES 3–12 years
OPENS Varies   CLOSES Midnight
FEE None   MEALS Lunch and dinner

EDGE   *All ships*

LOCATION Deck 2 Midship (*Magic, Wonder*), Deck 13 Forward (*Dream, Fantasy*)
AGES 11–14 years   OPENS Varies   CLOSES 1 a.m.
FEE None   MEALS None

VIBE   *All ships*

LOCATION Deck 11 Midship (*Magic, Wonder*), Deck 5 Forward (*Dream, Fantasy*)
AGES 14–17 years   OPENS Varies   CLOSES 2 a.m.
FEE None   REFRESHMENTS Sodas (free), smoothies (extra charge)
EXTRAS Sun deck with splash pools (*Dream, Fantasy*)

WHEN IT COMES TO ENTERTAINING CHILDREN, Disney Cruise Line has no equal. Youth clubs, designed for infants to 17-year-olds, open as early as 7:30 a.m. for babies and close as late as 2 a.m. for teens. Kids can participate in organized activities, ranging from craft-making to trivia contests and dance parties, or they can play individually with computer games, board games, books, and craft materials. Most of the organized activities last 60–90 minutes, so a new event will likely start soon after your child arrives; this means kids become part of the group quickly. Based on reader feedback, it's far more likely that your child will not want to leave his or her kids' club than not want to go to it in the first place.

Outside of the kids' clubs, there's plenty for children and families to do. Much like the Disney theme parks, the DCL cruise ships offer a contained environment that allows tweens and teens to enjoy some autonomy to roam on their own. Wave Phones (a mobile phone you may use free of charge on the ship and Castaway Cay for calls, voice mail, and text messaging, only from Wave Phone to Wave Phone) mean that you'll always be able to reach your children, and the food offerings on the pool deck mean that there's no worrying about finding something to eat (or how to pay for it).

Younger children (and older ones who aren't yet pretending they don't know you) and their families have activities scheduled throughout the day, from karaoke to character greetings; check your *Personal Navigator* for times and locations. Even the not-yet-walking crew can get in on the fun, with "diaper derbies" that happen in the ships' atria—these are lots of fun to watch, even if you don't have a child participating.

unofficial **TIP**

Be careful about cruising during times when school is in session: Some cruises have so few teens and tweens traveling that the youth clubs can be kind of a bust.

Other activities include minigolf (*Dream* and *Fantasy*), the arcade (**Quarter Masters** on the *Magic* and *Wonder*; **Arr-cade** on the *Dream* and *Fantasy*), and the sports decks, all topside.

SPECIAL CONSIDERATIONS

INFANTS In 2014, Disney increased to 6 months the minimum age for infants to sail on most Alaskan, Bahamian, Caribbean, and other cruises of seven nights or less. For longer cruises, such as transatlantic and other repositioning cruises or Hawaiian cruises, infants must be 1 year old.

TWEENS AND TEENS Don't worry that your preteen or teenager is "too cool" for a Disney cruise. Based on both our own experiences and those of other parents, teens will practically forget you exist once they get a feel for the clubs and activities. In fact, before you even set foot on the ship, you should set some ground rules for how often your teen needs to check in with you. Our rule was that everyone had to eat two meals per day together during sea days and stay together during shore excursions. On Castaway Cay, we reserved morning activities for family time, and the teens were allowed to explore the island on their own after lunch.

ONLY-CHILD SITUATIONS The middle- and high-school kids' clubs are seamless for kids who are traveling with similarly aged siblings, cousins, or friends. They have a built-in companion for activities and can sample the club offerings at will, with no fear of being the odd man out. Our (multiple) children were able to pop in and out of the teen clubs whenever an activity seemed interesting, never feeling alone or out of place.

For a middle-schooler or teen traveling as the only one of his/her age group in the family, the youth clubs can be more challenging, as was the case with one of our teens on a recent trip. She was completely fine joining in the introductory games during the Sail-Away

Celebration, where the fun was orchestrated by a counselor. Several other times, however, she dropped in at Vibe and found just a few kids obviously paired off into subgroups. Because of this—coupled with the fact that the counselors at the tween/teen clubs occasionally seem more invested in stamping out juvenile delinquency and covert smooching than actively engaging the kids—our normally social and extroverted daughter had trouble slotting herself in.

Our teen's observation was that the "single" kids who did best at Vibe were the ones who participated in absolutely every activity there, including the teen activities on Castaway Cay, thus giving them the opportunity to pair off with someone. Because she was doing so much stuff with us, she found it harder to participate at Vibe on an ad hoc basis. For solo teens and tweens, then, the youth clubs might best be thought of as an all-or-nothing proposition: Those who just want to sample the clubs, as opposed to immersing themselves in the activities, should expect the social scene to be harder to break into.

ACTIVE KIDS As a parent, you're the best judge of how much physical activity your child needs. We've rarely seen truly bad behavior on the Disney ships, but when we have, it's usually been an active child running in circles around other guests after sitting in passive activities all day.

To make sure that your kids burn off their excess energy in a positive way, keep an eye out for ways to add physical activity to their day, particularly if you're spending several consecutive days at sea. The pool and sports deck are obvious solutions, but these may sometimes be unavailable due to weather or temporary maintenance issues. The many onboard dance parties can be a good way for an active child to let off steam; also carefully check your *Personal Navigator* for movement opportunities.

The activities at the kids' clubs are marked with a color-coded Mickey-head symbol. For example, the yellow "In the Spotlight" activities focus on stage presence and performance, while the black "Solve It" activities focus on problem solving and puzzles. If you have a child who needs to move a lot, steer him or her toward the green "Jump Up" activities, which include group games and movement.

YOUTH CLUBS

THE BULK OF DCL'S CHILDREN'S ACTIVITIES take place at the youth clubs on the ships. They're organized by age group, as follows:

- **Flounder's Reef Nursery** (*Wonder*) and **It's a Small World Nursery** (*Magic, Dream,* and *Fantasy*), for infants and toddlers up to age 3
- **Oceaneer Club** and **Oceaneer Lab,** for children ages 3-12
- **Edge,** for ages 11-14
- **Vibe,** for ages 14-17

We provide profiles of the clubs starting on the next page, orga-nized by ship and ordered from the youngest to oldest age groups.

Children in the following age groups may choose which club they wish to participate in: 3-year-olds can choose the nursery or (as long as they're potty-trained) Oceaneer Club/Lab, 11- and 12-year-olds can choose between Oceaneer Club/Lab and Edge, and 14-year-olds can choose Edge or Vibe. This flexibility is helpful when siblings who are close in age want to be in the same club. Once a choice is made, how-ever, it may not be changed. Disney is also strict about making sure that kids stick to the club for their age group—that is, no sneaking into Vibe if they're not old enough, or if they're even slightly too old.

Children in the nurseries, Oceaneer Club, and Oceaneer Lab will be asked to wear a wristband while they're on the premises, and par-ents will be given an electronic pager. The wristbands look somewhat similar to the MagicBands now in use at Walt Disney World, but they work differently. Parents will see a $12.95 charge per band on their bill if the bands are not returned at the end of the sailing.

Sensors at each club's doors will trigger an alarm if your child tries to leave without a parent to deactivate the wristband. In the event that Disney or your child needs to contact you, club staff will call you on your Wave Phone, a mobile phone you can use aboard the ship.

Youth registered at the Edge and Vibe clubs (ages 11–17) are free to come and go as they please—there's no check-in or checkout. If your kids get bored, they may leave to visit a character greeting, go to the pool, grab a snack, go back to the room, or just roam around. (Rest assured that they won't be allowed to leave the ship without adult accompaniment.) Parents who are considering a little conjugal time while the kiddos are supposed to be occupied should be aware that they might be interrupted unexpectedly.

For some kids this is an unprecedented amount of freedom, which may cause discomfort for the parent or child. Be sure to set ground rules for your kids about notifying you where they are; these might include periodic check-ins via Wave Phone or notes on a whiteboard posted on your cabin door.

All kids must be registered to use the clubs. Parents can sign up their children either before boarding through online check-in (see page 21) or on embarkation day in the clubs' open houses. Signing up online has the advantage of giving busy cruisers one less thing to worry about after boarding the ship. Open houses are a great way to check out the various clubs. (*Warning:* The spaces are so well themed that adults will be sad when they have to leave.) Once a child is registered for a club, he or she may use its facilities for the entire cruise.

Some activities, such as board games, computer games, and crafts, are generally available on an ad hoc basis; kids can do them when-ever they're in the club. Throughout each day there are also planned themed activities, which will be noted in your *Personal Navigator.* Some of the listed activities are self-explanatory: You can easily figure out what "Magic Show" or "Dance Party" means. Other activities may be more cryptic, such as "Nemo's Coral Reef Adventure" or "4th Pigs Pasta Palace" (we're still not sure what that one was about). If you're not sure whether a particular planned activity will appeal to your child, or if your child has emotional or sensory-processing issues that might be exacerbated by certain stimuli, check with the club counselors for more details.

Nurseries

These operate under a reservation system and charge an hourly rate for services; parents will need to book specific times. The charge is $9 an hour for the first child and $8 an hour for each additional child in the same family. You should bring milk, formula, and baby food, along with diapers and wipes, a change of clothes, and a blanket and pacifier if your child needs these to nap.

Space is limited at each nursery; reservations are required and are first come, first served:

- Concierge guests and Platinum Castaway Club members can make reservations 120 days in advance.
- Gold Castaway Club members can make reservations 105 days in advance.
- Silver Castaway Club members can make reservations 90 days in advance.
- All other guests can make reservations 75 days out.

If you haven't made nursery reservations by the time you board, either stop by before dinner or call from your stateroom: Dial ☎ 7-5864 on the *Magic, Dream,* and *Fantasy* or ☎ 7-18500 on the *Wonder.*

Hours vary, especially when the ship is in port, but on most sea days the nurseries are open 9 a.m.–11 p.m., with open-house tours 8–9 a.m.; check your *Personal Navigator* for details. The nurseries are sometimes open noon–3 p.m., and usually 5:30–11 p.m. on the first afternoon of your cruise.

The *Magic*'s Youth Clubs

It's a Small World Nursery   LOCATION: Deck 5 Aft

OVERVIEW This is the *Magic*'s onboard nursery for infants and toddlers ages 6 months–3 years (some longer sailings may require children to be 12 months or older). Trained staff play with the children throughout the day. Unlike the activities at the clubs for older kids and teens, activities at the nursery are unstructured but may include movies, story time, crafts, and occasional visits from Disney characters.

DESCRIPTION AND COMMENTS Too cute. Decorated with brilliantly colored murals inspired by the art of Mary Blair, the Disney animator who designed It's a Small World at Disneyland and Walt Disney World, the nursery is cleverly divided into three sections. Up front is the "acclimation zone," a welcome area where kids can get used to their surroundings; this leads to a long, narrow, rectangular, brightly lit play area, off of which is a darkened, quiet room for naps. The play area is stocked with pint-size activities, including a 2-foot-tall playground slide on a padded floor, a small basketball hoop, plenty of leg-powered riding vehicles, play mats with large toys, and adorable miniature craft tables that you'd swear came from the Lilliput IKEA. A one-way mirror lets parents check up on their tots discreetly.

Around the corner, at the far end of the nursery, is the resting room, with six cribs and three glider chairs (sort of like rocking chairs, except they move linearly). Murals in soothing blues and golds adorn the walls. This room is kept dark most of the day, and the staff ensures that activities in the main room happen far enough away that noise isn't a problem. Just outside are a sink and changing area.

ACROSS THE SHIPS The *Dream* and the *Fantasy* also have It's a Small World Nurseries. The only real difference from the version on the *Magic* is that the nap room is larger, with more than twice as many cribs. The *Wonder* has **Flounder's Reef Nursery** (see page 148)—the basic setup is the same, but the theme is *The Little Mermaid* and the nap room is smaller.

Oceaneer Club and Oceaneer Lab   LOCATION: Deck 5 Midship

OVERVIEW The Oceaneer Club and Oceaneer Lab are connected spaces that host the 3- to 12-year-old set. Activities for older kids usually take place in the Lab and are often educational or participatory in nature (such as cooking demonstrations or science experiments). Younger children's programs are generally held in the Club and include story time, character greetings, and movement activities. Disney designates 7 as the border age for the Club and Lab and provides details in your *Personal Navigator* about each area's different activity tracks. During open houses, one side remains open for activities while the other side is open to the public. Lunch and dinner are provided.

Parents must check kids up to age 7 years in and out of the club. With parental permission, 8- to 12-year-olds may check themselves in and out—just designate your preference when you register your kids.

DESCRIPTION AND COMMENTS Newly redesigned on the *Magic,* the Oceaneer Lab and Club are separate areas connected by a short private hallway, allowing children to go from Lab to Club and back. Besides providing kids twice as much space, this arrangement separates younger and older children while giving siblings of different ages the chance to stay in contact.

The Oceaneer Club consists of four distinct sections branching off from a central "library" decorated with oversize children's books and outfitted with a huge plasma TV for movie screenings. **Andy's Room** is *Toy Story*–themed and is for smaller children. Its main feature is a tall, circular, gentle playground slide in the shape of Slinky Dog. There's also a large pink Hamm (the piggy bank) sitting in the middle of the play floor, and a giant Mr. Potato Head with equally large plug-in pieces, all scattered about.

The **Mickey Mouse Club,** the second themed room, serves as the Oceaneer Club's primary activity center. Done in black-and-white square tiles, with red tables and accents and pictures of Mickey and friends on the walls, the room has a large video screen on one wall and game consoles lining another.

The Mickey Mouse Club connects to both Andy's Room and **Marvel Avengers Academy.** In the academy you'll find Thor's hammer, Captain America's shield, and a life-size Iron Man suit, as well as another video screen and computer collection.

Disney is using the *Magic* to try out a new concept, also called Marvel Avengers Academy. The activities follow a multiday story in which kids embark on a recruitment experience that has them team up with various Avengers, hang out with Captain America, and suit up like Iron Man to battle the evil Red Skull. (No word yet on whether you can rent out Captain America's costume for private parties.)

Opposite Marvel Avengers Academy is **Pixie Hollow,** a Tinker Bell–themed dress-up and play area with costumes, an activity table, and a few computer terminals with themed games.

The Oceaneer Lab is done in a 19th-century nautical theme, with lots of exposed woods, red-leather chairs, navigation maps, and sailors' tools. More than a third of the space consists of one long room, filled with kid-size tables and stools, which serves as the primary area for arts and crafts. At the far end of this space is a set of computer terminals.

Next to the craft space, in the middle of the Lab, is a large screen for watching movies. Facing the screen is a collection of comfortable beanbags. Finally, the left side of the Lab is a set of small rooms. A couple have computer terminals or video-game consoles; one is a smaller arts-and-crafts room, and another is an animation studio where kids can learn to draw Disney characters and create their own computer animations.

ACROSS THE SHIPS All DCL ships have an Oceaneer Club/Lab. On the *Dream* and the *Fantasy,* the Club is also subdivided into themed areas, but they differ somewhat from those on the *Magic.* The Lab has a similar nautical theme and layout but is distinguished by a central "interactive floor," composed of individual video screens surrounded by foot-operated touch pads and used to play different interactive games.

On the *Wonder,* the Club is *Peter Pan*–themed and doesn't have the individual themed areas of the Clubs on the other three ships; the Lab has a *Toy Story* theme and a more open layout. Also, given that the *Wonder* is the second-oldest ship and hasn't yet benefited from a renovation, both areas seem slightly dated. Finally, where kids on the other three ships can roam between the Club and Lab as they wish, kids on the *Wonder* must be escorted by a counselor from one space to the other.

Edge LOCATION: Deck 2 Midship

OVERVIEW Tweens and early teens rule at Edge. Unlike at the Oceaneer Club/Lab, kids can come and go as they please. Activities range from drawing and cooking classes to scavenger hunts and computer games.

Parents may be surprised to see that things are scheduled past midnight on some nights.

DESCRIPTION AND COMMENTS A three-section activity area, Edge is the basement rec room your kids dream of. One entire wall is stacked with computer terminals hooked up to various video-game consoles; another section of the room is filled with couches and pillows around a video screen for movies and television; a large middle section for playing board games and other activities rounds out the space.

Edge is likely to be the first of the youth clubs in which the staff will treat your kids as peers to interact with rather than as children to be supervised. The staff generally does a great job of getting to know each child and will even compete in games alongside the kids. If you ever want to feel old and slow, watch the cup-stacking competition, where the object is to stack and unstack a pyramid of 15 plastic cups as quickly as possible. Some kids can do both in under 10 seconds total.

ACROSS THE SHIPS All DCL ships have an Edge. The layout and amenities are more or less the same on the *Wonder.* On the *Dream* and the *Fantasy,* Edge is inside the ships' forward (nonfunctioning) smokestack. The decor and atmosphere are ultramodern and high-tech, versus the homier feel of Edge on the *Magic* and *Wonder.*

Vibe   LOCATION: Deck 11 Midship

OVERVIEW Vibe is one of the coolest spots on the *Magic.* Even if you don't have a kid traveling with you, it's worth checking out during an open house. Counselors lead the activities (dance parties, karaoke, group games, and the like), but teens are given plenty of autonomy in their structure. Parents should note that the only curfew for teens on board is whatever one they impose themselves. One rule of note that's strictly enforced: no public displays of affection.

DESCRIPTION AND COMMENTS Vibe sits up a flight of stairs in the ship's forward smokestack, but your teens probably won't mind the climb. Inside is a two-story-tall lounge with brick walls; overstuffed leather furniture; a smoothie bar; tons of quirky decorations; and board games, video consoles, and a small room off to the side for activities. It looks more like a well-appointed summer-camp lodge than anything nautical or tropical. We think there should be one of these for adults.

ACROSS THE SHIPS All DCL ships have a Vibe. The layout and amenities are more or less identical on the *Wonder.* On the *Dream* and the *Fantasy,* Vibe is dramatically different but just as cool. The theming and decor are urban ultralounge rather than funky rumpus room, and teens get an indoor/outdoor space, complete with a stylish sun deck and splash pool.

The *Wonder*'s Youth Clubs

Flounder's Reef Nursery   LOCATION: Deck 5 Aft

OVERVIEW This is the *Wonder*'s onboard nursery for infants and toddlers ages 6 months–3 years (some longer sailings may require children to be 12 months or older). Trained staff play with the children throughout the day. Unlike the activities at the clubs for older kids and teens, activities at the nursery are unstructured but may include movies, story time, crafts, and occasional visits from Disney characters.

DESCRIPTION AND COMMENTS The cruise industry's first nursery at sea, Flounder's Reef is divided into two sections. One is a narrow, rectangular, brightly lit play area; the other is a darkened, quiet area for naps. The play area is stocked with play mats, toys, books, a playground slide, baby swings and bouncy chairs, and a TV/DVD player. Sea creatures from *The Little Mermaid* (the nursery is named after Flounder, Ariel's best friend) decorate the walls; the floor has a wave motif. A one-way mirror outside lets parents check up on their tots discreetly.

At the back of the nursery is the resting area, furnished with cribs. This room is kept dark most of the day, and the staff ensures that activities in the main room happen far enough away that noise isn't a problem. A sink and changing station are adjacent.

ACROSS THE SHIPS The *Dream, Fantasy,* and *Magic* have **It's a Small World Nursery** (see page 145), with decor inspired by the theme park attraction. Of course, little ones will be too young to care about aesthetics, but It's a Small World is more colorful and creatively themed. Also, the nap area here is small, with room for only a few cribs and a glider, and there's no theming to speak of. Overall, Flounder's Reef feels more like a garden-variety day-care center with a few Disney touches here and there.

Oceaneer Club and Oceaneer Lab
LOCATION: Deck 5 Midship

OVERVIEW The Oceaneer Club and Oceaneer Lab are connected spaces that host the 3- to 12-year-old set. Activities for older kids usually take place in the Lab and are often educational or participatory in nature (such as cooking demonstrations or science experiments). Younger children's programs are generally held in the Club and include story time, character greetings, and movement activities. Disney designates 7 as the border age for the Club and Lab and provides details in your *Personal Navigator* about each area's different activity tracks. During open houses, one side remains open for activities while the other side is open to the public. Lunch and dinner are provided.

Parents must check kids up to age 7 years in and out of the club. With parental permission, 8- to 12-year-olds may check themselves in and out—just designate your preference when you register your kids.

DESCRIPTION AND COMMENTS The Oceaneer Club was designed to look like Captain Hook's ship from *Peter Pan*—wooden-plank floors, hanging ropes, barrels, and netting. The space on the *Wonder* is basically one big room without the individual themed areas of the Clubs on the other ships. Attractions include a "crow's nest" slide; a rope bridge; a computer nook; a stage; a dance floor; an area for arts and crafts; the Captain's Closet (a dress-up room); several TV sets; and, of course, plenty of toys, books, and games. Activities may range from dancing with Snow White to an audience with Captain Hook himself to a "boot camp" with Corporal Green and the Green Army Soldiers from *Toy Story.*

Separated from the Club by a sliding door, the Oceaneer Lab is *Toy Story*–themed, with figures of Buzz Lightyear and the Squeeze Toy Aliens, retro–space age tables and chairs, and floor-to-ceiling columns in the shape of planetary orbs. The open layout includes a reading area, computer stations, a science lab, work spaces for arts and crafts, and a demonstration kitchen. Activities might include cookie-making, building race cars, and learning to draw Disney characters.

ACROSS THE SHIPS We're pretty sure that kids who've experienced the Oceaneer Club/Lab on any of the other three ships would be let down by the *Wonder*'s version. The spaces seem a little worn and dated, and they're positively low-tech in comparison. Also, whereas the themed areas of the Clubs on the *Magic, Dream,* and *Fantasy* are bright and cheerful, the Club on the *Wonder* is a tad gloomy and drab with all that dark wood. Even the Club/Lab's restrooms are nicer on the other ships. We hope to see an upgrade here in the future.

Edge LOCATION: Deck 2 Midship

COMMENTS See profile of Edge on the *Magic* (see page 147) for details.

Vibe LOCATION: Deck 11 Midship

COMMENTS See profile of Vibe on the *Magic* (see page 148) for details.

The *Dream*'s and *Fantasy*'s Youth Clubs

It's a Small World Nursery LOCATION: Deck 5 Aft

COMMENTS See our profile of It's a Small World Nursery on the *Magic* (see page 145) for details.

Oceaneer Club and Oceaneer Lab LOCATION: Deck 5 Midship

OVERVIEW On the *Dream* and *Fantasy,* the Oceaneer Club and Oceaneer Lab are connected spaces that host the 3- to 12-year-old set. Activities for older kids usually take place in the Lab and are often educational or participatory in nature (such as cooking demonstrations or science experiments). Younger children's programs are generally held in the Club and include story time, character greetings, and movement activities. Disney designates 7 as the border age for the Club and Lab and provides details in your *Personal Navigator* about each area's different activity tracks. During open houses, one side remains open for activities while the other side is open to the public. Lunch and dinner are provided.

Parents must check kids up to age 7 years in and out of the club. With parental permission, 8- to 12-year-olds may check themselves in and out—just designate your preference when you register your kids.

DESCRIPTION AND COMMENTS The Oceaneer Lab and Club are separate areas connected by a short private hallway, allowing children to go from Lab to Club and back. Besides providing kids twice as much space, this arrangement separates younger and older children while giving siblings of different ages the chance to stay in contact.

The Oceaneer Club consists of four distinct sections branching off from a central rotunda painted royal blue; on the ceiling are "constellations" of Disney characters made up of small, twinkling electric lights. **Andy's Room** is *Toy Story*–themed and is for smaller children. There's a crawl-through tube—think a Habitrail for humans—in the shape of Slinky Dog, along with a giant pink Hamm (the piggy bank) sitting in the middle of the play floor, and a large Mr. Potato Head with equally large plug-in pieces, all invariably scattered about.

The next area is **Monsters Academy,** a brightly colored, *Monsters, Inc.*–themed space filled with all manner of interactive games, along with a climbing structure. Then there's **Pixie Hollow,** a Tinker Bell–themed dress-up and play area with costumes, an activity table, and a few computer terminals with themed games. Finally, **Disney's Explorer Pod** is a scaled-down submarine inspired by *Finding Nemo.* Inside are 16 interactive game stations.

The Oceaneer Lab is done in a 19th-century nautical theme, with lots of exposed woods, red-leather chairs, navigation maps, sailors' tools, and inlaid images of sea horses and compasses on the floor. The main hall features a celestial map on the ceiling and a huge "Magic Play Floor," composed of 16 high-definition video screens surrounded by foot-powered touch pads and used to play interactive games. (If you remember the piano from the movie *Big,* you get the idea.)

Surrounding the main hall are the **Media Lounge,** for relaxing and watching movies; the **Animator's Studio,** where kids can learn to draw Disney characters and create digital animations; **The Wheelhouse,** with computer stations and interactive games; the **Sound Studio,** where kids can record their own music; and the **Craft Studio.**

ACROSS THE SHIPS All DCL ships have an Oceaneer Club/Lab. On the *Magic,* the Club is subdivided into themed areas, but they differ somewhat from those on the *Dream* and *Fantasy;* the Lab has a similar nautical theme and layout but is missing the nifty interactive floor.

On the *Wonder,* the Club is *Peter Pan*–themed and doesn't have the individual themed areas of the Clubs on the other three ships; the Lab has a *Toy Story* theme and a more open layout. Also, given that the *Wonder* is the second-oldest ship and hasn't yet benefited from a renovation, both areas seem slightly dated, and they're positively low-tech in comparison. Finally, where kids on the other three ships can roam between the Club and Lab as they wish, kids on the *Wonder* must be escorted by a counselor from one space to the other.

Edge LOCATION: Deck 13 Forward

OVERVIEW Tweens rule at Edge. Unlike at the Oceaneer Club/Lab, kids at the Edge can come and go as they please. Activities range from drawing and cooking classes to improv-comedy sessions and ghost-hunting role-playing games. Parents may be surprised to see that things are scheduled past midnight on some nights.

DESCRIPTION AND COMMENTS Built into the *Dream*'s and *Fantasy*'s forward (nonfunctioning) smokestack, Edge has an open layout and a clean 21st-century feel. The walls are papered in a geometric Mickey-head design. The centerpiece of the space is a huge video wall, more than 18 feet wide and nearly 5 feet tall. Across from it are tables with built-in screens for playing interactive games, surrounded by bright-red seating that looks like something out of *The Jetsons;* behind those are cubbyholes outfitted with flat-panel TVs and Wii consoles. Recessed shelves between the game nooks are stocked with books and board games. Next to the game tables are an illuminated dance floor (think *Saturday Night Fever*) and a lounge area with beanbags arranged next to floor-to-ceiling windows. On the other side of the video wall are laptop stations loaded with video games and an onboard social-media app.

Edge is likely to be the first of the youth clubs in which the staff will treat your kids as peers to interact with rather than as children to be supervised. The staff generally does a great job of getting to know each child and getting in on the fun.

ACROSS THE SHIPS All DCL ships have an Edge. On the *Magic* and *Wonder,* it has a totally different layout and atmosphere—more like a family rec room than a high-tech hangout.

Vibe   LOCATION: Deck 5 Forward

OVERVIEW Up a flight of stairs from Deck 4 to Deck 5 Forward, Vibe is one of the coolest spots on the *Dream* and *Fantasy.* Even if you don't have a kid traveling with you, it's worth checking out during an open house. Counselors lead the activities (dance parties, karaoke, role-playing games, and the like), but teens are given plenty of autonomy in their structure. Parents should note that the only curfew for teens on board is whatever one they impose themselves. One rule of note that's strictly enforced: no public displays of affection.

DESCRIPTION AND COMMENTS Accessed through a neon-lit hallway, Vibe has a decidedly adult look and feel—if you didn't know better, you'd think you were in a trendy urban nightspot. The central indoor gathering spot is the theater–cum–TV lounge, accented with soft pink neon lighting and featuring a 103-inch flat-panel television. Two rows of couches are arranged in a semicircle in front of the screen; giant throw pillows scattered on the floor make for additional places to lounge. Behind the couches and built into the rear wall are a row of podlike, porthole-shaped nooks for playing video games, watching videos, or hooking up an iPod. Just off the row of pods is a smoothie bar with a multicolored floor in Day-Glo hues; ultramodern stools with low, curved backs; and white banquette seating.

Off the TV lounge is another sleek space for socializing. The walls are covered in alternating black and silver horizontal bars. Black leather-look benches line the walls; next to those are retro-mod tables and chairs arranged nightclub-style. Video-game booths stand nearby. Across from the seating area are a dance floor and DJ booth, a karaoke stage, and another large video screen.

The main attraction, though, lies outside: the **Vibe Splash Zone,** a private deck with two splash pools, chaise longues, sets of tables and chairs, and recessed seating. Furnishings and decor share the same ultramod style as the indoor spaces.

ACROSS THE SHIPS All DCL ships have a Vibe. On the *Magic* and the *Wonder,* Vibe is dramatically different but just as cool. Built into the ships' forward smokestack, the two-story-tall lounge features brick walls, overstuffed leather furniture, and quirky decor. It looks more like a well-appointed summer-camp lodge than anything you'd find on a cruise ship.

OTHER KIDS' ACTIVITIES ON BOARD

On the *Magic* and *Wonder*

Many activities take place in the **Promenade Lounge** on Deck 3 Aft, including the following.

- *Playhouse Disney* Dance Party
- Pirate Trivia Quest
- Pop Decades Dance
- Wildcat Bingo
- Pirate Scavenger Maps

On the *Dream* and the *Fantasy*

Midship Detective Agency is an interactive, self-guided game in which kids help Disney characters (the Muppets on the *Fantasy*) solve a mystery. Similar to Sorcerers of the Magic Kingdom at Walt Disney World, this is one of the most fun onboard activities in the fleet. You begin by signing up on a computer inside a small desk on Deck 5 Midship. There you'll obtain a small, numbered cardboard game piece. One side of the game piece holds a 2-D bar code and your agent number; the other side displays a detective's badge icon.

Along with your badge card, you'll receive a pamphlet describing each of the agency's suspects behind the mystery. The pamphlet also includes a map of the ship that shows where to find clues to solve the mystery. Once you've signed up and obtained your game material, you'll watch a short video that explains the mystery you're solving. You'll also be told where to go to find your first clue.

Each clue is presented on an "Enchanted Art" video screen somewhere on the ship. The amazing thing about the video screens is that they look like ordinary wall art to anyone not playing the game—it's only when you hold up your badge that the screen comes alive with video and sound. (The technology embedded behind the screens' frames includes a bar-code reader for your badge, speakers, and a network of computers to keep track of your accomplishments.) To obtain the clue, you'll first have to solve a simple puzzle or win a simple game. You do this by using your badge as a sort of game controller while you're playing, tilting and moving the badge to guide the action on the screen. It takes a little practice to get used to, so tell your kids before they start that their first try at each screen is just a dry run. You can repeat the action as often as needed.

Height and Age Requirements Around the Ships and Castaway Cay

ON BOARD

AquaDuck *(Dream and Fantasy)* 42" to ride, 54" to ride alone; kids under age 7 must be accompanied by someone age 14 or older

AquaDunk *(Magic)* 48" to ride

AquaLab *(Magic and Fantasy)* All ages; kids must be toilet-trained (no swim diapers)

Donald's Pool *(Dream and Fantasy)* All ages; children under age 16 must be supervised; little ones must be toilet-trained (no swim diapers)

Family hot tubs All ages; children under age 16 must be supervised; little ones must be toilet-trained (no swim diapers)

Goofy's Pool *(Magic and Wonder)* All ages; children under age 16 must be supervised; little ones must be toilet-trained (no swim diapers)

Mickey's Pool *(Dream, Fantasy, and Wonder)* and **Nephews' Pool *(Magic)*** Age 3 and up; must be toilet-trained (no swim diapers)

Mickey's Slide *(Dream, Fantasy, and Wonder)* Ages 4-14, 38"-64"

Twist 'n' Spout Slide *(Magic)* Age 4 and over; at least 38" tall

Mickey's Splash Zone *(Wonder)*, Nemo's Reef *(Dream and Fantasy)*, and **Nephews' Splash Zone *(Magic)*** Age 3 and younger only; swim diapers required

Quiet Cove Pool (all ships) Age 18 and over only

Satellite Falls *(Fantasy)* Age 18 and over only

ON CASTAWAY CAY

Pelican Plunge waterslide No height requirement listed; life jackets encouraged

The Hide Out Ages 14-17; must be registered for Vibe

Scuttle's Cove Ages 3-12; must be registered for the Oceaneer Club/Lab

Once you've obtained the clue, you can eliminate one of the suspects from the mystery; then it's off to another section of the ship to get another clue. Make no mistake: Playing this game involves climbing a lot of stairs. However, you get to see a lot of the ship, and it's good exercise for the kids. You'll see them playing at all times of the day and night, and lines often form in front of each video screen, especially on sea days.

The *Dream* has two separate games: **The Case of the Plundered Paintings** and **The Case of the Missing Puppies.** Both feature Mickey Mouse and his friends. On the *Fantasy,* the Muppets star in **The Case of the Stolen Show.** We think the latter is the most fun—the game's designers expertly incorporate the Muppets' humor into the scenes.

Exclusive to the *Fantasy*

Borrowing from Walt Disney World, the *Fantasy* added the very popular **Bibbidi Bobbidi Boutique** (Deck 5 Midship) for girls ages 3–12 who want the princess treatment. Makeover variations include Disney Diva,

Pop Princess, and Fairy Tale Princess. Young princes may sign up for the **Royal Knight Package.** On Pirate Night, the boutique becomes **The Pirates League** and gives buccaneer-themed makeovers to guests age 3 and up (guests 17 and younger must be accompanied by an adult). Packages range from $15.95 to $184.95 and can be prebooked; note that these slots fill fast. The other ships offer a less extensive version of these experiences in **Skulls & Scurry** and **Glitter & Go** on theme nights.

For the princess who has everything, there's the **Royal Sea Package,** which gets you three nights of makeovers plus a gift delivered to your stateroom. It can be yours for $595 and must be booked by e-mail; download a reservation form from **tinyurl.com/royalseaorderform,** or ask your travel agent for details.

CHILDREN'S PERFORMANCE OPPORTUNITIES

DURING MOST SAILINGS OF SEVEN DAYS OR MORE, the Oceaneer Club and Lab invite kids ages 3–12 to participate in a show performed on stage in the Walt Disney Theater. The show, often called *Friendship Rocks!,* mostly involves having the little ones sit on stage and sing along with a few Disney classics. Mickey will make an appearance. Many younger kids (and their parents) think that being on stage with Mickey makes them rock stars, while others will be completely overwhelmed by the experience—use your best judgment.

Kids with a real yen to perform should look for karaoke opportunities on most sailings or talent-show opportunities on many longer sailings (see "Family Nightclubs," page 140).

CHILDREN'S ACTIVITIES IN PORT

WHEN BOOKING PORT EXCURSIONS, look for activities that are specified for families. Some tours will be specially designated for those traveling with kids. All excursion descriptions (see Part Twelve) include a recommendation for ages (or a requirement, depending on the type of activity) and an indication of the amount of stamina needed to participate. Another option for days when you're in port is to stay aboard and enjoy the lower crowds at the pools and waterslides.

CHILDREN'S ACTIVITIES AT CASTAWAY CAY

DCL'S PRIVATE ISLAND (see Part Ten) has designated areas just for children and families. The teen area, **The Hide Out,** is tucked away, though not on the beach, and offers sports, such as volleyball and table tennis, and scheduled activities. **Scuttle's Cove,** a play area for young children, has youth-club counselors on hand to direct activities. Both The Hide Out and Scuttle's Cove are monitored by Disney cast members to ensure that only children and their parents enter.

CHILL SPA FOR TEENS

INSIDE SENSES SPA & SALON on the *Dream, Fantasy,* and *Magic,* Chill Spa is for guests ages 13–17 (a parent or guardian must be present during treatments). Services can be booked after boarding. If you don't want your teen to be offered any extra products to buy after treatment, note that when you make your reservation. Read more about the spas on page 167.

WHERE TO MEET CHARACTERS

DISNEY CHARACTERS ARE AVAILABLE for photos and autographs several times per day at various locations on the ships; they also make occasional visits to the nurseries and kids' clubs. A complete schedule is usually available at the Character Information Board in your ship's atrium. The schedule is printed in the "Character Appearances" section of each day's *Personal Navigator*; it's also available by calling ☎ 7-PALS (7257) from your stateroom phone.

unofficial **TIP**
Arrive at least a half-hour ahead of time to meet the Disney princesses. We've arrived 45 minutes ahead to get a spot for our kids to meet Belle, and we weren't the first people in line.

Lines can get very long to meet the most popular characters, such as the Disney princesses, and appearances are limited to around 30 minutes each. The line to meet a character will be closed once it's been determined that no more guests can be accommodated in the character's remaining time. If your child is intent on meeting a specific character, your best bet is to get in line 15–30 minutes before that character is scheduled to appear.

One of the most popular greetings is one that Laurel calls "The Princess Bomb," which explodes in the atrium several times per cruise. Your kids can meet and pose for photos with four to six of the usual suspects from the Princess Hit Parade. On some cruises each princess will have her own line, while on others everyone will queue for one big royal receiving line. Ask the character attendants when you arrive if it's not obvious which is happening on your night. The princess greetings often have the longest lines, with some guests lining up more than 30 minutes before they start, as this reader found out:

> We had a princess event at 9:30 in the morning. Parents started gathering in the atrium an hour ahead. Some hadn't had their coffee yet, and they were NOT happy.

DCL has been testing the distribution of timed tickets for some popular character greetings on board, most notably for the *Frozen* princesses Anna and Elsa, but we've seen this happen for some other characters as well. If you have any character greetings on your must-do list, be absolutely sure to check your first-day *Personal Navigator* for a note about character-greeting ticket distribution—tickets for specific greetings have been available for only a few hours on sail day and not at any point after that.

On the afternoon of your first day on the ship, many characters will be on stage at the family pool. On other days, you may see princesses in the ship's lobby around 11:30 a.m. An assortment of characters, including everyone from Mickey and Minnie to Captain Jack Sparrow, usually gathers in the ship's lobby starting about 75 minutes before each dinner seating—that is, 4:30 p.m. for the 5:45 p.m. dinner seating and 7 p.m. for the 8:15 p.m. seating.

On longer cruises, characters such as Mickey, Minnie, Donald, Goofy, and Pluto may make onboard appearances many times throughout the voyage (albeit usually in different attire). The lines for these Disney classics are typically shorter later in the trip, when most folks have already had their fill of photos with the Big Cheese and company.

Character photo ops, including the Fab Five (plus Chip 'n' Dale) in beach attire and Captain Jack Sparrow, happen on Castaway Cay close to the ship dock and family beach.

POOLS *and* WATER-PLAY AREAS

EACH SHIP HAS SEPARATE FRESHWATER POOLS designed for small children, families, and adults. All are heated to a minimum temperature of 75°F. Health regulations require that children be toilet-trained to use the pools, while swim diapers are mandatory in the water-play areas. You may bring water wings and other Coast Guard–approved flotation devices into the pools, but not rafts, floats, or those foam noodles you see every summer. Snorkels and masks covering the nose/mouth are also prohibited.

THE *MAGIC'S* POOLS

THE SHIP'S NEWEST WATER FEATURE is the **AquaDunk** waterslide, a variation on the AquaDuck slide found on the *Dream* and *Fantasy*. Short and mildly fast, with a vertical start, the AquaDunk starts with your entering a vertical tube. You lean against one side of the tube while a clear Plexiglas door closes opposite you to seal the tube. Suddenly, the floor drops away and you plunge nearly vertically down the tube, through a quick 270-degree turn and into a braking pool of water. The entire experience takes perhaps 7 or 8 seconds, but the initial sensation of falling is fun enough to make it worth repeating. The AquaDunk usually opens at 9 a.m. and closes around 11 p.m.

Because the AquaDunk has an hourly capacity of only around 120 riders, long lines will develop quickly; we've seen 80-minute waits posted. If you're not there first thing in the morning, try during lunchtime or the first dinner seating around 6:15 p.m.

AquaLab, the *Magic's* water-play area for small children (age 3 and up), is on Deck 9 Aft. It consists of four areas: AquaLab, the Twist 'n' Spout waterslide (age 4 and up and over 38 inches tall), the Nephews' Pool, and the Nephews' Splash Zone.

Every inch of AquaLab is covered in water, which comes out from both vertical and horizontal surfaces. Overhead buckets, slowly filling with water, will dump their contents periodically on anyone standing below, while sprays from faux ship-plumbing will drench anyone walking within 10 feet. Your kids will probably spend hours here, so it's a good thing that both covered seating and refreshments are available nearby.

Next to the main AquaLab area is the **Nephews' Splash Zone,** a water-play area for kids up to 3 years old. This Plexiglas-enclosed area has water spouting from pint-size Huey, Dewey, and Louie figures. Padding on the ground allows kids to jump and run around safely, and you'll find parents sitting and relaxing nearby while the little ones get soaked.

A new three-story spiral waterslide, **Twist 'n' Spout** is a lot longer and slower than AquaDunk, making it perfect for kids not quite tall enough for the big slide. Twist 'n' Spout starts above Deck 11 and ends on Deck 9 next to AquaLab. The top part of the slide isn't usually staffed, but a camera system there allows the attendant at the bottom of the slide to monitor both the start and the end simultaneously. Kids must be 4–14 years old and 38–64 inches tall to ride. There's plenty of nearby seating for parents to get some sun while watching the little ones splash around.

The **Nephews' Pool** is a shallow, circular pool in the middle of the deck, touching both AquaLab and the Nephews' Splash Zone. Small children can splash around to their hearts' content while parents sit on ledge seating. Just past the forward end of AquaLab is **Pete's Boiler Bites** snack bar, and on the aft end is **Daisy's De-Lites.**

Goofy's Pool, the *Magic*'s family pool, is on Deck 9 Midship. It's the focal point of outdoor activity on the ship. The pool is 4 feet deep at every point, and deck chairs and lounges are arranged on both sides along its length. At the forward end of the pool is the **Funnel Vision** LED screen, which plays movies, TV shows, and videos almost constantly. At the aft end are **Pinocchio's Pizzeria** and two covered whirlpools. Both Goofy's and Nephews' Pools are typically open 8 a.m.–10 p.m. every day; check your *Personal Navigator* for specific hours.

The adults-only **Quiet Cove Pool** is on Deck 9 Forward. Like Goofy's Pool, it's 4 feet deep throughout, and two adults-only whirlpools are nearby. Teak lounge chairs are provided for relaxing. Just past the aft end of the pool are **Signals** bar and **Cove Café.**

THE *WONDER*'S POOLS

ON THE WONDER YOU'LL FIND **Mickey's Pool,** for children age 3 and up, toward Deck 9 Aft. Divided into three smaller pools corresponding to Mickey's face and ears, the pool has a maximum depth of 2 feet, and the bright-yellow spiral **Mickey's Slide** rises about one deck high (about the same level as Deck 10). Kids must be 4–14 years old and 38–64 inches tall

unofficial **TIP**
The *Wonder*, alas, doesn't have anything like the AquaDuck or AquaDunk waterslides.

to use the waterslide. There's plenty of nearby seating for parents to get some sun while watching the little ones splash around. Just past the forward end of Mickey's Pool is **Pluto's Dog House** snack bar, and on the aft end is **Goofy's Galley.**

Children who don't meet the requirements for Mickey's Pool can play in the nearby **Mickey's Splash Zone,** on the port side of the pool. Surrounded by short walls and themed to *The Sorcerer's Apprentice,* this water-play area for kids age 3 and under features gurgling sprays, jets, and sprinkles of water bubbling up from fountains in the floor. Best of all, there's plenty of covered seating nearby. Kids playing in Mickey's Splash Zone must be supervised.

Goofy's Pool, the family pool, is on Deck 9 Midship. It's the focal point of outdoor activity on the ship. The pool is 4 feet deep at every point, and deck chairs and lounges are arranged on both sides along its length. At the forward end of the pool is the **Funnel Vision** LED screen, which plays movies, TV shows, and videos almost constantly. At the aft end are **Pinocchio's Pizzeria** and two covered whirlpools. Both Goofy's and Mickey's Pools are typically open 8 a.m.–10 p.m. every day; check your *Personal Navigator* for specific hours.

The adults-only **Quiet Cove Pool** is on Deck 9 Forward. Like the corresponding pool on the *Magic,* it's 4 feet deep throughout, and two adults-only whirlpools are nearby. Teak lounge chairs are provided for relaxing. Just past the aft end of the pool are **Signals** bar and **Cove Café.**

THE *DREAM'S* POOLS

LIKE THE FANTASY AND WONDER, the *Dream* has **Mickey's Pool** for children age 3 and up, roughly midship on Deck 11. Divided into three smaller pools corresponding to Mickey's face and ears, the pool has a maximum depth of 2 feet, and the bright-yellow spiral **Mickey's Slide** rises about one deck high (about the same level as Deck 12). Kids must be 4–14 years old and 38–64 inches tall to use the waterslide. There's plenty of nearby seating for parents to get some sun while watching the little ones splash around.

Children who don't meet the requirements for Mickey's Pool can play in the nearby **Nemo's Reef,** toward the aft end of the pool. Larger and wetter than the Nephews' Splash Zone on the *Magic* and Mickey's Splash Zone on the *Wonder,* this *Finding Nemo*–themed water-play area for kids age 3 and under features gurgling sprays, jets, and sprinkles of water bubbling up from fountains in the floor, as well as from kid-size replicas of some of the movie's characters. A set of restrooms is just behind Nemo's Reef.

Found on Deck 11 Midship is the *Dream's* family pool, **Donald's Pool.** Like Goofy's Pool on the *Magic* and *Wonder,* it's the center of outdoor activity on the ship. The rectangular pool is about a foot deep close to its edges; in the middle is a roughly circular section that drops to a maximum depth of around 5 feet. The different depths allow younger swimmers to relax in the shallows without having to get out of the pool. Deck chairs and lounges line both sides of Donald's Pool. At the forward end of the pool is the **Funnel Vision** LED screen, which plays movies, TV shows, and videos almost constantly. At the aft end is the Mickey Pool. Just beyond the Funnel Vision stage are the counter-service restaurants: **Fillmore's Favorites, Luigi's Pizza,** and **Tow Mater's Grill** on the starboard side and the **Eye Scream** ice-cream station on the port side. Both Donald's and Mickey's Pools are typically open 8 a.m.–10 p.m. every day; check your *Personal Navigator* for specific hours.

The adults-only **Quiet Cove Pool** is on Deck 11 Forward on both the *Dream* and the *Fantasy*. This pool is 4 feet deep throughout. Rather than wasting space on whirlpools, the *Dream*'s designers wisely placed an outdoor bar, **Cove Bar,** at one end of the Quiet Cove Pool. The area around the bar is a splash-friendly, nonslip surface, with white bench seating and a round ottoman-like seat in the middle; there are also a few seats directly at the bar. Behind the pool is the lovely **Cove Café;** on either side is covered seating with lounges and chairs.

unofficial **TIP**

The best time to visit the AquaDuck is between 5 and 7 p.m., when most families are either at dinner or getting ready to go. You'll also find smaller crowds on days when the ship is in port.

Both the *Dream* and the *Fantasy* have an **AquaDuck** waterslide, a 765-foot-long clear-plastic tube that's almost as popular as the Disney princesses. Riders board an inflatable plastic raft at the aft end of Deck 12. The raft is shot forward through the plastic tube by high-pressure water faucets below and to the sides, making the AquaDuck a water-powered miniature roller coaster. There's enough water pressure here to propel your raft up two full decks' worth of height, followed by a descent of four decks into a landing pool. Guests must be at least 42 inches tall to ride, and children under age 7 must ride with someone age 14 or older who also meets the height requirement.

The AquaDuck's track sits at the outside edge of Deck 12 and goes as high as one of the ship's smokestacks. If you can keep your eyes open (and your wits about you), it offers some awesome views of the surrounding ocean and any nearby islands.

THE *FANTASY'S* POOLS

LIKE THE DREAM AND WONDER, the *Fantasy* has **Mickey's Pool** for children age 3 and up, roughly midship on Deck 11. Divided into three smaller pools corresponding to Mickey's face and ears, the pool has a maximum depth of 2 feet, and the bright-yellow spiral **Mickey's Slide** rises about one deck high (about the same level as Deck 12). Kids must be 4–14 years old and 38–64 inches tall to use the waterslide. There's plenty of nearby seating for parents to get some sun while watching the little ones splash around.

Children who don't meet the requirements for Mickey's Pool can play in the nearby **Nemo's Reef,** toward the aft end of the pool. Larger and wetter than the Nephews' Splash Zone on the *Magic* and Mickey's Splash Zone on the *Wonder,* this *Finding Nemo*–themed water-play area for kids age 3 and under features gurgling sprays, jets, and sprinkles of water bubbling up from fountains in the floor, as well as from kid-size replicas of some of the movie's characters. A set of restrooms is just behind Nemo's Reef.

Found on Deck 11 Midship is the *Fantasy*'s family pool, **Donald's Pool.** Like Goofy's Pool on the *Magic* and *Wonder,* it's the center of outdoor activity on the ship. The rectangular pool is about a foot deep close to its edges; in the middle is a roughly circular section that drops to a maximum depth of around 5 feet. The different depths allow younger swimmers to relax in the shallows without having to get out of the pool.

Deck and lounge chairs line both sides of Donald's Pool. At the forward end of the pool is the **Funnel Vision** LED screen, which plays movies, TV shows, and videos almost constantly. At the aft end is the Mickey Pool. Just beyond the Funnel Vision stage are the counter-service restaurants: **Fillmore's Favorites, Luigi's Pizza,** and **Tow Mater's Grill** on the starboard side and the **Eye Scream** ice-cream station on the port side. Both Donald's and Mickey's Pools are typically open 8 a.m.–10 p.m. every day; check your *Personal Navigator* for specific hours.

Like the *Magic,* the *Fantasy* has an **AquaLab** water-play area. On Deck 12 Aft, it's similar to Nemo's Reef in that its entertainment is provided by water splashing out at you, but where the water comes up from the floor at Nemo's Reef, it comes from the sky at AquaLab. High above your head are water pipes filling buckets and buckets of water, which are counterbalanced so that they spill down on unsuspecting (and suspecting) kids below. In fact, water comes at you from every angle in AquaLab, and that's exactly the appeal. AquaLab is for kids too old or too large to play in Nemo's Reef.

The adults-only **Quiet Cove Pool** is on Deck 11 Forward on both the *Dream* and the *Fantasy.* This pool is 4 feet deep throughout. Rather than wasting space on whirlpools, the *Fantasy*'s designers wisely placed an outdoor bar, **Cove Bar,** at one end of the Quiet Cove Pool. The area around the bar is a splash friendly, nonslip surface, with white bench seating and a round ottoman-like seat in the middle; there are also a few seats directly at the bar. Behind the pool is the lovely **Cove Café;** on either side is covered seating with lounges and chairs.

Both the *Fantasy* and the *Dream* have an **AquaDuck** waterslide, a 765-foot-long clear-plastic tube that's almost as popular as the Disney princesses. Riders board an inflatable plastic raft at the aft end of Deck 12. The raft is shot forward through the plastic tube by high-pressure water faucets below and to the sides, making the AquaDuck a water-powered miniature roller coaster. There's enough water pressure here to propel your raft up two full decks' worth of height, followed by a descent of four decks into a landing pool. Guests must be at least 42 inches tall to ride, and children under age 7 must ride with someone age 14 or older who also meets the height requirement.

The AquaDuck's track sits at the outside edge of Deck 12 and goes as high as one of the ship's smokestacks. If you can keep your eyes open (and your wits about you), it offers some awesome views of the surrounding ocean and any nearby islands. The best time to visit is between 5 and 7 p.m., when most families are either at dinner or getting ready to go. You'll also find smaller crowds on days when the ship is in port.

Besides all this, the *Fantasy* has a water feature not found on any other ship: **Satellite Falls,** an adults-only splash pool and sun deck on Deck 13 Forward. Covered with long, vertical tiles in different shades of blue and green, the pool looks great at night. In the center, a structure that looks like a giant Doppler radar receiver (and mimics a pair of actual satellite receivers on either side of the pool) pours a gentle stream of water into the pool below.

ONBOARD SEMINARS

LED BY CREW MEMBERS and attended by a limited number of passengers, onboard seminars are 30- to 60-minute interactive talks. Topics vary, but most involve food, wine, shopping, fitness activities, or how the ship is run. The shopping seminars and tours of the ship are usually free of charge; some of the cooking demonstrations are also free. A small fee—usually $15 to $25—is charged for seminars involving alcohol, and for some of the fitness activities.

Cooking demonstrations where wine is served, along with fitness activities, are restricted to guests age 18 and up. Wine and spirit tastings are only for guests age 21 and up, except during cruises that sail solely in Europe, where participants may be 18 if a parent or guardian is traveling with them and has provided written permission for them to drink.

The crew members who lead these seminars generally also have duties related to the subject. Wine presentations, for example, are usually run by either a restaurant sommelier or an experienced bartender; cooking demonstrations are run by one of the ship's chefs. Not surprisingly, the crew members' presentation and speaking skills are the most important factor in determining the quality of the seminar. On one cruise, a well-versed chef butterflied three dozen shrimp in slow motion so we could all take notes on proper knife technique. On another cruise, a bartender apparently not used to public speaking ran us through seven tequila shots and margaritas in 35 minutes, rendering us useless for the rest of the afternoon (not that we minded).

Several **wine-tasting sessions** are usually held on most cruises, especially those of more than four nights. The first session is typically an introduction to wine and covers the basics: grape varietals, flavor characteristics, vocabulary, and such. Subsequent sessions may concentrate on a particular style of wine, or those from a particular region. Most tastings serve 2- or 3-ounce pours from four or five varieties. The Champagne bars on the *Dream* and *Fantasy* hold tastings too. In addition to wine, Champagne, and tequila, cruises may offer Cognac, whiskey, martini, mojito, and beer tastings as well as general classes on mixology.

The **cooking demonstrations** are some of the best presentations on board. Like the wine sessions, cooking demos often follow a theme: The first day, for example, may show how to prepare an appetizer; the second involves an entrée; and the third will be dessert. Each of these is led by a member of the kitchen staff, usually a chef. These presentations are typically held in one of the ship's nightclubs so more people can attend. To make it easy for everyone to see what the chef is doing, several video cameras are often mounted above the chef's work table, providing a view of the preparations.

We've attended many cooking demonstrations on the Disney ships, and they've all been presented better and had more interesting foods than comparable classes elsewhere. We're always amazed at the number of ingredients used in some of these dishes too. One shrimp-and-lobster appetizer we prepared involved 31 separate ingredients! You won't be making these for a church potluck.

If you're looking for exercise instead of food or shopping, the **walking tours** of the ships are a great way to keep moving and see the inner workings of the ship. Most tours begin somewhere on the pool deck and wind their way down and back up the ship. Areas covered may include the ship's bridge, engine room, kitchens and restaurants, and entertainment areas. One great thing about these tours is that you get to ask questions of the crew members staffing each section. If you want to know what it takes to prepare 800 appetizers at the same time, you'll find the person to ask on this tour.

Shopping seminars are usually held on sea days when the ship will be docked at a port the following day. (The seminars are also videotaped and available on your stateroom's television 24 hours a day.) Most seminars last 60–90 minutes, with multiple sessions held per day. Each session usually covers one kind of item, such as watches, or a particular kind of gemstone available at the next port. The seminar on diamonds, for example, explains how cut, color, carat, and clarity combine to form the basis of each stone's price.

Along with statements of fact, bear in mind that you may also hear more-specious information. During one shopping seminar on the *Wonder,* we heard the presenter say, "You don't really need to pay attention to things like clarity or gem imperfections if you love a stone, because no one will know about it except you." Of course, she didn't mention that it really *does* matter if you're buying the piece as an investment, or if you ever want to sell it or insure it. You also won't hear any negative statements about the products being shilled—while your presenter may extol the virtues of the bright-blue tanzanite, what she won't say is that this gemstone is too soft and scratch-prone to be worn regularly.

We don't understand why anyone would attend a shopping seminar. If you're considering a major purchase such as diamonds, jewelry, or an expensive watch, you're almost certainly better off postponing it until you're back at home and can do your own research. Further, with the vast array of goods available on the Internet (usually with better consumer protections), it's unlikely that you'll find many things with prices low enough to justify the risk. (See our "Shopping" section later in this chapter for more information.)

The spa and fitness center host **wellness seminars** most mornings. Topics include everything from stretching exercises and acupuncture to group cycling and Pilates. Many of the sessions, such as stretching and cycling, are free, although space is limited and you're strongly encouraged to sign up well in advance to guarantee a spot. Personal-training sessions, available in 30- or 60-minute increments, cost roughly $45–$80, respectively, before tip.

Finally, the **Disney Vacation Club (DVC)** hosts presentations on its Walt Disney World time-shares during the cruise; check your *Personal Navigator* for the schedule. A DVC representative is often stationed at a desk somewhere just off the lobby. On sea days, you'll probably find the rep roaming the halls of the ship to get the word out on an upcoming seminar. And while you may or may not want to sit through a time-share presentation on vacation, the DVC reps are very generous in giving out free stuff, as this reader found:

> We didn't want to sit through the DVC sales pitch, but we're suckers for swag. We stopped by the DVC desk and they practically threw goodies at us. Despite me saying that there were just two of us on board, the rep insisted on giving me four DVC baseball caps and four sturdy drawstring backpacks.

◼︎ **SPORTS** *and* **FITNESS**

EACH SHIP OFFERS AN ARRAY of outdoor and indoor sports and fitness options. While it's no substitute for your local megagym, there's enough equipment and variety on board for almost everyone to maintain muscle tone and cardio conditioning during the cruise.

*un*official **TIP**
The Fitness Center is on Deck 9 Forward on the *Magic* and *Wonder,* and on Deck 11 Forward on the *Dream* and *Fantasy.*

Use of the fitness center is generally limited to guests age 18 and up. While the Vibe teen club may bring a group of 14- to

17-year-olds to the gym for a group activity, a high school varsity athlete shouldn't expect to be able to use the equipment at a training level, even with parental permission or supervision.

Each DCL ship has a comprehensive **Fitness Center** with new, well-maintained weight machines, free weights, treadmills, stair-climbers, elliptical machines, stationary bikes, and more.

These gyms provide yoga mats, large plastic step-aerobics benches, exercise balls, and elastic bands for stretching. Also provided are a water fountain, a basket of fresh fruit, cloth towels, paper towels, and spray bottles of sanitizer to clean the equipment when you're done. Male and female locker rooms have showers, a sauna, sinks, robes, towels, personal-grooming items, and lockers with electric locks. There is no charge to use these facilities.

We've spent a lot of time in the gyms on every ship, and we've been happy with the variety of equipment available. Nautilus-style weight machines are available for working every major and minor muscle group. Virtually all of the electric cardio machines have video monitors so you can watch the ship's television while working out, along with plugs for your headphones.

The Fitness Centers are usually open from around 6 a.m. until 11 p.m.; check your *Personal Navigator* for the exact schedule. They tend to be most crowded in the morning between 8 and 11 a.m., and least crowded between 5 and 11 p.m. Group- and personal-training sessions are available, including weight training, Pilates, and other courses, for an additional fee. Group sessions start at around $12 per workout, typically about 45 minutes each. Individual training sessions cost around $40 per half-hour session.

The only thing we've found disconcerting in the gyms is that the treadmills on the *Dream* and *Fantasy* face the port (left) side of the ship, not the bow. If the ship is moving while you're running on one of these treadmills, the scenery in front of you will be passing from left to right, but your brain expects to see the scenery moving toward you. Some people—including Len—instinctively twist their bodies left in an attempt to line up the scenery with the way their minds think they should be going. This makes for awkward running (walking doesn't seem to be much of an issue). If you find yourself unable to run correctly on the treadmill, try the outdoor course described next.

unofficial **TIP**
If your itinerary includes a trip to Castaway Cay, Disney usually hosts a 5K run around the island starting at 9 a.m. There's no cost to run. Water is provided at several points throughout the course, and Disney usually hands out Mickey-shaped plastic "medals" to finishers. Check your *Personal Navigator* the night before your stop for where to meet on board.

Runners and walkers will appreciate the **0.3-mile track** circling Deck 4 of the *Magic* and *Wonder* and the **0.4-mile track** on Deck 4 of the *Dream* and *Fantasy*. One of the great things about running laps on the ship is the amazing scenery, which (almost) makes you forget that you're exercising while you're seeing it. We've run a few laps on both ships, and the track is certainly good enough to get in a few miles to start your day. Some sections take you through some relatively narrow corridors, and there's a good chance that you'll be running past groups of other tourists who are out enjoying the deck too. Finally, keep an eye open for water on the deck, which can make the track slick.

If running isn't your thing, every DCL ship has **outdoor basketball courts** surrounded by woven rope fencing to keep errant balls from leaving the ship. These are popular with kids and parents looking to shoot around a bit—we've never seen a competitive game played at one. The basketball courts can be converted to a miniature soccer field or volleyball court, too, if you can find enough people to play.

Each ship also has **shuffleboard courts** near midship on Deck 4; if you're up for a challenge, outdoor **tennis tables** are available too (Deck 9 Forward on the *Magic* and *Wonder; Deck 13 Aft on the *Dream* and *Fantasy*). Readers report that the windy conditions on deck make it difficult to play, but perhaps your game will benefit from a bit of unpredictability.

The *Dream* and *Fantasy* both have Disney-themed **miniature-golf courses** outdoors on Deck 13 Aft, and these are a lot of fun for the entire family. The *Dream* and *Fantasy* also have **Foosball tables** outdoors. As with the table tennis, we find it helpful to have the following list available when our game fails us:

HANDY EXCUSES FOR RECREATIONAL INEPTITUDE
• Gust of wind changed ball trajectory
• Rough seas caused ship to list suddenly
• Sunglasses aren't made for the UV rays at this latitude (*Note:* must be wearing sunglasses when saying this)
• Concentration broken by sound of pirate ship-cannon in distance
• Giant-squid tentacle was seen reaching up behind opponent

If you're looking to get in some individual practice time on the *Dream* and *Fantasy,* **virtual sports simulators** are available on Deck 13 Aft for golf, basketball, soccer, football, hockey, and baseball. These indoor facilities have a large movie screen set up in a dedicated room; a computer projects a simulated soccer field, basketball court, or other appropriate venue on the screen. You're given actual sports equipment to kick, throw, or swing. Your movements, and the movements of the ball, are tracked by computers and displayed on-screen—there's a slight lag in the display, but it's not enough to be distracting. Half-hour sessions cost $25 for golf and $12 for other sports; hour-long sessions are $45 for golf and $20 for other sports.

SPAS

SOME OF THE MOST RELAXING TIMES we've spent on DCL's ships have been in their spas. Whether you're looking for a massage, manicure, new hairstyle, or just some time to unwind in a hot sauna, you'll find it at the spa.

This section summarizes the major spa and salon services offered on each ship, but note that many more are available. We rec-ommend visiting the spa on your first after-

unofficial **TIP**
The best time to visit the spa is during dinner or when the ship is in port.

noon aboard to sign up for any last-minute treatments and check for specials. *Note:* Prices listed are approximate and do not include a tip, typically 15–20% of the cost of your treatment. There's a 50% can-cellation charge if you cancel within 24 hours of your appointment.

Salon services must be booked after 1 p.m. on your first day aboard—you can't book them online. If you're trying to book spa services before your cruise, Disney's website may not let you book some services, such as facials, for two people at the same time of day. (We think that the website assumes that only one person per ship is qualified to do these tasks, and that this person is unavailable once the first service is booked.) If you run into this problem, try booking the services online one after the other, and then visit the spa in person when you board to explain what you want done.

Along the same lines, one thing that's different about spa treat-ments on the Disney ships versus on land is that the same person is likely to be your masseuse, facialist, and manicurist—there's simply not enough room on the ship for a whole squadron of beauty experts, so roles have to be combined. Some readers like the continuity of hav-ing one person to talk with throughout their treatments; others think that one person can't provide the same level of service as multiple dedicated professionals.

ON THE *MAGIC*

ON DECK 9 FORWARD is **Senses Spa & Salon.** The reception area and check-in desk are just behind the forward elevator lobby, past the adult Quiet Cove Pool. Senses on the *Dream* and *Fantasy* have a hair salon, treatment rooms for individuals and couples, and a complex of steam baths and showers. Men's and women's locker rooms, shared with the Fitness Center, provide storage lockers with electric locks, showers, robes, slippers, and towels.

Formerly known as Vista Spa & Salon (the name still used for the *Wonder*'s spa), Senses got its current name after the ship's 2013 dry dock. The *Dream*'s and *Fantasy*'s spas are also named Senses, as well as those at the Grand Floridian and Saratoga Springs Resorts at Walt Disney World.

The changes to the *Magic*'s spa were mainly cosmetic, however, and Senses on this ship is much more akin to the *Wonder*'s Vista Spa than the other two Senses. The two major updates are a redesigned lobby and the addition of **Chill Spa** for guests ages 13–17, in line with the teen spas on the *Dream* and *Fantasy*. However, the *Magic*'s Chill Spa is nothing like those two—it's a single treatment room off the beauty salon. To call it a spa is laughable.

Senses' hair salon has services for men and women. Options for men include haircuts (around $35); the **Elemis Express Shave** with hot-towel wrap (around $45); and the wordy **Elemis Pro-Collagen Grooming Treatment with Shave** (around $95), billed as "the shave of all shaves"—an almost hour-long treatment including the towel wrap, a shave, a minifacial, and massages for your face, scalp, and hands. Men who use electric shavers for their daily toilette should be aware that a hand-held razor shaves much closer than an electric blade and can cause razor burn, even on men who aren't normally susceptible. Your face will be as smooth as a baby's bottom, though.

Women can get a literal head-to-toe makeover, starting with hairstyling. A simple shampoo and blow-dry runs about $32–$48 depending on hair length; adding a haircut is about $56–$75. Separate conditioning treatments are available: The **Frangipani Hair and Scalp Ritual,** which sounds like it's part of a tribal initiation, starts at around $30; most other standard conditioning treatments are around $50 each. Senses also offers a treatment for color-treated hair for around $30; hair coloring starts at about $55.

Waxing for eyebrows ($25), legs ($89), arms ($39), upper lip ($19), chin ($19), and bikini line ($29) is available too. If you're headed to Palo for dinner, you can get your makeup done for your big night out, starting at $75.

Manicures (around $50) and pedicures (around $70) come with a heated stone massage of your various digits. There seems to be no discount for doing both together. Additional services include adding polish ($25), removing polish ($20), paraffin baths ($15), and acrylic nails ($82).

Facials and massages are administered in private, individual treatment rooms or in one of the dedicated Spa Villas for singles and couples. Five different facials are offered, including ones with microdermabrasion, fruits and herbs, enzymes, and something that involves "amazing micro-currents applied at a high frequency" to your skin . . . voluntarily. Treatments cost $115–$170 for a 50-minute session.

Some treatment rooms at Senses on the *Magic* (and Vista Spa on the *Wonder*) sit directly under the basketball courts. If someone is playing, you'll hear through the ceiling every time someone bounces a ball or lands after jumping.

Massages include the traditional deep-tissue kind; a variation accompanied by heated, scented stones placed on various parts of your body; and another where warmed bamboo sticks are rolled over you in addition to the massage. Prices range from $129 for a basic 50-minute rubdown to $244 for 100 minutes. Besides these are massages combining hands-on therapy with slatherings of spices, minerals, and herbs designed to make you feel like a Thanksgiving turkey with a healthy glow. Among the offerings are the **Aroma Ocean Wrap with Half-Body Massage** ($188), the **Thai Herbal Poultice Massage ($195),** and the **Exotic Lime and Ginger Salt Glow with Half-Body Massage** (part of two $400-plus treatment packages for couples).

Services in the Chill Spa room for teens range from the **Magical Manicure** at the low end ($29) to the **Hot Chocolate Wrap** at the high end ($141).

Besides these spa services, 30-minute teeth-whitening treatments are available for individuals (around $150) and couples (around $260). They're not especially popular, though, probably because you're told to abstain from drinking coffee and wine after the whitening.

Our favorite spa experience is the **Rainforest,** which costs around $16 per person, per day. This gets you access to three separate steam rooms, arranged around a quiet tiled room with heated stone lounge chairs. Each steam room has its own scent, temperature, and steam setting. Outside the steam rooms are Rainforest showers, with push-button settings that allow you to vary the intensity, pattern, and temperature of the water flow.

unofficial **TIP**
We don't recommend the length-of-cruise Rainforest pass on the *Magic.* Get the cheaper one-day pass instead.

Unfortunately, the Rainforest at Senses on the *Magic* (along with the one at Vista Spa on the *Wonder*) isn't as nice as the versions on the *Dream* and *Fantasy:* It's considerably smaller and less spacious, with fewer showers and lounge chairs, and, unlike its larger siblings, it doesn't have outdoor hot tubs or ocean views. That said, it's still the most relaxing thing you can do on the *Magic*, and because DCL sells a limited number of passes per cruise—we've heard estimates of as few as 20 on the entire ship—you're unlikely to share the Rainforest with more than a handful of other people on any day. Also, a day pass at the Rainforest on the *Magic* and *Wonder* is less expensive than on the *Dream* and *Fantasy:* $16 versus $25 on the larger ships.

ON THE *WONDER*

ON DECK 9 FORWARD, **Vista Spa & Salon** largely mirrors Senses Spa & Salon on the *Magic.* Aside from the name, the only significant differences are that the interiors haven't been refurbished and the Chill Spa treatment room for teens is missing.

ON THE *DREAM* AND THE *FANTASY*

DISNEY'S TWO NEWEST SHIPS each have a **Senses Spa & Salon** on Deck 11 Forward. Both are gorgeous, incorporating dark woods and intricate tile and stonework, with comfortable leather chairs and soft bed linens. Senses on the *Dream* and *Fantasy* is much larger than Vista Spa & Salon on the *Wonder* and slightly larger than the *Magic*'s Senses. Some of the treatment rooms and spa areas afford sweeping views out over the sides of each ship; also, Senses on the *Dream* and *Fantasy* has two covered outdoor whirlpools available to those with a Rainforest pass. On the *Magic* and *Wonder,* ocean views and outdoor features are available only to those who book a pricey treatment in one of the private Spa Villas.

Salon services, facials, and massages are about the same as those offered at the spas on the *Magic* and *Wonder.* Here are the major differences:

*un*official **TIP**
Bring a towel to sit on in the saunas, and wear sandals—the seats and floors are very hot.

More luxurious than its counterparts on the two smaller ships, the **Rainforest** (about $25 per person, per day) gives you access to three saunas with varying levels of heat and humidity: the Laconium, a dry sauna with mild heat and low humidity; the Caldarium, with medium heat and humidity; and the Hamam, a full-on steam bath, with the hottest temperatures and lots and lots of steam. In addition to different levels of steam, each sauna has its own scent and music.

We enjoy hopping between these saunas and the nearby Rainforest showers—tiled circular cutouts hidden behind the walls along the path leading to the saunas. Each shower has different options for water temperature, pressure, and spray pattern, each of which you select by pushing a button. For example, one option might be a light, cool mist, perfect for when you've just jumped out of the sauna. Another is like a warm, steady downpour in a tropical jungle.

Had enough of the steam rooms and showers? Then repair to one of the two covered outdoor whirlpool tubs or one of the stone lounge chairs in an adjacent room. The ocean views here are perhaps the biggest selling point over the Rainforests on the *Magic* and *Wonder.*

The best thing about the Rainforest package is that Disney sells only a limited number of them per cruise. We hear that number can be as low as 40 people on the *Dream* and *Fantasy.* Not 40 at a time, not 40 per day—40 people on the entire ship. While we're not sure if that number is correct, we do know that we've never seen more than two other people in this part of the spa on any cruise. It's the single most relaxing thing you can do on board.

*un*official **TIP**
Parents should note that our unaccompanied teens were upsold more than $200 in beauty products during one trip to the spa. When making an appointment for your teen, specify up front whether they can buy products and, if so, how much they can spend.

Finally, exclusive to the *Dream* and *Fantasy* is the teens-only **Chill Spa,** a spa-within-a-spa entirely inside Senses. (The *Magic* also has something it calls Chill Spa, but it's a single treatment room.) Designed for guests ages 13–17, Chill has its own array of facial, massage, exfoliating, and mani–pedi packages. Prices start at around $90 for a massage, $95 for a facial, and $45 and $65 for manicures and pedicures, respectively. Hairstyling and fitness sessions in the gym are also available.

Parent–child massages are offered as well ($99 for half-body, $195 for full-body). Let us know if you've tried these with your teens, please: When we told ours about them, one replied, "Gross!" and the other gave us a look like she'd prefer being rubbed with angry ferrets.

SHOPPING

WHETHER YOU'RE AT SEA OR IN PORT, your daily *Personal Navigator* handout highlights your shopping opportunities for the day.

ONBOARD SHOPPING

ONBOARD SHOPS GENERALLY AREN'T OPEN when the ship is in port. If there's any possibility that you're going to run out of something critical during the day, be sure to stock up on it while the shops are open.

As Disney-theme-park fans, we were surprised at the relatively modest amount of space dedicated to retail stores on the Disney ships. Each ship has dedicated retail spaces for children, women, and men. Look for them on Deck 4 Forward on the *Magic* and *Wonder* and Deck 3 Forward on the *Dream* and *Fantasy,* on either side of the walkway to the Walt Disney Theatre.

The shops sell a little bit of everything, from T-shirts and stuffed animals to snacks, bathing suits, and towels. You'll also find sunscreen, aspirin, toothpaste, diapers (in limited sizes), and other travel supplies. The onboard shops may also stock location-specific items; for example, during our Alaskan cruise, the shops stocked mittens, knit caps, binoculars, and books about local wildlife. In addition, an onboard store sells duty-free alcohol by the bottle, including wines and spirits served on board, though you won't be able to take possession of your purchase until the last night of your cruise.

In case you neglected to pack your eye patch for Pirate Night, the shops can outfit the entire family head to toe, buccaneer-style. You'll find a variety of the same merchandise

unofficial TIP
A note about the "Shopping Consultants" on board: You'll note that their name tags look different from other crew members'. This is because they're not Disney employees. Both DCL and the consultants receive money back from shops that have been recommended in the *Personal Navigator* handout when guests buy something there. This is not to say you shouldn't buy from these shops, but remember that the shopping recommendations aren't entirely unbiased.

found in Disney theme parks as well as DCL-specific souvenirs. Some of our favorites are china and spreaders from Animator's Palate—the cynics among us wonder if this wasn't in response to these items walking off the ships on their own—and the DCL-exclusive AquaDuck Vinylmation. A separate retail space sells jewelry, including midpriced

IS IT REAL?

YOU PROBABLY REALIZE the "Louis Vuitton" bag on sale for $25 at the Straw Market is a fake. Also remember that perfume and sunglasses are among the most counterfeited items out there. Many luxury brands, such as Gucci and the aforementioned Louis Vuitton, do have actual stores in the Caribbean and European ports, so you can buy with confidence there (though to one author's despair, Hermès doesn't have an outpost in the Bahamas). Another thing to look out for is out-of-season merchandise being sold at full price: On one trip to Nassau, we found an authentic Kate Spade bag being sold at MSRP, but it could be found 30–50% off stateside because it was from the previous season. With all purchases, do your due diligence ahead of time to know what a fair price is for anything you're considering buying.

We find that the amount of time spent bargaining in port isn't worth any potential savings, and so we don't spend a lot of time shopping on our cruises. That said, our Ports section (see Part Eleven) highlights any especially good deals we've been able to find along the way.

watches, earrings, rings, and gold and silver chains by the inch. As we say elsewhere, we're hesitant to buy expensive things on the ship or in port. The concern we have with jewelry is that it's difficult both to comparison-shop for similar items and to assess the quality of what you're looking at.

Besides the retail spaces, each ship has an art gallery with limited-edition Disney-character and theme-park art, along with **Shutters** photo gallery, where you can purchase snaps from your cruise.

The most commonly heard advantage to buying on board or in port is that you don't pay US or local sales taxes, which can be significant on large purchases. US residents are still required to declare these purchases when they return to the States, and they may be subject to import duties. See page 60 for more details.

CASTAWAY CAY

THE SHOPS HERE SELL SOME ITEMS that are exclusive to the island, such as T-shirts and beach towels. We've purchased last-minute cords for our sunglasses, water-resistant pouches for our phones, and other beach supplies on Castaway Cay. Note that no sales tax is charged on the island or on board, which makes purchases cheaper than if you bought them at a Disney park.

IN PORT

MANY TRAVELERS FIND SHOPPING IN PORT as essential to the cruising experience as gambling is to the Las Vegas experience. If you approach buying things with this attitude, you won't be disappointed. You'll be surrounded by retail opportunities at each port from the moment you step off the ship; bargaining is expected, so assume that the price you're quoted the first time you ask isn't the final one. If you need T-shirts, duty-free booze, or handmade woodcrafts to bring back as inexpensive souvenirs, you'll have no trouble finding them within a few hundred yards of the ship.

JEWELRY Buying jewelry in port is popular with many cruisers. The problem we have with doing this is that fair prices vary greatly with the quality of the gems purchased, and you really need to be an informed shopper to know what's a good price for an item. Our recommendation is to pre-shop online (**Amazon** and **bluenile.com** are great places to start) to know the going prices for gems of the weight and quality you're interested in. One brand in particular, **Effy,** is already sold on Amazon and through its own website (**effyjewelry .com**), so check it out before you leave.

RELIGIOUS SERVICES

CRUISES OF SEVEN NIGHTS or longer hold a nondenominational Christian service on Sunday mornings and a Shabbat service on Friday evenings. Worship times depend on when the ship is in port or, in the case of Jewish services, when sunset occurs. There are no dedicated chapels on the ships—services are typically held in a lounge or theater, depending on the number of guests on board and the ship's other offerings. Guest Services can recommend houses of worship in port.

PART TEN

CASTAWAY CAY

CASTAWAY CAY IS LIKELY TO BE your favorite island on your Bahamian or Caribbean cruise. The weather is almost always gorgeous; the shore excursions are reasonably priced (mostly); and, as is the case with Walt Disney World, there's little of the "real world" to get in the way of a relaxing day. And that's before the free food and (nonalcoholic) drinks. We provide additional coverage of Castaway Cay in Part Eleven, Ports, and Part Twelve, Port Adventures.

 ## WHAT *to* BRING

THE SUN AND HEAT ARE INTENSE, so bring plenty of high-SPF sunscreen and water. Insulated sports bottles are a great idea. Other solar protection you may need includes light-colored, long-sleeved, lightweight shirts; sweatpants; swimsuit cover-ups; hats; lip balm; and sunglasses.

Disney will provide you with medium-size towels for use while on Castaway Cay—as many as you can carry. If you'd prefer a full-size beach towel, bring one of your own or purchase one while you're on the island.

Disney also provides life jackets (free) for use while on the island. Strollers, wagons, and sand-capable wheelchairs are available for rent on a first-come, first-served basis.

OTHER ITEMS YOU MAY FIND USEFUL TO BRING TO CASTAWAY CAY

- **A watch or cell phone** for checking how long everyone has been in the sun and when it's time to reapply sunscreen. Also useful for knowing whether the island's restaurants are open (usually 11 a.m.–2 p.m.).
- **An underwater or waterproof camera** for taking photos while swimming, snorkeling, or participating in other activities.
- **A small cooler** to keep medicine, baby formula, and other perishables cool. Fill it with ice before you leave the ship, and refill it from the restaurants' ice machines on the island. The cooler must be soft-sided and no larger than 12 by 12 by 12 inches; larger coolers are not allowed to be brought on the ship when boarding.

OTHER ITEMS YOU MAY FIND USEFUL TO BRING TO CASTAWAY CAY

- **Water shoes** will protect your feet from sharp rocks and coral and provide some insulation from hot sand and pavement.
- **Small beach toys,** such as a shovel and pail, though pails might present some packing issues. Toys are also available for purchase on the island.
- **Your own snorkeling gear** if you already have it, or if the idea of sharing a snorkel tube just grosses you out. DCL provides flotation vests for free.
- **Swim diapers,** if you have little ones who like the water.
- **A hairbrush or comb.** It's windy on the island, and you'll want to look good in your vacation photos.
- **Insect repellent.** Disney keeps the bug population under control, and we've never been bothered by anything. In case your family is especially sensitive to bites, however, it's a good idea to bring something like Off or Repel.
- **Something to read—a book or e-reader.** Be careful, however, about leaving expensive electronics alone on the island.
- **A portable music player.** Especially useful if you're going for a jog around the island's 5K course.
- **Athletic shoes and socks.** If you want to play basketball on the island, you'll also want proper footwear.
- **A change of clothes.** While Castaway Cay's sun will dry your swimsuit in a hurry, you may want dry clothes to wear while you're walking around the island, sitting down for meals, or riding bikes. You can also return to the ship to change, but going through security takes time.
- **A small amount of cash.** Castaway Cay has its own official Bahamian post office from which you can mail home postcards and letters. The post office takes cash only (no room charges), so bring a few dollars for postage. (This is the only place on the island for which you'll need cash.)

WHAT *to* DO

THERE ARE MORE THINGS TO DO than you'll have time for in a single day or even two. A list of our favorite Castaway Cay shore activities follows; see Part Twelve for details.

- **Castaway Ray's Stingray Adventure** affords you the opportunity to pet and feed small and medium-size stingrays in a dedicated lagoon.
- The **snorkeling lagoon** features underwater sights, such as a replica of the *Nautilus* submarine from *20,000 Leagues Under the Sea,* other shipwrecks and shipping artifacts, plus statues of Minnie and Mickey. Common marine life seen in the snorkeling lagoon includes stingrays, blue tang, and yellowtail snapper (plus the occasional barracuda).
- Rent **sailboats or paddleboats, personal watercraft,** or **inflatable floats and tubes.**
- Runners may want to start their day with the **Castaway Cay 5K,** a free (as in no-cost) jog through the developed parts of the island.
- Single-speed **bicycle rentals** allow you to fully explore the island, including the island's observation tower and trails, which can be accessed only on foot or bike.

Continued on page 178

Castaway Cay

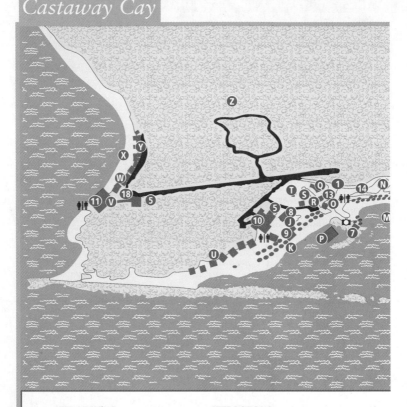

ATTRACTIONS

A. Arrival Plaza
B. Post Office
C. Marge's Barges and
    Sea Charters Dock
D. Boating Harbor
E. Scuttle's Cove
F. Boat Beach
G. Monstro Point
H. Castaway Ray's
    Stingray Adventure
I. Gil's Fins and Boats
J. Gazebos
K. Castaway Family Beaches
L. Snorkeling Lagoon
M. Swimming Lagoon
N. In-Da-Shade Games
O. Flippers and Floats
P. Pelican Plunge

ATTRACTIONS

Q. The Hide Out (teens only)
R. Bike Rentals
S. Beach Sports
T. Spring-a-Leak
U. Family Cabanas 1–21
V. The Windsock Hut
W. Massage Cabanas
X. Serenity Bay Adult Beach
Y. Adult Cabanas 22–25
Z. Observation Tower

FOOD AND DRINK

1. Pop's Props and Boat Repair
    (Covered Seating)
2. Dig In (Covered Seating)
3. Cookie's BBQ
4. Conched Out Bar

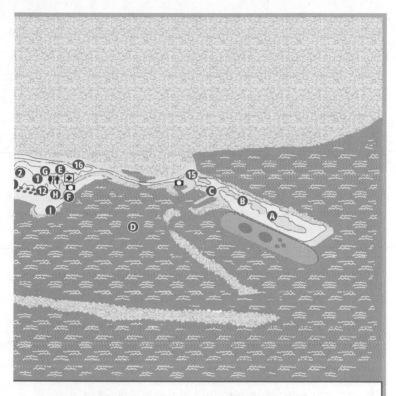

FOOD AND DRINK

5. Outdoor Seating
6. Gumbo Limbo (Covered Seating)
7. Heads Up Bar
8. Grouper (Covered Seating)
9. Sand Bar
10. Cookie's Too BBQ
11. Castaway Air Bar

SHOPPING

12. She Sells Sea Shells . . .
    and Everything Else
13. Buy the Seashore
14. Bahamian Retail

MISCELLANEOUS

15. Kargo Handling Tram Stop
16. Scuttle's Cove Tram Stop
17. Pelican Point Tram Stop
18. Serenity Bay Tram Stop

⊞ First Aid
♦♦ Restrooms and
    Outdoor Showers
◘ Photo Opportunities
■ Bike/Nature Trail

Continued from page 175

Castaway Cay's lagoons are shallow, with small, gentle waves. Anchored within a short swim from shore is **Pelican Plunge,** a floating platform with two waterslides and a water-play area. The waterslides begin on the platform's second story (accessed by stairs) and end with a splash back into the lagoon. Each slide offers a different experience: One is a long, open slide with moderate turns, while the other is a shorter, enclosed slide with plenty of tight turns and twists.

Along with the slides, Pelican Plunge's water-play area includes pipes, nozzles, and plumes of water spraying out from every direction. The main feature is a giant overhead bucket, which is constantly being filled with water from the lagoon. The bucket is counterbalanced so that when the water reaches a certain level, the bucket tilts over suddenly, pouring gallons of water on anything nearby.

If you have small children who enjoy water but you're concerned about ocean currents, consider letting the little ones run around at the inland **Spring-a-Leak** water-play area, just beyond the Pelican Point tram stop, near the middle of the family beaches. Like Pelican Plunge, Spring-a-Leak has plenty of burbling, spraying, misting water to keep kids wet and happy all day long.

Scuttle's Cove, an additional area for the little ones, offers supervised activities, yet another water-play area, and a giant-whale-bone excavation site.

Teens have their own dedicated area inland: **The Hide Out,** with volleyball, tetherball, and other activities. Be aware that some teens may not like the fact that The Hide Out is away from the beach and has no water features or water-play areas.

Height and Age Requirements at Castaway Cay

- **Pelican Plunge waterslide:** No official height requirement listed; life jackets encouraged
- **The Hide Out:** Ages 14–17; must be registered for Vibe on board
- **Scuttle's Cove:** Ages 3–12; must be registered for the Oceaneer Club/Lab on board

▌▌ WHERE *to* RELAX

CASTAWAY CAY IS ALSO A GREAT PLACE to sit back, listen to the ocean, feel the sea breeze on your face, and smell the salt air. Two family beaches are available, while adults ages 18 and up have **Serenity Bay,** a private beach with its own outdoor barbecue, bar, rental cabanas, and more.

FAMILY BEACHES Most of Castaway Cay's developed beachfront is reserved for families. If you're taking the tram from the dock, get off at the first stop, **Pelican Point,** and you'll find yourself in the middle of both family beaches.

A small, hook-shaped peninsula juts into the lagoon and effectively separates the family beaches. If you're going to rent floats or boats or do some snorkeling, you'll want to head to the left of the peninsula once you're off the tram. If you're going to play in the water, especially at the Pelican Plunge waterslide, bear right.

Both family beaches offer free lounge chairs and towels, with restrooms, food, and drink dispensers a short walk away. The Pelican Plunge side of the beach also has 21 private cabanas for rent ($549 per day; Serenity Bay has 5 cabanas that rent for $399 per day). These are so popular that they're all generally reserved by concierge and Platinum Castaway Club members before the general public gets a crack at them. On the off-chance that a cabana is available, ask at the Port Adventures desk as soon as you board the ship.

PART ELEVEN

PORTS

THE FOLLOWING SECTION outlines the ports visited by Disney Cruise Line (DCL). Grouped geographically, each profile summarizes the port's history, weather, port information, tourist highlights, food, and shopping opportunities.

Just for the record, some ports as classified by DCL aren't technically part of the geographic area in which they're listed; rather, they're part of an itinerary with a significant part or a majority of its route within that area. For example, Dover, United Kingdom, is listed under "Mediterranean Ports" because it's on an itinerary that begins there; heads south along the Atlantic coast, visiting Vigo, Spain, and Lisbon, Portugal; and travels north and east along the Mediterranean coast from Gibraltar to Barcelona, Spain. Also, note that a few ports are listed in multiple areas—Dover, for instance, also appears in "Northern European Ports."

Our Itineraries Index (page 265) lists the specific itineraries that visit the ports described here and also includes maps of each area.

ALASKAN PORTS

Juneau, Alaska

LANGUAGES English and Tlingit

HISTORY Juneau began as a mining camp. Gold mining was the major industry from the 1880s until the 1940s, when the last official gold mine was closed. Juneau has been the capital of Alaska since 1906, first as a district and then remaining as the government seat when Alaska became a state in 1959. Growth accelerated in the 1970s with the building of the Trans-Alaska Pipeline. Central Juneau is close to sea level and is surrounded by natural elements, including mountains, glaciers, and the Gastineau Channel. There are no roads leading in or out of town. Travel to other areas is almost exclusively by boat or plane.

WEATHER Disney cruises dock in Juneau May–August. Average daytime highs during this period range from the mid-50s to the low 60s. (*Note:*

All temperatures listed are in degrees Fahrenheit.) Nighttime lows during these months are in the low-to-mid-40s. Precipitation is fairly steady throughout the year. Typical rainfall is 4–5 inches per month during the summer.

THE PORT All ships dock within walking distance of downtown Juneau. Within a mile, you'll find the **Federal Building,** the **Governor's House,** the **State Capitol,** the **Alaska State Museum,** the **Visitor Center,** and other attractions. Shuttles and taxis service key attractions beyond downtown.

TOURIST HIGHLIGHTS The **Mendenhall Glacier** is a primary attraction. Check at the visitor center for a guide to walking trails maintained by the US Forest Service. In addition to natural features, you may see bears fishing for salmon in glacial streams. The **Mt. Roberts Tramway** ferries guests 1,800 feet up the peak for scenic views and hiking. Points of historic interest include **St. Nicholas Russian Orthodox Church,** the oldest operating church in Alaska. Also stop by the **Red Dog Saloon,** a remnant of the mining era with an Old West atmosphere. For a walking tour that covers many of these points of interest, see page 250.

WHAT TO EAT Fresh fish is a key part of menus throughout the area. Salmon and halibut are most common, but shellfish is also easy to find. Our favorite restaurant in Alaska is **Tracy's King Crab Shack,** just steps from the dock. A moderately covered outdoor venue with a view of the harbor, Tracy's serves Alaskan king crab significantly bigger than your head. We opted for the sampler platter of crab chowder, crab cakes, and a monster crab leg, washed down with an Alaskan Brewing Company ale. If you ask the cook nicely, he may let you hold a crab for a fun photo op. It's a little pricey, but delish.

WHAT TO BUY Carved Alaskan jade is abundant in souvenir shops. Also look for native arts and crafts that use natural elements such as stone, wood, and fur.

Ketchikan, Alaska

LANGUAGE English

HISTORY Ketchikan was first settled by native tribes lured by the seaside location. The area has one of the world's largest collections of standing totem poles, found both in town and scattered throughout the region, most created by the town's native founders. In the late 1800s and early 1900s, fishing and fish processing, along with lumber and lumber processing, began to attract settlers from other parts of the world. The town embodied a freewheeling, frontier spirit with plentiful saloons and brothels. Today, Ketchikan is known in Alaska as the Salmon Capital of the World and caters to a booming tourist trade.

WEATHER Disney cruises dock in Ketchikan May–August, when average daytime highs range from the mid-50s to the mid-60s and nighttime lows from the low 40s to the low 50s. While precipitation is lowest during the summer months, Ketchikan is in a maritime-rainforest area, with abundant rainfall and cloud cover. Expect to get wet: Typical rainfall is 6–9 inches per month during May, June, July, and August.

THE PORT Ships dock adjacent to the center of town. The town itself is only three blocks wide with most points of interest easily accessible from the port.

TOURIST HIGHLIGHTS An in-town highlight is the seasonal lumberjack show, where professional lumberjacks demonstrate ax throws, log rolling, and pole climbing. Those wishing to stay near the port can enjoy several small museums, including the **Totem Heritage Center,** the **Tongass Historical Museum,** and the **Southeast Alaska Discovery Center.** (For a walking tour that covers these and other points of interest, see page 251.) Take a ride on the **Cape Fox Lodge** funicular, which affords spectacular views of the port and surrounding areas. Outdoor activities include kayaking, hiking, and wildlife observation.

WHAT TO EAT The local fresh fish is a must-try. Fishermen bring in frequent hauls of salmon, shrimp, crab, octopus, and more.

WHAT TO BUY Alaskan crafts such as miniature carved totems, silver and bronze sculptures, wool clothing, and regional foods are typical Ketchikan souvenirs. Our favorite souvenir purchased on any vacation is the beaver pelt we got at **Tall Tale Taxidermy,** run by the Szurley family, longtime Ketchikan residents. A stop at Tall Tale convinced Erin, a squeamish New Yorker, that taxidermy is a true art form.

Skagway, Alaska

LANGUAGE English

HISTORY Skagway was originally settled by the native Chilkoot and Chilkat peoples. Beginning in the late 1800s, Skagway became a center for gold exploration. In 1896 gold was found in the region, leading to an influx of prospectors, miners, and associated service providers. Competition among prospectors was fierce, leading to a lawless, Wild West atmosphere. The gold rush was over by 1900, but the spectacular wilderness inspired many to stay and maintain the new town.

WEATHER Disney cruises dock in Skagway May–August. Average daytime highs during these months range from the mid-50s to the mid-60s, with nighttime lows averaging from the low 40s to the low 50s. Typical rainfall is 1–2 inches during the summer.

THE PORT There is no passenger terminal—cruise ships dock alongside industrial sea vessels. The dock is an easy walk from town; there are also inexpensive buses. The entire town is accessible from one main street, Broadway. For a walking tour that covers the area, see page 253.

TOURIST HIGHLIGHTS At the **Klondike Gold Rush National Historical Park,** the visitor center has educational materials about the area's mining heyday. For more-hands-on learning, try panning for gold yourself at the **Liarsville Gold Rush Trail Camp** (see page 249 for details). **White Pass and Yukon Route Railroad,** a narrow-gauge train line, offers scenic views of mountains, waterfalls, and gorges; in **Haines,** a ferry ride away, you can enjoy watching the whales and American bald eagles. Other outdoor adventures include horseback riding, hiking, rock climbing, and dog sledding.

WHAT TO EAT Fresh fish appears on menus throughout the area. Also try the local Alaskan king crab and elk meat. Due to the cost of shipping nonlocal food to this remote location, prices may be higher than otherwise expected.

WHAT TO BUY Skagway is a small town, catering mostly toward the tourist trade, with abundant small souvenirs. Typical finds include mining and railroad artifacts, hand-knit woolen garments, ceramics, carved wood, and jewelry made by local artisans. Most shops in Skagway don't open until 9 a.m. at the earliest, and there are few notable breakfast spots in town. Unless you have an early excursion, feel free to sleep a little late without feeling like you're missing something.

Tracy Arm, Alaska

HISTORY Tracy Arm is a fjord—a long, narrow inlet with steep cliffs on both sides, created by glacial movement. Part of the Tongass National Forest, Tracy Arm is more than 30 miles long, and ice covers about one-fifth of the area. In the summer, the fjord may have significant icebergs floating in its waters.

WEATHER The weather is similar to Juneau's: Average daytime highs May–August range from the mid-50s to the low 60s, nighttime lows during these months are in the low-to-mid-40s, and typical rainfall is 4–5 inches per month.

THE PORT Ships do not dock at Tracy Arm—there is no port or town. The experience is the view from aboard your ship.

TOURIST HIGHLIGHTS Tracy Arm is all about the scenery of the **Sawyer Glaciers.** Take in the granite cliffs, icebergs, and forested mountains. You may spot wildlife such as bears, whales, bald eagles, mountain goats, and more. About once per hour, the glaciers calve, sending massive ice sheets into the waters below. The impact of the glaciers is vastly different on different decks. Soaring vistas are best viewed from Decks 9 and 10; to spot animals, try the outdoor areas of Deck 4. If your stateroom is on a lower deck, look out your porthole from time to time. Periodically vary your location on the ship for a fuller experience.

Vancouver, British Columbia

LANGUAGE English

HISTORY Europeans first visited Vancouver in the late 1700s. The gold rush in the late 1800s brought the initial long-term settlers. Early industry focused on logging, mining, and transportation, due to the natural port. Immigrants came from England, Scotland, Ireland, and Germany, followed by an influx from China and other areas of Asia. Vancouver is now a major industrial center and cosmopolitan city bustling with high-rises, shopping, restaurants, and entertainment.

WEATHER Cruises depart from Vancouver during the summer and early fall. The average daytime highs May–September range from the low 60s to the low 70s. Average nighttime lows during those months range from the mid-40s to the mid-50s. This moderate climate makes Vancouver one of the warmest cities in Canada. Vancouver's rainfall is lowest in the summer, averaging less than 3 inches per month May–September.

THE PORT Disney cruises embark at the **Canada Place Cruise Terminal,** adjacent to downtown Vancouver. Within walking distance you'll find the **Pan Pacific Hotel,** along with many restaurants and bars.

TOURIST HIGHLIGHTS The **Vancouver Lookout,** near Harbour Centre, affords a panoramic overview of the city. For additional visual stimulation, check out the **Vancouver Art Gallery,** which displays more than 10,000 pieces of art. Other local attractions include **Science World,** with interactive exhibits and an Omnimax theater, and the **Vancouver Aquarium,** home to 70,000 sea creatures and where whale, dolphin, and sea otter shows happen daily. The **Dr. Sun Yat-Sen Classical Chinese Garden** is the first authentic Chinese garden built outside of China. A 15-minute SkyTrain ride from Vancouver will take you to **Metropolis at Metrotown,** British Columbia's largest shopping center.

WHAT TO EAT You can find nearly every cuisine represented in the restaurants of Vancouver. Local seafood is a must. For authentic Asian dishes, visit the **Chinatown** district. **Granville Island** is a public market with fresh local seafood and produce; walk among the dozens of stalls to taste the best from local vendors.

WHAT TO BUY No trip to Canada is complete without the purchase of something maple—syrup, candy, and even maple mustard. Find silk robes in Chinatown, local crafts at Granville Island, and gear representing the Vancouver Canucks hockey team everywhere.

BAHAMIAN *and* CARIBBEAN PORTS

Castaway Cay, Bahamas *(also see Parts Ten and Twelve)*

LANGUAGE English

HISTORY DCL entered into a 99-year lease agreement with the Bahamian government in 1999, giving the cruise line the rights to develop what was then known as Gorda Cay. Renamed Castaway Cay by Disney, the island measures about 1.5 square miles and sits in the Atlantic Ocean, roughly 80 miles north-northeast of Nassau, at about the same latitude as Fort Lauderdale, Florida (100 miles to the west).

WEATHER Castaway Cay is a year-round destination, but no matter when you visit, it's either warm or hot. Average high temperatures gradually increase from around 76° late December–January to a peak of 89° in August, before they drop again. Low temperatures are also moderate, from 62° in late January to 76° throughout the summer. Rain patterns follow the Atlantic hurricane season, with peak rainfall occurring late August–early November. Precipitation is lightest December–May.

TOURIST HIGHLIGHTS Less than 10% of Castaway Cay has been developed for cruise guests, but Disney packs a lot of activities into that relatively small space, including two family beaches; one adults-only beach; separate lagoons for boating and snorkeling; a teens-only hangout; basketball, soccer, and volleyball areas; and bike trails. Two open-air trams connect the dock with these areas.

WHAT TO EAT Castaway Cay has three all-you-care-to-eat outdoor restaurants: **Cookie's BBQ, Cookie's Too,** and **Serenity Bay BBQ.** Each restaurant serves the same menu of grilled hot dogs, hamburgers, veggie burgers, chicken, fish, and ribs. Sides include corn on the cob, coleslaw, various salads, and similar picnic food, plus cookies and soft-serve ice cream for dessert. They're generally open 11 a.m.–2 p.m. Serenity Bay BBQ is at the adults-only Serenity Bay beach—no guests under age 18.

All of Castaway Cay's bars serve similar drinks. **Conched Out Bar,** near the gazebo, is the largest bar but has only outdoor seating.

Sand Bar, near the Castaway Cay family beach, is a small shack with a couple of serving windows, specializing in beer and frozen drinks. A limited amount of shaded bench seating is available. **Castaway Air Bar,** near the Serenity Bay adult beach, is the quietest of Castaway Cay's bars, and the view is pretty good too. **Heads Up Bar,** near Castaway Ray's Stingray Adventures, sits at the far end of the pier. The one downside to Heads Up is the lack of shade. It can get very hot very quickly out here, so lingering with a drink isn't always possible. The views are great here, though.

WHAT TO BUY Castaway Cay offers minimal opportunities for shopping. Two Disney-operated souvenir stands offer merchandise similar to what you'll find in the onboard shops, such as t-shirts, flip-flops, and baseball caps, as well as fun-in-the-sun basics, including plastic buckets, sunscreen, and goggles. If you're looking for something that specifically says "Castaway Cay" on it, buy it on the island. In addition to the Disney shops, one building houses a few stalls run by Bahamian merchants. You'll find items here much like you'd find at the Straw Market at Nassau: bags, sun hats, and figurines. The one item that many guests find to be a true must is a postage stamp. The island's teeny post office will imprint your letters with a special Castaway Cay postmark. The post office accepts cash only (US currency is fine), not your Key to the World Card, so be sure to carry a few dollars onto the island.

Cozumel, Mexico

LANGUAGE Spanish

HISTORY Cozumel was a Mayan outpost from the first century. Mayan legend describes Cozumel as the home of Ixchel, a love and fertility goddess. The story says that when temples were dedicated to her, she released her favorite birds, swallows, as a symbol of her gratitude. (*Cozumel* is derived from *Cuzamil,* Mayan for "Land of the Swallows.") The Spanish arrived in the early 1500s, bringing disease that decimated the Mayan population. For years after this, the region was besieged by pirates. In the late 1800s, Abraham Lincoln briefly explored the possibility of making Cozumel a relocation point for freed American slaves. Popularity as a tourist region exploded in the 1960s after explorer Jacques Cousteau mentioned it in a documentary as one of the most beautiful areas in the world for scuba diving.

WEATHER Temperatures are constant throughout the year. Average daytime highs are in the 80s in every season. Average nighttime lows range from the high 60s to the mid-70s year-round. Precipitation, on the other hand, varies widely during the year. The driest season is October–March, with an average of less than 5 inches of rainfall during each of those months. Rainfall increases to an average of 8 inches per month in the spring, and an average of up to 10 inches per month in the summer.

THE PORT Disney ships generally dock at the **Punta Langosta Pier,** at the southern end of the downtown area. There is skybridge access to the **Punta Langosta Mall,** across the street from the dock; here you'll find basic services, including shops, restaurants, and a Starbucks. Taxis travel to all outlying points.

TOURIST HIGHLIGHTS It's all about the water in Cozumel. Snorkeling and diving in the coral reefs are a popular draw, particularly at **Cozumel Reefs National Marine Park.** For history buffs, the pre-Columbian ruins at **Xelha, Chichén Itzá,** and **Tulum** offer a look into the Mayan culture. **Chankanaab National Park** offers opportunities to interact with marine animals, as well as walking trails that wind among a large iguana population. Cozumel is also the perfect place to enjoy the sun as you lounge at one of its many beaches.

WHAT TO EAT Fish is plentiful here, with grilled mahimahi on many menus. You'll also find familiar Mexican fare such as fajitas, tacos, and enchiladas. Many restaurants offer barbecued pork. Margaritas are found in most watering holes, and you may find that some spots have their own house-made tequila. Also try the local *michelada,* beer mixed with lime juice.

WHAT TO BUY Jewelry, Mexican handicrafts, and tourist T-shirts are all sold close to the cruise terminal. You may find good-quality leather sandals, bags, and hammocks. For food gifts, look for tequila or vanilla, or try the local liqueur Xtabentún, made from honey.

Falmouth, Jamaica

LANGUAGES English and Patois

HISTORY Falmouth was founded in 1769. During the late 18th century, it served as a major distribution point for rum, sugar, coffee, and molasses. In trade for crops, Falmouth received many Africans. The port's business declined with the end of slavery in the 1800s, but tourism brought a resurgence of visitors in the late 1900s.

WEATHER Temperatures in Falmouth are consistent throughout the year. In all months, the average daytime high is in the 80s, and the average nighttime low is in the 70s. Falmouth averages less than 3 inches of rain per month January–April. Rainfall picks up later in the year, with an average of about 6 inches per month May–November. Rainfall decreases again in December, to about 4 inches.

THE PORT Falmouth's cruise port opened in 2011 to much fanfare. When ships are docked, local vendors set up stalls nearby to sell local wares. The terminal also offers several permanent shops and duty-free vendors. Walking about 5 minutes past the port will bring you to the town of Falmouth and access to restaurants and more shops.

TOURIST HIGHLIGHTS The **Good Hope Great House** is a former sugar plantation; estate tours are a highlight of a Falmouth visit. The property also offers horse and buggy rides, dune buggy excursions, river tubing, and zip lining. Many of these activities are also available at **Mystic**

Mountain adventure park. **Dunn's River Falls** is a spectacular natural phenomenon. As you walk through town, stop to see the **Water Square Fountain,** the **Anglican Parish Church,** and **Falmouth Court House.** A few beaches are within a 10-minute taxi ride away; **Montego Bay**'s party beaches are about a 30-minute taxi ride away.

WHAT TO EAT Jerk-style preparations are a staple of Jamaican cuisine. Meat, chicken, or fish is rubbed with spices and sugars and then grilled over a wood fire. Rice and beans is a typical side dish. To cool off, try fresh local mango, guava, and the national fruit, ackee. Also look for Jamaican patties, pastries stuffed with meat. With many yam farms nearby, you'll also find yams on many restaurant menus. Rum and rum punches are a potent way to jump-start your relaxation. The national beer, Red Stripe, is served throughout the area.

WHAT TO BUY Many visitors bring home jarred spices and jerk seasonings; rum and coffee are also good souvenirs. Local artwork, jewelry, woodcarvings, and woven goods are also popular items.

Galveston, Texas

LANGUAGE English

HISTORY Galveston Island was first inhabited by the Karankawa and Akokisa Indians. The Spanish first explored the area in the early 1500s, and the French held force there for much of the 1600s. In 1816, the first permanent European settlement was founded by pirates, who used Galveston as a base of support for the Mexicans against the Spanish in the region. By 1860, Galveston was part of the Republic of Texas and a major port in the slave trade. Later, it became the first city in Texas to provide a secondary school for African Americans. Galveston has been subjected to several major hurricanes, including a catastrophic 1900 storm that remains the deadliest natural disaster in US history.

WEATHER Disney cruises depart from Galveston October–December. The average daytime high in October hovers around 80°, with average nighttime lows in the high 60s. Daytime highs in November and December average in the 60s, with nighttime lows in the high 40s and low 50s. Precipitation is fairly constant: Expect average rainfall of 2–4 inches per month.

THE PORT The cruise terminal has basic services. About two blocks from the terminal, you'll find several hotels with shops and restaurants.

TOURIST HIGHLIGHTS **Pleasure Pier,** on the Galveston Seawall, is a low-key carnival area. For more thrills, head over to **Schlitterbahn** water park. **Moody Gardens** is a botanical preserve and theme park with 3-D and 4-D theaters. Small museums in the area include the **Railroad Museum,** the **Texas Seaport Museum,** and the **Offshore Drilling Rig Museum.** If you're spending time in **Houston** before cruising, check out the **Houston Zoo,** the **Houston Museum of Natural Science,** the **Downtown Aquarium,** and of course the **Johnson Space Center.**

WHAT TO EAT Look for seafood in Galveston, particularly crab and shrimp. For a Texas-style meal, keep an eye out for barbecue brisket and chicken. The area has several Cajun restaurants, with jambalaya and New Orleans–influenced po'boys on the menu. Plus, more than a dozen steakhouses call the region home, so you'll have no problem finding beef prepared just the way you like it.

WHAT TO BUY Along the beach, you'll find shops selling the requisite T-shirts and sunglasses, along with jewelry made from shells or coral, beachwear, wind chimes, and beach toys. If you're visiting Houston before your cruise, look for NASA-related items and clothing emblazoned with the logos of the city's sports teams.

Grand Cayman, Cayman Islands

LANGUAGE English

HISTORY Christopher Columbus accidentally discovered these islands during a voyage in 1503. The Caymans came under British control following the 1670 Treaty of Madrid; during this time, they also saw an influx of settlers from Jamaica, and slaves were brought to the island beginning in the 1730s until slavery was abolished in 1834. The region underwent periodic attacks from pirates into the late 18th century. Jamaica (a British colony at the time) governed the islands until 1962, when Jamaica became independent and the Caymans elected to stay under British rule.

WEATHER Temperatures are consistent throughout the year. Daytime highs average in the 80s and nighttime lows in the 70s. Precipitation, however, varies considerably: During December–April, you can expect an average of less than 3 inches of rainfall per month, while May–August experiences an average of about 6 inches of rainfall per month. September–November may have up to 9 inches of rainfall per month.

THE PORT Grand Cayman is a tender port—you have to take a smaller vessel to get from the ship to land. The tender brings you to the edge of downtown **George Town**. Shops and restaurants are within walking distance of the dock.

TOURIST HIGHLIGHTS Stingray City offers opportunities to swim with rays. The **Cayman Turtle Farm** is a research facility that studies green sea turtles; here, you'll be able to observe the 16,000 inhabitants and watch the turtle hatchlings feed. Water lovers will find abundant scuba and snorkeling opportunities, including excursions to swim near the wreck of a sunken 1940s schooner. History buffs will enjoy the **Pedro St. James Historic Site** and the **Cayman Islands National Museum**. A nearby seaside village named **Hell** lures many visitors who just want to say they've been there. Numerous nearby beaches afford opportunities for sunning and relaxation.

WHAT TO EAT Seafood—including the traditional national dish, turtle—is plentiful here. Look for rock shrimp and conch in many dishes. Jerked meats are popular on the island, as are many grilled meats. Many of the desserts, such as sticky pudding and rum cakes, have a British influence. Other sweets may include fruit, honey, and coconut.

WHAT TO BUY Decorative conch shells make a nice reminder of the area. If you've interacted with the stingrays or turtles, a carved replica of these creatures may make a good souvenir. Also look for local artwork and woven hats and bags. Gourmets will want to bring home some Tortuga rum cake.

Key West, Florida

LANGUAGE English

HISTORY The original inhabitants of the area were the Tequesta and Calusa peoples. Juan Ponce de León was the first recorded European visitor, arriving in 1521. Cubans and British used the island as a fishing spot before it was claimed by Spain; however, Spain exerted little control over the area. In 1822 Matthew C. Perry claimed the Keys for the United States. The islands became more prosperous when they were connected to mainland Florida by an overseas railway bridge in 1912.

WEATHER Daytime temperatures average in the 80s April–November, with nighttime lows during that time in the 70s. December–March, daytime temperatures average in the 70s, with nighttime lows in the 60s. Precipitation is lowest in the winter and spring, with average rainfall of less than 3 inches per month November–May. The summer gets wetter, with average rainfall of 3–5 inches per month in June and July. August, September, and October average 5–7 inches of rain per month.

THE PORT The entire island measures only 2 miles by 4 miles, so many services are within distance of a brisk walk from port. **Mallory Square,** on the waterfront near the docks, offers bars, restaurants, and basic shopping. To get around the area without walking, rent golf carts, bicycles, or a pedicab near the port. The **Conch Tour Train** allows visitors to hop on and off for personalized island touring. For less kitsch and more charm, be sure to explore a bit beyond the immediate port area.

TOURIST HIGHLIGHTS The must-do for literary types is a stop at the **Ernest Hemingway Home and Museum.** See Hemingway's studio and visit with the colony of cats descended from the author's many feline companions. For excellent views of the Keys, visit the nearby **Lighthouse and Keepers Quarters Museum.** Nature experiences are available at the **Key West Aquarium** and the **Key West Butterfly Conservancy.** And no trip to Key West would be complete without some relaxation time on the beach.

WHAT TO EAT Fresh seafood is abundant here, with oysters, clams, lobster, grouper, and shrimp appearing on many menus. Conch fritters are a specialty at many restaurants. There is a large Cuban influence in the food culture here: Look for sandwiches on Cuban bread stuffed with meats and cheeses. Beef stews, plantains, and yellow rice are all served with a Cuban flair. Of course the most popular regional dessert is Key lime pie, made with the juice of local fruit. In addition to pie, you're likely to find dozens of other lime-accented foods during your visit, including cookies, candy, salsa, and barbecue sauce. Rumrunners, mojitos, and margaritas are all available to help you ease into the island lifestyle.

WHAT TO BUY Most of the shopping is casual and beach-oriented. Look for T-shirts, sunglasses, swimsuits, and surf- and sun-related trinkets. Epicureans may take home a bottle of Key lime juice to use in their own cooking. If you want a permanent souvenir, you could get a tattoo at one of the many shops on the island.

Miami, Florida

LANGUAGES English and Spanish

Miami, Florida *(continued)*

HISTORY The Tequesta Indians inhabited the area until Spain claimed it in 1566. Spain ceded Florida to the United States in 1819. Miami, named after the Miami River, became a force to be reckoned with following the 1896 southward expansion of Henry Flagler's Florida East Coast Railroad. The population boomed until the Great Depression, and after a pause, the area saw another surge in population from 1960s Cuban exiles.

WEATHER Average daytime highs are in the 80s May–October, with nighttime lows in the 70s. Average daytime highs are in the 70s December–April, with average nighttime lows in the 60s. Precipitation is greatest during the summer. November–April, expect an average monthly rainfall of about 3 inches or less. May, July, and October average 4–5 inches of rainfall per month, while June, August, and September see average rainfall of 6–9 inches per month.

THE PORT The Port of Miami is 9 miles from Miami International Airport and about 5 minutes from downtown. **Bayside Market,** a shopping and dining center, is a 15-minute walk from the port. A park with a small sand beach is also nearby. Major hotels and restaurants are within walking distance.

TOURIST HIGHLIGHTS **South Beach** is where the beautiful people go. Take a stroll there to see the Art Deco architecture, and stop in a bar or club for a drink. Another interesting neighborhood is **Little Havana,** imbued with old-world charm. Learn about Miami's immigrant history at the **Cuban Museum of the Americas.** Gardeners will like the **Fruit and Spice Park,** which grows more than 500 species of edibles, while kids will love exploring the **Miami Children's Museum** and the **Seaquarium.** And, of course, you can soak in the sun at the area's many beaches.

WHAT TO EAT Many local establishments serve food with a Cuban flair. Look for stewed chicken or lamb and grilled fish or pork accompanied by tomatoes, vegetables, and rice. Seafood gumbo with rice is also popular, as are stuffed Cuban sandwiches. For a pick-me-up, try strong Cuban-style coffee. For a slow-me-down, try sangria, mojitos, or other fruit-based drinks.

WHAT TO BUY Miami is a major cosmopolitan city with luxury chains and chic boutiques in abundance. There are also the requisite beachside T-shirt and trinket shops. For off-the-beaten-path ideas, try the **Tropicana Flea Market,** open on weekends. Sports fans may want to pick up a Miami Heat jersey or gear from the University of Miami. Hand-rolled cigars are sold in many areas of Miami. A classic, and classy, choice for gentlemen would be a *guayabera,* the loose-fitting Cuban-style shirt. Ladies can start their cruise with some new swimwear.

Nassau, Bahamas

LANGUAGE English

HISTORY Originally called Charles Town, Nassau was destroyed by fire in 1684 during an attack by the Spanish. It was rebuilt and renamed 10 years later by the Dutch and English. Over the next few decades, the Bahamas became a pirate stronghold. In 1718 the Brits ousted the pirates and reclaimed the area. During the American Revolutionary War, there was a brief occupation by Americans and then another Spanish occupation in 1782. The Spaniards surrendered the land back to England a year later. In 1807 the slave trade was outlawed, and thousands of freed slaves eventually made the island their home. Today, Nassau is a major tourist destination.

WEATHER Daytime highs average in the 80s March–November. Temperatures drop slightly in winter, with daytime highs averaging in the 70s December–February. Nighttime lows average in the 70s June–October and in the 60s November–May. Precipitation is lowest in the winter, with average monthly rainfall of less than 3 inches November–April. A moderate rise occurs in May with average monthly rainfall of less than 5 inches. Precipitation increases substantially in the summer and fall, with up to 9 inches of rainfall per month June–October.

THE PORT Ships dock at **Prince George Wharf,** on which is located the **Festival Welcome Center** with basic tourist services. Downtown Nassau is a 10-minute walk away.

TOURIST HIGHLIGHTS Our walking tour (see page 254) takes in such points of interest as the **Queen's Staircase,** the **Government House,** and **John Watling's Distillery.** Museum and history lovers will enjoy the **National Art Gallery of the Bahamas,** the **Pirate Museum,** and **Fort Charlotte.** Numerous beach, water-sports, and animal-encounter excursions are available here. Casinos offer the full range of opportunities to lose your shirt.

WHAT TO EAT For a taste of typical Bahamian food, try conch, fish stew, or crawfish. These are often served with a side of grits, rice, macaroni and cheese, or potato salad. Desserts may include pastries flavored with pineapple, guava, or coconut.

WHAT TO BUY There is no shortage of trinket vendors aimed at the tourist trade. You'll find inexpensive T-shirts on every corner. If you visit the **Straw Market,** make sure to look for handmade straw pieces rather than those imported from China. Other popular items include decorated conch shells or carved wood. Foodies may desire rum cakes or guava jams and jellies.

Philipsburg, Sint Maarten

LANGUAGES Dutch, French, and English

HISTORY The island was originally occupied by the Carib Indians. Christopher Columbus later found and named it for the medieval bishop St. Martin of Tours, which is now aptly fitting. In the early 1600s, Dutch colonists used the island as a source of salt for export. The Dutch were then ousted by the Spanish, who were subsequently removed by the French. In 1648 a treaty divided the area in half, with shared control and occupancy. Parts of the territory changed hands between the Spanish and the Dutch 16 times in about 200 years. At several points in the early 1800s, British pirates attacked and brought the area under English rule. The slave trade was a large part of the island's economy in the 17th and 18th centuries; when slavery was abolished, plantation owners imported low-wage earners from China and the East Indies. The island is currently divided and called by two names: Saint-Martin, controlled by the French, and Sint Maarten, controlled by the Dutch. It is one of the smallest landmasses overseen by more than one country. English is widely spoken on both sides of the island.

WEATHER The climate is mild, with average year-round temperatures between 82° and 89°. August–November are typically the wettest months, with 4–5.5 inches of rain per month. The water temperature just off the island rarely dips below 80°.

THE PORT A 5-minute walk from the port is a small marina called **Dock Maarten** (LOL), with a few shops and a restaurant. One mile away, accessible on foot and by taxi, is downtown Philipsburg, which is a large duty-free shopping destination.

TOURIST HIGHLIGHTS Gamblers will enjoy the many casinos in Saint-Martin–Sint Maarten. Be sure to brush up on the rules of roulette, baccarat, craps, blackjack, and poker before you arrive. Guests looking to get their gamble on will find casinos on the Dutch side of the island near the airport and Simpson Bay, and around downtown Philipsburg. The Boardwalk area on **Great Bay,** on the Dutch side, offers beachside lounging and a long string of bars and restaurants. From **Maho Beach,** also on the Dutch side, watch planes fly incredibly low to land at the nearby airport. (The signage letting you know that getting too close to the aircraft could kill you just adds to the fun.) Water sports available here include snorkeling, scuba diving, and fishing. **Lucky Stables** offers horseback-riding opportunities.

For a quieter and more European experience, catch a cab right off the dock (as opposed to the nonlicensed "tour operators" in downtown Philipsburg) to **Marigot,** on the French side of the island. At **Orient Beach,** women can go topless, and some sections allow you to bare it all, but the posteriors on display are more Joe the Plumber than Jennifer Lopez.

See page 257 for our St. Maarten walking tour.

WHAT TO EAT Seafood, particularly conch fritters, is plentiful here. Other dishes may have West Indian, French, and Dutch influences. More than 40 Chinese restaurants are also on the island. You may encounter the regional favorites callaloo (beef- and crab-based), crab cakes, and johnny-cake biscuits. Dessert often includes coconut pies and guava tarts.

WHAT TO BUY St. Maarten is known for its shopping, particularly electronics, cameras, liquor, fragrances, and cigarettes. These will likely be large European brands. If you're looking for local flavor, you'll find typical tourist souvenirs such as artwork, carvings, and woven goods.

Port Canaveral, Florida

LANGUAGE English

HISTORY In 1929 Congress approved construction of a deepwater port at Port Canaveral, completed and dedicated in 1953. Initially this was a cargo center, with a primary mission of taking orange juice to the North. Concurrent with the rise of shipping in the area was the building of the nearby space center. The first passenger ships arrived in the 1970s to see the area's newly developed theme parks on their ports of call. The first home-ported cruise ship sailed from Port Canaveral in 1982.

WEATHER Expect it to be hot in Port Canaveral during in the summer. May–October, average daytime highs range from the mid-80s to the low 90s. Nighttime lows during that period are in the upper 60s to low 70s. November–April, expect average daytime highs in the low 70s to low 80s, with nighttime lows in the low 50s to low 60s. Precipitation varies considerably throughout the year. The dry season is November–May, with average monthly rainfall of about 3 inches or less. June–October, monthly rainfall averages 5–8 inches. Summer storms are common.

THE PORT Disney cruises dock at **Berth 8,** at a comfortable dedicated terminal with basic facilities. **Jetty Park,** just east of the port, offers a lifeguard-patrolled beach, a snack bar, and a playground. The **Cove** area at Port Canaveral is home to several restaurants and shops.

TOURIST HIGHLIGHTS The main attraction here is the **Kennedy Space Center.** Visitors can tour the facilities, ride in a space simulator, and participate in special programs with astronauts. Beach lovers will want to head over to **Cocoa Beach** and relax in the sun. Twenty minutes away, in Titusville, you'll find the **Brevard Museum of Natural History and Science,** the **Great Florida Birding Trail,** and the **US Space Walk of Fame.** Of course, the Orlando theme parks are about an hour west of Port Canaveral. Many cruisers make a pre- or postvoyage visit to **Walt Disney World, Universal Studios,** or **SeaWorld.**

WHAT TO EAT Seafood is served at most restaurants. Look for oysters, conch, and grouper. Many other cuisines, including Italian, Cuban, Asian, and German, are represented in the waterfront area. Fast food such as burgers and pizza is readily available too.

WHAT TO BUY Look for souvenirs related to the American space program: model rockets, patches depicting moon missions, and pieces of meteorites. For a unique food experience, buy a package of dehydrated astronaut ice cream. Near the beach, stock up on swimsuits, sunglasses, sunscreen, flip-flops, and other last-minute cruising essentials. You'll find that prices on land are significantly lower than in the shops on board. And if you're visiting the theme parks before or after your trip, you'll find a nearly limitless supply of related T-shirts and toys to take home.

San Juan, Puerto Rico

LANGUAGES Spanish and English

HISTORY Juan Ponce de León was the first European explorer to mention visiting the island of Puerto Rico. The city of San Juan was founded in 1521 by Spanish colonists who used it as a stopover on their way to the Americas. Throughout the 17th and 18th centuries, the island withstood various attacks by the English, including Sir Francis Drake, and the Dutch. In 1815 the island was opened to immigration as part of the Royal Decree of Graces. In 1898 United States warships attacked San Juan, eventually resulting in Spanish cession of Puerto Rico to the United States in the Treaty of Paris. In 1917 Puerto Ricans were granted American citizenship. Not quite a state—although 61% of its residents favored statehood in a 2012 referendum—the island sends a nonvoting representative to Congress and also maintains a local legislature.

WEATHER As is the case elsewhere in the Caribbean, weather here stays consistent year-round. Average daytime highs are in the 80s throughout the year, with average nighttime lows in the 70s. Precipitation is lowest in the winter, with an average of less than 4 inches of rainfall per month January–March. During the rest of the year, rainfall averages 4–6 inches per month.

THE PORT The DCL dock is in Old San Juan, across the street from a Sheraton hotel and just steps away from the main city.

TOURIST HIGHLIGHTS History buffs will want to explore **El Morro,** a fortress built to protect the island from attack by sea, and **El Castillo de San Cristobal,** designed to protect San Juan from overland attacks. Musicians may want to stop by the **Museo de Pablo Casals,** which houses the Spanish cellist's manuscripts and personal documents. The **Museum of Contemporary Art** showcases modern artists from Latin America and the Caribbean. For some fun in the sun, explore the beaches in the nearby towns of **Condado** and **Isla Verde.** Many visitors will want to stop by the **Casa Bacardi** distillery (also known as the Cathedral of Rum) for a tour and a taste.

WHAT TO EAT Puerto Rican cuisine is a melting pot of Spanish, Cuban, Mexican, African, and American flavors. To start your meal, try conch fritters or *empanadillas* (pastry filled with meat or seafood). Entrées include meat or seafood stews, fried steak or veal, barbecued pig, broiled chicken, or grilled seafood. Beans, rice, and plantains are often found as accompaniments. Dessert will likely include coconut or caramel flan (custard). Sweets may also be flavored with guava, papaya, or mango. You'll find that coffee or local rum is the beverage of choice.

WHAT TO BUY Dominoes is a popular game here, and a domino set makes a nice souvenir. Also look for hand-tooled leather, scented soaps, and woven hats and bags. For a take-home treat, buy some rum or coffee. Discount outlet shops for American brands include **Ralph Lauren** and **Coach.**

St. Thomas and St. John, US Virgin Islands

LANGUAGE English

HISTORY The original occupants of the Virgin Islands were the Ciboney people. Christopher Columbus first sighted the islands in the late 1400s, and the Dutch West India Company created a settlement here in 1657. This was shortly followed by occupation by the Danish West India and Guinea Company. Sugarcane, harvested by slaves on St. Thomas and the nearby islands of St. John and St. Croix, became the primary export. In 1848 slavery was abolished and the sugar trade declined. In 1917 the United States purchased St. Thomas, St. John, and St. Croix from Denmark as a means of controlling the Panama Canal during World War I, and the islands remain a US territory today (the other Virgin Islands are now under British control).

WEATHER Temperatures are constant throughout the year. Daytime highs average in the high 80s year-round, with nighttime lows in the 70s.

Precipitation is lowest in the winter, with an average monthly rainfall of less than 3 inches December–April. A moderate rise occurs May–August, with an average monthly rainfall of less than 4 inches. Precipitation increases to about 6 inches per month September–November.

THE PORT The cruise docks are a 10-minute taxi ride to **Charlotte Amalie,** the main city on St. Thomas. If you wish to walk rather than take a cab, just follow the waterfront path for around 20 minutes to downtown. Pedestrians should note that although this is a US territory, cars drive on the *left* side of the road—watch carefully when crossing streets.

Directly at the dock, you'll find outposts of many local shops, as well as some American chain stores. Some cafés, a bank, and a pharmacy are also in the immediate dock area.

TOURIST HIGHLIGHTS The **Paradise Point Skyride** offers views of the harbor. At the top, enjoy lunch and walk along trails inhabited by local wildlife. For another beautiful scene, beachgoers will want to visit the popular **Magens Bay. Coral World** is a nearby attraction with an underwater observatory, animal interaction with sharks and stingrays, and water sports such as parasailing. For history lovers, **Fort Christian** is a great spot. This museum houses local artifacts in a 17th-century Danish fortress. Another historic site is **Blackbeard's Castle,** which was used as a lookout by Danes to protect the harbor from early pirates. (For a walking tour that takes in these two historic sites and other points of interest, see page 259.)

WHAT TO EAT Local dishes include fresh seafood such as conch and lobster. Stewed beef, goat, and chicken are also popular. For a quick bite, try a meat *pate* (pastry filled with ground pork and beef). Side dishes may feature plantains, yams, rice, beans, and lentils. Fruit and fruit juices are available in abundance. If you're drinking alcohol here, it's likely rum made from sugar and molasses grown in the Caribbean.

WHAT TO BUY St. Thomas is the largest shopping port in the Caribbean. Most goods, including electronics, fragrances, jewelry, tobacco, crystal, china, and liquor, are widely available in the States. If you're planning to shop for these, you should be familiar with discount pricing from vendors at home. For local treasures, shop in the open-air markets for artwork, carved wood, and hand-pieced leather. Foodies will want to take home Caribbean rum-ball candy.

CALIFORNIA COAST PORTS

Cabo San Lucas, Mexico

LANGUAGE Spanish

HISTORY Native inhabitants of the Cabo San Lucas region include the Pericu peoples. European influence was minimal until the early 1800s. Industry and trade took hold in the early 1900s, when commercial fishing companies began to capitalize on the local tuna. The 1970s saw a surge in tourism, due in part to the completion of Mexican Federal Highway 1, linking Cabo to other parts of Mexico.

WEATHER Disney cruises visit Cabo San Lucas in May and October. Average daytime highs during those months are in the mid-80s–low 90s, with average nighttime lows in the low-to-mid-70s. Precipitation is typically low in May, averaging about 1 inch for the month. Rainfall in October is moderate, about 5.5 inches total.

THE PORT Cruise ships anchor in the harbor and tender guests into the marina. Once at the marina, the downtown area is a 10- to 15-minute walk away. Taxis are also readily available. A large mall near the marina has basic services, as well as an array of luxury-brand outposts such as **Tiffany** and **Cartier.** For those looking to stock up on necessities, there's a **Walmart** at Plaza San Lucas.

TOURIST HIGHLIGHTS The cruise ship anchors in the harbor and tenders guests into the marina, where nearby lie a large mall and luxury brand outposts. White-sand beaches are the major attraction—relax on the sand or take part in active water pursuits such as snorkeling, sailing, parasailing, or sport fishing. For those wishing to be active and dry, Cabo is a golf paradise, boasting numerous world-class courses. Zip lining is a wonderful excursion for guests with a daredevil streak. Whale watching and interactive dolphin experiences are popular activities. Those looking to enjoy art and culture will want to visit the **Vitro-fusion Glass Blowing Factory** to watch artisans create recycled glassworks, or stay in town to explore the **Iglesia de San Lucas,** a Spanish mission with many original features still intact.

WHAT TO EAT While you can find food from many nationalities, the local Cabo cuisine is, of course, Mexican. Try the street-vendor versions of tacos, quesadillas, and tortas. Rocker Sammy Hagar's **Cabo Wabo Cantina** is a must-stop spot for many visitors. The menu features a dozen different shrimp dishes, as well as catch-of-the-day specials, served with a heaping earful of rock and roll on the side.

WHAT TO BUY Along with typical seaside tourist trinkets, shirts, caps, and shot glasses emblazoned with the Cabo Wabo logo are an obligatory purchase for many visitors. Foodies will want to take home the local hot sauce, a Mexican tequila, or Damiana, a liqueur made with an herb known for its supposed aphrodisiac qualities. Look for soaps and lotions made with imitation turtle oil or scented with local spices.

Ensenada, Mexico

LANGUAGE Spanish

HISTORY The Yuma Indians were the first known inhabitants of the region. Portugal's João Rodrigues Cabrilho conducted the first European exploration of the area in the mid-1500s. Ensenada was founded September 17, 1542, as San Mateo. In 1602 it was renamed Ensenada de Todos Santos ("Bay of All Saints") by Sebastián Vizcaíno, a Spanish explorer and diplomat. The Jesuits were the city's first permanent settlers, in the 17th century. Following a Jesuit ouster in 1768, Dominicans took control of the region. Ensenada became the capital of Baja California in 1882; its growth was interrupted by the Mexican Revolution. In the 1920s, prohibition of alcohol in the US played a role in the eventual rebound of the area, as thirsty Americans began to look south for a source of booze. Today, tourism and fishing are prominent industries.

WEATHER Disney Cruise Line visits Ensenada in May and October. Average daytime highs during both these months are in the mid-70s, with variable precipitation and average nighttime lows in the mid-to-high 50s. Rainfall averages less than 2 inches a month throughout the year.

THE PORT Cruise ships dock in the same area as commercial and fishing vessels. Near the dock, numerous pop-up vendors sell typical tourist items; there is also a drugstore and a few cafés. From here you're a 15-minute walk to the **Avenida Lopez Mateos** tourist area. Taxis and shuttles are also available.

TOURIST HIGHLIGHTS **La Bufadora** is a natural marine blowhole about 20 miles south of town. The best beaches are 5 miles south of Ensenada, in the small town of **Chapultepec.** Activities there include horseback riding, surf fishing, and Jet Skiing. **Riviera del Pacífico,** formerly an exclusive and glamorous hotel (and, according to local lore, the birthplace of the margarita), is now a civic center. If you're in the mood for some culture, try the **Museo de Historia** or the **Estero Beach Museum** for a look at local art and artifacts.

WHAT TO EAT Fresh fish is on the menu in Ensenada. Look for halibut, clams, oysters, abalone, tuna, and more. The area's signature dish is the fish taco, typically prepared with battered, fried white fish; shredded cabbage; avocado; and a spicy mayonnaise. (If you order from a stand or a street cart, exercise caution—if there's a crowd, indicating rapid turnover, then the food is generally safe to eat.) When it comes adult beverages, you'll find a large selection of beers in most restaurants, as well as the ubiquitous margarita in all its many forms. Or pick up a bottle of *vino* at one of the area wineries.

WHAT TO BUY Tacky-T-shirt stands abound near the dock. Make a game of trying to find the most entertaining examples. You'll also find the usual piñatas, painted maracas, and straw hats. Blankets, leather goods, and logoed shot glasses are everywhere. Note that many items advertised as silver are really tin or other soft metal. Several stores sell Cuban cigars; puff yours while you're in Mexico. Many cruisers use a stop in Ensenada to stock up on medications for which you need a prescription in the US but not in Mexico—use your best judgment.

San Diego, California

LANGUAGE English

HISTORY San Diego is the site of the first European settlement in what is now California, a result of exploration conducted in 1542 by João Rodrigues Cabrilho of Portugal. Subsequent European visitors were primarily from Spain. The first permanent mission in the area was established in 1769, with a population of Spanish settlers arriving in 1774. In 1821 Mexico claimed the area in the Mexican War for Independence. In 1850 California became part of the United States. Significant American naval presence began in 1901, which solidified San Diego as a major West Coast port. San Diego is now a center of high-tech industry.

WEATHER Disney cruises visit San Diego in May, September, and October. The average daytime high temperature in May is in the high 60s, with average nighttime lows in the high 50s. Average daytime highs in September and October are in the mid-70s, while average nighttime lows are in the mid-to-low 60s. Precipitation during all three months is minimal, with an average of less than 1 inch of rainfall per month.

THE PORT Cruise ships dock at the **B Street Cruise Terminal,** directly adjacent to downtown. An upscale mall, **Horton Plaza,** featuring a flagship Nordstrom store, is a 10-minute walk away. Public transportation and taxis are readily available for more-distant jaunts.

TOURIST HIGHLIGHTS **Balboa Park** is home to gorgeous gardens and 15 different museums, including the **San Diego Museum of Art** and the **San Diego Natural History Museum.** The **San Diego Zoo** is one of the few places in the United States where you can see pandas. Theme park fans will want to visit **SeaWorld** and **Legoland.** The **Gaslamp Quarter** and the San Diego missions provide insight into the history of the area. **Tijuana, Mexico,** is 17 miles south of San Diego; be sure to check on legal restrictions if you plan to drive there.

WHAT TO EAT San Diego is a major metropolitan area with all major cuisines represented. The offerings at many local restaurants are influenced by nearby Mexico—quesadillas, tacos, burritos, enchiladas, and such. Because of the city's seaside location, fresh fish is another local menu staple. A regional favorite is cioppino, a stew with fish, clams, shrimp, squid, and mussels, often served with toast. Tequila-based drinks and local wines are popular with adult drinkers.

WHAT TO BUY Sports fans will want to purchase jerseys of the local Padres baseball, Chargers football, or San Diego State Aztecs football or basketball teams. Pick up clothing or shell-based jewelry, or choose some art reflecting the surf culture. Local tequila is a common food gift.

San Francisco, California

LANGUAGE English

HISTORY The first European settlers in the area were Spaniards, who arrived in 1769 and established the Presidio of San Francisco in 1776. By the early 1800s, the Bay Area had become part of Mexico. In 1846 the United States claimed California in the Mexican-American War, and two years later, the gold rush brought an influx of miners and prospectors to the West, resulting in massive and rapid growth of the area. In 1906 a major earthquake and fire destroyed much of the city. Many edifices were rebuilt in a grand Beaux Arts style. The Golden Gate and Oakland Bay Bridges were built in 1936–37, allowing further expansion to outlying areas. In the 1950s and '60s, San Francisco's North Beach and Haight-Ashbury neighborhoods became the Meccas of America's counterculture.

WEATHER DCL visits San Francisco in May. The weather is moderate year-round. When you visit, you can expect average daytime highs in the 60s and average nighttime lows in the upper 40s to mid-50s. Rainfall in May is light, with slightly more than half an inch for the month. The (in)famous San Francisco fog doesn't hit until summer.

THE PORT Disney cruises dock at **Pier 35,** which has minimal services. Steps away, you'll find the **Fisherman's Wharf** shopping and dining area. Also nearby, taxis, buses, and the **Bay Area Rapid Transit** system can take you into the heart of the city, a 10-minute ride away.

TOURIST HIGHLIGHTS Watch the ships, eat the snacks, and gaze at the Golden Gate Bridge from Fisherman's Wharf. For a look into American penal history, take the nearby ferry over to the infamous **Alcatraz** penitentiary. Wander into **Chinatown** to dine and shop. Take in a museum, such as the **San Francisco Museum of Modern Art,** the **Fine Arts Museum of San Francisco,** or the **Walt Disney Family Museum.** For an outdoor experience, take a hike among the giant redwoods of **Muir Woods National Monument.** Or take a drive out of town for a visit to the Napa and Sonoma wine country. To immerse yourself in the city's famed gay culture, visit the **Castro District.** Of course, no trip to San Francisco would be complete without a ride on a cable car past **Lombard Street,** said to be the crookedest street in the world.

WHAT TO EAT Virtually all major cuisines are represented in San Francisco. Along Fisherman's Wharf, look for seafood in all forms, particularly chowder. Sourdough bread is an area specialty, often serving as a chowder bowl as well as a side dish. The vineyards north of the city make San Francisco a wine lover's paradise. Authentic Chinese dishes abound in the Chinatown district. The **Ghirardelli** chocolate factory no longer offers tours, but the ice-cream shop is still out of this world.

WHAT TO BUY For children, a toy cable car is a fun gift. Pick up some silks or carved stone in Chinatown. Sports fans will want jerseys representing the local teams, and foodies will want to pick up some Ghirardelli chocolate, a sourdough starter, or a fabulous bottle of wine.

Vancouver, British Columbia *(See page 183 for full profile.)*

Victoria, British Columbia

LANGUAGE English

HISTORY British settlement in Victoria began in the mid-1840s as a Hudson Bay trading post. Not long after this, the Fraser Canyon Gold Rush brought an influx of prospectors. The port then became a naval base and the commercial center of British Columbia. Victoria was designated the capital of British Columbia after the territory became a Canadian province in 1871. Today the city is home to thriving fishing and shipbuilding industries and is a nascent technological hub. The scenic harbor is also a major tourist destination.

WEATHER DCL cruises visit Victoria in September, when daytime highs average in the high 60s and nighttime lows in the high 40s. September rainfall averages slightly more than an inch.

THE PORT The Victoria ship terminal is about 1 mile from downtown but has no facilities. Take a scenic walk through **Beacon Hill Park,** or take a shuttle or taxi.

TOURIST HIGHLIGHTS For lovers of flora, the sunken garden at **Butchart Gardens** is just one of the popular destinations in Victoria, known as the City of Gardens. Many remnants of Victoria's British heritage—including double-decker buses and horse-drawn carriages—remain, and the **Empress Hotel** serves a proper English tea. **Craigdarroch Castle,** a 19th-century edifice, boasts panoramic city vistas and an impressive collection of antique furnishings. For a dose of history, visit the **Royal British Columbia Museum,** which owns more than 7 million artifacts, including an intact woolly mammoth. Outdoors enthusiasts will enjoy walking trails along the Pacific Ocean, as well as scuba diving, kayaking, and marine life observation. Victoria is also home to a vibrant **Chinatown.**

WHAT TO EAT Victoria is a modern city, with restaurants featuring most major cuisines. Pacific cod, salmon, and halibut are on menus throughout Victoria. For Asian favorites such as noodles and broth, venture into Chinatown.

WHAT TO BUY Look for native crafts such as jewelry and carvings. You can find tea and tea-service items in the Anglophile shops. **Fort Street** is known as Antique Row due to the many older trinkets for sale in the shops along this thoroughfare. Visit Chinatown for silks, fans, and Asian ornaments.

HAWAIIAN PORTS

Hilo, Hawaii

LANGUAGES English, Hawaiian, and Pidgin

HISTORY Hilo is the largest city on the island of Hawaii, a.k.a. the "Big Island." Archeological evidence indicates settlement by Polynesian peoples from the Marquesas Islands as early as AD 300. Centuries-old local chiefdoms were consolidated under the Hawaiian Islands' first monarch, King Kamehameha the Great, in 1782. The late 18th century also saw the arrival of British Captain James Cook as well as explorers and traders from China. In the 1820s, US missionaries arrived in Hilo, further complicating the cultural influences. During the mid-1800s, sugar plantations thrived, and sugar became a key export. In 1893, a coalition of American and European business and political leaders forced Hawaii's last monarch, Queen Lili'uokalani, to step down, and in 1898 the islands were annexed by the United States. The early 1900s saw a major influx of Japanese immigrants, followed by the arrival of many Korean immigrants. The mid-20th century saw several natural upheavals, including earthquakes, volcanic eruptions, and tsunamis. Hawaii became the 50th state in 1959. The closure of area sugar plantations during the 1990s led to a downturn in the local economy, but tourism has been fueling the rebound.

WEATHER DCL visits Hilo in September. Average daytime highs during this period are in the low-to-mid 80s, with average nighttime lows in the high 60s to low 70s. Precipitation on the Big Island is heavy throughout the year, with September rainfall averaging about 10 inches for the month.

THE PORT Cruise ships dock at piers on Kuhio Street, about 2 miles east of downtown Hilo. There is very little in the way of services near the dock. Taxis into town are available, as well as a public bus system.

Shuttles take guests to the local farmers' market or to **Hilo Hattie,** a retailer of Hawaiian-themed clothing.

TOURIST HIGHLIGHTS The **Pacific Tsunami Museum** chronicles the 1946 and 1960 tsunamis that destroyed much of the town. A wave machine lets you experience the feel of rushing water. The **Lyman Museum** features exhibits about Hawaiian geography and history. Nature enthusiasts will want to visit **Hawaii Volcanoes National Park,** home of Kilauea—the most active volcano on the planet—and Mauna Loa. If you're looking for natural beauty with little exertion, **Rainbow Falls** is small but close to downtown and requires no hiking. The **Mauna Loa Macadamia Nut Factory** offers tours and tastings.

WHAT TO EAT If you visit the large farmers' market, look for unfamiliar fruits such as mangosteen, durian (*warning:* an acquired taste!), or rambutan; many vendors will allow you a small taste before buying. Some stalls sell prepared foods such as taro pastries or *musubi,* a sushilike snack made with Spam (a Hawaiian delicacy), chicken, or hot dogs. Most menus will have local fish served grilled, broiled, or in tacos. Tropical fruits abound: pineapple, bananas, guava, papaya, mango, and coconut. A great beachside refresher is shave ice, a tropical take on a snow cone that's topped with a variety of sweet, fruity sauces and sometimes ice cream or sweetened condensed milk. Kona coffee is especially delicious. Macadamia nuts are sold all over the island—try some dipped in chocolate.

WHAT TO BUY Typical Hawaiian souvenirs include floral shirts (match the whole family!), art prints of the local scenery, carved wooden objects, ukuleles, and hula accessories such as skirts and leis. Food finds are everywhere: macadamias in every form, jams and jellies, and packaged Kona coffee beans.

Honolulu, Hawaii

LANGUAGES English, Hawaiian, and Pidgin

HISTORY The capital of Hawaii and both the southernmost and westernmost major city in the United States, Honolulu is located on the island of Oahu. Archeological evidence indicates settlement of the Hawaiian Islands by Polynesian peoples from the Marquesas Islands as early as AD 300. The first known foreigner to enter Honolulu Harbor was William Brown, captain of the English ship *Butterworth,* in 1794. King Kamehameha I (The Great), who conquered the islands in 1782, moved his court from the "Big Island" of Hawaii to Waikiki in 1804; he relocated to what is now downtown Honolulu five years later. In 1820, a group of New England missionaries arrived, bringing with them their religion, education, and economics. Later immigrants from Asia, Portugal, and Puerto Rico helped make Hawaii a true cultural melting pot. King Kamehameha III proclaimed Honolulu the capital city of his kingdom in 1850. In 1893, the US overthrew the monarchy and in 1898 annexed the islands, creating the Territory of Hawaii. In 1941, the Empire of Japan bombed the Pearl Harbor military base just west of Honolulu, prompting America to enter World War II. Hawaii became the 50th state in 1959.

WEATHER DCL visits Honolulu in September. Average daytime highs during this period are in the high 80s, with average nighttime lows in the low 70s. Precipitation on Oahu is minimal at this time of year, with September rainfall averaging less than an inch for the month.

THE PORT Cruise ships dock adjacent to **Aloha Tower Marketplace,** which includes shops, restaurants, and all basic services. The top floor of this 10-story building houses an observation deck (free admission) offering panoramic views of the harbor. Taxis and rental cars are readily available, and a reliable public bus system covers much of Oahu. The **Waikiki Trolley** is similar to the San Francisco cable-car system.

TOURIST HIGHLIGHTS The main draw in Oahu for many guests is the **World War II Valor in the Pacific National Monument** at Pearl Harbor, encompassing the **USS *Arizona* Memorial** and a museum complex. Tours are a must, and tickets may be purchased in advance (call ☎ 877-444-6777 or visit **recreation.gov**). **Chinatown** is a vibrant area with many unique shops and restaurants. In the Capitol District, visit historic **Iolani Palace,** the only royal residence in the United States. Culture mavens will enjoy the **Hawaii State Art Museum,** which features Hawaiian art across all media. Nature lovers will enjoy the **Lyon Arboretum,** with walking paths that border more than 600 plant species, more than 80 of which are rare or endangered. If you'd like to learn about pineapple production, the **Dole Plantatio**n is a nearby excursion. The **Waikiki Beach** area is a buzz of hotels, shops, and restaurants flanked by the distinctive **Diamond Head** crater. Disney fans may want to check out the company's **Aulani Resort & Spa,** part of the larger Ko Olina resort complex about 45 minutes west of Honolulu.

WHAT TO EAT Hawaiian cuisine reflects the state's natural bounty as well as its diverse cultural heritage. Most menus will have local fish served grilled, broiled, or in tacos. Tropical fruits abound: pineapple, bananas, guava, papaya, mango, and coconut. Sticky rice serves as the base for everything from a *loco moco* (a burger and fried egg over rice) to the ubiquitous Spam *musubi* (think sushi, but with Spam). If you visit a luau, you're sure to encounter *kalua* pig served with a side dish of *poi* (mashed taro root). Sweets include desserts and candies based on the locally grown macadamia nut. A great beachside refresher is shave ice, a tropical take on a snow cone that's topped with a variety of sweet, fruity sauces and sometimes ice cream or sweetened condensed milk. Kona coffee is especially delicious. Kids will love POG (passion fruit, orange, and guava) juice. Bars and restaurants serve the requisite fruity cocktails, often accompanied by a paper umbrella. Hey, when in Honolulu . . .

WHAT TO BUY There's no more iconic souvenir than the classic Hawaiian shirt. If you're looking for something other than the typical floral print, the gift shop at the USS *Arizona* Memorial often sells Hawaiian-style shirts with military-themed prints. Foodies will want to bring home macadamia-nut candies, Hawaiian sea salt, tropical fruit jams, or a package of local coffee beans. Other popular items include carvings or housewares made from koa wood, leis made from shells, and recordings by Hawaiian musicians.

Kahului, Hawaii

LANGUAGES English, Hawaiian, and Pidgin

HISTORY Kahului is located on the island of Maui. Polynesian and Tahitian settlers were among the first known inhabitants. Until the late 1400s, the island was ruled by tribal chiefdoms, which were united in the mid-1550s under the rule of a single royal family. Europeans began to visit in the mid-1500s, but they did not become a significant presence until the early 1800s. In the 1820s, Christian missionaries began teaching and preaching, altering the island's traditional religious and educational systems. The 1800s saw massive deaths among the indigenous peoples due to the introduction of Western illnesses. Crops such as sugar and pineapple became mainstays of the local economy in the mid-to-late 19th century. Maui served as a recreation and training base during WWII, and the first tourist hotel was built here in 1946. Hawaii became the 50th state in 1959.

WEATHER DCL visits Kahului in September. Average daytime highs during this period are in the high 80s, with average nighttime lows in the low 70s. Precipitation on Maui is minimal at this time of year, with September rainfall averaging less than an inch for the month.

THE PORT Kahului is an industrial port. Within a 15-minute walk you'll find the **Maui Mall**, which houses a grocery store, movie theater, and other shops. A public beach is also within walking distance. Taxis service the harbor, but there is little public transportation—a rental car may be more efficient and less expensive. Shuttles can take you to the Kahului Airport, which has desks for most major auto-rental agencies.

TOURIST HIGHLIGHTS The **Road to Hana** is an internationally famous leisure drive. The narrow, twisting road requires skilled driving, and perhaps some Dramamine. Along the route you'll see tropical vegetation, waterfalls, sea caves, and swimming holes. Many guests will want to explore **Lahaina,** a historic town with numerous art galleries, shops, restaurants, and bars. For shopping and snorkeling, venture to **Ka'anapali,** which features an upscale outdoor mall called **Whalers Village** and the **Pu'u Keka'a (Black Rock)** ocean-diving area. For a look at plantation life, visit the **Maui Tropical Plantation,** which offers tram tours of the 112-acre property. For panoramic views, take a **helicopter tour** of the region's volcanoes and waterfalls.

WHAT TO EAT Fresh fish abounds on most menus. Look for coconut shrimp, fish tacos, ahi tartare, ahi *poke* (a raw-tuna salad), and sushi of every sort. The Road to Hana is populated by fresh fruit stands and vendor shacks that sell delicious banana bread. Pork is often prepared shredded with a sweet sauce on the side. Typical side dishes include pounded taro, rice, or macaroni salad. The locally made potato chips have a cult following (the Kitch'n Cook'd brand is particularly addictive). For a refreshing treat, try shave ice topped with fruit-flavored sauces. Favorite beverages include coffee-based drinks and cocktails made with rum and fruit.

WHAT TO BUY Typical Hawaiian souvenirs include wearables such as Aloha shirts, sarongs, and swimwear, along with recordings by local musicians and prints by local artists. Look for crafts made from koa wood such as carvings, bowls, or hair ornaments. Gourmands will want to buy unusual flavors of Spam (a beloved regional delicacy), coffee beans, macadamia-nut candies, and jams made from local fruits.

Nawiliwili, Hawaii

LANGUAGES English, Hawaiian, and Pidgin

HISTORY Nawiliwili is located on the island of Kauai. Indigenous peoples have inhabited the island since at least AD 1,000. Continuous European visitation began following Captain James Cook's landing in 1778. The mid-1800s saw an expansion of agricultural trade. Nawiliwili Harbor officially opened in 1930. Hawaii officially joined the United States in 1959. Kauai's beautiful scenery has served as a backdrop for numerous Hollywood films, including *South Pacific* (1958), *Raiders of the Lost Ark* (1981), *Jurassic Park* (1993), and *The Descendants* (2011).

WEATHER Disney Cruise Line visits Nawiliwili in September. Average daytime highs during this period are in the mid-80s, with average nighttime lows in the mid-70s. Precipitation is moderate at this time of year, with September rainfall averaging about 2 inches for the month.

THE PORT There is little in the way of services directly at the port. The shops and restaurants of the **Harbor Mall** and **Anchor Cove Shopping Center** are within walking distance. Free shuttles are also provided. **Kalapaki Beach** is adjacent to the malls and provides an area for sunning and water sports. Taxis service the port, but a rental car may be the most efficient way to see the area.

TOURIST HIGHLIGHTS Nawiliwili Beach Park provides beaches for sunning and swimming. The natural wonders of Kauai are also evident at **Waimea Canyon** and **Koke'e State Park. Kilohana Plantation** provides a look into the lavish lifestyles of Hawaii's sugar magnates; a train trip around the plantation functions as a guided tour. Lovely **Wailua Falls** was featured in the opening shots of the 1970s TV staple *Fantasy Island*. The **Kilauea Point Lighthouse** offers sweeping ocean views, and the **Kilauea Point National Wildlife Refuge** offers prime bird-watching.

WHAT TO EAT In a word, fish. Look for *poke,* a raw-seafood salad made with *tako* (octopus) or ahi tuna; *lomi-lomi* salmon, a raw-salmon-and-tomato salad; fish tacos; and *poi,* or mashed taro root. Locals favor *musubi* (Spam or other meat served over sushi rice) or *saimin* (a noodle soup similar to ramen or lo mein). Many meat dishes show an Asian influence. Typical sides include rice, potato salad, and macaroni salad. Fresh fruit, particularly local guava, pineapple, and coconut, is found in abundance. Regional sweets include *lilikoi* (passion fruit) pie, shave ice (like a snow cone), and *haupia* (a rich coconut pudding that's often used as a pie filling). Coffee and fruit-based drinks are excellent here.

WHAT TO BUY A prized—and pricey—local purchase is a Ni'ihau shell lei, handcrafted from shells found on a lightly inhabited nearby island. Musicians may be interested in buying a handcrafted ukulele or CD of local songs. Aloha shirts and hula skirts are great for guests who want to wear a bit of the islands at home. Look also for candies, cookies, and jams made from locally grown fruits and nuts.

Vancouver, British Columbia   *(See page 183 for full profile.)*

MEDITERRANEAN PORTS

Barcelona, Spain

LANGUAGES Catalan and Spanish

HISTORY Barcelona was founded as a Roman city. Subsequently, Visigoths and then Moors controlled the area until the early 800s. Franks held the region through the 10th and 11th centuries. From the 12th century, Barcelona and Catalonia became allied with the Kingdom of Aragón, and the Port of Barcelona became a trading thoroughfare. A period of decline ensued with the arrival of the Black Death in the 14th century, followed by the expansion of the Hapsburg monarchy as well as the rise of Turks in the region. The early 1700s brought a rejuvenation of the Barcelona dock system and then the arrival of the industrial age in the 1800s. By the mid-1800s, Barcelona was again a flourishing European port. Periods of unrest and rebuilding took place throughout the early 1900s, with stability constant since 1977, when the Catalan government was restored. Barcelona hosted the 1992 Summer Olympics, a boon for the entire region.

WEATHER Disney cruises visit in August and September. Daytime highs average in the low 70s–low 80s, with nighttime lows in the mid-to-low 60s. Even when temperatures peak, coastal breezes typically keep things comfortable. Precipitation is usually minimal these two months, with an average of less than 3 inches of rain per month.

THE PORT There is little here to entice tourists, but a 5-minute taxi ride or brisk 20-minute walk from the port brings you to **La Rambla,** a pedestrian mall lined with restaurants, boutiques, and major international clothing chains. Taxis are plentiful.

TOURIST HIGHLIGHTS The premier attractions are La Rambla and **La Boqueria,** an open-air market with dozens of food stalls. The influence of artist Antoni Gaudí is in evidence throughout the area, principally in the can't-miss **Sagrada Família** cathedral and the **Park Güell** garden complex. (Our walking tour of Barcelona, page 263, includes a stop at the church.) Gothic architecture abounds in the old section of town. Art aficionados will enjoy the **Salvador Dalí Theatre and Museum,** the world's largest Surrealist object (*trippy* doesn't begin to describe it). Foodies will relish the **Museu de la Xocolata** (Museum of Chocolate). The **Poble Espanyol,** a walled city within the city, showcases architecture, artisans, and food from each of Spain's 15 regions. Sun worshippers appreciate the city's public beaches.

WHAT TO EAT In a word: *¡Tapas!* Most restaurants offer some version of these small plates. Look for seafood, olives, artichokes, egg dishes, breads, and local hams and sausages. La Boqueria's many sweets vendors offer intricately shaped chocolates and marzipans.

WHAT TO BUY You can find almost anything in Barcelona, from high-end leather goods and shoes to handblown glassware. Great choices are packaged foodstuffs, such as candy, olives, olive oil, and wine, or sportswear featuring the local football (soccer) teams and Antonio Gaudí–inspired artwork.

Civitavecchia, Italy

LANGUAGE Italian

HISTORY Rome is a major metropolis with a lengthy past. Legend has it that the city was founded by the mythological twins Romulus and Remus, who were abandoned as infants and suckled by a wolf until a shepherd found them and raised them as his own. From 290 BC to AD 235, Rome was the dominant force in the Western world, controlling most of Europe and the Mediterranean. Later the Bishop of Rome (the Pope) established the city as the center of the Catholic Church. During the Renaissance, Rome became a hub for art and invention.

WEATHER Summers in Rome are hot. Average daytime highs in August, when Disney cruises visit, are in the low-to-upper 80s; temperatures in the high 90s are not unusual. Nighttime summer lows average in the low 60s. Summer is the dry season in Rome, with rainfall in August averaging less than 2 inches for the month.

THE PORT The pier doesn't offer anything of note. It's a 10-minute walk from here to the train station, from which it's a 90-minute journey to Rome by bus or train.

TOURIST HIGHLIGHTS It's impossible to take in all Rome has to offer in a day—choose one or two highlights and plan to come back. Among the main attractions are **Vatican City,** with the **Sistine Chapel** and **St. Peter's Basilica;** the **Colosseum;** the **Spanish Steps;** the **Pantheon;** the **Trevi Fountain;** the **Catacombs;** the **Arch of Constantine;** and the numerous museums.

If you choose not to visit Rome or the countryside, you'll find smaller sights in Civitavecchia itself. The most popular local attraction is **Fort Michelangelo,** built in 1503 to protect the village from invaders. Another spot in town is the ancient baths, **Terme Taurine,** which were built around natural hot sulfur springs. A seafront market—offering souvenirs, food, and, of course, gelato—is open during the summer. A public beach is near the Civitavecchia promenade.

WHAT TO EAT Pizza is available almost everywhere, as is pasta in almost every conceivable shape and size. Roasted or fried artichokes are a popular side dish. Salt cod, zucchini blossoms, and fresh and aged cheeses may be served as an appetizer. For dessert, gelato is a specialty—look for unique flavors such as licorice, melon, apple, or hazelnut.

WHAT TO BUY With every major fashion designer represented in Rome, haute couture and leather goods abound. In and around the Vatican, you'll find religious artifacts, books, and artwork for sale. Sports enthusiasts will want to purchase jerseys of the local soccer teams.

Dover, United Kingdom

LANGUAGE English

HISTORY Renowned for its stark white seaside cliffs, Dover has an enviable location in the south of England, about a 2-hour drive from London and a Chunnel trip of less than an hour to France. The city's proximity to France has made it a strategic stronghold for centuries, with evidence of occupation by various tribes and sects dating back to medieval times. During the Tudor years, Dover was fortified to withstand Continental invasion. The Napoleonic Wars saw the development of further defenses against the French. In the mid-1800s, Dover endeavored to become a tourist center with seaside amenities. During the 20th century, the city saw extensive fighting during both world wars as it defended the English Channel, with the aforementioned white cliffs inspiring a hit song during World War II.

WEATHER Disney cruises visit Dover during the summer. In May, average daytime highs are brisk, in the high 50s, with nighttime lows in the mid-40s. June, July, and August bring warmer temperatures during the day, averaging in the low 70s, with nighttime lows remaining in the 50s. Pack a jacket for the evening. Precipitation is low throughout the year, with typically less than 2 inches of rain per month during the summer.

THE PORT The town center is about a mile from the docks, which offer basic services. Taxis and a shuttle bus are readily available. Stop at the **Visitor Information Centre,** inside the Dover Museum on Old Town Gaol Street, for directions. Bus and train transportation, within a mile of the town center, provide access to London, 2 hours away.

TOURIST HIGHLIGHTS If you're staying in town, a visit to **Dover Castle,** atop those famed white cliffs, is a must. Explore secret wartime tunnels, or interact with costumed docents who reenact aspects of King Henry II's court. **Canterbury Cathedral,** the site of religious pilgrimages since the 14th century, is about a half-hour away by car.

Many guests make their stay in Dover brief and focus instead on the sights of **London.** Must-sees there include the bustling **West End** theater district, **Buckingham Palace** and the changing of the guard, **Westminster Abbey,** the **British Museum,** the **Tower of London,** the giant **London Eye** Ferris wheel, and much, much more.

WHAT TO EAT British food isn't limited to fish-and-chips and meat pies—to the contrary, it's quite cosmopolitan. Restaurants serve most global cuisines: French, Italian, Spanish, Indian, and more.

WHAT TO BUY In Dover, look for mugs, T-shirts, and books related to the castle and the cliffs. London, of course, has shops offering nearly everything imaginable. Woolens such as sweaters and caps are popular items, as are depictions of the royal family and the famed red double-decker buses. And no trip to London would be complete without a stop at **Harrods,** where you can buy everything from gourmet meats and cheeses in the downstairs food halls to haute couture and pet puppies upstairs.

Gibraltar, United Kingdom

LANGUAGES English, Spanish

HISTORY Gibraltar is a British territory on the Iberian Peninsula, at the mouth of the Mediterranean. The massive Rock of Gibraltar is the region's principal landmark. The first known inhabitants of the area were the Phoenicians, with later occupations by the Carthaginians, Romans, Vandals, and Visigoths. During the 1200s–1500s, ownership of Gibraltar was contested by the Nasrids of Granada, the Marinids of Morocco, and the Catholic kings of Castile. In 1501, rule passed to the Spanish crown. In 1704, an Anglo-Dutch force captured Gibraltar. Under the subsequent Treaty of Utrecht, the British were given permanent sovereignty and turned the area into a prominent naval base. During WWII, the civilian population was evacuated, and the Rock became a fortress. Today, Gibraltar's primary industries are tourism, shipping, financial services, and gaming.

WEATHER In May, when DCL visits Gibraltar, average daytime highs are in the mid-70s, while average nighttime lows are in the mid-50s. Precipitation is low in May, with typically less than an inch of rain falling during the month.

THE PORT Cruise ships dock at Gibraltar's recently built terminal, about a mile from the center of town. The terminal is in an industrial area, but a quick shuttle ride or walk will take you to the major sights.

TOURIST HIGHLIGHTS Traveling to the top of the Rock is *the* must-do activity, easily accomplished via cable car. A nature preserve at the top is home to native wild Barbary apes and Barbary partridges. The monkeys—they're not technically apes despite the moniker—roam free and are quite tame due to decades of interaction with humans. Note that feeding them is forbidden and guests are urged not to eat around them—they're not too proud to beg, and they've even been known to swipe ice-cream cones from unsuspecting kids.

The **Gibraltar Museum**'s exhibits chronicle the territory's storied history. Proper English tea is served at the **Caleta Hotel.** Nature enthusiasts will enjoy exploring **Cathedral Cave.**

WHAT TO EAT Because Gibraltar fuses English and Spanish cultures, you'll find both pub food and tapas throughout Gibraltar. The local dishes include *calentita* and *panissa,* breadlike dishes made with a chickpea base, and *rolitos,* rolls of thinly sliced beef stuffed with herbs, olives, bacon, eggs, and vegetables.

WHAT TO BUY Gibraltar Crystal glassware is produced in town. Choose from wineglasses, bowls, vases, candy dishes, and candlesticks. Children will gravitate to stuffed toy monkeys, a reminder of their interaction with the Barbary apes. Linens, leather, and other goods of Spanish influence are sold in town at an outpost of the British retailer **Marks & Spencer.**

La Spezia, Italy

LANGUAGE Italian

HISTORY Florence and Tuscany are considered the birthplace of the Italian Renaissance. From about 1300 to 1500, it was the most important city in Europe. Its factious history includes several changes of government, including a period of rule by the storied Medici family. For a part of the 1700s, Tuscany became an Austrian territory and then later a prefecture of the French *département* of Arno. In the 1800s Italian rule returned. In modern times Tuscany has been a center of tourism, trade, and financial services.

WEATHER August, when Disney swings through, is hot, with average daytime highs in the mid-70s to upper 80s. Temperatures approaching 100°

are not uncommon. Precipitation is fairly constant throughout the year, with average rainfall being about 2–4 inches per month in every season. **THE PORT** Cruise ships dock at the **Molo Garibaldi.** The train station and La Spezia proper are a 15-minute walk away. **TOURIST HIGHLIGHTS** La Spezia is a sweet town with several cafés and public beaches. The most popular attraction in the port city is the **Cinque Terre,** five small villages built into the rocks between the water and the hills. The villages are connected by a walking trail at **Riomaggiore,** a brief train ride away. La Spezia is also easily accessible by boat to the elegant resort of **Portofino.** Florence is a 2-hour auto trip from the port; Pisa is a 1-hour auto trip.

Museums abound in Florence, with the most famous being the **Uffizi Gallery.** Other museums include the **Bargello, Pitti Palace, Museo dell'Opera del Duomo,** and **Gucci Museum.** The symbol of the city is the **Duomo di Firenze.** For a fee, you can climb to the top of the cathedral for a bird's-eye view of the city. A stroll along the **Ponte Vecchio** is perfect for romance. The **Boboli Gardens** offer lush plantings and an interesting sculpture garden. In Pisa you must see the **Leaning Tower.** The cathedral there is constructed of colorful hand-carved marble. **WHAT TO EAT** Try antipasto, often thinly sliced salami, pickled vegetables, and crostini. Most menus will include pasta or risotto, salads, grilled meats, and olives. Florentine desserts may include gelatos, *schiacciata con l'uva* (a sweet grape bread), or *castagnaccio* (chestnut cake). **WHAT TO BUY** Florence is a city of high fashion, with most major luxury retailers in evidence. Leather goods are sold everywhere. Look for jackets, gloves, wallets, briefcases, and handbags in traditional and boldly colored dyes. Gold jewelry is often lovely here, but watch for extreme pricing. Crafty types may enjoy hand-marbled papers or wax letter seals. Murano glassware and jewelry are popular purchases. Marionettes are wonderful takeaway items for kids.

Lisbon, Portugal

LANGUAGE Portuguese
HISTORY Lisbon has long been a major trading port between Europe and North Africa. Its first inhabitants were pre-Celtic peoples, during the Neolithic Era; successive centuries brought occupations by the Iberians, Phoenicians, Greeks, Carthaginians, Romans, and Visigoths. During the eighth century AD, Islamic Moors gained control of the region and ruled until Christian Crusaders arrived about 400 years later. Maritime exploration was a primary focus until the early 1700s.

In 1755, a major earthquake, along with related fires and tsunamis, destroyed most of the city's buildings; for this reason, much of Lisbon's architecture is newer than that of other large European cities. The area was rebuilt under the leadership of then–Secretary of State Sebastião José de Carvalho e Melo. Napoleon occupied Lisbon from 1807 until 1814, after which a new constitution was developed and the territory of Brazil was granted independence.

The early 20th century was a time of unrest, beginning with the assassination of King Carlos in 1908. In 1910, a coup d'état overthrew the constitutional monarchy and established the Portuguese Republic. The next 20 years saw more than 40 separate changes of government. The dictatorial Estado Novo regime ruled from 1926 to 1974, when it was deposed in a military coup known as the Carnation Revolution. In 1986, Portugal joined the European Community, a decision that spurred major redevelopment.

WEATHER Disney Cruise Line visits Lisbon in August, when daytime highs average in the low 80s and nighttime lows in the low-to-mid 60s. Summers are dry, with average rainfall of less than an inch per month. Expect sunny skies.

THE PORT The terminal, with basic shops, ATMs, and a few cafés and restaurants, lies on the Tagus River, a 20-minute walk from tourist sites. Shuttles and taxis are readily available, as are light-rail and bus service.

TOURIST HIGHLIGHTS The **Alfama** neighborhood is a hilly enclave composed of tiny shops, restaurants, and clubs where traditional *fado* music (think Portuguese blues) is played and sung. While you're in the area, visit the **Castelo de São Jorge,** a Moorish church on Lisbon's highest hill—the views are spectacular. Reach it using **Tram 28,** Lisbon's version of a San Francisco cable car.

The **Belem** section of town is home to several notable attractions, including the **Monastery of Jerónimos,** the **Monument to the Discoveries,** and the **Museu Nacional dos Coches,** home to the world's largest collection of royal vehicles. The **National Tile Museum** displays painted works as well as intricate mosaics. The **Oceanarium,** Europe's largest indoor aquarium, features birds as well as fish and is popular with kids. **Casa das Histórias,** in the seaside suburb of Cascais, features works by Surrealist artist Paula Rego.

WHAT TO EAT Fish and shellfish dominate many menus. The national dish is *bacalhau,* or salt cod. You can find it prepared with vegetables or fried with rice, eggs, onions, and olives. *Porco alentejana* is pork loin cooked with clams and potatoes. Warm up with *caldo verde* ("green soup"), made with cabbage, onions, potatoes, and *chouriço* sausage. Snack on *presunto,* a dry, cured ham that's somewhat like Italian prosciutto, along with local cheese made from cow, sheep, or goat milk. For a sweet treat, try *pasteis de nata,* egg-custard tarts that are typically topped with cinnamon and powdered sugar; try to get some fresh from the oven. Adult beverages include *ginjinha,* a strong sour-cherry liqueur that's sometimes served from a chocolate shot glass. And of course, no trip to Lisbon would be complete without sampling some port or the many other varieties of fortified wine.

WHAT TO BUY Ceramic tiles are a typical Portuguese souvenir; look for hand-painted tiles in shops throughout Lisbon. Variations may included framed ceramic artwork or coasters. Portugal is a major exporter of cork; take-home treasures made with it include housewares and handbags. Fragrant Claus Porto soaps are a thoughtful gift to bring back for your housesitter—not only do they smell wonderful, but the ornate wrapping paper adds visual appeal. Foodies will want to take home local olive oils or bottles of port.

Naples, Italy

LANGUAGE Italian

HISTORY Naples has been continuously inhabited since at least the second millennium BC. During the first century BC, Naples played a role in the merging of Greek and Roman cultures. Following the fall of the Western Roman Empire, Naples became the capital city of the Kingdom of Naples and remained so from the late 1200s to the early 1800s. During World War II, Naples was the most bombed Italian city. Many of the outer buildings in the area were constructed as part of the restoration.

WEATHER Daytime highs during August, when DCL visits, range from the mid-70s to the mid-80s. Nighttime lows during that period fall into the low 60s. Precipitation averages less than 2 inches for the month.

THE PORT There are few services directly at the port, but from here it's a 15- to 20-minute walk into town.

TOURIST HIGHLIGHTS In the city of Naples, see the **Museo Archeologico Nazionale.** Other historic sites include the **Castel Nuovo,** the **Museo di Capodimonte,** and the **Duomo di Napoli.** Fifteen miles southeast of Naples are the ruins of **Pompeii,** where you can wander the streets of an ancient town preserved in time by the volcanic eruption of Mt. Vesuvius. If you're in the mood for a beach day, take a hydrofoil boat to the island of **Capri.**

WHAT TO EAT Naples is the birthplace of pizza, and **Antica Pizzeria Port'Alba** (founded in 1738) is the first establishment to serve it, though certainly not the only one you should consider. The classic version is the pizza margherita, a simple pie of tomato, basil, and fresh mozzarella. Neapolitan cuisine is also rich in seafood, often sauced with tomatoes, garlic, and olive oil. You will find house-made mozzarella available in many shops. Limoncello (lemon liqueur) is the adult beverage of the region; sip it alone or mixed into juices for a refreshing cocktail. Regional desserts include baba (a cake, perhaps soaked in liqueur), zeppole (like a doughnut, often filled with custard), and sfogliatelle (shell-shaped pastry). The local chocolatier, **Odin-Gay,** is a city favorite.

WHAT TO BUY Bring home some of the local limoncello if you want to taste Naples at home. If you're looking for jewelry, artisans here work in 18-karat gold and carved coral. Many visitors bring home replicas of the historical artifacts they see in Pompeii. Various shops sell locally carved wooden Christmas ornaments. In Capri, handmade sandals are a popular find.

Vigo, Spain

LANGUAGES Galician and Spanish

HISTORY Vigo is the largest city in Spain's autonomous region of Galicia, which borders Portugal and shares cultural similarities with its neighbor to the south. Organized occupation of the area was first documented in the 15th century. Various invaders attacked Galicia in succession from the 15th through 19th centuries. These included the Celts, the Romans, the Visigoths, the Moors, the Turks, the French, and the British. One notable invader was Sir Francis Drake, who occupied Vigo in 1589. During the mid-17th century, the citizens of Vigo attempted to stem the constant attacks by building a wall around the area, portions of which still stand. In 1808, Napoleon annexed Spain, but a year later Vigo's citizens successfully expelled the French Army, an event now celebrated annually as the Reconquista ("reconquest") around March 28. Vigo grew rapidly in the 19th and 20th centuries, becoming a well-known fishing port.

WEATHER DCL cruises visit Vigo in August, when daytime highs average in the high 70s and nighttime lows in the high 50s to low 60s. Summer is the dry season—in August, total rainfall averages about 2 inches.

THE PORT Ships dock at the **Muelle de Transatlánticos,** a 5-minute walk from the main city, across the Avenida del Castillo. Many attractions are accessible on foot. Taxis are readily available; for details about bus service, stop by the information kiosk adjacent to the port. Shopping and other services are available at a large shopping mall next to the dock area. Guests with mobility issues should note that Vigo is exceptionally hilly—they may want to take taxis even to destinations close to the ship.

TOURIST HIGHLIGHTS Architectural highlights include the **Citadel,** an ancient fort, and the 17th-century **Castrelos Palace,** which now houses a museum. Take a stroll through **Castrelos Park**'s immaculately maintained neoclassical gardens. The **Museo de Arte Contemporáneo de Vigo** displays works by up-and-coming Spanish artists. Foodies will want to visit the **Mercado de Berbes,** a noted fish market that sells dozens of varieties of seafood, including Galicia's famed oysters. The **Iglesia Concatedral de Santa María** is one of several churches in the area dating from the Renaissance. A good bet for kids is the **Vigo Zoo,** which is home to more than 1,000 animal species and offers lovely views of the region. If you're in the mood for sun, the surrounding area has more than 40 beaches—including 3 that are clothing-optional.

WHAT TO EAT Bordered by the Atlantic Ocean to its north and west, Galicia is renowned for its seafood. Selections may include spider crabs, monkfish, turbot, octopus, and squid, which you'll find broiled, fried, or cooked in stews. *Percebes* (goose barnacles), a local delicacy, are a unique treat. Meat eaters will be interested in the *jamón ibérico,* thinly sliced ham, as well as the local salami and chorizo sausages. Tapas-style vegetable dishes, accompanied by local bread, make a tasty snack. A popular small plate is *pimientos de Padrón,* fried green peppers sprinkled with sea salt and drizzled with olive oil—though they're generally sweet and mild, they can occasionally surprise you with their heat, a phenomenon that's been described as "Spanish roulette." For a sweet treat, try *tarta de Santiago,* an almond cake flavored with lemon or brandy and "stenciled" with powdered sugar using a cutout in the shape of the Cross of St. James. (St. James, or Santiago, is the patron saint of Spain and is buried in the Galician town of Santiago de Compostela.)

WHAT TO BUY The traditional souvenir of the Galician region is a pilgrim's walking stick; look for hand-carved versions. The local symbol is a scallop shell, which you can find depicted on numerous items, including artwork, jewelry, clothing, and ceramics. Foodies will want to buy some Tetilla cheese or Galician wine.

Villefranche, France

LANGUAGES French and Italian

HISTORY The Greeks were the first organized human presence on what is now known as the French Riviera. They were followed by the Romans in the eighth century BC. Before the Dark Ages, the region saw invasions from Visigoths, Burgundians, and Ostrogoths, which were later followed by threats from the Saracens and Normans. Stability came in the 13th century with the House of Grimaldi, which took power in what is now Nice, Antibes, and Monaco. Tourism became a major influence in the area beginning in the late 1700s, when wealthy Brits began arriving to take advantage of the climate and fine air quality.

WEATHER Disney cruises visit the French Riviera in August, when it's warm and dry. Daytime highs average in the low 70s–low 80s; nighttime lows average in the mid-60s. Precipitation is low, with less than 2 inches of rainfall for the month.

THE PORT Disney cruises anchor in the harbor and tender to the terminal in central Villefranche. Several small shops and cafés, along with train and bus stations, are within walking distance. A soap factory in town, **La Savonnerie de Villefranche,** lets visitors watch its work. If you're staying in port and looking for relaxation, the public beach is about a 10-minute walk away from the old town

TOURIST HIGHLIGHTS Most major and minor points on the French Riviera are accessible with less than an hour of travel away from the port. In **Nice,** stroll along the **Promenade des Anglais** or visit the **Cours Saleya** market for sweet and savory treats. In **Cannes,** look for art galleries on the **Rue d'Antibes. Monte Carlo** is famous for luxury shopping, the upper crust, and the **Grand Casino.** Try your hand here if you're in the mood for gambling. **Èze** is a medieval-era hilltop village from which you can see into France, Monaco, and Italy. Nearby **Grasse,** known as the fragrance capital of the world, offers tours of the **Fragonard** perfume factory.

WHAT TO EAT You'll find less butter and cream in food along the French Riviera than you would in other parts of France. Look here for *bouillabaisse* (fish stew), *salade niçoise* (a composed salad of tuna, tomato, eggs, and olives), the pizzalike *pissaladière,* crepes, and, of course, plenty of pastry.

WHAT TO BUY In Monte Carlo, look for souvenirs associated with Princess Grace and other members of the Grimaldi family, as well as trinkets representing the Grand Prix auto race. In Cannes, you'll find many items emblazoned with the film-festival logo. Throughout the area, look for wines, linens, and fragrances.

NORTHERN EUROPEAN PORTS

Akureyri, Iceland

LANGUAGE Icelandic

HISTORY The first known Viking settlement in Iceland occurred in the ninth century AD. Transient fishing camps formed and dissipated for many hundreds of years, with the first permanent settlement established in 1778; even so, the population numbered less than 100 for many more years. Growth in earnest began in the mid-1800s, when Icelanders began to appreciate the sound natural port and fine agricultural conditions. During World War II, the island served as an air base for British and Norwegian troops, and the US Air Force maintained a presence there until 2006. (Iceland, however, has no armed forces of its own and is considered the most peaceful country in the world.) Today, fishing and fish processing are the main industries, with tourism an area of growth. Perhaps its best-known export is Björk, the famously quirky and widely acclaimed singer-songwriter.

With a population of just under 20,000, Akureyri is a small town by US standards, but it's the second-largest urban area in Iceland.

WEATHER They don't call it "Iceland" for nothing, but Disney cruises visit in May and June, when the average daytime highs are rather mild—in the mid-40s–mid-50s. Nighttime lows in early summer average in the mid-30s–mid-40s. Precipitation is typically minimal during this time of year, with monthly rainfall estimated at less than 2 inches per month.

THE PORT Services at the port are minimal, but much of Akureyri is accessible by foot or bicycle. Taxis and free buses will take you on the short ride to town, where bike rentals and bike tours are available.

TOURIST HIGHLIGHTS Akureyri is home to several small but notable museums, including the **Safnasafið New Folk and Outsider Art Museum,** the **Aviation Museum,** and the **Industry Museum.** For an outdoor experience, try whale-watching, fishing, horseback riding, or taking a dip in a geothermal pool.

WHAT TO EAT Not surprisingly, seafood is a specialty of many restaurants in this fishing nation. Salmon, char, and mussels are particularly popular. Fish is prepared sushi-style or in traditional smoked, salted, and cured forms. (*Hákarl,* or fermented shark, is best left to Andrew Zimmern wannabes.) Beef and dairy are also popular. *Skýr* is a tangy dairy product native to Iceland—similar in flavor and consistency to Greek yogurt, it's technically a cheese. Burgers are easy to find; locals like them topped with béarnaise sauce and French fries. You can also try more-exotic game such as puffin, reindeer, and whale. Several local bakeries sell a variety of breads, pastries, and doughnuts. The only microbrewery in Iceland, **Kaldi,** is a 20-minute drive from Akureyri.

WHAT TO BUY A popular stop is the **Christmas Garden** shop, which offers a wide array of candles, ornaments, decorations, and ginger-scented snacks. Viking and troll memorabilia can be found almost everywhere. Knit textiles such as sweaters and mittens make for cozy mementos of your trip. You can even buy a reindeer hide to serve as a rug or blanket back home.

Ålesund, Norway

LANGUAGE Norwegian

HISTORY Ålesund has existed as a fishing village since Viking times. According to local lore, the Viking chief Rollo hailed from the area. In 1904, a major fire destroyed much of the town, leaving nearly 10,000 residents homeless. Germany's Kaiser Wilhelm assisted in the rebuilding effort by sending ships full of construction materials. Many of the structures that stand today were built circa 1904–07 in an Art Nouveau style. But despite Germany's influence, Ålesund sided with the Allies during World War II. Today, fishing is its primary industry.

WEATHER DCL visits Ålesund in June. Average daytime highs during this period are in the mid-to-upper 50s, with average nighttime lows in the mid-to-upper 40s. Precipitation is minimal at this time of year, with less than an inch of rain during June.

THE PORT Ålesund's port is small, but within an easy 10-minute stroll you'll find shops, cafés, and local points of interest.

TOURIST HIGHLIGHTS Trek up the stairs from the town park to **Fjellstua,** a mountaintop lodge and café, for panoramic views of the harbor. **Vasset Outdoor and Sports Park** offers fishing and horseback riding. The **Sunnmøre Museum** displays numerous styles of fishing boats as well as 40 historic structures. The municipal **Aalesunds Museum** provides information and exhibits about the city and about the Arctic in general.

WHAT TO EAT This being Scandinavia, seafood is a given. Try the local delicacy *klipfish*—split, salted, and dried cod. Salted smoked herring is also popular. Adventurous types can buy prawns directly from the fishing boats and eat them raw on the docks. Cheeses and game meats are readily available as well. If you're not in the mood for Norwegian food, several local places serve pizza.

WHAT TO BUY Hand-knit woolen hats, mittens, and sweaters are easy to find in Ålesund. Blown glass and pottery stock the shelves in shops and galleries. Depictions of trolls and moose adorn all manner of objects. Foodies will want to take home some local jam or honey.

Bergen, Norway

LANGUAGE Norwegian

HISTORY Bergen, the second-largest city in Norway, with about a quarter-million people, was founded circa AD 1030 as a Viking settlement and served as the national capital during the 13th century. It was only superseded in population by the current capital of Oslo (see page 222) in the mid-1800s. Over the centuries, Bergen has withstood a number of challenges: In the 1300s, it was decimated by the Black Plague; English and Dutch forces battled in its harbor in the 17th century; a series of fires spanning hundreds of years devastated it; and Germany occupied it for several years during World War II. Bergen has long been a Scandinavian center of trade, in particular the seafood industry.

WEATHER Disney cruises visit Bergen in June, when average daytime highs are in the mid-to-upper 60s and average nighttime are in the mid-to-upper 50s. Precipitation is typically minimal, with less than an inch of rainfall in June.

THE PORT The port is within a 10-minute walk of town. Restaurants, cafés, and shops are all nearby, as are many of the Bergen's tourist attractions. Taxis are plentiful, but many people choose to walk. The wharf area is particularly photogenic.

TOURIST HIGHLIGHTS Many visitors enjoy browsing in the local fish market. Others take the funicular to **Mt. Floyen** for breathtaking views of the surrounding islands. **Bergenhus Festning,** at the entrance to Bergen's harbor, is one of the oldest, best-preserved castles in Norway, with dungeons on the ground floor. **Bryggens Museum** displays archeological finds from the 12th century. **Bergen Aquarium** houses one of Europe's largest collections of fish and invertebrates from the North Sea. The **Fantoft Stavkirke,** about 3 miles from town, is a painstakingly reconstructed 12th-century stave church: It was built around 1150 in the town of Fortun, moved to Bergen and reassembled in 1883, burned by arsonists in 1992, and finally reopened in 1997 after an extensive restoration. Classical-music enthusiasts will want to visit **Troldhaugen,** the home of composer Edvard Grieg, which is preserved in its 1907 state, complete with Grieg's own Steinway piano.

WHAT TO EAT As a seaport, Bergen specializes in many forms of seafood, including prawns, octopus, salmon, and even smoked whale. Cod plays a starring role in fish cakes, fish balls, and fish pudding (tastes better than it sounds). Root vegetables such as carrots, potatoes, turnips, and onions are a common accompaniment. Pork and game meats are served in the form of chops, meatballs, or in stews. Berries are popular for breakfast or dessert. Several British-style pubs serve beer and ale in a cozy atmosphere—they'll also have a bottle or three of aquavit behind the bar. For the homesick, there's even a TGI Friday's in town.

WHAT TO BUY Knit woolens abound in every form: sweaters, caps, mittens, and socks. Trolls are depicted on every possible item, including clothing, kitchenware, and knickknacks. Also look for unique cheese knives and pewter serving pieces.

Copenhagen, Denmark

LANGUAGE Danish

HISTORY Copenhagen was founded as a Viking fishing village in the 11th century AD. The first fortresses in the area were built circa 1160. In the mid-1400s, the city was designated as the capital of Denmark, the country's first king (Christian I) was crowned, and the University of Copenhagen was founded. The mid-1600s and early 1700s were a period of turmoil and destruction, with a siege by Sweden and a series of devastating fires. In the early 1800s, Copenhagen withstood an attack by Britain. Most of the 1800s and early 1900s were a period of growth, with art and public beautification as a focus; the Tivoli Gardens amusement park and the writings of the beloved Danish author Hans Christian Andersen also came about during this time. The Nazis occupied the city during World War II, following which came another period of artistic growth and development of infrastructure.

WEATHER DCL visits Copenhagen in May–July. Average daytime highs in May are typically in the mid-50s, with nighttime lows in the mid-40s.

In June and July, daytime highs are in the mid-to-high 60s, with night-time lows in the low 50s. (Copenhagen's highest recorded temperatures have reached only the mid-80s.) Precipitation is minimal in the summer, averaging less than an inch of rain per month.

THE PORT The **Frihavnen (Freeport) Terminal,** about 2 miles from town, offers little in the way of services. Taxi stands are nearby, or you can take a 15-minute walk to the nearest train station to get to local sights. Copenhagen Airport is less than 10 miles from the port, making for an easy transfer.

TOURIST HIGHLIGHTS Children will enjoy a visit to **Tivoli Gardens,** an intricately landscaped amusement park that provided inspiration to Walt Disney during a 1950s visit. The park offers charming, gentle rides as well as thrills for braver souls. Speaking of Disney inspirations, a visit to Copenhagen wouldn't be complete without a stop at Edvard Eriksen's iconic *Little Mermaid* statue, near the harbor. **Rosenborg Castle** houses artifacts of Danish royalty, including many of the crown jewels. The **Latin Quarter** makes a nice walk; pass the oldest church and synagogue in the city, as well as the university. The **Staten Museum for Kunst** is the country's premier fine-art repository, and the **Nationalmuseet** is Denmark's largest museum of cultural history. Fans of **Hans Christian Andersen**'s fairy tales will want to visit one of the many places he called home in Copenhagen or pay their respects at his gravesite.

WHAT TO EAT Not surprisingly, Danish pastries are the thing to get for breakfast. Look for local breads and jams as well as *snegl* (snail), a type of buttery cinnamon roll. Seafood, including scallops, cod, salmon, whiting, and oysters, is served fresh, smoked, salted, and pickled. Sausages, cheeses, and deli-style meats are popular, too, particularly as part of a *smørrebrød,* or open-faced sandwich. Pork or veal meatballs, accompanied by boiled or roasted potatoes, are Danish comfort food. Side dishes are often cabbage- or onion-based. The local beer is **Carlsberg;** the brewery holds daily tours and tastings during the summer.

WHAT TO BUY **Legos** were invented in Denmark; look for unique sets that aren't available back home. Danish fashion is gaining a reputation as world-class, thanks to hot designers like **Baum und Pfergarten, Bruuns Bazaar, Henrik Vibskov,** and **Stine Goya.** Clean lines and eco-friendly materials have long been the hallmark of Danish furniture and housewares. **Royal Copenhagen** porcelain is a perennial favorite of collectors. Viking-themed toys, statuary, and books are popular souvenirs.

Dover, United Kingdom *(See page 206 for full profile.)*

Geiranger, Norway

LANGUAGE Norwegian

HISTORY Geiranger was quite isolated, inhabited by only a handful of native people, until the mid-1800s, when the first steamships and tourist boats stopped to take in views of the fjords, which are now listed as a UNESCO World Heritage Site. During the late 1800s, construction began on several hotels so that visitors could stay to enjoy the natural wonders for longer periods. Since then, Geiranger has functioned as a tourist destination from May to October each year, but it reverts to a typical Norwegian small town in the winter, with fewer than 500 permanent residents.

WEATHER Disney cruises visit Geiranger in June. Average daytime highs during this period are in the high 50s–mid 60s, with nighttime lows averaging in the high 40s–low 50s. Precipitation is typically minimal at this time of year, with less than an inch of rain for the month.

THE PORT Ships anchor in the harbor and tender into port. Geiranger is tiny—you can walk from one end of town to the other in less than 20 minutes, or you can take a taxi. Several shops and cafés are steps away from the docking area.

TOURIST HIGHLIGHTS The natural beauty of the fjords is the main attraction of the area; explore it by biking or hiking. **Brudesløret (The Bridal Veil)** is one of the most scenic waterfalls in Norway. Take in the views from the **Dalsnibba** mountain plateau or from **Flydalsjuvet,** a jutting rock formation. History buffs may enjoy **Herdalssetra,** a 300-year-old goat farm that provides a modern view into an ancient agrarian lifestyle; the goats are adorable, too. **Geiranger Church** is a lovely example of traditional architecture. Geiranger is also home to the **Norwegian Fjord Center** as well as a small local art gallery.

WHAT TO EAT Local markets sell cloudberries, strawberries, fruit juice, *sylte* (head cheese), cheese, goat meat, *mør* (a form of preserved meat), and preserved sausage. Restaurants and cafés serve traditional Norwegian dishes, including fish prepared in many styles, smoked whale, venison, and elk. Pastry lovers will enjoy the local sweet waffle served with berries and cream.

WHAT TO BUY Geiranger shops sell the ubiquitous Norwegian knit goods and troll souvenirs. Also look for carved rock jewelry, painted wood, and tin kitchenware.

Helsinki, Finland

LANGUAGES Finnish and Swedish

HISTORY Helsinki was founded in 1550 by King Gustav I of Sweden as a trading port. During its early years, the city was plagued by war, poverty, fires, and, yes, the plague. More prosperous times began with the construction of a naval fortress during the 18th century. In 1809, Russia annexed Finland after defeating Sweden in the Finnish War. Czar Alexander I of Russia named Helsinki the capital to reduce Swedish influence and bring the seat of Finnish government closer to St. Petersburg. Finland declared its independence in 1917, which was followed by a brief period of unrest and a longer period of growth and renewal. A highlight of the modern era was Helsinki's hosting of the 1952 Summer Olympics.

WEATHER Disney cruises visit Helsinki in May, June, and July. Temperatures during this period range from an average daytime high near 60° in late May to average daytime highs in the low-to-mid-70s throughout July. Average nighttime lows in the summer range from the low 40s to the low 50s. Precipitation is typically minimal at this time of year, with average rainfall of less than an inch per month.

THE PORT Services at the port are basic—a few souvenir shops, an ATM, and a currency exchange. Taxis and shuttles are available to take you to **Kauppatori (Market Square),** about 2 miles away. Once you're in town, you'll find many attractions within walking distance.

TOURIST HIGHLIGHTS Market Square contains many open-air stalls featuring food and flowers. Also note the architecture, which shows both Swedish and Russian influences. To get a feel for the native culture, visit a public sauna, where you can wear your birthday suit and sweat with the locals. Museum lovers have plenty of options here. The **Designmuseo** spotlights Finnish design; **Kiasma Museum of Contemporary Art** showcases art, design, and technology (note: closed for renovations until March 2015); and the **National Museum of Finland** focuses on the nation's history. Area churches of note include the **Lutheran Cathedral of Finland,** a palatial white Neoclassical structure topped with green copper domes, and the **Uspenski Cathedral,** an Eastern Orthodox house of worship with a traditional golden onion-shaped dome. **Suomenlinna (Finland's Fortress),** a UNESCO World Heritage Site, is a 15-minute ferry trip from town; dating from 1748 and built on six islands, it comprises not only a fortress, museums, and gardens but also a residential community where about 800 people live year-round. Children will like **Linnanmäki,** an amusement park, or the **Helsinki Zoo.**

WHAT TO EAT Smoked and salted fish of every sort is available on menus throughout Helsinki. Look for herring, salmon, perch, and whitefish. Cheese is a staple. *Leipäjuusto* ("bread cheese"), a Finnish specialty, is a rich cow's milk cheese that's baked or grilled as part of the manufacturing process; the browning makes it resemble a pizza or flatbread. Typical meats include lamb, elk, reindeer, duck, and goose. Potatoes, carrots, turnips, and mushrooms are frequently served side dishes. Summer fruits include strawberries, blueberries, lingonberries, and cloudberries.

WHAT TO BUY Among the most recognizable souvenirs are bags, clothing, and housewares from the internationally famous Finnish design house **Marimekko.** The bold colors and patterns are unmistakable. All manner of reindeer-related products can be found in Helsinki—blankets and rugs, as well as practical and decorative objects made from bone and horn. Canned reindeer meat is a unique takeaway. Finnish sweet-and-salty black licorice is another popular purchase.

Kirkwall, United Kingdom

LANGUAGE English

HISTORY Kirkwall, a small town with a population of less than 10,000, is the capital of the Orkney Islands, just to the north of Scotland. Archeological evidence dates human habitation of the Orkneys to approximately 3500 BC. Residents during the Iron and Medieval Periods included the Picts, the Norse, and the Scots. The area was under Norwegian rule from the 9th to 13th centuries AD. In 1468, Orkney was promised by Christian I, king of Denmark, Norway, and Sweden, as collateral against a dowry to be paid to James III of Scotland, who was betrothed to Christian's daughter, Margaret. Scotland has largely retained rule (the dowry was never paid). In the late 1600s, Oliver Cromwell's troops were stationed in Orkney and taught the locals various industrial arts and methods of agriculture. The Orkneys held naval bases in both world wars.

WEATHER Disney Cruise Line visits Kirkwall in July, when daytime highs average in the high 50s to low 60s and nighttime lows in the mid-40s. Summer is the dry season, with an average of about 2.5 inches of rain during July.

THE PORT Most cruise ships tender into port. Basic services and cafés can be found with walking distance of the dock. Free shuttle service is available from the terminal into town, about 2 miles away. There's also an auto-rental service near the dock, but availability is limited, so book early. Most of the town can be easily explored on foot.

TOURIST HIGHLIGHTS **St. Magnus Cathedral** is a stone masterpiece dating from 1137. The **Orkney Museum** features historical artifacts from the region. **Highland Park Distillery,** the northernmost distillery in the UK, offers samples at the end of its tour. **Skara Brae,** a UNESCO World Heritage Site, is a well-preserved Stone Age village. The **Orkney Wireless Museum** focuses on the history of radio and recorded sound. The **Ring of Brodgar** is a Stonehenge-like assemblage of 36 gigantic stones. Ferry service is available to other nearby islands.

WHAT TO EAT Fresh seafood is on many Kirkwall menus. Look for oysters, clams, lobster, and scallops, as well as less-familiar local favorites such as torsk, sea witch, and megrim. Meats include local beef, pork, and lamb; in particular, the meat from North Ronaldsay sheep, which feed mainly on seaweed, is a popular treat for visitors. Typical sides include root vegetables and potatoes. Many meals are accompanied by cheese and oat cakes (like crackers or flatbread). Orkney fudge is a prized treat, as are scones with rhubarb jam. Beer, ale, and spirits are easy to find; try the output from the two local breweries or the nearby Highland Park Distillery. The **Orkney Wine Company** produces naturally fermented wine from fruit such as raspberries and elderberries.

WHAT TO BUY Typical Kirkwall souvenirs include hand-knit woolen goods such as sweaters and mittens. Carved wooden objects and handcrafted jewelry are also popular. Take home a taste of the islands with some Orkney fudge, whiskey, or oat cakes.

Kristiansand, Norway

LANGUAGE Norwegian

HISTORY Archeological evidence suggests that the Kristiansand area has been inhabited since at least 6500 BC. Most of the settlement was small farms until the development of an active trading port in the 1400s. In the mid-1600s, the town was named in honor of King Christian IV (-*sand* refers to the sandy headland on which the city is built). The late 1700s were boom times, with Kristiansand serving as a center of shipbuilding. Like many Norwegian cities, Kristiansand suffered a series of devastating fires in the 18th and 19th centuries that destroyed parts of the town, necessitating rebuilding. In the early 1900s, mining and mineral processing became key industries. Recent years have seen a surge in technology and offshore drilling.

WEATHER DCL visits Kristiansand in early July. Average daytime highs during this period are in the low-to-mid-60s, with average nighttime lows in the low 50s. July rainfall averages about an inch.

THE PORT The cruise terminal lies within walking distance to the city center and the **Strandpromenaden (Boardwalk).** You'll find shops, cafés, and basic services within a 10-minute stroll of the ship. Taxis and buses service the port as well.

TOURIST HIGHLIGHTS Children will enjoy **Dyrepark,** a combination zoo–amusement park that is the most frequently visited attraction in Norway. **Posebyen** is the oldest part of town, featuring many lovely buildings that have withstood past fires. The **Setesdalsbanen,** a railway between Kristiansand and the town of Byglandsfjord, offers rides on a vintage steam train. The Neo-Gothic **Kristiansand Domkirke (Cathedral)** is a center of community activity as well as a house of worship. If the sun is out, walk over to the sandy beach area for some relaxing people-watching. The Strandpromenaden features shops and a fish market.

WHAT TO EAT The quayside area is home to many cafés and restaurants, as well as an open-air market and indoor stalls. Look for seafood offerings such as smoked salmon, mackerel, and cod cakes. Snack like a local and buy some prawns (shrimp) from the market and eat them while you enjoy the harbor view. You'll find moose, elk, venison, and other game meat on many menus. Expect to find a variety of cheeses for sale as well. Several varieties of berries are offered for breakfast and dessert.

WHAT TO BUY Kristiansand retailers sell many of the traditional Scandinavian souvenirs such as knit goods, carvings, and metalwork. Trolls, moose, and elves adorn all manner of trinkets. Jam made from local cloudberries makes a tasty gift.

Molde, Norway

LANGUAGE Norwegian

HISTORY Known settlement of Molde (MOHL-deh) dates to at least the Battle of Sekken in 1162. The area slowly grew into a trading port over the next several hundred years. During the 1600s, the region faced and eventually rebuffed an occupation by Sweden. During the 18th and 19th centuries, textile work became a key industry. Tourists discovered the town in the late 1800s. One third of the city was destroyed in a fire in 1916; additional destruction happened at the hands of the Germans during World War II. Following the war, Molde turned to banking, higher education, and tourism for growth.

WEATHER Disney cruises visit Molde in late June. Average daytime highs during this period are in the low-to-mid-60s, with nighttime lows averaging in the low 50s. Precipitation is minimal at this time of year, averaging less than an inch of rainfall for the month.

THE PORT The area directly next to the port is rather nondescript, but you'll find several small shops within a 10-minute walk. Taxis and buses serve the area.

TOURIST HIGHLIGHTS Molde takes great pride in its nickname, "The Town of Roses"—the relatively temperate climate makes for bountiful crops and flora. The **Romsdal Museum** features an extensive collection of Norwegian folk art displayed both indoors and outdoors. **Fiskerimuseet** focuses on the fishing trade and local culture. For natural beauty, visit **Mardalsfossen,** the longest freefalling waterfall in northern Europe. The nearby **"Troll Church"** is an area with limestone caves, waterfalls, and grottoes.

WHAT TO EAT Not surprisingly, fresh seafood appears on many menus, with salmon a particular favorite. Game meats such as venison, duck, and moose abound. Local lamb is said to be particularly tasty; find it served in stews, in meatballs, and roasted. The local soft drink, called Ananasbrus, is a lightly carbonated pineapple beverage. Fresh strawberries are a delicacy in the summer months. For breakfast try *brunost,* a caramelized brown cheese (think a sweet-savory fudge).

WHAT TO BUY Popular souvenirs are hand-knit sweaters, hats, and mittens. Decorated and practical pieces made from pewter, silver, and tin line the shelves of many shops. In addition to the usual troll and elf motifs, you'll find many rose-themed items in Molde. Goat or reindeer skins make great rugs, wall hangings, or blankets.

Olden, Norway

LANGUAGE Norwegian

HISTORY Olden is a sleepy little village of about 500 year-round residents. In ancient times, it was home to fishing camps. Permanent settlement began in the mid-1600s. In the late 1990s, Olden became a popular tourist destination.

WEATHER Disney Cruise Line visits Olden in late June, when daytime highs average in the low 60s and nighttime lows in the 50s. Precipitation is typically minimal at this time, with less than an inch of rainfall during the month.

THE PORT Olden is a tender port. The tenders dock at the edge of the main village, which measures slightly more than half a mile square. You can get anywhere you want to go in town quickly and easily.

TOURIST HIGHLIGHTS Natural beauty is the draw here—you won't find much in the way of cultural sites, architecture, dining, or shopping. Olden is the gateway to the **Briksdal Glacier**—the largest glacier on the European mainland—in **Jostedal Glacier National Park.** Be sure to bring your camera to capture the stunning scenery. "Troll cars," small motorized vehicles reminiscent of golf carts, take tourists around town and up to the glacier (in recent years, they replaced the more traditional horse-drawn carriages).

WHAT TO EAT A few restaurants in town serve seafood and sandwiches. For a more substantial meal, visit the restaurant at the **Olden Fjordhotel,** which offers a typical Scandinavian *smörgåsbord.*

WHAT TO BUY A few shops sell local handicrafts, and there's a boutique or two; otherwise, it's outdoor stalls selling the typical tourist tchotchkes.

Oslo, Norway

LANGUAGE Norwegian

HISTORY A city of about 600,000 people (1.5 million including its suburbs), Oslo is the capital of Norway and also its economic, commercial, and social center. It was founded around AD 1000, and while it has changed names—and nations—a few times, it has served as a seat of government since 1300. Like many other European cities, Oslo lost much of its population (about 75%) to the Black Death during the Middle Ages. As a consequence, church membership and income dropped significantly, allowing merchants and traders to take over Oslo's economy—a role they never relinquished.

From about 1500 to 1905, Norway was a possession first of Denmark and later of Sweden. It achieved independence from Sweden in 1905. Germany occupied Norway during World War II, establishing its own government from 1940 until the German surrender in 1945.

Like many European countries, Norway is politically much more liberal than the United States. (The Høyre, Norway's conservative party, for example, supports a generous welfare state, universal health care, marriage equality, and membership in the European Union.) Unlike many ports visited by DCL, Oslo is not heavily dependent on tourism; shipping, oil and gas production, fishing, manufacturing, and services are the main drivers of Norway's economy. As a result, there's much more to see in Oslo than, say, Disney's typical Caribbean port.

WEATHER DCL visits Oslo in May and June. Daytime highs range from the high 50s to low 70s, with nighttime lows in the mid-40s–low 50s. Summer is the rainy season in Oslo, with about 15–17 rainy days per month. Bring a lightweight waterproof jacket and a pair of moisture-wicking socks with you to explore the city.

THE PORT Cruise ships dock at the southern end of downtown Oslo, within half a mile of the **Central Station,** which provides bus, subway, taxi, and train service throughout the city. Public transportation is clean and efficient.

TOURIST HIGHLIGHTS Oslo is one of Len's favorite cities. The city has adapted the sleek Scandinavian aesthetic to otherwise-typical European architecture. The tree-lined streets have wide, spotless sidewalks. You could spend the entire day just walking around and have a perfectly lovely time.

If you're a fan of Walt Disney World and of Epcot in particular, try our walking tour of Oslo (page 261), which will help you find the original inspirations for three World Showcase icons: The **Gol Stave Church,** in Oslo's Norwegian Museum of Cultural History, is the model for the stave church in front of the Norway Pavilion; **Castle Akershus,** near the port of Oslo, is the inspiration for Restaurant Akershus; and the **Viking Ship Museum,** part of the University of Oslo Museum of Cultural History (a different museum from the one that houses the stave church), was seen in the old *Spirit of Norway* film that was shown after the now-defunct Maelstrom boat ride.

Art and architecture fans should take a short walk west along the waterfront, to the **Tjuvholmen** neighborhood, which features cafés, restaurants, art galleries and museums, outdoor sculpture, and some really interestingly shaped buildings.

Finally, within a short walk of the cruise port, at the west end of Karl Johans Gate (Oslo's main thoroughfare), is the 173-room **Royal Palace,** the official residence of Norway's royal family. For information on guided tours, visit **royalcourt.no** (click "The Royal Residences," then "Palace Tours").

A short walk from the Royal Palace is the **Nobel Peace Center,** which awards the annual Nobel Peace Prize. The Center includes a museum with displays honoring past winners, along with multimedia presentations on current projects. See **nobelpeacecenter.org/en** for hours and admission prices.

WHAT TO EAT You'll find familiar cuisines represented in the cafés and restaurants along Karl Johans Gate—everything from northern European to North American, and a fair bit outside. (A friend of ours swears that the best chimichanga he's ever eaten was in Oslo, at **Taco República.**)

Len recommends dining at one of the **Grand Hotel**'s two restaurants. The **Grand Café** serves a modern interpretation of the Norwegian breakfast, including smoked herring, wild salmon, and local lamb; Sunday brunch is served from 1 to 4:30 p.m. Expect to pay around $50 per person for the regular breakfast and $65 for brunch; visit **tinyurl.com/grandcafeoslo** for reservations. If you're walking around during the morning, try the **Palm Court** restaurant for afternoon tea, which includes three plates of pastries, cookies, and sweets, plus tiny sandwiches and, of course, as much tea as you care to drink. Cost is around $65 per person. Visit **tinyurl.com/palmcourt tea** for reservations.

WHAT TO BUY Oslo's main shopping district is along **Karl Johans Gate,** about a quarter-mile from the port. Here you'll find Norwegian brands such as **Helly Hansen** (for clothing, especially cold-weather outerwear). For a multitude of retail and dining options, try the **Oslo City Shopping Centre** (Stenersgata 1; open Monday–Friday, 10 a.m.–10 p.m., Saturday, 10 a.m.–8 p.m., closed Sunday), which looks like a Norwegian space port. For high-end threads, try the **Eger Karl Johan** department store (23-B Karl Johans Gate; open Monday–Friday, 10 a.m.–7 p.m., Saturday, 10 a.m.–6 p.m., closed Sunday).

Reykjavík, Iceland

LANGUAGE Icelandic

HISTORY The year AD 871 brought the first recorded settler to Iceland: Ingólfur Arnarson, a fugitive from Norway. Almost no development beyond basic farming happened for the next 900 years. Industry and infrastructure picked up steam in the mid-1700s with the development of a textile industry based on tanning, wool harvesting, dyeing, and weaving; other early industries included fishing and shipbuilding. The first Icelandic constitution was adopted in 1874, and the island achieved independent statehood in 1904 under the crown of Denmark. Iceland asserts neutrality in global conflicts but did house Allied forces during World War II. Full independence was reached in 1944 when the first president of Iceland was elected. In more recent times, finance and technology have become key industries. A city of about 120,000 people, Reykjavík is currently the world's northernmost capital of a sovereign state.

WEATHER Disney cruises visit Iceland in May and June. Average daytime highs during this period are in the mid-40s–mid-50s; nighttime lows average in the mid-30s–mid-40s. (The highest recorded temperature is 78°). Precipitation is typically minimal at this time of year, with an average rainfall of less than an inch per month. The sun barely sets during the summer, so expect to see folks out and about well into the night.

THE PORT The **Skarfabakki** cruise dock is about 2 miles from the center of town. There is little of interest near the dock itself, but taxis and a free shuttle will take you to the commercial district. The **Cruise Welcome Center** can direct you as well as provide information about local attractions. Once you're in Reykjavík proper, most attractions are accessible on foot.

TOURIST HIGHLIGHTS Reykjavík has a wonderful mix of urban sophistication and outdoor adventure. Because the island is nearly treeless, many Icelandic buildings are constructed from materials such as driftwood, corrugated iron, volcanic rock, and sod, making for an eclectic and innovative architectural mix. In town, visit the **Menningarmiðstoð Kópavogs,** a cultural complex with a natural-history museum; the **Hafnarborg,** a modern-art museum; or the **Hallgrimskirkja,** a Lutheran cathedral built in the Expressionist style. About 30 miles from the city, the **Blue Lagoon** mineral spa has interesting geothermal features. An active volcano, **Hengill,** is within a 20-minute drive and features natural hot springs. Wildlife excursions afford opportunities to see whales, birds of prey, and thousands of the island's charming native puffins.

WHAT TO EAT Seafood stews, chowders, and kabobs are local specialties. Lobster, crayfish, salmon, trout, and scallops are abundant. Sushi-style restaurants are popular. Whale meat is a treat for the adventurous. Meats may include duck, horse, and eel, as well as pork and veal served in thin slices or as cold cuts. For those in need of something familiar, pizza and burgers are easy to find. Pastries, bread, and eggs are morning staples. Cheese and yogurt made from both cow and sheep milk are popular. Vegetarianism is relatively rare in Iceland, with the most prevalent plant foods including potatoes, cabbage, turnips, rutabagas, and other root vegetables. Hot chocolate and coffee are ubiquitous.

The local firewater is *brennivín,* a powerful unsweetened schnapps fermented from potatoes and flavored with caraway, cumin, and other botanicals. It packs a wallop, and thank goodness for that—*brennivín* is the traditional beverage to accompany the Icelandic specialty *hákarl,* or fermented shark meat.

"Fermented" doesn't really tell the whole story, though. A Greenland shark is cleaned, buried in sand and weighted with stones, and then left to cure (read: decompose) for 6–12 weeks. Then the flesh is cut into strips and hung up to dry for several months. The reason for all this advance, um, preparation? The meat is poisonous when it's fresh.

If you still think you might like to sample *hákarl* after reading this far, we'd be remiss if we didn't apprise you of the following: (1)

Wikipedia advises, "Those new to it will usually gag involuntarily on the first attempt to eat it because of the high ammonia content." (2) A food blogger who was brave enough to try it likened the taste to "a tramp's sock soaked in urine." (3) It made Gordon Ramsay retch.

WHAT TO BUY Puffins, trolls, and elves are depicted on everything from clothing to housewares. Fine-quality Icelandic wool sweaters are a prized souvenir. Look for hand-knit items as well as jewelry and carvings made from area driftwood, lava, and found items. Note that shopping in Iceland can be expensive due to elevated taxes and tariffs, so be sure to ask the full price before buying.

St. Petersburg, Russian Federation

LANGUAGE Russian

HISTORY The area that is now St. Petersburg has been occupied since at least the ninth century AD by a series of Slavs, Finns, Swedes, and other ethnic groups. Real turbulence in the area began during the 16th century with a series of border disputes between Russia and Sweden. Russia gained control of the region, and the city proper was founded in 1703 by Tsar Peter the Great. After Peter died in 1725, several rulers jostled for position. Eventually Peter's daughter, Elizabeth, took the crown and a period of growth and prosperity occurred in what was now the Russian capital. Catherine the Great assumed power following a 1762 coup d'état. Her reign saw the growth of trade and a flourishing of the arts. Subsequent rulers Paul I and Alexander I modified the government into a more bureaucratic structure. Bureaucracy further increased under Nicholas I in the early to mid-1800s. The next ruler, Alexander II, was assassinated in 1881 and the country entered a period of capitalism. Uprisings in the early 1890s were followed by revolution and destruction during the first World War. Communism prevailed post–World War I, and the city's name was changed to Leningrad in 1924. After a German siege in 1941, food was scarce and famine common. The Soviets resumed control in 1944, but the effects of World War II lasted until well into the 1960s. With the fall of Communism in Russia in 1991, the city's original name was restored.

WEATHER DCL visits St. Petersburg in June and July. Average daytime highs in June are in the low-to-high 60s, with nighttime lows averaging in the mid-40s–low 50s. In July, daytime highs are in the high 60s–mid-70s, with nighttime lows averaging in the mid-50s. Precipitation is typically minimal during the summer, with less than an inch of rainfall per month. During the "White Nights" of summer, the sun barely sets.

THE PORT A port terminal finished in 2011 houses passport control, a café, several shops, an ATM, and other basic services. Taxis are at the ready to take you on the 15-minute drive into town or to the transportation arranged by your port-adventure escort. Guests visiting St. Petersburg on organized excursions (such as DCL's port adventures) are not required to have a visa. If you'd like to explore on your own, however, you must have a valid Russian tourist visa, obtained in advance of your trip.

TOURIST HIGHLIGHTS Many visitors consider the **State Hermitage Museum** their highest priority. The scope and quality of the collections are easily comparable to those of the Louvre or the Metropolitan Museum of Art. The **Peter and Paul Fortress** houses a museum of Russian history. **St. Isaac's** is the largest domed cathedral in the world. The **Church of the Savior on Spilled Blood** houses a gorgeous display of mosaics.

WHAT TO EAT You'll find many cuisines represented in the restaurants of St. Petersburg. For Russian fare, try one of the many soups, either cold ones such as beet-based borscht or warm ones made with meat and cabbage. You'll often find meat boiled, served cold, or minced in a pastry or pie. Carp, salmon, pike, and trout are typical seafood offerings. Blinis and pancakes are used as a base for fillings ranging from eggs, chopped meat, and onions, to cottage cheese and jam. Most Russians drink tea on a daily basis. A popular beverage is *kvass,* which is made from fermented bread; it has an extremely low alcohol content and is sometimes flavored with fruit or spices. Vodka is plentiful, natch.

WHAT TO BUY Russian nesting dolls, or *matryoshka,* are a near-mandatory purchase. Bargaining is common in outdoor stalls. Lacquered papier-mâché boxes, painted with scenes from Russian folk tales, are a popular purchase. Look for jewelry made with amber or detailed silver filigree. Those knowledgeable about rugs or antiques may encounter some unique finds, but always ask about shipping before you buy. Pick up a book or two on local art and architecture. Of course, you'll want to take home a bottle of vodka.

Stavanger, Norway

LANGUAGE Norwegian

HISTORY Stavanger has been a fishing port since the time of the Vikings. The town's official founding date is AD 1125, which coincides with the building of the local cathedral. Fishing and small-village life continued for centuries until the development of the petroleum industry, which today is a key employer in the region. The mainland base for several offshore-drilling operations, Stavanger has one of the lowest unemployment rates in all of Europe.

WEATHER Disney cruises visit Stavanger in June, when daytime highs average in the high 50s–mid-60s and nighttime lows in the 40s. Rainfall is minimal, with less than an inch of rain during June.

THE PORT Ships dock just at the edge of town. Many services and points of interest are within a 10-minute walk. Taxis, buses, and bike rentals are all nearby.

TOURIST HIGHLIGHTS Stavanger's Old Town is home to charming whitewashed cottages, perfect for photo opportunities. For those interested in the local fishing industry, a visit to the **Norwegian Canning Museum** is in order. Other area educational sites include the **Maritime Museum, Printing Museum,** and **Petroleum Museum.** Visitors interested in religious history may want to visit **Utstein Abbey,** Norway's only preserved medieval monastery.

WHAT TO EAT Fish, shellfish, lamb, beef, and cheese figure prominently in local menus, as do moose, reindeer, and duck. Locally grown vegetables include tomatoes, cucumber, potatoes, and parsley. Look for lamb ragout and fish stew at the scenic **Flor & Fjære** restaurant, on the nearby

island of Sør-Hidle. Popular cafés in town include **Ostehuset (Cheese House),** where the raclette is locally sourced, and **Sjokoladepiken (Chocolate Girl),** which serves chocolate in nearly every form imaginable. A number of pubs in town serve beers from around the world.
WHAT TO BUY Textiles, knitwear, and handwoven items are popular purchases. Pewter goods are readily available, with the most notable items being the *ostehovel,* a distinctive cheese slicer that was invented in the area. The work of area glassblowers and potters is also popular.

Stockholm, Sweden

LANGUAGE Swedish
HISTORY The area was first settled by Vikings in about AD 1,000. In the 13th century, nearby mines made Stockholm a center of the iron trade, and it subsequently served as a prominent cultural and economic center for northern Europe. During the early 1500s, Sweden and Denmark battled for control of Stockholm, resulting in much loss of life. In 1634, Stockholm became the official capital of Sweden. A period of prosperity was dampened by a great plague in 1710. By the mid-18th century, Stockholm was again a center of trade. Throughout the 19th and 20th centuries, art, design, and technology gained footholds.
WEATHER DCL visits Stockholm in June and July. Average daytime highs during these months are in the mid-60s–mid-70s, with nighttime lows averaging in the mid-40s–mid-50s. Precipitation is typically light in the summer, averaging less than an inch of rainfall per month.
THE PORT The **Frihamnen** docks include a modern passenger terminal with some basic shops and an ATM. The port is a 15-minute taxi, bus, or shuttle ride away from town.
TOURIST HIGHLIGHTS Stockholm is a city of museums. Some notable ones include **Fotografiska,** showcasing contemporary photography; the **Nationalmuseum,** with prominent Rembrandt and Nordic-art collections; and **Moderna Museet**, which houses works by Dalí, Picasso, Kandinsky, and others. **Kungliga Slottet,** the royal palace, has exhibits on weaponry and the crown jewels, as well as a charming changing of the guard. For a taste of the outdoors, visit **Rosendal's Garden,** where you can pick your own flowers from lush beds, paying by weight, as well as enjoy a light meal at the café. Children will enjoy **Junibacken,** an indoor park celebrating the life and work of Astrid Lindgren, the author of the *Pippi Longstocking* books, or **Tivoli Gröna Lund,** a small amusement park.
WHAT TO EAT Seafood, beef, and pork are on many menus in Stockholm. Red meat is often found in the form of meatballs, typically served with a brown cream sauce. The traditional accompaniment is a lingonberry tart and boiled or mashed potatoes. Open-faced sandwiches made with cheese, cold cuts, or hard-boiled eggs are a typical Swedish lunch. Smoked salmon and pickled herring are other usual offerings. Dark, crisp breads are served throughout the day, while sweeter rolls and pastries are served in the morning. For celebrations, Swedes like to spread out a buffet-style *smörgåsbord.* Aquavit, *punch* (a sweet liqueur made with sugarcane, rum, and spices), and beer are typical adult libations.

WHAT TO BUY If you're in the mood for wearables, Swedish clogs are a hot item; look for game-animal leathers and hand-painted designs. Swedish glass and crystal are of particularly high quality. Other typical souvenirs are trays embellished with a repeating-triangle pattern based on the one in the pavement of Sergels Torg (Stockholm's main public square) or brightly painted Dalahäst horses carved from wood. For a relatively small country, Sweden has had an outsized influence on global pop music (not just ABBA); look for CDs from local rising performers. Carved pipes are a common gift in Sweden—even if you're not a smoker, some are lovely to display. Foodies will want to take home tinned herring, ginger cookies, pots of berry jam, or salty licorice. Finally, if you love **IKEA** back home, you'll want to fit in a visit to Stockholm's flagship store.

Tallinn, Estonia

LANGUAGE Estonian

HISTORY The first known large-scale building in Tallinn was the construction of a fortress in 1050. Danes ruled this trade port, then known as Reval, during the 1200s. During the Protestant Reformation in the 1500s, Swedes controlled the region. In the early 1700s, Russians took control. Following World War I, Estonia declared independence in 1918, but this ended during World War II, when the Soviet Union annexed the region. Estonia regained its independence in 1991, with the collapse of the USSR. In 2004, the Baltic nation joined the European Union.

WEATHER Disney Cruise Line visits Tallinn in June and July. Average daytime highs throughout the summer range from the low 60s to the low 70s, with average nighttime lows ranging the mid-40s to low 50s. Precipitation is typically light during summer, with less than an inch of rain per month.

THE PORT Completed in 2012, the cruise terminal houses ATMs, a currency exchange, several small shops, and a tourist-information desk; free Wi-Fi is provided. The center of town is about 15 minutes away on foot. Once you get there, most attractions are easily walkable within a 0.6-square-mile area.

TOURIST HIGHLIGHTS **Raekoja Plats** is Tallinn's Town Hall Square. The weathervane atop the Town Hall has been in place since 1530. **Kiek-in-de-Kök** (meaning "peep in the kitchen") is a grand six-story structure housing historical displays and an art museum; built as an artillery tower in 1475, it gained its name because soldiers could see into neighboring houses from its upper floors. **Toompea Castle** is a lovely example of medieval architecture. The top floor of the **Sokos Hotel Viru** was once a secret lair where the KGB eavesdropped on guests; today it houses a small spy museum. If you'd like to get away from the city, coastal **Pirita** offers boat excursions.

WHAT TO EAT Estonian cuisine is heavy on meat (particularly pork) and potatoes, and on seafood in coastal areas. Soups, both broth- and cream-based, are popular as starters and main courses alike. Cabbage and dark rye bread are typical accompaniments. Local delicacies include marinated eel, *sült* (jellied pork), sliced tongue, and blood sausage served with berry jam. *Kali* is a lightly carbonated nonalcoholic beverage similar to unfermented beer. *Kama,* a dairy drink made with kefir (like liquid yogurt) and ground grain, has a milkshake-like texture. The local adult beverage is Vana Tallinn, a rum-based, heavily spiced liqueur with an alcohol content of up to 50%.

WHAT TO BUY Handcrafted woolens are a popular take-home item. Look for sweaters, caps, mittens, and scarves adorned with geometrics or reindeer-related designs. Simple linen shirts and tunics are typical of the area. Area craftspeople expertly carve wooden items, particularly from juniper. Also look for local pottery and blown glass. **Kalev** is the biggest candy manufacturer in Estonia; pick up a box of chocolate to bring home. You may also find Soviet-era artwork and antiques, and you may see Cuban cigars for sale (smoke up while you're in port).

Warnemünde, Germany

LANGUAGE German

HISTORY A town of about 8,400 people on the Baltic coast, Warnemünde has been an established village since about AD 1200 and remained a small fishing village for centuries. In 1323, it was annexed by nearby Rostock to safeguard the latter town's access to the Baltic Sea. Once completely dependent on the fishing industry, Warnemünde's economy is now driven by shipbuilding and tourism (the town first became popular as a seaside resort in the mid-1800s). Since the construction of its cruise terminal in 2005, Warnemünde has become the most important cruise port in Germany. The capital city of **Berlin** is about 153 miles to the south.

WEATHER Disney cruises visit Warnemünde in July, when average daytime highs are in the high 60s–mid-70s and average nighttime lows are in the high 50s. Precipitation is typically negligible, with less than an inch of rainfall for the month.

THE PORT The Warnemünde cruise terminal has only limited services. However, the train station is about 5 minutes away on foot. The train to the town of Rostock takes about 20 minutes. A train trip to Berlin takes about 2 hours and 45 minutes. You could also rent a car, but you'll want to reserve in advance and make sure that you have the proper driving certification.

TOURIST HIGHLIGHTS If you're staying close to port, the **Monastery of the Holy Cross,** in Rostock, displays medieval art and functions as the local history museum. Also in Rostock, see **St. Mary's Church,** with a Baroque organ and an astronomical clock dating back to 1472.

In Berlin, the imposing **Brandenburg Gate** is a must-see for many visitors. The **Reichstag** is likewise a potent symbol of German history. The **Unter den Linden** area has lovely gardens as well as Germany's largest history museum. Visit the **Berlin Wall Memorial** on **Bernauer Strasse;** when Berlin was a divided city, the Wall ran along this street. **Potsdamer Platz** is a major shopping and restaurant district. Sports fans will want to check out the **Olympic Stadium.** Children will enjoy the **Berlin Zoo.**

WHAT TO EAT German cuisine is typically meat-and-potatoes comfort food: *schnitzels* (pork, veal, or chicken cutlets), roasts, and dumplings served with boiled or mashed spuds and a side dish of mushrooms or onions. You'll also find *wursts* (sausages) of all sorts, often served with pastalike *spaetzle.* Large, soft pretzels are a popular snack. A famous pastry is the Berliner, which is much like a jelly doughnut. (Contrary to popular belief, JFK didn't goof and say "I am a doughnut" when he declared, *"Ich bin ein Berliner."*) Other desserts are apple- or caramel-based. Beer, not surprisingly, is the beverage of choice. In addition, global cuisines such as Chilean, French, Indian, and Turkish are well represented in Berlin's thriving restaurant scene.

WHAT TO BUY Bring home a beer stein, a purchase that's both practical and decorative. Cuckoo clocks and pewter serving items are popular purchases as well. Teddy bears and Haribo gummy candies are good choices for children. The cook in the family will appreciate a jar of spicy German mustard.

Here's a treat that you and your kids can enjoy only while overseas: the **Kinder Surprise,** a chocolate egg molded around a plastic capsule containing a small toy, such as a car or a miniature Disney character. The eggs are wildly popular with children and collectors all over Europe, and the toys really are cute. Unfortunately, many Americans are unaware that they can't bring Kinder Surprises home: They're *verboten* in the United States due to a longstanding FDA regulation banning "embedded non-nutritive objects" in foods. (For what it's worth, the labels have prominent safety warnings, and the plastic shell seems like a sensible safeguard.) At best, US Customs will seize the eggs if you get caught smuggling them in; at worst, you could be detained and slapped with a fine of $2,500 . . . *per egg.*

❚❙ PANAMA CANAL PORTS

Cabo San Lucas, Mexico *(See page 195 for full profile.)*

Cartagena, Colombia

LANGUAGE Spanish

HISTORY Cartagena has been inhabited since 4000 BC. Spanish explorers founded the city proper during the early 1500s. This was followed by periodic plundering by pirates and privateers from France and England, and later by a major invasion from Englishman Sir Francis Drake. During the 17th century, the Spanish constructed a series of fortresses to protect the city. Throughout the 17th and 18th centuries, Cartagena was a major trading outpost. In 1811 the region declared its independence from Spain, resulting in nearly a century of crisis. Today Cartagena is a prosperous tourist destination.

WEATHER DCL visits Cartagena in May and October, but it's hot here year-round. Expect daytime highs in the upper 80s and average nighttime lows in the 70s. Average precipitation is a moderate 3–4 inches during in May but up to 8 inches during October, which is part of the rainy season.

THE PORT The cruise terminal has basic services but not much else. A landscaped park near the dock gates has a café and small shops. Buses and taxis are available to take you to the main part of town.

TOURIST HIGHLIGHTS **Old Town** is a popular exploration spot. Look for the **Plaza de Bolívar** and the giant bronze statue of Simón Bolívar, who helped Colombia and other South American countries secure independence from Spain. Nearby are the **Museo del Oro y Arqueologia** and a 16th-century cathedral. The fortress **Castillo San Felipe de Barajas** presents a look into the area's past. The **Palacio de la Inquisición** exhibits artifacts from the Spanish Inquisition, including some very creative torture devices. For outdoor fun, Cartagena offers many beaches within a 10- to 20-minute taxi ride away from town. Divers will find scuba and snorkel equipment available for rent.

WHAT TO EAT Restaurants here serve food from most major cuisines. Traditional foods include grilled fish, meat, and rabbit; rice, cassava, and plantains are common side dishes. Street vendors sell *butifarras* (meatballs), *buñuelos* (cheese balls), and *arepas de huevo* (fried dough with an egg inside). Try the *mote de queso*, a local soup made from yams, eggplant, and cheese. Fruit juices are available in abundance, both in restaurants and in street shacks. The local beer is Club Colombia.

WHAT TO BUY You'll find plenty of jewelry, particularly emeralds, for sale here. Many vendors are open to bargaining. Ornate (and often obscene) woodcarvings are common finds. For local flavor, search out loose-fitting traditional dresses, baskets, or handmade musical instruments. Java junkies will naturally want to take home some Colombian coffee.

Cozumel, Mexico   *(See page 185 for full profile.)*

Galveston, Texas   *(See page 187 for full profile.)*

Key West, Florida   *(See page 189 for full profile.)*

Panama Canal, Panama

HISTORY The Spanish government initially authorized construction of the Panama Canal in 1819. Progress was scattershot for several decades thereafter, with planning beginning in earnest in 1876 and construction starting in 1881. Engineering struggles plagued early efforts to dig the canal, eventually resulting in the plan for a system of raised locks. Continued disease and construction difficulties caused the bankruptcy of the original funders and a long stall in the work process. The project was revived following strategic interest from US President Theodore Roosevelt, with the United States taking formal control over the region in 1904. Several years were spent creating an infrastructure capable of supporting the materials and labor force required to complete the task. Lock building commenced in 1909 and was finished in 1913. In 1914 a French boat, the *Alexandre La Valley,* became the first to completely traverse the canal. The Panama Canal subsequently revolutionized world trade patterns, cutting nearly 8,000 miles off a sea journey from New York to San Francisco. In 1977 the United States began to reduce its role in the region, and today the Panama Canal Authority oversees the canal, which continues to be improved. Currently the locks cannot accommodate the size of the largest ships, and in 2007 a project began to create a new wider lane of locks.

WEATHER Warm and wet. Because it's close to the equator, temperatures vary little in Panama, with lows throughout the year around 75° and highs around 90°. Disney ships generally visit in May and September, which average 24–26 days of rain per month, with humidity above 90%. (On the upside, we hear big hair is coming back in style.)

THE PORT The ship moves through the canal without stopping to let off passengers.

TOURIST HIGHLIGHTS The highlight of the voyage is watching how the canal's locks fill and release water to move the ship up and down through the terrain. It takes 8–10 hours to get through all of the locks, so you have plenty of time to catch the action.

Puerto Vallarta, Mexico

LANGUAGE Spanish

HISTORY The native settlers were the ancient Aztlán peoples. European influence began in the early 1500s, when Spaniards, including Hernán Cortés, took control of the region. During the 17th and 18th centuries, the area was a known shelter for pirates and smugglers. Organized trade began to blossom in 1859, when the Union en Cuale mining company started operating in the region. In the early 1900s, the mining trade gave way to fruit farming, which then ceded influence to the growing tourism industry. Since the 1950s, Puerto Vallarta has been a resort and cruise destination.

WEATHER Disney cruises visit Puerto Vallarta in May and October. Average daytime highs during those months are in the mid-80s–low 90s, with average nighttime lows in the low-to-mid-70s. Precipitation is relatively low in May, averaging less than 2 inches of rainfall. October is slightly wetter, averaging about 3 inches for the month.

THE PORT From the **Marina Vallarta Terminal,** you're an easy walk to several restaurants, small shops, and hotels with bars. A full **Walmart** is about a 10- to 15-minute walk from the port, allowing you to pick up any basic necessity at a relatively reasonable price. Downtown Puerto Vallarta is about 3 miles from the port, accessible via taxi or bus.

TOURIST HIGHLIGHTS The beaches are the big draw here. Snooze by the waves or enjoy more-active pursuits such as snorkeling or biking. Animal lovers can enjoy dolphin excursions or watch whales and turtles. **El Centro,** Puerto Vallarta's downtown, features churches with charming colonial detail. Tequila manufacturing and tasting is a big draw to this area. Be sure to sample several varieties; you'll be amazed at the differences.

WHAT TO EAT Not surprisingly, you'll find tacos, taquitos, tostadas, and enchiladas on local menus, along with fresh seafood (try red snapper or marlin served with spices and lime). Those in the mood for adult beverages will find no shortage of margaritas, daiquiris, and beer.

WHAT TO BUY Puerto Vallarta shopping caters to the tourist trade. You'll find silver, ceramics, leather, and woven goods in many forms, as well as the ubiquitous T-shirts and trinkets portside. Haggling is common with vendors by the beaches, so if you don't like the price you see, feel free to propose something lower. Several modern malls in the area sell major-brand cruise wear at typically reasonable prices. Foodies will want to bring home local chocolates or Mexican spices.

San Diego, California *(See page 197 for full profile.)*

TRANSATLANTIC PORTS

Barcelona, Spain *(See page 205 for full profile.)*

Castaway Cay, Bahamas *(See page 184 for full profile.)*

Copenhagen, Denmark *(See page 216 for full profile.)*

Funchal, Madeira, Portugal

LANGUAGE Portuguese

HISTORY Funchal is the capital of Portugal's Autonomous Region of Madeira, about 250 miles north of the Canary Islands in the Atlantic Ocean. Settlement began in the early 1400s, and Christopher Columbus was an early resident. During the late 15th century, the sugar industry expanded in Madeira, making this an important trading port. During the 16th century, Funchal was a stopping point for ships traveling from the Indies to the New World. The 1800s saw a period of upheaval, with control of the island of Madeira passing from the British to the Portuguese. In 1976 Portugal granted political autonomy to Madeira.

WEATHER September, when DCL visits Funchal, is pleasant and mild. Average daytime highs are in the mid-70s, while average nighttime lows are in the mid-60s. Precipitation is typically low at this time of year, averaging about 1 inch of rainfall for the month.

THE PORT Services are limited at the port itself. A few small souvenir stalls pop up when ships are in port, offering the most basic souvenirs and snacks. The center of town is about half a mile away, accessible on foot, by cab, or by shuttle bus.

TOURIST HIGHLIGHTS For breathtaking vistas of the harbor, the **Monte Cable Car** will take you from the old town area to high hills. For outdoor strolling, try the **Jardins do Palheiro,** a British Colonial–style park. Many plantings here bloom virtually year-round. For a more strenuous hike, explore the *levadas,* a system of aqueducts, many with views of the natural wonders of the area. Museum lovers will enjoy the **Museum of**

Natural History or the **Sacred Art Museum.** Animal enthusiasts will want to look into day trips for whale- and dolphin-watching.

WHAT TO EAT Garlic is present in nearly all savory dishes in the region. Try the local tomato-and-onion soup, espada (a native fish), codfish, scabbard fish served with banana, or *espetada* (grilled marinated beef). You'll also find rabbit and goat on many menus. Traditional pastries include the *bolo de mel,* or honey cake. And don't forget to try the locally produced sweet wines.

WHAT TO BUY Madeira is famous for its embroidery. You can find intricately decorated fabric and clothing throughout the area. Madeira dessert wine is often a prized purchase; bring home several of the local varieties. Wicker and baskets are also sold everywhere. Visit the **Mercado dos Lavradores** for handicrafts and local packaged treats.

Miami, Florida   *(See page 189 for full profile.)*

New York, New York

LANGUAGE English

HISTORY With a population of 8.4 million in the city proper and 23 million in the greater metro area, New York is the largest city in the United States and the eighth-largest urban agglomeration in the world. Many would also argue that it's the world's most important and most exciting city.

The first European exploration of the New York area began in the mid-1500s. Henry Hudson re-discovered the area in 1609, later claiming it for the Dutch East India Company. Permanent European presence in the area took root in the mid-1600s. New York was a center of conflict during the Revolutionary War, falling to British invaders in the late 1700s. By the early 1800s, the city had become one of the largest ports in North America, and its famed grid system of streets and avenues was developed. Immigrants from all over Europe arrived throughout the 1800s, creating unique ethnic enclaves. Along with immigration came the additional influx of commercial enterprise and cultural dominance in areas such as art, publishing, and fashion. New York's pivotal moment in recent history, of course, was the destruction of the World Trade Center in lower Manhattan on September 11, 2001.

WEATHER DCL cruises stop in New York in May. The weather at this time of year is often lovely, with daytime highs in the mid-70s and nighttime lows in the mid-50s. Average precipitation is consistent throughout the year, with typical rainfall in May of about 4.5 inches.

THE PORT Cruise ships dock in midtown Manhattan, on the West Side. Within a 10-minute walk you'll find restaurants, shops, banks—you name it. The port itself is served by taxis and buses, and the subway is just a few blocks away, giving you access to the entire metropolitan area.

TOURIST HIGHLIGHTS We only have space to scratch the surface. The bustling **Times Square** theater district is just a few blocks from the port; keep an eye out for the **Naked Cowboy.** Museum lovers have their pick of the **Museum of Natural History,** the **Museum of Modern Art,** the **Metropolitan Museum of Art,** the **Guggenheim,** and scores more. **Central Park** and its zoo are a moderate walk or a short cab ride from midtown. **Columbia** and **New York Universities** are nearby. And of course, the **Statue of Liberty,** the **Empire State Building,** and the **World Trade Center Memorial** areas are must-dos for many visitors. For a bird's-eye view of Manhattan, visit **Top of the Rock** in **Rockefeller Center.**

WHAT TO EAT If you can eat it, someone in New York can cook it. You truly can find nearly every cuisine in the world represented in the kitchens of New York restaurants. Try dim sum in Chinatown, Greek specialties in Queens, soul food in Harlem, sushi on nearly every corner, and the only North American outposts of Paris's famed **Ladurée** macaron shop on the Upper East Side and in SoHo. For an "only in New York" experience, eat a "dirty-water dog" and a hot pretzel from a cart in Central Park, try the pastrami-on-rye from the **Carnegie Deli,** and grab some real coal-oven thin-crust pizza from **Patsy's,** and choose something to nosh on from the appetizing counter at **Zabar's** on the Upper West Side—for bagels, lox, knishes, blintzes, and sour pickles, this is THE place. And *shhhh,* don't tell anyone else, but our favorite cookies in the universe come from **Levain Bakery,** on 74th Street near Columbus Avenue. They're big enough to share . . . but why would we?

WHAT TO BUY As if we even needed to say it, New York is home to major department stores, art galleries, designer-sample sales, luxury-goods purveyors, specialty shops of every persuasion, and bodegas filled with endless trinkets. Whatever you want to buy, you can get it here. Shoppers who like to haggle should visit the diamond and jewelry district in midtown. Classic New York gifts include memorabilia from Broadway shows, Yankees or Mets jerseys, and coffee-table books describing the collections of the many local museums.

Oslo, Norway   *(See page 222 for full profile.)*

Port Canaveral, Florida   *(See page 192 for full profile.)*

Reykjavík, Iceland   *(See page 224 for full profile.)*

St. John's, Newfoundland and Labrador

LANGUAGE English

HISTORY St. John's takes pride in its status as one of the oldest settlements in North America. Sir Humphrey Gilbert claimed the area as England's first overseas colony in 1583, and the English maintained control for about the next hundred years. During the 1700s, the area saw attacks by Dutch and French forces. A period of growth followed, with St. John's serving as a trading port and naval base. Today, its chief employers are educational institutions and the oil-and-gas industry.

WEATHER Disney Cruise Line visits St. John's in May, when average daytime highs are in the low 50s and average nighttime lows in the mid-30s. Precipitation is light, with less than an inch of rain for the month.

THE PORT Services directly at the pier are minimal. The cruise dock is about 5 minutes from town by foot. Taxis are also available.

TOURIST HIGHLIGHTS **Signal Hill** is a rocky point offering expansive views of the harbor. Nearby **Johnson Geo Centre** includes an insightful exhibit on the sinking of the *Titanic*. **Cape Spear** is the easternmost point in North America. Whale-watching is a great activity for nature lovers. The **Railway Coastal Museum** showcases several vintage train cars.

WHAT TO EAT With Newfoundland being one of Canada's Maritime Provinces, fresh fish is a given. Find it baked, fried, or in stews and cakes. Moose meat is regularly eaten here as well, often served with boiled potatoes and carrots. The region's longstanding British influence has given St. John's a thriving pub community, where you'll find a multitude of beers and ales as well as pub grub such as meat pies and lamb stew. Afternoon tea is another English-influenced tradition.

WHAT TO BUY A native mineral is labradorite, used in jewelry and decorative items. Local potters and woodworkers offer unique handcrafted works. Foodies will want to take home a jar of local cloudberry jam.

PART TWELVE

PORT ADVENTURES

DISNEY CRUISE LINE OFFERS more than 600 shore excursions—"port adventures," in Disney-speak—for families to experience while their ship is docked. While it's impossible for us to have tried them all, we have embarked on quite a few. We've also interviewed scores of families and DCL employees to learn which are the most popular and which ones they'd recommend to friends.

Because most Disney cruises stop at Castaway Cay (see Part Ten), this section includes detailed reviews of its port adventures. These generally last 1–3½ hours; others, such as snorkeling or biking, are self-guided. Disney staff leads most (but not all) of these excursions.

Beyond Castaway Cay, most port adventures last 3–6 hours, including transportation time, and all are designed to fit comfortably into the ship's schedule. Third-party companies based near the port run virtually all of the port adventures, except those on Castaway Cay. On the day of your activity, you'll be instructed to gather somewhere on the ship, such as a restaurant or lounge, at a predetermined time. Once you're there, a Disney cast member will ensure that you have the correct port-adventure tickets and identification to reboard the ship. You may also be asked to sign a liability waiver to participate in a particular activity.

When those tasks are complete, everyone signed up for the activity will be escorted by cast members off the ship to a meeting point on the port's docks. There, representatives of the third-party company running the port adventure will meet you. You'll be in their care until you're returned to the port after your activity.

FINDING PORT ADVENTURES

IF YOU'VE BOOKED A CRUISE, you can see your port-adventure options in the Disney Cruise Line Planning Center for your voyage (see page 21). But before you book, you can also see full lists of options that may help you choose a specific itinerary.

DCL lists its port adventures at **disneycruise.disney.go.com /cruises-destinations.** Click on the region where you'll be cruising—Alaska, for example—and click "Ports of Call." In most cases, clicking the name of the port will bring you to a page with tabs labeled "Overview," "Places to Explore," "Port Adventures," and "Travel Information" (a few port pages have just the "Overview" and "Port Adventures" tabs).

"Port Adventures" will bring you to some, but not all, of your options for a particular port. The options shown first are usually some of the more expensive headliner activities. Scroll down to the bottom of the page to check for a "Search All Port Adventures" link; if it's there (not all ports have it), click to see all your options—some ports offer dozens of choices at a wide range of price points and activity levels.

Of course, you're not limited to Disney's offerings: You can explore on your own (see Part Eleven, Ports, for general suggestions in the profile for each port), or you can book an alternative excursion through another vendor. If you don't see something that strikes your fancy on the DCL website, check the shore-excursion information for other cruise lines. There will likely be overlap, but Norwegian or Carnival, for example, may have identified a third-party excursion vendor that better suits your style.

Still another option is to try our **custom walking tours,** new for this edition. See page 249 for details.

Finally, remember that you're under no obligation to participate in *any* organized adventures. Feel free to hang out on the ship or just amble aimlessly around the port city. Your vacation, your call.

EVALUATING A PORT ADVENTURE

THE PORT ADVENTURES OFFERED through Disney Cruise Line have all been vetted by DCL staff for quality and reliability. When you book your excursion through DCL, it's unlikely that you'll end up with an experience that's *completely* without merit. However, just because an excursion is right for one person doesn't mean it's right for you. If you ask yourself the questions in the chart on the next page, you should increase your odds of choosing the best option for your needs.

Our research shows that two of the largest factors affecting a guest's enjoyment of an excursion are the weather in port and the quality of the guide. Even with the best planning, you may find that a sudden storm or an inexperienced guide dims the quality of the adventure. Of course, if the excursion turns out to be a total wash or the guide behaves unprofessionally, you should speak to the tour provider and to Disney, but try not to let normal ups and downs derail your enjoyment.

20 QUESTIONS TO ASK WHEN CHOOSING A PORT ADVENTURE

1. Have I looked at all the physical requirements of the excursion?

2. Does this excursion's price make sense to me?

3. Are there hidden fees that increase the cost of the excursion—for example, add-on photo packages or meals?

4. How does the price of this individual excursion fit into my overall excursion budget?

5. What percentage of the excursion will be spent in transportation?

6. What percentage of the excursion will be spent with a guide versus on my own?

7. Is there an adult-only or teen-only version of this excursion? Do those variations make more sense for me?

8. Does the excursion's mode of transportation make sense for me? (Guests who get motion sickness or are afraid of heights, for example, may want to avoid helicopter excursions.)

9. Is a meal or snack provided as part of the excursion? Do I want there to be?

10. Will adverse weather conditions drastically affect my enjoyment of the excursion?

11. Does the excursion take place in a port where guests tender to shore? (Tender excursions are more likely to be canceled.)

12. Are there similar excursions at other ports during my itinerary? (For example, numerous ports have dolphin encounters—is this particular port the best for such an excursion?)

13. Are there similar excursions at the same port? (For example, several dogsledding variations are available in Juneau—consider which one appeals to you the most.)

14. How long is the excursion? What percentage of my day will it encompass? Are there other things I'd rather do in port?

15. Is a similar experience available close to home or at another frequently visited vacation spot? (For example, zip-line and go-kart experiences are available in several ports—ask yourself whether you want to spend cruise time for these when you could easily do them elsewhere.)

16. What is the level of activity involved in this excursion?

17. Is this excursion too similar to something I'm doing in another port?

18. Will the timing of the excursion interfere with my child's dining or nap schedule?

19. Can I bring a stroller on the excursion?

20. Are there elements of the excursion specifically designed with children in mind?

CANCELING A PORT ADVENTURE

DEPENDING ON YOUR CASTAWAY CLUB LEVEL (see page 28), you may make port-adventure reservations up to 120 days in advance. Once you make a reservation, you may cancel it with no penalty up to three days before you sail—after that, there are no refunds. Of course, you're not charged if Disney or the tour provider cancels the excursion due to weather or other unforeseen circumstances.

The only other exception to the cancellation penalty occurs if you decide to upgrade your excursion. You may change a previously booked port adventure to one that's more expensive. You'll simply pay the difference in excursion fees without any penalty. You may upgrade on board at Guest Services or at the Port Adventures desk.

Port adventures booked on your own or through other vendors may have different cancellation policies, so always ask when booking.

PORT ADVENTURES
on CASTAWAY CAY

WE CONSIDER CASTAWAY CAY'S SHORE EXCURSIONS among the best values of any that DCL has to offer. Here's a quick rundown of what's available.

BICYCLE RENTALS

THESE SINGLE-SPEED ROAD BIKES with plump tires are good for getting some exercise while exploring the island. Men's and women's models are available, and the seats are designed for comfort. The seats can be adjusted up and down to suit your leg length, although years spent on the island have rusted many of the metal cams used to loosen the seats. Ask a cast member to help (they have wrenches!) if yours won't budge.

unofficial TIP
The **Castaway Cay Getaway** and **Extreme Getaway Packages** include activities listed here and are cheaper than purchasing à la carte, but we don't recommend them—trying to fit all that adventure into one or two days seriously cuts into your relaxation (and eating!) time.

Pick up your bicycles just past the Pelican Point tram stop, near the middle of the family beaches. You can also rent bikes next to the Serenity Bay adult beach, just behind the Castaway Air Bar. Cost is $10–$13 per hour, though no one on the island seems to keep track of how long you've had your bike.

BOAT RENTALS

VARIOUS WATERCRAFT, including one- and two-seat kayaks, sailboats, and paddleboats, are available for rent in half-hour increments. Costs range from $14 for a single-seat kayak to $27 for a Hobie Cat catamaran. The paddleboats require an extraordinary amount of leg power to get anywhere, and 30 minutes is going to be plenty for most people. Previous sailing experience is required to rent a sailboat.

CASTAWAY CAY 5K RUN

ONE OF THE BEST PORT ADVENTURES to start your day on Castaway Cay is fun, well organized, and absolutely free. Runners and walkers who wish to participate in the 5K meet around 8:15 on the morning the ship arrives at the island. The meeting location is almost always at one of the bars in the adult area of the ship because that's the way the best races begin; check your *Personal Navigator* the night before for details on when and where to meet.

Sign up for the 5K at the Port Adventures desk anytime; you can also just show up at the designated meeting place on the morning of the race. Two cast members will meet you there and make sure you have your Key to the World Card and ID. They'll give you a runner's bib (a nice touch for this unchipped race) and safety pins; then you'll walk off the ship with the rest of the runners toward the start of the race, by the Pelican Point tram stop. Parents who need to drop their kids off at Scuttle's Cove will be given time to do so on the way.

Once you arrive at the start, everyone is given a chance to hit the restroom and drop anything they don't want to run with in the storage area by the bike rentals. This is unsecured, so don't leave your gold doubloons, but other stuff is fine.

Once everyone is ready, you're off and running. The route includes a trip up and down the airstrip and two loops out to the viewpoint. You'll be sharing the road with the trams as well as folks on bicycles, so be aware of your surroundings. One cast member will be at the entrance to the loop with water—take advantage of it, because this run is hot.

The other cast member will be by the digital timer at the end of the race to congratulate you on your spectacular finish and give you a medal. Wear it proudly for the other folks who were still at the breakfast buffet while you were out running 3 miles in the heat.

The 5K and snorkeling are the two port adventures that we always do on the island. They're two fun and affordable ways to enjoy your day.

5K RUN FAQS

What should I pack? Don't forget your running shoes and clothes.

Can my kid join me? Sort of. Disney officially restricts participants to folks age 12 and older, so your child won't get a bib or medal. Because of the informal setup of the race, though, there's no way to stop kids under 12 from running along with you. Parents are given time during the walk to the race start to drop off kids at Scuttle's Cove.

Is it a race? This 5K brings out people of all abilities and seriousness about their running. Take it at your own pace and just enjoy it.

Is there a time limit? Not officially, but the cast members would probably appreciate it if you're done within 40-45 minutes. (There's also a Castaway Cay Power Walk if that's more your speed.)

Can I buy a souvenir? Yes. When RunDisney began sponsoring this event, we got "medals" (plastic) and the opportunity to purchase T-shirts at the end (in addition to the race bibs you receive). The T-shirts, while attractive, are cotton instead of tech material.

Can I shower after the race? There are no private showers on the island, just the ones by the restrooms for knocking off the sand. If you didn't bring a swimsuit with you and don't plan to get right into the water, you'll need to walk back to the ship to shower in your cabin.

How's the weather? Hot. Drink lots of water. Wear sunscreen. Eating at Remy or Palo the night before probably isn't the best idea. Did we mention that it's hot?

What about itineraries with two stops at Castaway Cay? You get two opportunities to run. Yay! You can do both or either.

Is water available? Yes. Not only does a cast member offer water on the course, but the 5K also begins and ends by a regular water stop for the island. Drink lots!

BOTTOM FISHING

A 3-HOUR CATCH-AND-RELEASE FISHING EXCURSION ($139 per person) takes place in the waters around Castaway Cay, with Disney-provided fishing rods and bait. Your boat's captain will take you into the waters around the island; the most commonly caught species are yellow jack, grouper, various porgies, and snapper. It's not unheard of to hook a barracuda or small shark, too. Most charters leave around 9 a.m. and are back in time for lunch. Readers prone to seasickness shouldn't take this excursion, and kids must be age 6 or older to participate.

CASTAWAY RAY'S STINGRAY ADVENTURE

THIS IS YOUR CHANCE TO PET AND FEED small- and medium-size stingrays in a supervised, structured setting on the shore of the Stingray Lagoon. Disney keeps dozens of these stingrays in a sectioned-off part of Castaway Cay's lagoon, and the stingrays are trained to use a special feeding platform at mealtimes. The cost is $45 for guests age 10 and up, $36 for kids ages 5–9.

Holding a specially formulated pellet of food between two fingers, you'll place your hand, palm down, on the platform. A stingray will swim up to the platform, glide over your hand, and grab the food in its mouth. You'll also have the chance to pet each ray as it swims by. There's plenty of food and plenty of stingrays for everyone. Besides the feeding, you'll get a brief introduction to stingrays, skates, and sharks before you begin, when a cast member reviews rules and procedures.

Many children are worried about being bitten by the stingrays, and let's face it: The word *sting* in their name doesn't exactly make rays the poster children for cuddly animals. But the rays don't have teeth, and the only thing that seems to get them excited is the prospect of feeding time. Calling them rays may help your kids find these animals more approachable. Kid fears might also be assuaged by a mention of the friendly Mr. Ray in *Finding Nemo*.

FLOAT AND TUBE RENTALS

INNER TUBES AND RECTANGULAR FLOATS are available for $10 for one day or $13 for two days. You can swap out one type for the other during the day.

GLASS-BOTTOM-BOAT EXCURSION

GUESTS BOARD A SMALL MOTORIZED WATERCRAFT that holds about 25 people and that ventures about 15 minutes out into the ocean. You can observe sea life below through several "windows" in the floor of the boat. During the trip, you're accompanied by a local guide who discusses the fish and other natural elements you'll encounter.

The highlight of the tour takes place at approximately the mid-point of the journey: Guests are given a cup filled with about 1 ounce of oatmeal, which they toss overboard to attract fish. During the feeding portion of the tour, several hundred tropical fish of various species surround the boat, and the guide points out the characteristics of as many fish as possible. The feeding lasts about 5 minutes, after which the fish will disappear quickly. Sightings of fish at other points of the tour are sporadic.

The trip takes about 45 minutes to an hour (about 15 minutes out, 15 minutes back, and around 15 minutes parked at viewing spots along the reef adjacent to Castaway Cay). Cost is $37 for adults and $25 for kids ages 0–9. Guests must be able to climb five steps to board and debark the boat to participate, and guests will stand aboard the boat for the duration of the excursion.

PARASAILING

GUESTS LOOKING FOR A BIRD'S-EYE VIEW OF PARADISE should check out this excursion. Floating hundreds of feet in the air, you're master of all you survey, or at least it seems that way for several minutes.

You board a speedboat and travel several hundred yards away from land. Then, in singles or pairs, you stand at the back of the boat and are harnessed to a line-bound parachute that is slowly let out until you and the parachute are 600–1,000 feet above the water. Enjoy panoramic views of your ship, Castaway Cay, and beyond.

Each excursion takes about 10 people onto the boat. There are no ride-alongs; every guest on the boat must pay. Your actual parasail event will last about 5–7 minutes. Depending on the number of other guests, the entire experience lasts 45 minutes–1 hour.

Open to guests age 8 and up, parasailing excursions cost $95 for both adults and kids. Guests must weigh between 90 and 375 pounds; those who weigh less than 90 pounds may be able to ride if they fly in tandem with another guest, but their combined weight may not exceed 375 pounds. Determination of single or tandem rides is fully at the discretion of the staff.

Kids under age 13 must be accompanied by a paying adult age 18 or older. Guests ages 13–17 may go on the excursion unaccompanied but must be escorted to the Marge's Barges excursion meeting site by an adult age 18 or older. All guests must sign a safety waiver.

You must leave your shoes on the dock and are strongly discouraged from wearing a hat or glasses during your sail; there is a storage area on the boat for your personal belongings. Wheelchairs and other wheeled mobility devices cannot be accommodated.

No photography service is provided during the excursion—you're welcome to bring cameras onto the boat, but you assume all liability for the loss of anything you bring up with you. Understandably, anything dropped into the ocean can't be retrieved.

SNORKELING

THIS IS ONE OF THE LEAST EXPENSIVE, most rewarding shore excursions offered on a Disney cruise. We recommend it for every family. Cost is $14 for kids ages 5–9 for one day, $18 for two days; $29 for age 10 and up for one day, $36 for two days.

First, find some chairs on the family beach, where you can store your stuff while you're in the water. If possible, choose something near a vertical landmark such as a tree; it will be easier to find when you come back to shore.

Next, pick up your snorkeling gear at Gil's Fins and Boats, a short walk from Scuttle's Cove, the island's first tram stop. You'll be given a mask, snorkel, fins, and an inflatable buoyancy vest to make swimming easier. Also pick up a blue-mesh gear bag, which makes it easier to haul your stuff back to your beach chairs.

Put on your vest before you get in the water, but don't inflate it just yet. Wait until you're in hip-high water to put on your flippers because it's impossible to walk in them on shore (and they'll get sandy). Keep your mask off until you get into the water.

If you're snorkeling with younger children, plan on spending 10–15 minutes adjusting the fit of masks and vests. Inflate their vests by blowing into the vertical tube on the left side of the vest, adding just enough air to keep the top of their heads above water. (If you overinflate the vests, they'll have trouble getting their masks below the surface.) Also practice using the flippers, which work best with slow, deliberate leg movements.

Once everyone's gear is working, take one last look at the lagoon to get your bearings. Disney has placed orange-and-white buoys above the underwater sites, so head for those.

There usually aren't a lot of fish in the first 30–40 yards nearest the shore, though it's possible to see almost anything once you're in the water. Fish species in the lagoon include yellowtail snapper, sergeant major, banded butterfly fish, blue tang, and barracuda. Obviously, you shouldn't try to catch any of these fish with your hands.

If you've snorkeled before and you enjoy it, Castaway Cay offers another snorkeling excursion in the waters off the island. You board the *Seahorse*, a large catamaran, and head for the northwest side of the island, about a mile offshore from the Serenity Bay adult beach, where you're able to snorkel in the open ocean for 2–2½ hours. Cost is $55 for adults, $36 for kids ages 5–9.

WALKING AND KAYAK NATURE ADVENTURE

THIS PORT ADVENTURE BEGINS at Marge's Barges, where everyone boards a tram to the Serenity Bay adult beach. Next you walk behind the adult beach cabanas to a nature trail, which leads to the beach beyond. During the walk, your guide will point out interesting plants and animals and talk about the history of the Bahamas.

Upon reaching the beach, participants don their life jackets and head out in their kayaks. This is the part where you're at Mother Nature's whim. We took this tour after a friend raved about it. She headed out in the morning and was able to kayak to the interior of the island. Our own tour was later in the afternoon as the tide was going out. The interior of the island was inaccessible by kayak, and the tides made piloting our single kayak very difficult. We wouldn't book this adventure in the afternoon again, even if it were the only time available.

Even if you're able to book this in the morning, however, the tour is 3–3½ hours long—time you could spend snorkeling, biking, or lazing on the beach. Ideally, you would book this on the morning of the second stop of a five-night Castaway Cay cruise.

Be sure to bring walking shoes, sunglasses, a hat, sunscreen, and an underwater or water-resistant camera; consider gloves for paddling to avoid blisters. Wear a swimsuit under your clothes for swimming. You must stow your belongings on the beach for the kayaking, so leave the doubloons in the cabin. Water is provided. Cost is $64 for guests age 10 and up.

WATERCRAFT SKI ADVENTURE

BOOKING THIS PORT ADVENTURE is the only way that guests can use WaveRunner watercraft on Castaway Cay, and that fact alone makes it worth your while if you're willing to spend the money.

Riders begin at the Boat Beach (the beach closest to where the ship docks), where they're given life jackets and a safety briefing. While you must be at least 18 years old to drive the WaveRunner, kids as young as 8 may ride along. Our advice for two adults is for each to ride as singles unless one is truly afraid of piloting a craft alone—a single rider will go much faster than two adults due to the weight difference. If you've never piloted a WaveRunner before, don't worry; it's fairly easy. It's actually easier to maneuver once you get up to speed than when you're idling or going slowly at the beginning of the excursion. If you're familiar with driving a motorcycle or Vespa, you've got this down. Most participants get the hang of things quickly.

As you head out, riders will start in single file with a guide leading and one more assistant bringing up the rear. Try to avoid hitting the wake of the craft in front of you because the bumpiness can be a little scary when you're up to speed, which tops out at a little more than 30 mph at full throttle.

Unless you choose to swim or tip your craft, you won't get especially wet, though you will want to wear waterproof shoes or sandals or go barefoot. Flip-flops aren't allowed, as they're likely to come off in the water (along with hats). You may store anything that you don't want to take with you in an unlocked chest at the beginning of the tour. We recommend taking a waterproof camera for photos on the beach; just secure it around your neck for the trip out.

Disney says the hour-long tour may have two stops, but ours had one—the same beach you visit on the Walking and Kayak Nature Adventure. The fact that you can visit this beach on the WaveRunner without having to kayak there is a plus, but perhaps we're still bitter about the blister we got kayaking. The other stop is an island opposite the beach.

When you arrive, your tour guide will give you a very brief history of the islands and point out any interesting flora and fauna, much like an abbreviated version of the Walking and Kayak tour. Then you can swim in the ocean for a bit before heading back to the Boat Beach to end your port adventure. The piloting of the WaveRunners, not the nature talk or the beach visit, is the real highlight.

Would we book this again? *Maybe.* This is one of the more expensive port adventures for its length. The WaveRunners are fun, but the Boat Beach is far enough away that just getting there and back will cut into your time on the island. If you have the chance, you may want to book this for earlier in the day as you're just getting off the ship, or late as you're heading back. Price is $95 for a single rider, $160 for two riders.

OUR RECOMMENDATIONS
Beyond CASTAWAY CAY

DOLPHIN ENCOUNTERS

ACCORDING TO OUR SOURCES, dolphin encounters are the most popular shore-excursion choice for families. Every port in Mexico, along with Nassau, Falmouth, Grand Cayman, and St. Thomas, offers one. If your Caribbean or Bahamian cruise includes a port besides Castaway Cay, you'll almost certainly have a chance to book one.

Because of the dolphins' popularity, these port adventures aren't cheap, generally starting at around $180 for adults and $160 for children, or roughly $700 for a family of four.

Most dolphin-related port adventures last 4–7 hours, of which roughly 30 minutes are spent in the water with a dolphin and 10–20 other tourists. During our visits, we took turns with the rest of the group in petting, feeding, and taking photos with the dolphin. In hindsight, the remarkable thing is that we spent perhaps 1 minute each in direct contact with the animal.

The rest of the time is transportation to and from the port, a background class and instruction on how to interact with the dolphin, a short show during which the dolphins demonstrate their jumping skills and tricks, and some beach or pool time once your encounter is done.

Dolphin Alternatives

IF $700 SOUNDS EXPENSIVE for a few minutes with any intelligent mammal, allow us to suggest some alternatives. One is **Castaway Ray's Stingray Adventure** (see page 243), which includes almost an hour of in-the-water time feeding and petting dozens of small, gentle stingrays in a special section of Castaway Cay's lagoon. Snorkel equipment is provided for your day on the island, where you may also see stingrays through-out the lagoon.

That said, if your kids have their hearts set on dolphins and your vacation schedule has room for an extra day, consider a visit to Sea-World's **Discovery Cove** in Orlando (**discoverycove.com**). Prices for Discovery Cove's all-day Dolphin Swim Day package runs $229–$319 per person and includes a 30-minute dolphin experience, plus the following:

- Snorkeling equipment for SeaWorld's man-made Grand Reef, home to stingrays and dozens of fish species
- Access to an oasis-themed freshwater pool, where you can observe (but not touch) otters and marmosets
- An aviary where you can feed birds
- Access to a man-made beach and lazy river

Breakfast, lunch, and unlimited snacks and beverages (including alcohol) are included in the price, along with locker rentals, sunscreen, and admission to SeaWorld for the two weeks around your vacation dates.

MAYAN PYRAMIDS

DCL TOURS OF TULUM MAYA RUINS take place in **Cozumel, Mexico.** Be aware that the trip involves considerable transportation time: 4 of its 7½ hours are spent on ferries or buses. Prices are $129 ages 10 and up, $99 ages 5–9.

NASSAU

THE BIG DRAW HERE is **Atlantis,** a Las Vegas–style resort about a 20-minute drive from the port (☎ 888-877-7525; **atlantis.com**). Activities include golf, snorkeling, man-made beaches, a water park, and various dolphin encounters. Beyond those, Atlantis has a casino, spa, rock-climbing wall, and fishing charter boats. Atlantis's shore excursions start at $95 per adult and $59 per child for access to the beaches and grounds (but not the waterslides), including lunch.

Beyond Atlantis and the dolphin encounters, we've tried port adventures including harbor cruises, city tours, and chocolate and wine tastings. All were pleasant enough, but none of them was something we'd do again.

NASSAU WALKING TOUR If you want to tour Nassau inexpensively, try our walking tour on page 254. The tour takes around 3 hours and costs around $20 per person, including lunch and drinks. Highlights include the **Queen's Staircase, Fort Fincastle, John Watling's Distillery,** and a local fish fry for lunch. The tour includes time for a swim on the beach.

SKAGWAY, ALASKA

ANNOYINGLY LONG-WINDED NAME ASIDE, the **Liarsville Gold Rush Trail Camp and Salmon Bake Featuring Exclusive Disney Character Experience** is a fun port adventure for families (2½–3 hours; $89 ages 10 and up, $49 ages 3–9). Guests board a bright-yellow school bus and take a 15-minute drive through downtown Skagway to Liarsville, a re-created mining camp at the foot of White Pass. When you arrive, you're greeted by "locals" dressed in period attire and escorted to the Hippodrome, a covered pavilion where you'll see a puppet show that highlights the history of the Gold Rush in Alaska, including how Liarsville came to receive its name.

After the show, you'll receive instructions on how to pan for gold—scoop, swirl, spill—before you're released to your very own "handler" and set out to seek your fortune. The pans are prepared and handed out as you approach the mining troughs. Getting the hang of the technique isn't as easy at it looks, but your handler is there to help. While you're panning, Chip 'n' Dale stop by to steal some gold, and Donald, dressed in flannel and a hunting cap, pays a visit. Gold in every pan is guaranteed, but even the most successful panning won't make you rich, or even earn you enough to help pay off your stateroom balance.

The salmon bake is set up across the way, buffet-style. Guests trickle over to the food after they strike it not-so-rich, so crowds aren't a problem. Choose from rotisserie chicken, baked beans, rice pilaf, coleslaw, and salads, plus bread and blueberry cake. Wild-caught salmon is served from an open-air grill; the fish is tasty, but be aware that it contains small bones—we guess that's what makes it wild.

This reader liked (but didn't love) the experience:

> *The Liarsville gold panning was fun, and it was a huge hit with my stepson (age 8). I felt the price could have been a bit more affordable, the puppet show a bit shorter, and the gold panning a bit longer and more involved. For us it was a one-time experience, but an enjoyable one.*

WALKING TOURS

FOR THOSE WHO WANT TO STEP OFF THE BEATEN PATH of organized excursions, we've created our own walking tours of Disney Cruise Line ports around the globe. Each tour includes not only things to see and do but also recommendations for places to eat. These tours are less expensive than almost any port adventure, offer a more flexible schedule, allow you to see a great deal of the port, and offer a wider choice of dining options.

Alaska
Juneau Walking Tour

Duration About 3 hours depending on your walking pace, how much you stop to shop, and how long it takes you to eat. Add another 1–2 hours if you decide to take the tram to Mt. Roberts. **Walking distance** About 2.5 miles. **Cost** Lunch varies. If you decide to take the Mt. Roberts Tramway, the cost is $32 for adults, $16 for kids ages 6–12, and free for kids age 5 and under. **Accessibility** This is a walk up paved roads with several large hills. Nothing is specifically inaccessible, but guests using wheelchairs might find the route somewhat strenuous. **Kid-friendliness** Best for adults— kids will likely get bored hiking past municipal buildings and museums; plus, we've included an optional detour into a bar. **Map** See **tinyurl.com/downtownjuneaumap.**

STEP 1 Depending on which dock the ship is using, you're about 0.75 mile down a nondescript service road from the port to town. You can walk the road or take the free shuttle bus that continuously ferries cruisers from the ship. Start touring at the **Downtown Public Library** (292 Marine Way); pop in and use their free Wi-Fi if you need a fix and didn't purchase Internet access on the ship. Nearby, look for the bronze sculpture of city founders **Joe Juneau, Richard Harris,** and **Chief Kowee.**

STEP 2 Proceed toward town up South Franklin Street. Depending on the time of day, you may need some fortification to start your tour. If that's the case, the **Red Dog Saloon** (278 S. Franklin St.) has so-so food, but the Duck Fart layered shot—Kahlúa, Bailey's, and Crown Royal—is one of those things you just have to try in Juneau.

STEP 3 Continue up South Franklin, stopping in whatever shops strike your fancy along the way. We like **Alaska Brew Company Depot** (219 S. Franklin St.) for T-shirts and to see the brewery information upstairs; **Alaskan Fudge Company** (195 S. Franklin St.) to check out and sample the creatively named candies (puffin paws, sea otter paws, husky paws, and huckleberry jelly sticks); and the **Mt. Juneau Trading Post** (151 S. Franklin St.) for pelts and native artwork. If you have room in your luggage, you can buy a wooly-mammoth tusk. Be sure to pop your head in the **Alaskan Hotel** bar (167 S. Franklin St.) to see the Victorian-era decor.

STEP 4 South Franklin becomes North Franklin after Front Street. Proceed up North Franklin to Fifth Street and make a right to see **St. Nicholas Russian Orthodox Church** (326 Fifth St.), built in 1894. Walk back down Franklin and take a left onto Fourth Street. The **Alaska State Capitol** will be a few steps up on your left, at 120 E. Fourth St. Cross Main Street and see the **Juneau-Douglas City Museum** (114 W. Fourth St). Note the large totem pole out front, and spend a few minutes checking out the exhibits. (Open Tuesday–Saturday, 10 a.m.–4 p.m.; free admission.)

STEP 5 Bear right at the end of Fourth Street as it turns into Calhoun Avenue. At Calhoun and Seventh Street, see the **Alaska Governor's Mansion** (716 Calhoun Ave). No, you can't see Russia from this house.

STEP 6 Continue on Calhoun, making a left onto Capitol Avenue. Follow Capitol until it dead-ends at Willoughby Avenue. Take a left onto

Willoughby and a quick right onto Whittier Street. The **Alaska State Museum** (395 Whittier St.) is currently closed and is projected to reopen in May 2016 as the State Library, Archives and Museum.

STEP 7 Continue down Whittier Street to Egan Drive. The **Centennial Hall Convention Center** (101 Egan Drive) is a good source for maps and general information.

STEP 8 Egan Drive turns into Marine Way. Note **Juneau City Hall** at the corner of Marine and Seward. Continue on Marine Way to end up back at the Downtown Public Library. Continue down Marine and bear right as Marine turns into the lower part of South Franklin Street—you've walked a large circle.

STEP 9 If you want to eat light, grab something at one of the food carts near the port, but we prefer to stop in at **Tracy's King Crab Shack** (406 S. Franklin St., behind the Trove boutique and gift shop), our favorite Alaskan cruise-stop restaurant. The Crab Shack Combo (about $32) will feed one hungry or two not-so-hungry people with a cup of crab chowder, a giant king crab leg, and four mini-crab cakes. Add a side of slaw and you can definitely feed two. Seating is at covered outdoor picnic tables. While you're waiting for your order, pop behind the order-prep station to watch the cooks tend to the 9- to 10-pound crabs. Ask nicely and they'll probably let you hold one of these monsters for a terrific photo op.

STEP 10 If you're tuckered out, grab the shuttle back to the ship. If not, head to the **Mt. Roberts Tramway** station (490 S. Franklin St.; open daily, 8 a.m.–9 p.m.). Buy tickets for the tramway and take the 5-minute ride to the top of Mt. Roberts. While you're at the top, check out the film in the visitor center, snap photos of the view, scout for bald eagles, or take a brief nature hike. Back at the tramway station, you'll see the ship; take the shuttle from there or walk back.

Ketchikan Walking Tour

Duration About 2–3 hours. **Walking distance** About 3 miles. **Cost** About $30 per person, including admission to the Tongass Historical Museum, admission to Dolly's, and a chowder or sandwich along the way. If you're taking in the Great Alaskan Lumberjack Show, add $40 for each adult and $20 for each child. **Accessibility** Not technically wheelchair-inaccessible, but this is a walk of several miles, up several steep hills. **Kid-friendliness** Little kids may get antsy during Steps 6–8. **Map** See **tinyurl.com /ketchikanmap.**

STEP 1 Exit the ship and head to the end of the pedestrian-only dock area. Start at the corner of Mill and Front Streets, near the **Fish Pirate's Saloon.** Walk one block down Mill Street and turn right down Main Street to the **Southeast Alaska Discovery Center** (50 Main St.), operated by the US Forest Service. Check out the exhibits on the Alaskan rainforest, native peoples, and natural resources; there may also be classes or lectures for kids. (Admission is $5 for adults, free for kids age 15 and younger; see **tinyurl.com/seakdiscovery** for hours.) While you're at the Discovery Center, note that you're adjacent to the **Great Alaskan Lumberjack Show**

(420 Spruce Mill Way); if you're so inclined, buy tickets for a show later in the afternoon (see Step 10).

STEP 2 Go back to the corner of Mill and Front Streets. If you need maps or information, stop at the **Ketchikan Visitors Bureau** (131 Front St.). Proceed up Front Street, away from the ships, to Mission Street. Turn left onto Mission and take a photo under the big KETCHIKAN: THE SALMON CAPITAL OF THE WORLD sign.

STEP 3 Step back on Front Street and stop at **Alaska Fine Art** (224 Front St.) to see the incredible carved mammoth tusk by sculptor Eddie Lee. Look for eagles, bears, mountain goats, and other carved animals.

STEP 4 If you're hungry, grab a bite at **Annabelle's Famous Keg & Chowder House** (326 Front St.). The three-chowder sampler is a popular choice. When you're done, take a look farther down Front Street to see the **Ketchikan Tunnel.** Locals like to brag about the tunnel because it was once noted in the *Guinness Book of World Records* as the only tunnel in the world that you could go completely through, over, and around. To us, it looks like a minor traffic pass-through. Just on the other side of the tunnel is a restaurant called **Burger Queen** (518 Water St). Every local we talked to raved about it, but we thought the food was just so-so, and there's zero ambience.

STEP 5 Go back down Front Street to Mission Street, and head down Mission away from the water. If you find yourself in need of some canned salmon, buy some at the **Salmon Market** on the corner of Mission and Main. At 503 Mission St., note **St. John's Episcopal Church,** which has stood in its current location since 1904. Turn around and enter the **Cape Fox Marketplace** at 500 Mission St. Inside this (very) mini-mall, you'll find **Tall Tale Taxidermy,** a family-run furrier and taxidermist. We bought a beaver pelt.

STEP 6 Proceed back up Mission Street and bear left as it turns into Dock Street. Just ahead, at 629 Dock St., visit the **Tongass Historical Museum.** Pay the small admission fee ($3 for adults May–September, free October–April; free for kids age 12 and younger; see **tinyurl.com/tongass historicalmuseum** for hours). View artifacts and photos of Ketchikan's history as a fishing port and mining center. Check out the native totem pole out front.

STEP 7 Proceed up Dock Street and follow it as it turns into Bawden Street. Bawden soon forks—take the right fork onto Park Avenue. Continue on Park to see the **salmon-spawning river.** In season, see salmon struggle to get back to their native streambed; a concrete "fish ladder" aids their passage.

STEP 8 Continue on Park, past Venetia Avenue, Harris Street, and Freeman Street, then turn right at Woodland Avenue (Herring Way will be on the left). Continue on Woodland until it dead-ends at Deermount. Turn right onto Deermount Street. Along the way, you'll pass one of Ketchikan's Alaska Native–American Indian communities. Deermount dead-ends into Stedman Street—turn right and proceed along Stedman. Pass the **Sun Raven Totem Pole,** just beyond Inman Street, and the **University of Alaska Southeast** campus.

STEP 9 Continue on Stedman Street until you get to Thomas Street. Turn left down Thomas to view the harbor from the wood-planked dock. Continue on Stedman until you get to the red trestle bridge, just past the New York Hotel. Instead of crossing the bridge, take the small path on the right that turns into boardwalked **Creek Street,** the old red-light district, which once had more than 30 houses filled with "working girls." Stop in at **Dolly's House** (24 Creek St.), where local madam Dolly Arthur and her staff plied their trade, to see period artifacts and photos. (Open daily, 8 a.m.–4 p.m. when ships are in port; closed in winter. Admission is $10.)

STEP 10 Exit Creek Street onto Dock Street, back near the Tongass Historical Museum. Proceed down Dock toward the water. Make a left onto Bawden Street, then a right onto Mill Street. If you've had enough, head back to the ship. Or if you want some more Alaska fun, make a left onto Main Street and head back to the **Great Alaskan Lumberjack Show** (to see the schedule, go to **alaskanlumberjackshow.com** and click "About the Show," then "Reserve Now!"). The lumberjacks impress with their feats of skill, and certain tourists will find them easy on the eyes—one online reviewer sums them up as "hot guys with chainsaws." If you're hungry, make a pit stop next door at the **Alaska Fish House** (5 Salmon Way) for a cod burger or halibut tacos.

Skagway Walking Tour

Duration About 3 hours, depending on the timing of any shows/presentations you partake of. **Walking distance** About 2 miles. **Cost** About $45 per person; includes $20 fee for the *Days of '98* show, $10 fee for a Red Onion Saloon brothel tour, a burger lunch, and a beer at the end. **Accessibility** Most of Skagway is on level surfaces. Wheelchair users shouldn't find it a problem. **Kid-friendliness** Skip the brothel tour if you have younger kids in tow. **Map** See **tinyurl.com/skagwaymap.** The entirety of Skagway is about seven blocks long by two blocks wide—you can see the ship from anywhere in town, so there's really no likelihood of getting lost. **Special comments** Be aware that while the ship will dock at about 7:30 a.m., most of the shops in town, including the restaurants, won't open until after 9 a.m., so unless you have an excursion, there's no reason to rush in the morning. If you want to go farther afield, stop by the **Chilkoot Trail Center,** on Broadway between First and Second Avenues. Run by the US National Park Service and Parks Canada, it can offer maps and advice on day hikes in the surrounding area (open daily, 8 a.m.–5 p.m. June 1– Labor Day weekend).

STEP 1 Assume that you're exiting the ship from the Ore Dock (the most likely option). Directly ahead, you'll see the White Pass & Yukon Route train tracks.

STEP 2 Follow the tracks up Broadway until just before First Avenue. Take a photo at the WELCOME TO SKAGWAY, ALASKA sign. Walk forward about 30 feet to view the old **Yukon Engine #52** (1881) and **Rotary #1 Snowplow** (1899), which was capable of clearing up to 12 feet of snow off the tracks.

STEP 3 Proceed up Broadway and turn right onto Second Avenue. Stop into the **White Pass & Yukon Route headquarters,** at the corner of Second and Spring, and see the exhibits about Alaskan train travel (open weekdays, 8 a.m.–5 p.m.). You'll find slightly less-tacky souvenirs here than elsewhere. If you haven't booked a train excursion on board the ship and would like to do one, purchase your tickets here.

STEP 4 Also on Second Avenue is the **Klondike Gold Rush National Historical Park Visitor Center.** Check out the exhibits discussing the Gold Rush experience in the Klondike Region. Stay for the free 30-minute movie, *Gold Fever: Race to the Klondike,* or a 45-minute ranger presentation. Rangers are also available to answer general questions about Alaska and mining. (Open daily, 8 a.m.–6 p.m. May–September; open weekdays, 8 a.m.–5 p.m. October–April.)

STEP 5 Head back out to Broadway and walk toward Sixth Avenue, browsing in the shops along the way. Poke your head into the **Mascot Saloon** (corner of Broadway and Third Avenue), a National Park Service reproduction of a Gold Rush–era watering hole. If you've forgotten any basics for your trip, stop in **Skagway Hardware,** on the corner of Fourth Avenue and Broadway. They have everything from mouthwash to suitcases and power strips.

STEP 6 On the corner of Broadway and Sixth Avenue, take in the hourlong *Days of '98* stage show. This campy musical tells the tale of Soapy Smith, a notorious con man who duped many prospectors during the late 1800s (see **thedaysof98show.com** for showtimes). If you have time to kill before the next show, grab a muffin at the best bakery in town, **Bites on Broadway,** directly across Sixth Avenue. Or cross to the other side of Broadway to snap a photo in front of the **Skagway Post Office,** which has one of the highest zip codes in the country: 99840.

STEP 7 After the show, turn right down Sixth Avenue (away from town) and take a look at the **William and Ben Moore Cabin & Homestead,** a National Park Service–restored Gold Rush–era home.

STEP 8 Back on Broadway, find the **Skagway Bazaar,** on the post-office side of the street between Fifth and Sixth Avenues. Scoot down the narrow passageway to find the **BBQ Shack,** which serves caribou, elk, buffalo, and venison burgers, as well as halibut or smoked-salmon chowder.

STEP 9 Return to Broadway, heading back toward the ship. Stop in the **Red Onion Saloon,** formerly Skagway's whorehouse of choice, at the corner on Second Avenue. Relax with an Alaska Brewing Company beer on tap, or try the Fire Dance, an Alaskan-moonshine shot sprinkled with real gold flakes. The curious can take one of the various bordello tours, which offer a look at the upstairs "cribs." Free garters with every tour! (See **redonion1898.com/restaurant-bar-menu** for hours and schedules.)

STEP 10 Pop back into any interesting shops, then return to the ship via Broadway.

Bahamas and the Caribbean
Nassau Walking Tour

Duration About 3 hours. **Walking distance** 4.5 miles. **Cost** Around $20/person (including lunch and a cocktail at the distillery). **Accessibility** Good except for the Queen's Staircase, which can't be navigated in a wheelchair. **Kid-friendliness** Best for adults—while children are allowed on the distillery tour, they'll probably be bored to tears there and at the various cultural sites. **Map** See next page for a map coded to the steps below, or pick up a city map in Festival Place as you leave the port. **Special comments** Wear good walking shoes, and bring swimwear if you intend to enjoy the beach.

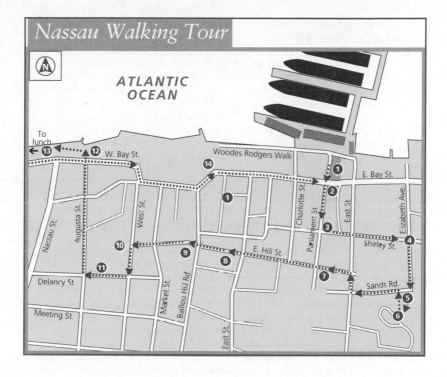

STEP 1 Exit the ship through Festival Place. You can pick up a map of Nassau here.

STEP 2 Outside Festival Place, take Parliament Street across Bay Street to Parliament Square.

STEP 3 Continue on Parliament Street to Shirley Street, and take a left.

STEP 4 Continue on Shirley Street across East Street to Elizabeth Avenue.

STEP 5 Take a right onto Elizabeth Avenue to continue to the base of the **Queen's Staircase.** Named for Queen Victoria, this is perhaps the most tranquil spot on our tour. Enjoy the cool shade, the junglelike greenery, and the artificial waterfall cascading to the left of the stairway before ascending the 65 steps to the entrance of Fort Fincastle. The stairs, while steep, aren't overly challenging, but alternatively you can take East Street to Prison Lane to the top of the staircase. Be careful, though, because there's no sidewalk along this route.

STEP 6 Climb the Queen's Staircase to reach the **Water Tower** and **Fort Fincastle.** Pay a small admission fee ($1 per person) to enter the fort, built in 1793 by Lord Dunsmore, a.k.a. Viscount Fincastle, then-royal governor of the Bahamas. Intended to protect Nassau from invasion and constructed to resemble the bow of a paddlewheeler, the fort never actually saw battle. (Open every day except Monday, 8 a.m.–4 p.m.)

The Water Tower, built in 1928, no longer holds any water, but the views of the island are worthwhile. (At press time, it was closed for repairs; call ☎ 242-322-2442 before you go to see if it's open.) At 126 feet, the observation deck, reached by elevator or 216 stairs, is the highest point in not only Nassau but also the entire island of New Providence. It's a great landmark to let you know early on that you were headed in the right direction to reach the staircase and the fort.

Note: Self-appointed tour guides at the fort and observation deck, as well as the Water Tower's elevator operator, may try to hustle you for tips. Give only if you feel like it.

STEP 7 Descend the staircase and take a left on Sands Road. Follow Sands Road to East Street, and make a right. Visit the **General Post Office,** at the corner of East Street and East Hill Street. Postage stamps make a nice, inexpensive souvenir whether you're a collector or not; US currency is accepted.

STEP 8 Continue on East Hill Street and take a right on Market Street. Take a left on Duke Street to **Government House**, the seat of the Bahamian government—you can't miss this pink-stucco, white-columned building with the big statue of Christopher Columbus out front. The Government House is mostly closed to the public but hosts a once-monthly English high tea for tourists and locals. If your cruise schedule coincides with the event, it's a charming way to spend an afternoon and make some new friends. Proper attire is required to enjoy the *veddy* proper repast of scones, clotted cream, cucumber sandwiches, and different types of tea. (Held the last Friday of the month, January–November, at the Government House Ballroom, 4–5 p.m.; reservations required. Go to **tinyurl.com/governmenthousetea** for booking information.)

STEP 9 Across Blue Hill Road from Government House is the **Graycliff Hotel** (8–12 W. Hill St.). Tour the grounds and check out the gardens and pools. There's a chocolate shop on-site.

STEP 10 Continue along West Hill Street to West Street. Here you'll find the **National Art Gallery of the Bahamas** and **St. Francis Xavier Cathedral.** The oldest Catholic church in the Bahamas, the cathedral is currently undergoing an extensive renovation but is still open to the public. Beautiful in its simplicity, the church is a nice stop along the way for rest and reflection. (Open to visitors weekdays, 9 a.m.–4:30 p.m.)

STEP 11 After touring the cathedral, head south (away from the water) on West Street to **John Watling's Distillery,** on your right at 17 Delancy St. The only distillery in the Bahamas, John Watling's makes rum on-site in a fantastically restored colonial estate. Tour the distillery and try a generous sample at no charge. The gift shop sells liquor and offers tastings; lunch is also served in the on-site pub. (Open daily, 10 a.m.–6 p.m., until 9 p.m. Friday.)

STEP 12 Return to West Bay Street and take a left, continuing west, away from the cruise terminal. Walk along the public beach. If you've packed a swimsuit, enjoy some time in the water.

STEP 13 (LUNCH) Instead of going to the Fish Fry, a cluster of tourist restaurants on Arawak Cay near the terminal, follow our advice and eat with the locals at the **food trucks** across the street—you'll know you're there when you see Bahamians buying food there. Picnic tables are available.

A large lunch plus drink runs about $10. The food is made to order, so relax and enjoy yourself. This was the freshest seafood we'd ever eaten—don't be thrown off if your fish arrives with its head still attached.

STEP 14 Return to the ship via **Bay Street,** the center of duty-free shopping in Nassau. We don't find the goods worth haggling over, but you may enjoy browsing. Jewelry and accessories are the big draws here, as is liquor. Two shops we like are **The Linen Shop,** which sells a nice selection of kitchen linens and Christmas decor, and **Cole's of Nassau** (Bay and Parliament Streets), for women's fashions.

Stop at Bay Street's **Straw Market** only if you feel you must in order to say you've been. Once upon a time, Laurel lived in the Bahamas, and going to Nassau was a trip to the big city. The market sold high-quality straw goods that were tasteful and well made—Laurel has bowls that still look like new after 40 years—but, sadly, that's no longer the case. You may still find a few nice locally made pieces among the ones imported from China, but mostly it's the same old tacky, overpriced T-shirts, beach towels, baseball caps, and fake designer bags you can get at any port.

Sint Maarten/Saint-Martin Walking Tour

Duration 4–7 hours. **Walking distance** About 1 mile not counting the time you'll spend in taxis. **Cost** About $35 per person for the Dutch side, plus an all-day taxi rental, which usually runs $120–$140 (plus tip) for 4–6 people. The French side of the island uses the euro as its currency, so you should also bring about €40 per person for lunch and drinks. **Accessibility** Most taxi drivers are happy to accommodate passengers who use wheelchairs. Fort Louis, however, can be accessed only by climbing stairs. Shops and restaurants in Marigot and Philipsburg are at ground level, but many require navigating a step or two out front. Most public restrooms have doorways that are too narrow to accommodate a wheelchair. **Club Orient** resort, which isn't on our tour, has beach wheelchairs—the catch is naked people. A good resource is **stmaarten.org/challenged-tourists-tips.** **Kid-friendliness** Recommended for everyone; parents with young children should skip Maho Beach and start at Marigot. Also, the stairs at Fort Louis are too taxing for little ones. **Map** See **tinyurl.com/stmaarten walkingtour.** **Special comments** Bring water, sunscreen, bathing suits, and a change of clothes.

Note: This is a walking tour only in the loosest sense—because you'll be visiting a large swath of the island, you'll need to hire a taxi driver for the day. Typical rates are $120–$140 for four people, plus gratuity, for a safe, relatively modern, air-conditioned ride. Drivers are generally very friendly and occasionally hilarious, as this reader found:

> *My partner was champing at the bit to check out the clothing-optional section of Orient Beach. (Myself, not so much.) When he told the driver where we wanted to go, she replied, "Ah, so ya wanna go to the NEKKID beach!"*

Our friend Matt Hochberg, who runs **royalcaribbeanblog.com,** recommends **Leo Brown** (☎ 721-524-4290); we've also heard great things about **Gerard France** (☎ 721-553-4727), who charges around $260 for the day.

STEP 1 It's a 25-minute cab ride from the port in Philipsburg to the Dutch side's **Maho Beach,** a tiny strip of sand maybe 600 feet long and 50 feet wide, on the west side of the island. What makes Maho Beach unique is that it sits on the other side of a small two-lane road from the main landing strip of Princess Juliana International Airport. Most planes landing on the island pass directly over the beach at no more than a couple hundred feet of altitude and land at the edge of the runway directly across. Watching the approach of small planes is a thrill; watching the big jets land is terrifying. You'll love it. Check **flightaware .com/live/airport/sxm** for the airport's arrival and departure schedule.

Because of the island's prevailing winds, planes taking off start at the end of the runway closest to the beach, too. The propeller and jet wash from the engines are enough to push adults back on their heels and knock over small children. That's lots of fun, too, but be careful.

Sunset Bar & Grill (2 Beacon Hill Road), a small outdoor restaurant at the far end of the beach, serves burgers, sandwiches, and drinks of all kinds. At the opposite end of the beach is the **Sonesta Maho Beach Resort** (Rhine Drive), and nearby are plenty of shopping and dining options.

STEP 2 When you're ready for lunch, hop in your cab for the 20-minute ride to the middle of **Marigot,** on the French side. The main drag, the **Boulevard de France,** has some of the island's best dining and shopping. It's also home to the marina and to **Fort Louis,** built in 1767.

If you're looking for island cuisine, try **Rosemary's,** on Boulevard de France near the marina and Fort Louis. Rosemary's is a *lolo*— a grill serving fresh seafood, stews, and other local favorites. The food is tasty, and service is very friendly. While the menu is priced in euros, they'll usually accept a one-for-one exchange of US dollars, giving Americans a 30% discount.

If you're in the mood for a quick bite of French food, grab a *croque monsieur* or other sandwich at **Sarafina's,** a *pâtisserie* about a block from Rosemary's on Boulevard de France. Usually crowded, Sarafina's serves a surprisingly large selection of fresh French pastries, sandwiches, and desserts. We suggest grabbing a baguette sandwich to go and eating it while you window-shop along the boulevard.

The hike up to Fort Louis, northeast of the Boulevard de France, is strenuous, especially in the sun, but it does offer the best views of this side of the island. (Open daily, sunrise–sunset; free admission.) To keep up your energy levels, pick up a quick something from Sarafina's after you return.

STEP 3 Here's your chance to work in some beach time. Skip **Orient Beach,** which is overcrowded with tourists and not the best choice if you're uncomfortable with toplessness or nudity. (On the upside, the beach at **Club Orient,** a naturist resort, provides special wheelchairs for guests with disabilities.) We recommend one of these instead:

Baie de L'Embouchure is off Rue du Coconut Grove, on the east side of the island, about 20 minutes from Marigot and half a mile south of Orient Beach. A crescent-shaped bit of beach about half a mile long, the beach is protected by an offshore reef that dampens the incoming waves. This, along with its relatively small crowds, makes it great for families with young children.

Mullet Bay Beach, about a 15-minute taxi ride southwest of Marigot, has a wide, sandy shore. The south side of the beach sits across from the Mullet Bay Golf Course, so there's no string of high-rise hotels to hamper your view.

Baie Longue is on the northwest side of the island, about a 15-minute taxi ride from downtown Marigot. Again, it's much less crowded than Orient Beach; the one downside is that the shoreline is filled with coral, making it unsafe for small children to play in. But it is pretty.

St. Thomas Walking Tour

Duration 3–5 hours. **Walking distance** About 6 miles on foot, 3 miles if you take a taxi back to the port, or less than a mile if you take a taxi both ways. **Cost** $22–$27 per person, including lunch; add $4 each way if using a taxi. **Accessibility** The first two steps in the tour are out of the question for wheelchair users. **Kid-friendliness** Recommended for children ages 6 and up; parents with small children should bring a stroller and use a taxi to get to Blackbeard's Castle and back to the ship. **Map** See **tinyurl.com/stthomaswalkingtour. Special comments** Bring water and sunscreen; swimsuits and towels are optional if you want to use the pools at Blackbeard's Castle.

STEP 1 It's a pleasant walk from the port to **Blackbeard's Castle,** on Blackbeard's Hill; if you take a taxi instead, the fare should be around $4 per person. Depart the ship at the West Indian Company Dock and walk northeast toward Edward Wilmot/Long Bay Road. Follow the road as it runs along the coast, and bear left toward the water when it becomes Veterans Drive. One block past the DeLugo Federal Building, turn right on Hospital Gade and walk north about four blocks; then turn left on Prindsens Gade. Turn right on Lille Taarne Gade and look for the signs.

There's no evidence that the British pirate whose real name was Edward Teach ever laid a boot upon "Blackbeard's Castle"—the reference is pure marketing (it's part of a hotel). What's more, the "castle" is a lookout tower, never meant for habitation: Its original name was Skystsborg Tower, and it was built far up on the hill by 17th-century Danish settlers to spot incoming ships that wouldn't be seen from Fort Christian farther down.

However, a climb to the top of the tower will get you a lovely panoramic view of the harbor and the town laid out in front of you, and of the mountains behind you. If you're a small group, the scenery alone is probably worth the $10 admission. If the view isn't enough, your admission also includes access to the adjacent hotel's pools and tours of two restored Colonial-era homes nearby, and you can return later for those. (Tour hours are usually 9 a.m.–2 p.m. Tuesdays and Wednesdays, but check at **blackbeardscastle.com** before you go; you can also book your tour at the website.) Before you climb the tower's narrow stairs, you're asked to watch an extremely cheesy, almost certainly apocryphal, but mercifully brief retelling of Blackbeard's death. We find it easier to get through by imagining that the "actor" is wearing tights and holding a human skull, à la Hamlet.

STEP 2 Follow the signs from Blackbeard's Castle south, toward the harbor, to the **99 Steps.** These stone-and-concrete stairs built into the side of the mountain afford good views of the harbor and town. (For the fact-checkers among us, there are actually more than 100 steps.)

STEP 3 Turn left and walk one block east to the **Government House.** Built in the 1860s, it holds the offices of the island's governor (currently John de Jongh Jr.), and tourists may visit the first two floors of the building. Besides Colonial architecture, on display are two small works by Camille Pissarro, a Danish-French Impressionist painter who was born on St. Thomas in 1830. (Open 8 a.m.–5 p.m. weekdays; closed holidays; free admission.)

STEP 4 From Government House, head south one block on Torvets State Road, then turn right on Norre Gade. About 100 feet ahead, on your right, is **Frederick Lutheran Church** (open daily, 9 a.m.–5 p.m.; free admission). Built in 1666, it's the oldest church in St. Thomas and one of the oldest Lutheran churches in the New World. The church's simple, elegant architecture features a vaulted ceiling. A narrow set of stairs leads to better views from the second floor's musician's area. Before you leave, donate a couple bucks and light a candle to commemorate making a pig of yourself at the ship's buffets.

STEP 5 From the church entrance, turn right and walk to the corner of Norre Gade and Fort Pladsen. Turn left on Fort Pladsen, toward the harbor; about 75 feet down the road, on your left, is **Emancipation Park,** which commemorates the emancipation of slaves in the Danish West Indies following the Danish revolution of 1848. Inside the park is a memorial to the emancipation; a memorial to King Christian IX of Denmark, who brought parliamentary rule to the island; and a copy of the United States's Liberty Bell, which commemorates the temporary landing on St. Thomas, in April 1607, of British settlers bound for Virginia. (Bonus fact: Every US state and territory has a copy of the Liberty Bell. Find yours at **tinyurl.com/statelibertybells.**)

Jen's Island Café is across the street from the northeast corner of the park, at the intersection of Tolbod Pladsen and Forte Strade. The food is fresh and tasty, with friendly service. A full meal takes about an hour, so we recommend a quicker stop at the bar for a fast sandwich and drink.

Adjacent to Emancipation Park and Jen's Island Café is **Fort Christian,** the oldest building on St. Thomas. Completed around 1680, it served as government residence, church, and prison before being converted to a museum in the 1970s. Unfortunately, it's been closed since 2005 due to an unfinished renovation project, with no reopening in sight. Even so, the fort is impressive to look at from the outside and makes for a nice photo op.

STEP 6 On the west side of the park, follow Fort Pladsen street north, away from the harbor, to Tolbod Pladsen, which turns into Kongens Gade after about a block. Stay on Kongens Gade, which will change names to Main Street, then Dronningens Gade, then Curaçao Gade, then Kronprindsens Gade, all within the half-mile walk to **Saints Peter and Paul Cathedral.** You'll see the church's high school, on the corners of Kanal Gade and Kronprindsens, just before you get to the church. The church will be on your right. The oldest Catholic church on the island and the seat of the Diocese of St. Thomas, the present building was dedicated in 1848, although previous buildings on the site date back to 1802. Inside, columns support vaulted arches, giving the sanctuary a Gothic-inspired island feel; the stained-glass windows depict various scenes from the Old and New Testaments. (See **cathedralvi.com** for hours; call ☎ 340-774-0201 to schedule a guided tour.)

STEP 7 Upon exiting the church, walk down either Brond State Road or Stoners Alley one block toward the harbor. You'll end up on Veterans Drive; look for taxis heading east toward the port. Note that there are two ports in St. Thomas, so make sure that you're on the correct ship. The fare should be about $4 per person back to the port.

By foot, we recommend following Veterans Drive, which hugs the waterfront on your right, all the way back to the ship. You'll find plenty of spots for shopping, food, and drinks along the sidewalk on the left side of the street. With a bit of luck, you'll catch a seaplane landing or taking off at the nearby seaport. The walk is around 1.8 miles.

Europe
Oslo-Meets-Epcot Walking Tour

Duration 4–7 hours. **Walking distance** 1–5 miles, depending on how much public transportation is used. **Cost** About $50–$100 per person. **Accessibility** The points of interest here have only limited wheelchair access. **Kid-friendliness** Recommended for ages 8 and up; parents with young children should use the bus to get to and from the Folk Museum. **Map** See Step 2. **Special comments** This tour visits the inspirations for three iconic landmarks at Epcot's Norway Pavilion.

BEFORE YOU GO The **Oslo Pass** includes admission to all of the featured attractions and public transportation between them (subject to regular schedules). Cost is around $48 US per adult and $24 US per child, and vouchers are available at **visitoslo.com.** You'll need to exchange the vouchers for real passes at the Oslo Central Station (5 Fridtjof Nansens Plass, near City Hall about a mile north of the cruise terminal). You can also buy direct, with no need to pick up physical tickets, using the **Oslo Pass app** for iOS or Android. However you buy it, the pass saves $5–$20 per person for this tour.

Norway's currency is the krone, one of which is worth about 15¢ US at current rates. If you need to convert a few dollars, pounds, or euros to kroner, you'll find a number of ATMs around the port and at the Oslo Central Station hub.

STEP 1 Follow the signs from the port less than 0.5 mile to **Akershus Fortress,** parts of which date from the 1300s. The outer set of walls, known as the

Outer Fortress, was built in the 17th and 18th centuries and holds government offices and the **Norwegian Armed Forces Museum.** The Inner Fortress holds **Akershus Castle,** including an impressive set of entertainment halls—still used by the Norwegian government for formal events, and the most likely inspiration for Epcot's Akershus Royal Banquet Hall—along with a chapel that is the resting place for several Norwegian kings and queens. Many other rooms are also accessible within the fortress; these display period furniture, paintings, and artifacts.

Hours vary seasonally; check **tinyurl.com/akershusfortress** before you visit. Admission is about $12 US for adults, $5 US for kids.

STEP 2 From the fortress, it's 3 miles to the **Norwegian Museum of Cultural History (NMCH)** and the **Gol Stave Church**—a walk of a little more than an hour or a 25-minute bus ride. By foot, the route travels mostly along pretty, tree-lined streets such as Bygdøy Allé, past shops, restaurants, and apartments (see **tinyurl.com/oslowalkingtour** for a map of the route). The nearest bus stop is at Wessels Plass, about five blocks northeast of the fortress; pick up the #30 bus toward Bygdøy Allé via Bygdøynes. (Wessels Plass is a couple of blocks southwest of Karl Johans Gate, the main shopping area in town. You'll be returning to this area later.)

The NMCH is a massive collection of artifacts spanning Norway's history from 1300 to the present. Just as at a typical museum, NMCH has paintings, sculpture, clothing, and other examples of decorative arts, representing every period in the country's history. Unlike most museums, however, NMCH's collection includes more than 160 buildings, most of which you can enter and which show the evolution of Norway's architecture. (Much of that apparently involves using grass for rooftops.) Don't miss the apartment building representing life in the 18th, 19th, and 20th centuries.

The **Gol Stave Church,** built around the year 1200 in the city of Gol in central Norway, was relocated to the museum site in the early 20th century. It inspired the stave church at the Norway Pavilion in Epcot (another replica stands in Minot, North Dakota). Made almost entirely of wood, the church is much larger than you'd expect inside, and remarkably detailed. The walls are filled with painted representations of various scenes from the Bible, including the Last Supper. A small wooden altar, supported by a floor of unfinished planks, gives the place a simple solemnity. We've visited many of Europe's most celebrated churches, and this tiny one ranks with the best of them.

The museum is open daily, but hours vary seasonally; check **norskfolkemuseum.no/en** before you visit. Admission is about $18 US for adults, $5 US for children.

STEP 3 (OPTIONAL) About 800 feet south of the NMCH is the **Viking Ship Museum.** At the beginning of Epcot's old *Spirit of Norway* film, which played following the Maelstrom boat ride (which closed in late 2014 to make way for an attraction themed to the hit Disney movie *Frozen*), a small child runs up to a large black Viking ship on display in a museum. This is the museum, and the *Oseberg,* built sometime before the year AD 834 (yes, 834), is the ship. (The film can still be seen on YouTube.)

The museum holds three antique ships in all, and touring probably won't take you more than 30 minutes. The museum's days and hours of operation vary, so check **khm .uio.no/english** before you visit. Admission is about $10 US for adults, $5 US for kids.

STEP 4 By foot, follow the path you took in Step 2 in reverse, but when you're almost back to the fortress, turn left (northeast) on Kongens Gate where it intersects Myntgata and walk four blocks to **Karl Johans Gate.** Or take the #30 bus back to Wessels Plass—from here it's about five blocks southwest back to the port or a couple of blocks northeast to Karl Johans Gate. (See the Google map referenced in Step 2.)

Karl Johans Gate is the thoroughfare where shopping, dining, and nightlife are concentrated in downtown Oslo. You'll find a wide selection of Norwegian clothing, accessories, and art on every street. (At the far end of the street sits Norway's Royal Palace, so you know the shopping is good.) Disney/Epcot geeks will recognize Karl Johans Gate as the location of the parade in the *Spirit of Norway* film—the parade was filmed in 1987 on Norway's Constitution Day (May 17).

Two More Easy Options

BARCELONA WALKING TOUR: CHURCHES, MEATS, AND CHEESES
Several of DCL's Mediterranean cruises begin or end in **Barcelona, Spain.** If you've got a few hours to spare, here's a quick side trip into the heart of Barcelona. (See **tinyurl.com/barcelonawalkingtour** for a map and bus/subway options.) Beginning at the Port of Barcelona, walk to the Paral-lel L2 subway stop on the Avinguda del Paral-lel. Take the L2 to the Monumental station and walk four blocks northwest to the **Sagrada Família** church.

Construction on the church, designed by Spanish architect Antoni Gaudí as a blend of Gothic and Art Nouveau themes, was begun in 1882 and is scheduled to be finished around 2026. Along with Paris's Notre Dame and London's Westminster Abbey, this is one of Europe's great churches; it's also the most airy and colorful. The church is open daily, 9 a.m.–8 p.m. Admission is around $26 US per person, giving you access to one of the towers, which affords spectacular views of the city. For more information, see **sagradafamilia.cat/sf-eng.**

Next, pick up supplies for a picnic lunch by heading for **Croissantería Forn de Pa** (34 Carrer de Sant Antoni Maria Claret), a 13-minute walk from the church. You'll find delicious, French-quality croissants, baguettes, and pastries here, which is exactly *not* what you'd expect in the middle of Barcelona. Next, make the 10-minute walk to **Charcutería Simón** (392 Carrer de València), a small neighborhood store stocked with delicious meats, cheeses, and olives. If Sagrada Família is our kids' favorite part of Barcelona, then Forn de Pa and Charcutería Simon are numbers two and three on their list. Pick up some drinks from any nearby grocer, head around the corner from Charcutería Simón to **Plaça**

de la Sagrada Família park (12 Plaça de la Sagrada Família), find some shade, and enjoy your meal in the shadow of the church.

SAUNTER AROUND SAN JUAN In **San Juan, Puerto Rico,** DCL offers a very popular guided tour of the **Castillo de San Cristóbal,** a Spanish fort built in 1783, and the largest Spanish-built military structure in the New World. Disney's tour costs around $54 per person; however, the US National Park Service runs the fort, which is part of the **San Juan National Historic Site,** and admission through the NPS is only $5 per person. Free guided tours are also available—check **nps.gov/saju/index .htm** for details. A cab ride between the fort and the port shouldn't run more than $20, so a family of four can save a lot of money this way.

When you're done touring San Cristóbal, step out of the fort and into **Old San Juan.** Take a walk down Avenida Juan Ponce de León, heading west. It'll turn into Calle Fortaleza, where you'll find lots of good restaurants for lunch, from all different cuisines. It's a nice walk, a little more than a mile one-way. Take a cab back to the port when you're done.

Also in San Juan, we'd avoid the $31-per-adult **Casa Bacardí** tour, which doesn't actually tour the rum distillery itself. It's little more than a marketing presentation with a couple of drinks—nothing like, say, the excellent tour of **John Watling's Distillery** in Nassau (see page 256).

ITINERARIES INDEX

DISNEY CRUISE LINE'S FOUR SHIPS serve six main geographic areas: Alaska, the Bahamas, the California coast, the Caribbean, the Mediterranean, and northern Europe. DCL also offers "repositioning" cruises when it needs to move a ship between the United States and Europe or from the Atlantic to the Pacific.

To appeal to as wide an audience as possible, Disney cruises vary in length (and price) within each geographic area. Guests interested in visiting the Bahamas, for instance, can choose from cruises of three, four, or five nights.

There's even more variation, however, since Disney's ships visit the same ports as every other cruise line's ships, and the destination ports can't dock every line's ship at the same time. (Disney's Castaway Cay is a good illustration—it can dock just one ship at a time.)

To help fit its ships into the ports' schedules, DCL offers multiple versions of most itineraries, each of which visits exactly the same ports, but in different order. As an example, consider a four-night Bahamian cruise out of Port Canaveral, which visits Nassau and Castaway Cay and usually includes a day at sea. Disney offers at least five separate itineraries:

SHIP AND ITINERARY VERSION				
	NIGHT 1	NIGHT 2	NIGHT 3	NIGHT 4
Dream A	Port Canaveral	Nassau	Castaway Cay	At Sea
Dream B	Port Canaveral	Nassau	At Sea	Castaway Cay
Dream C	Port Canaveral	Castaway Cay	Nassau	At Sea
Dream I	Port Canaveral	At Sea	Nassau	Castaway Cay
Dream J	Port Canaveral	Castaway Cay	Nassau	Castaway Cay

Taking these variations into account, Disney's four ships sail more than 50 distinct itineraries, listed in the following section. We've also included maps of the ports for each geographic area. To keep things simple, the maps show only the ports visited along the ships' routes, not the order in which each port is visited.

See Part Eleven for detailed port information.

ONLINE FARE TRACKER

OUR WEBSITE HAS AN INTERACTIVE TOOL that demonstrates how Disney Cruise Line fares vary by date, stateroom type, and the size of your party. Access it here: **touringplans.com/disney-cruise-line/tools /fare-tracker.**

By viewing this data, you can get a sense of the best time(s) to book a cruise, and you can see which cruises are likely to have last-minute discounts. Full access to the Fare Tracker and other Disney Cruise Line content is available as an add-on to a **touringplans.com** subscription; the fees are nominal, and owners of the current edition of *The Unofficial Guide to Disney Cruise Line* get a substantial subscription discount. If you aren't satisfied for any reason, we offer a 45-day money-back guarantee.

NEW ITINERARIES

DISNEY USUALLY ANNOUNCES its ships' schedules in seasonal blocks (spring, summer, and so on), around 14 or 15 months in advance of the first sailings. Thus, you should expect to hear about summer 2016 itineraries in early spring 2015, and fall 2016 itineraries a few months later.

ITINERARY CHANGES

BE AWARE THAT WHILE CHANGES to itineraries are not frequent, they are also not unheard of. We've seen port stops changed in advance due to issues in a foreign country. We've also seen them cancelled midtrip due to weather conditions. For example, during a 2013 family trip on the *Fantasy,* ocean conditions became too rough for tender travel; therefore, a scheduled stop in Grand Cayman was cancelled and became a day at sea instead. We weren't charged for the port adventures we'd booked, and the onboard entertainment offerings were expanded.

Less common are cancellations or reschedulings of entire sailings. A few published sail dates for 2015 were cancelled and rescheduled due to issues with a planned regular maintenance dry dock of the *Dream.* Notice of the cancellations came nearly a year in advance, but some guests who were booked on these voyages had their plans impacted by the change. Guests who had been booked on the cancelled dates were offered assistance with rebooking and given a $250 onboard credit.

Nevertheless, you may want to consider whether this information affects the purchase of trip insurance or the timing of when you buy your airline tickets.

ALASKAN CRUISES *(see map page 268)*
Disney Wonder

7-NIGHT ALASKAN CRUISE: ITINERARY A
ITINERARY Day 1 Vancouver, British Columbia; Day 2 at sea; Day 3 Tracy Arm, Alaska; Day 4 Skagway, Alaska; Day 5 Juneau, Alaska; Day 6 Ketchikan, Alaska; Day 7 at sea; Day 8 Vancouver, British Columbia.
2015 SAIL DATES May 25–June 1, June 1–8, June 8–15, June 15–22, June 22–29, June 29–July 6, July 6–13, July 13–20, July 20–27, July 27–August 3, August 3–10, August 10–17, August 17–24, August 24–31, August 31–September 7.

BAHAMIAN AND CARIBBEAN CRUISES
(see map pages 270–271)
Disney Magic

3-NIGHT BAHAMIAN CRUISE: ITINERARY E
ITINERARY Day 1 Miami, Florida; Day 2 at sea; Day 3 Castaway Cay, Bahamas; Day 4 Miami, Florida.
2015–16 SAIL DATES December 31, 2015–January 3, 2016.

4-NIGHT BAHAMIAN CRUISE: ITINERARY A
ITINERARY Day 1 Miami, Florida; Day 2 Castaway Cay, Bahamas; Day 3 Nassau, Bahamas; Day 4 Key West, Florida; Day 5 Miami, Florida.
2015 SAIL DATES September 30–October 4, October 14–18, October 28–November 1, November 11–15, November 25–29, December 9–13.

4-NIGHT BAHAMIAN CRUISE: ITINERARY D
ITINERARY Day 1 Miami, Florida; Day 2 Nassau, Bahamas; Day 3 Castaway Cay, Bahamas; Day 4 Key West, Florida; Day 5 Miami, Florida.
2015 SAIL DATES December 27–31.

4-NIGHT BAHAMIAN CRUISE: ITINERARY E
ITINERARY Day 1 Miami, Florida; Day 2 Castaway Cay, Bahamas; Day 3 at sea; Day 4 Key West, Florida; Day 5 Miami, Florida.
2015 SAIL DATES December 23–27.

5-NIGHT BAHAMIAN CRUISE: ITINERARY B
ITINERARY Day 1 Port Canaveral, Florida; Day 2 Castaway Cay, Bahamas; Day 3 Nassau, Bahamas; Day 4 Key West, Florida; Day 5 at sea; Day 6 Port Canaveral, Florida.
2015 SAIL DATES May 10–15.

5-NIGHT WESTERN CARIBBEAN CRUISE: ITINERARY A
ITINERARY Day 1 Miami, Florida; Day 2 at sea; Day 3 Cozumel, Mexico; Day 4 at sea; Day 5 Castaway Cay, Bahamas; Day 6 Miami, Florida.
2015 SAIL DATES October 4–9, October 18–23, November 15–20, November 29–December 4, December 13–18.

Alaskan Ports of Call (Wonder)

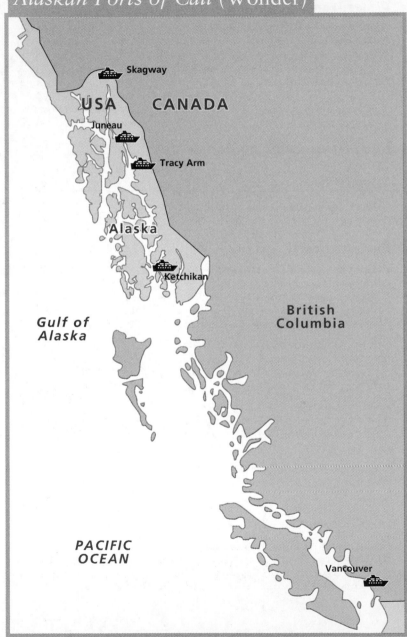

5-NIGHT WESTERN CARIBBEAN CRUISE: ITINERARY B

ITINERARY Day 1 Miami, Florida; Day 2 at sea; Day 3 Grand Cayman, Cayman Islands; Day 4 Cozumel, Mexico; Day 5 at sea; Day 6 Miami, Florida.
2015 SAIL DATES October 9–14, October 23–28, November 6–11, November 20–25, December 4–9, December 18–23.

7-NIGHT WESTERN CARIBBEAN CRUISE: ITINERARY A

ITINERARY Day 1 Port Canaveral, Florida; Day 2 Key West, Florida; Day 3 at sea; Day 4 Grand Cayman, Cayman Islands; Day 5 Cozumel, Mexico; Day 6 at sea; Day 7 Castaway Cay, Bahamas; Day 8 Port Canaveral, Florida.
2014 SAIL DATES December 7–14, December 21–28.
2015 SAIL DATES January 4–11, January 18–25, February 1–8, February 15–22, March 1–8, March 15–22, March 29–April 5, April 12–19, April 26–May 3.

7-NIGHT WESTERN CARIBBEAN CRUISE: ITINERARY B

ITINERARY Day 1 Port Canaveral, Florida; Day 2 at sea; Day 3 Cozumel, Mexico; Day 4 Grand Cayman, Cayman Islands; Day 5 Falmouth, Jamaica; Day 6 at sea; Day 7 Castaway Cay, Bahamas; Day 8 Port Canaveral, Florida.
2014 SAIL DATES December 14–21.
2014–15 SAIL DATES December 28, 2014–January 4, 2015.
2015 SAIL DATES January 11–18, January 25–February 1, February 8–15, February 22–March 1, March 8–15, March 22–29, April 5–12, April 19–26, May 3–10.

Disney Wonder

4-NIGHT BAHAMIAN CRUISE: ITINERARY B

ITINERARY Day 1 Miami, Florida; Day 2 Castaway Cay, Bahamas; Day 3 Nassau, Bahamas; Day 4 Key West, Florida; Day 5 Miami, Florida.
2014 SAIL DATES December 3–7, December 17–21.
2015 SAIL DATES January 14–18, January 28–February 1, February 11–15, February 25–March 1, March 11–15, March 25–29, April 8–12, April 22–26.

4-NIGHT BAHAMIAN CRUISE: ITINERARY E

ITINERARY Day 1 Miami, Florida; Day 2 at sea; Day 3 Nassau, Bahamas; Day 4 Castaway Cay, Bahamas; Day 5 Miami, Florida.
2014 SAIL DATES December 26–30.

5-NIGHT BAHAMIAN CRUISE: ITINERARY C

ITINERARY Day 1 Miami, Florida; Day 2 Castaway Cay, Bahamas; Day 3 Nassau, Bahamas; Day 4 at sea; Day 5 Key West, Florida; Day 6 Miami, Florida.
2014–15 SAIL DATES December 30, 2014–January 4, 2015.

6-NIGHT BAHAMIAN CRUISE: ITINERARY A

ITINERARY Day 1 Galveston, Texas; Day 2 at sea; Day 3 Key West, Florida; Day 4 Castaway Cay, Bahamas; Days 5 and 6 at sea; Day 7 Galveston, Texas.

Continued on page 272

Bahamian and Caribbean Ports of Call

USA

Galveston

Port Canaveral

Florida

Gulf of Mexico

Key West

Miami

Grand Cayman

Cozumel

MEXICO

PACIFIC OCEAN

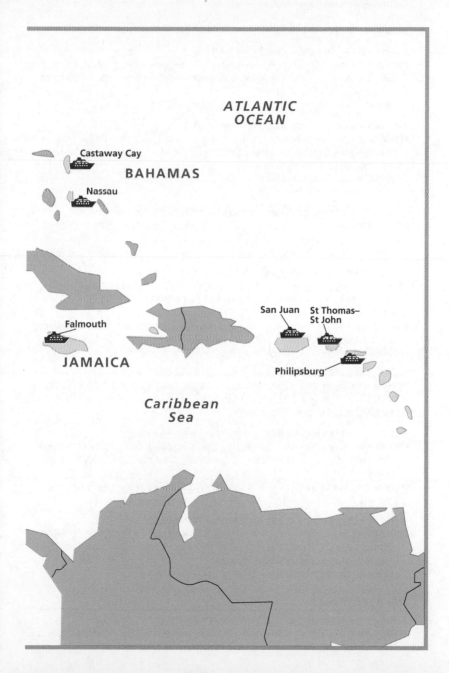

Continued from page 269

2015 SAIL DATES December 18–24.

7-NIGHT BAHAMIAN CRUISE: ITINERARY A
ITINERARY Day 1 Galveston, Texas; Day 2 at sea; Day 3 Key West, Florida; Day 4 Castaway Cay, Bahamas; Day 5 Nassau, Bahamas; Days 6 and 7 at sea; Day 8 Galveston, Texas.
2015 SAIL DATES November 13–20, December 11–18.

7-NIGHT BAHAMIAN CRUISE: ITINERARY B
ITINERARY Day 1 Galveston, Texas; Day 2 at sea; Day 3 Key West, Florida; Day 4 Nassau, Bahamas; Day 5 Castaway Cay, Bahamas; Days 6 and 7 at sea; Day 8 Galveston, Texas.
2015–16 SAIL DATES November 20–27, December 4–11, December 28, 2015–January 4, 2016.

4-NIGHT WESTERN CARIBBEAN CRUISE: ITINERARY A
ITINERARY Day 1 Galveston, Texas; Day 2 at sea; Day 3 Cozumel, Mexico; Day 4 at sea; Day 5 Galveston, Texas.
2015 SAIL DATES December 24–28.

5-NIGHT WESTERN CARIBBEAN CRUISE: ITINERARY A
ITINERARY Day 1 Miami, Florida; Day 2 at sea; Day 3 Cozumel, Mexico; Day 4 at sea; Day 5 Castaway Cay, Bahamas; Day 6 Miami, Florida.
2014 SAIL DATES December 7–12, December 21–26.
2015 SAIL DATES January 4–9, January 18–23, February 1–6, February 15–20, March 1–6, March 15–20, March 29–April 3, April 12–17, April 26–May 1.

5-NIGHT WESTERN CARIBBEAN CRUISE: ITINERARY B
ITINERARY Day 1 Miami, Florida; Day 2 at sea; Day 3 Grand Cayman, Cayman Islands; Day 4 Cozumel, Mexico; Day 5 at sea; Day 6 Miami, Florida.
2014 SAIL DATES December 12–17.

5-NIGHT WESTERN CARIBBEAN CRUISE: ITINERARY C
ITINERARY Day 1 Miami, Florida; Day 2 at sea; Day 3 Grand Cayman, Cayman Islands; Day 4 at sea; Day 5 Castaway Cay, Bahamas; Day 6 Miami, Florida.
2015 SAIL DATES January 9–14, January 23–28, February 6–11, February 20–25, March 6–11, March 20–25, April 3–8, April 17–22.

7-NIGHT WESTERN CARIBBEAN CRUISE: ITINERARY A
ITINERARY Day 1 Galveston, Texas; Days 2 and 3 at sea; Day 4 Falmouth, Jamaica; Day 5 Grand Cayman, Cayman Islands; Day 6 Cozumel, Mexico; Day 7 at sea; Day 8 Galveston, Texas.
2015 SAIL DATES November 6–13.

Disney Dream

3-NIGHT BAHAMIAN CRUISE: ITINERARY A
ITINERARY Day 1 Port Canaveral, Florida; Day 2 Nassau, Bahamas; Day 3 Castaway Cay, Bahamas; Day 4 Port Canaveral, Florida.

2014 SAIL DATES December 12–15, December 19–22, December 26–29.

2015 SAIL DATES January 2–5, January 9–12, January 16–19, January 23–26, January 30–February 2, February 6–9, February 13–16, February 20–23, February 27–March 2, March 6–9, March 13–16, March 20–23, March 27–30, April 3–6, April 10–13, April 17–20, April 24–27, May 1–4, May 8–11, May 11–14, May 22–25, May 29–June 1, June 5–8, June 12–15, June 19–22, August 7–10, August 14–17, August 21–24, August 28–31, September 4–7, September 11–14, September 18–21, September 25–28, September 28–October 1, October 1–4, October 30–November 2, November 6–9, November 13–16, November 20–23, November 27–30, December 4–7, December 11–14, December 18–21, December 21–24, December 28–31.

4-NIGHT BAHAMIAN CRUISE: ITINERARY A

ITINERARY Day 1 Port Canaveral, Florida; Day 2 Nassau, Bahamas; Day 3 Castaway Cay, Bahamas; Day 4 at sea; Day 5 Port Canaveral, Florida.

2014 SAIL DATES December 1–5, December 8–12, December 15–19, December 22–26.

2015 SAIL DATES January 5–9, January 12–16, January 19–23, January 26–30, February 2–6, February 9–13, February 16–20, February 23–27, March 2–6, March 9–13, March 16–20, March 23–27, March 30–April 3, April 6–10, April 13–17, April 20–24, April 27–May 1, May 4–8, May 18–22, May 25–29, June 1–5, June 8–12, June 15–19, August 3–7, August 10–14, August 17–21, August 24–28, August 31–September 4, September 7–11, September 21–25, October 26–30, November 2–6, November 9–13, November 16–20, November 23–27, November 30–December 4, December 7–11.

4-NIGHT BAHAMIAN CRUISE: ITINERARY B

ITINERARY Day 1 Port Canaveral, Florida; Day 2 Nassau, Bahamas; Day 3 at sea; Day 4 Castaway Cay, Bahamas; Day 5 Port Canaveral, Florida.

2014–15 SAIL DATES December 29, 2014–January 2, 2015.

4-NIGHT BAHAMIAN CRUISE: ITINERARY C

ITINERARY Day 1 Port Canaveral, Florida; Day 2 Castaway Cay, Bahamas; Day 3 Nassau, Bahamas; Day 4 at sea; Day 5 Port Canaveral, Florida.

2015 SAIL DATES December 14–18.

4-NIGHT BAHAMIAN CRUISE: ITINERARY I

ITINERARY Day 1 Port Canaveral, Florida; Day 2 at sea; Day 3 Nassau, Bahamas; Day 4 Castaway Cay, Bahamas; Day 5 Port Canaveral, Florida.

2015–16 SAIL DATES May 14–18, September 14–18, December 24–28, December 31, 2015–January 4, 2016.

4-NIGHT BAHAMIAN CRUISE: ITINERARY J

ITINERARY Day 1 Port Canaveral, Florida; Day 2 Castaway Cay, Bahamas; Day 3 Nassau, Bahamas; Day 4 Castaway Cay, Bahamas; Day 5 Port Canaveral, Florida.

2015 SAIL DATES June 22–26, July 1–5, July 15–19.

Disney Fantasy

7-NIGHT EASTERN CARIBBEAN CRUISE: ITINERARY A
ITINERARY Day 1 Port Canaveral, Florida; **Days 2 and 3** at sea; **Day 4** Philipsburg, Sint Maarten; **Day 5** St. John–St. Thomas, US Virgin Islands; **Day 6** at sea; **Day 7** Castaway Cay, Bahamas; **Day 8** Port Canaveral, Florida.
2015 SAIL DATES May 23–30, June 6–13, June 20–27, July 4–11, July 18–25, August 1–8, August 15–22, August 29–September 5, September 12–19, September 26–October 3, October 10–17, October 24–31, November 7–14, November 21–28, December 5–12, December 19–26.

7-NIGHT EASTERN CARIBBEAN CRUISE: ITINERARY B
ITINERARY Day 1 Port Canaveral, Florida; **Days 2 and 3** at sea; **Day 4** St. John–St. Thomas, US Virgin Islands; **Day 5** San Juan, Puerto Rico; **Day 6** at sea; **Day 7** Castaway Cay, Bahamas; **Day 8** Port Canaveral, Florida.
2014 SAIL DATES December 13–20.
2014-15 SAIL DATES December 27, 2014–January 3, 2015.
2015 SAIL DATES January 10–17, January 24–31, February 7–14, February 21–28, March 7–14, March 21–28, April 4–11, April 18–25, May 2–9.

7-NIGHT EASTERN CARIBBEAN CRUISE: ITINERARY C
ITINERARY Day 1 Port Canaveral, Florida; **Days 2 and 3** at sea; **Day 4** Philipsburg, Sint Maarten; **Day 5** San Juan, Puerto Rico; **Day 6** at sea; **Day 7** Castaway Cay, Bahamas; **Day 8** Port Canaveral, Florida.
2014 SAIL DATES December 6–13, December 20–27.
2015 SAIL DATES January 3–10, January 17–24, January 31–February 7, February 14–21, February 28–March 7, March 14–21, March 28–April 4, April 11–18, April 25–May 2, May 9–16.

7-NIGHT WESTERN CARIBBEAN CRUISE: ITINERARY A
ITINERARY Day 1 Port Canaveral, Florida; **Day 2** at sea; **Day 3** Cozumel, Mexico; **Day 4** Grand Cayman, Cayman Islands; **Days 5 and 6** at sea; **Day 7** Castaway Cay, Bahamas; **Day 8** Port Canaveral, Florida.
2015 SAIL DATES November 28–December 5, December 12–19.

7-NIGHT WESTERN CARIBBEAN CRUISE: ITINERARY C
ITINERARY Day 1 Port Canaveral, Florida; **Day 2** at sea; **Day 3** Cozumel, Mexico; **Day 4** Grand Cayman, Cayman Islands; **Day 5** Falmouth, Jamaica; **Day 6** at sea; **Day 7** Castaway Cay, Bahamas; **Day 8** Port Canaveral, Florida.
2015-16 SAIL DATES May 16–23, May 30–June 6, June 13–20, June 27–July 4, July 11–18, July 25–August 1, August 8–15, August 22–29, September 5–12, September 19–26, October 3–10, October 17–24, October 31–November 7, November 14–21, December 26, 2015–January 2, 2016.

CALIFORNIA COAST CRUISES (see map opposite)
Disney Wonder

2-NIGHT WEEKEND GETAWAY CRUISE
ITINERARY Day 1 San Diego, California; **Day 2** at sea; **Day 3** San Diego, California.
2015 SAIL DATES May 15–17, October 9–11, October 16–18.

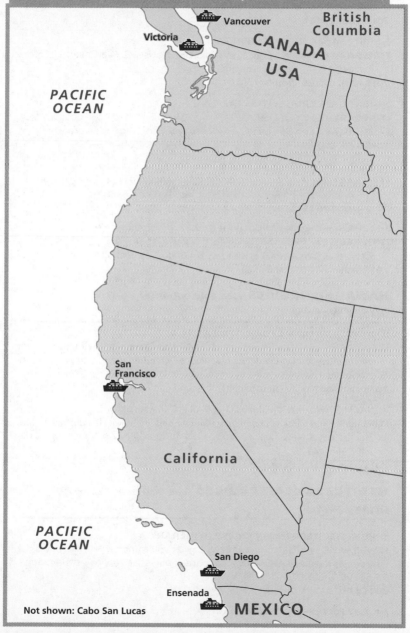

California Coast Ports of Call (Wonder)

3-NIGHT GETAWAY CRUISE
ITINERARY Day 1 San Diego, California; Day 2 Ensenada, Mexico; Day 3 at sea; Day 4 San Diego, California.
2015 SAIL DATES May 17–20.

3-NIGHT BAJA CRUISE: ITINERARY A
ITINERARY Day 1 San Diego, California; Day 2 at sea; Day 3 Ensenada, Mexico; Day 4 San Diego, California.
2015 SAIL DATES October 1–4.

5-NIGHT BAJA CRUISE: ITINERARY A
ITINERARY Day 1 San Diego, California; Day 2 Ensenada, Mexico; Day 3 at sea; Day 4 Cabo San Lucas, Mexico; Day 5 San Diego, California.
2015 SAIL DATES October 4–9, October 11–16, October 18–23.

4-NIGHT VANCOUVER–SAN DIEGO CRUISE *(Repositioning)*
ITINERARY Day 1 Vancouver, British Columbia; Day 2 Victoria, British Columbia; Days 3 and 4 at sea; Day 5 San Diego, California.
2015 SAIL DATES September 27–October 1.

5-NIGHT SAN DIEGO–VANCOUVER CRUISE *(Repositioning)*
ITINERARY Day 1 San Diego, California; Day 2 at sea; Day 3 San Francisco, California; Days 4 and 5 at sea; Day 6 Vancouver, British Columbia.
2015 SAIL DATES May 20–25.

HAWAIIAN CRUISES *(see map opposite)*
Disney Wonder

10-NIGHT HAWAIIAN CRUISE: ITINERARY A
ITINERARY Day 1 Vancouver, British Columbia; Days 2–6 at sea; Day 7 Hilo; Hawaii; Day 8 Nawiliwili; Hawaii; Day 9 Kahului; Hawaii; Days 10 and 11 Honolulu; Hawaii.
2015 SAIL DATES September 7–17.

10-NIGHT HAWAIIAN CRUISE: ITINERARY B *(Repositioning)*
ITINERARY Day 1 Honolulu; Hawaii; Days 2 and 3 Kahului; Hawaii; Day 4 Hilo; Hawaii; Day 5 Nawiliwili; Hawaii; Days 6–10 at sea; Day 11 Vancouver, British Columbia.
2015 SAIL DATES September 17–27.

MEDITERRANEAN CRUISES *(see map pages 278–279)*
Disney Magic

5-NIGHT MEDITERRANEAN CRUISE: ITINERARY A
ITINERARY Day 1 Barcelona, Spain; Day 2 Villefranche, France; Day 3 La Spezia, Italy; Day 4 Civitavecchia, Italy; Day 5 at sea; Day 6 Barcelona, Spain.
2015 SAIL DATES August 10–15.

7-NIGHT DOVER–BARCELONA CRUISE

Hawaiian Ports of Call (Wonder)

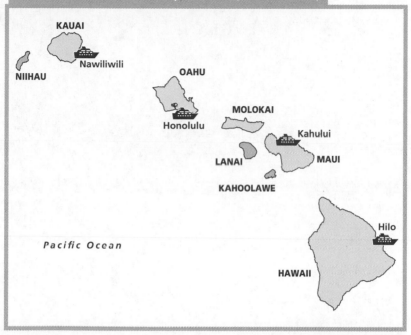

ITINERARY Day 1 Dover, United Kingdom; Days 2 and 3 at sea; Day 4 Vigo, Spain; Day 5 Lisbon, Portugal; Day 6 Gibraltar, United Kingdom; Day 7 at sea; Day 8 Barcelona, Spain.
2015 SAIL DATES August 3-10.

7-NIGHT MEDITERRANEAN CRUISE: ITINERARY B
ITINERARY Day 1 Barcelona, Spain; Day 2 at sea; Day 3 Naples, Italy; Day 4 Civitavecchia, Italy; Day 5 La Spezia, Italy; Day 6 Villefranche, France; Day 7 at sea; Day 8 Barcelona, Spain.
2015 SAIL DATES August 15-22, August 22-29, August 29-September 5.

NORTHERN EUROPEAN CRUISES *(see map pages 280-281)*
Disney Magic

7-NIGHT NORTHERN EUROPE CRUISE: ITINERARY A
ITINERARY Day 1 Copenhagen, Denmark; Day 2 at sea; Day 3 Tallinn, Estonia; Day 4 St. Petersburg, Russian Federation; Day 5 Helsinki, Finland; Day 6 Stockholm, Sweden; Day 7 at sea; Day 8 Copenhagen, Denmark.
2015 SAIL DATES May 30-June 6, June 13-20.

Continued on page 282

Mediterranean Ports of Call (Magic)

Northern European Ports of Call (Magic)

Norwegian Sea

ICELAND
Akureyri
Reykjavík

Molde
Ålesund
Bergen
Stavanger

Kirkwall

North Atlantic Ocean

North Sea

DI

UNITED KINGDOM
Dover

English Channel

Continued from page 277

7-NIGHT NORWEGIAN FJORD CRUISE: ITINERARY A
ITINERARY Day 1 Copenhagen, Denmark; Day 2 at sea; Day 3 Stavanger, Norway; Day 4 Ålesund, Norway; Day 5 Geiranger, Norway; Day 6 Bergen, Norway; Day 7 at sea; Day 8 Copenhagen, Denmark.
2015 SAIL DATES June 6–June 13.

9-NIGHT NORWEGIAN FJORD CRUISE: ITINERARY A
ITINERARY Day 1 Copenhagen, Denmark; Day 2 at sea; Day 3 Stavanger, Norway; Day 4 Ålesund, Norway; Day 5 Geiranger, Norway; Day 6 Molde, Norway; Day 7 Olden, Norway; Day 8 Bergen, Norway; Day 9 at sea; Day 10 Copenhagen, Denmark.
2015 SAIL DATES June 20–June 29.

11-NIGHT NORTH NORWEGIAN FJORDS AND ICELAND CRUISE: ITINERARY A
ITINERARY Day 1 Copenhagen, Denmark; Day 2 Oslo, Norway; Day 3 Kristiansand, Norway; Day 4 Stavanger, Norway; Day 5 at sea; Day 6 Akureyri, Iceland; Days 7 and 8 Reykjavík, Iceland; Day 9 at sea; Day 10 Kirkwall, United Kingdom; Day 11 at sea; Day 12 Dover, United Kingdom.
2015 SAIL DATES June 29–July 10.

12-NIGHT NORTHERN EUROPE CRUISE: ITINERARY A
ITINERARY Day 1 Dover, United Kingdom; Day 2 at sea; Day 3 Copenhagen, Denmark; Day 4 Warnemünde, Germany; Day 5 at sea; Day 6 Stockholm, Sweden; Day 7 Helsinki, Finland; Days 8 and 9 St. Petersburg, Russian Federation; Day 10 Tallinn, Estonia; Days 11 and 12 at sea; Day 13 Dover, United Kingdom.
2015 SAIL DATES July 10–22.

12-NIGHT NORTHERN EUROPE CRUISE: ITINERARY B
ITINERARY Day 1 Dover, Day 4 Warnemünde, Germany; Day 5 at sea; Day 6 Stockholm, Sweden; Day 7 Helsinki, Finland; Days 8 and 9 St. Petersburg, Russian Federation; Day 10 Tallinn, Estonia; Days 11 and 12 at sea; Day 13 Dover, United Kingdom.
2015 SAIL DATES July 22–August 3.

PANAMA CANAL CRUISES *(see map pages 284–285)*
Disney Wonder

14-NIGHT EASTBOUND PANAMA CANAL CRUISE: ITINERARY A
(Repositioning)
ITINERARY Day 1 San Diego, California; Day 2 at sea; Day 3 Cabo San Lucas, Mexico; Day 4 Puerto Vallarta, Mexico; Days 5–8 at sea; Day 9 Panama Canal, Panama; Day 10 Cartagena, Colombia; Days 11 and 12 at sea; Day 13 Cozumel, Mexico; Day 14 at sea; Day 15 Galveston, Texas.
2015 SAIL DATES October 23–November 6.

14-NIGHT WESTBOUND PANAMA CANAL CRUISE: ITINERARY A
(Repositioning)

ITINERARY Day 1 Miami, Florida; Day 2 at sea; Day 3 Cozumel, Mexico; Days 4 and 5 at sea; Day 6 Cartagena, Colombia; Day 7 Panama Canal, Panama; Days 8–11 at sea; Day 12 Puerto Vallarta, Mexico; Day 13 Cabo San Lucas, Mexico; Day 14 at sea; Day 15 San Diego, California.
2015 SAIL DATES May 1–15.

TRANSATLANTIC CRUISES *(see map pages 286–287)*
Disney Magic

11-NIGHT WESTBOUND TRANSATLANTIC CRUISE: ITINERARY A
(Repositioning)
ITINERARY Day 1 Barcelona, Spain; Days 2 and 3 at sea; Day 4 Funchal, Portugal; Days 5–10 at sea; Day 11 Castaway Cay, Bahamas; Day 12 Miami, Florida.
2015 SAIL DATES September 19–30.

15-NIGHT EASTBOUND TRANSATLANTIC CRUISE: ITINERARY A
(Repositioning)
ITINERARY Day 1 Port Canaveral, Florida; Days 2 and 3 at sea; Day 4 New York, New York; Days 5 and 6 at sea; Day 7 St. John's, Newfoundland and Labrador; Days 8–10 at sea; Day 11 Reykjavík, Iceland; Days 12 and 13 at sea; Day 14 Oslo, Norway; Days 15 and 16 Copenhagen, Denmark.
2015 SAIL DATES May 15–30.

Panama Canal Ports of Call (Wonder)

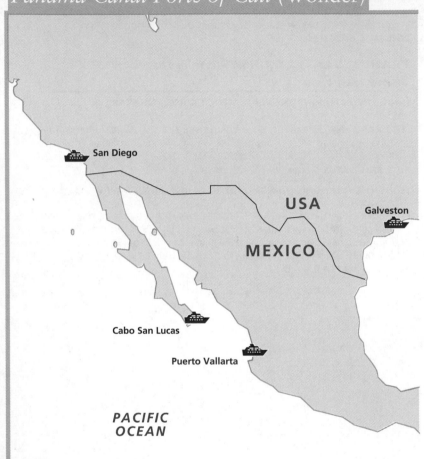

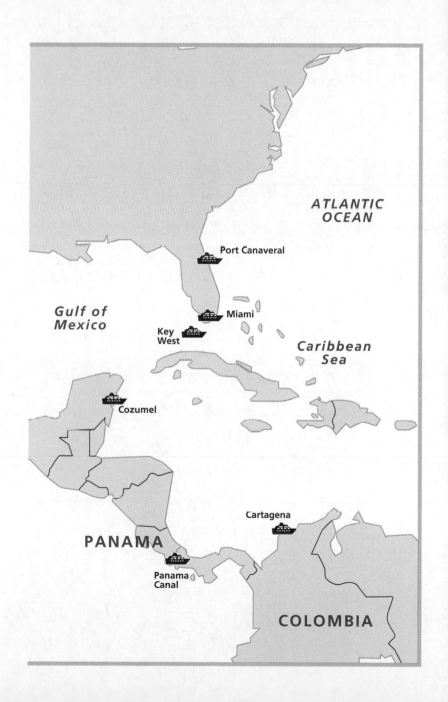

Transatlantic Ports of Call (Magic)

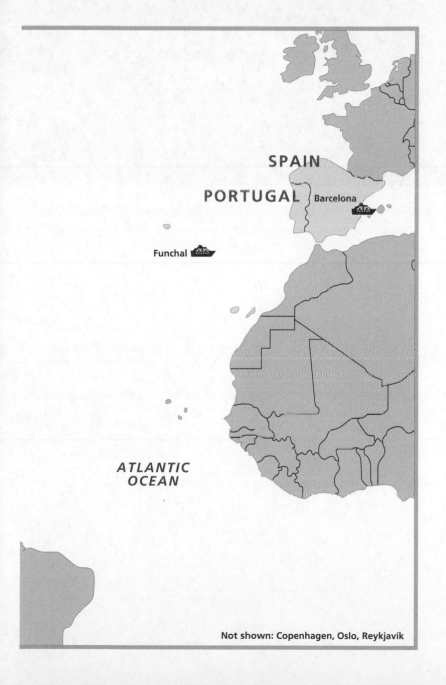

SPAIN

PORTUGAL Barcelona

Funchal

*ATLANTIC
OCEAN*

Not shown: Copenhagen, Oslo, Reykjavík

SUBJECT INDEX

DISCARD